GERMANY AND CHINA

GERMANY AND CHINA

How Entanglement Undermines Freedom, Prosperity and Security

Andreas Fulda

BLOOMSBURY ACADEMIC
LONDON • NEW YORK • OXFORD • NEW DELHI • SYDNEY

BLOOMSBURY ACADEMIC
Bloomsbury Publishing Plc
50 Bedford Square, London, WC1B 3DP, UK
1385 Broadway, New York, NY 10018, USA
29 Earlsfort Terrace, Dublin 2, Ireland

BLOOMSBURY, BLOOMSBURY ACADEMIC and the Diana logo are trademarks of
Bloomsbury Publishing Plc

First published in Great Britain 2024

Library of Congress Cataloging-in-Publication Data

Names: Fulda, Andreas, 1977- author.
Title: Germany and China: how entanglement undermines freedom,
prosperity and security / Andreas Fulda.
Description: London; New York: Bloomsbury Academic, 2024. |
Includes bibliographical references.
Identifiers: LCCN 2023053076 (print) | LCCN 2023053077 (ebook) | ISBN 9781350357013
(hardback) | ISBN 9781350357020 (paperback) | ISBN 9781350357037 (epub) |
ISBN 9781350357044 (ebook)
Subjects: LCSH: Germany–Foreign relations–China. | China–Foreign relations–Germany.
Classification: LCC DD120.C6 F85 2024 (print) | LCC DD120.C6 (ebook) |
DDC 327.43051–dc23/eng/20240212
LC record available at https://lccn.loc.gov/2023053076
LC ebook record available at https://lccn.loc.gov/2023053077

ISBN: HB: 978-1-3503-5701-3
PB: 978-1-3503-5702-0
ePDF: 978-1-3503-5704-4
eBook: 978-1-3503-5703-7

Typeset by Deanta Global Publishing Services, Chennai, India
Printed and bound in Great Britain

To find out more about our authors and books visit www.bloomsbury.com and sign up for
our newsletters

EARLY PRAISE

'China matters to Germany, Europe and the world. Getting our policy towards a resurgent China right is important to Germany, Europe and other democracies. Andreas Fulda has raised serious questions about the German establishment's engagement with China in this book. It should be required reading for policy makers and others interested in how we should engage China.'

Steve Tsang, Director of the SOAS China Institute, UK

'Even in uneventful times, *Germany and China: How Entanglement Undermines Freedom, Prosperity and Security* would be a very important book. Andreas Fulda masterfully dissects a series of Germany's pathological self-deceptions which hamper effective foreign policy, trade, and security. Chief among them is the assumption that trade can be made into a unidirectional sort of soft power vector, bestowing a democratization process on totalitarian nation states but remaining ineffectual against their counterpart. These self-deceptions, as Fulda convincingly argues, are not merely accidents of the political process but rather the result of a complacent reliance on simplistic (and instrumental) but inconsistent mental models. The book's most important message is arguably its wake-up call on the vulnerabilities arising from such incoherent mixtures of mercantilist optimism and political naïveté. Facing increasing hybrid threats from aspiring superpowers Russia and China, Germany must not only strengthen its economy by reducing dependency, but also buffer its political and academic system against interference. Exercising an impressive degree of self-reflection and impartiality, Fulda shows how a moralized, dysfunctional style of debate helped sustain obsolete policy images. The book thus offers the rare feat of not only a meticulously researched problem analysis, but also an applied example of how a robust implementation of transparency in political debates may be implemented.'

Pascal Jürgens, Professor of Computational Communication Science, Trier University, Germany

'*Germany and China: How Entanglement Undermines Freedom, Prosperity and Security* is a tour de force. Grounded in 25 years of research and on-the-ground experience, Andreas Fulda's third book provides an ominous critique of Germany's economic and psychological dependence on China, and the subsequent threat posed to Germany's national security. Fulda contextualises his epic account in a rich socio-political history of Germany and China relations, offering both a philosophical and pragmatic critique. He builds on this with concrete case examples, to demonstrate the extent to which the German political structure and economy has become reliant on the whims of Beijing. The real value in the book is not just in showing how the relationship between the two state parties has evolved, but more significantly, the work draws out the threat posed by China's encroachment on German state sovereignty. This prolific work should serve as a warning for our times. In an era where China's global dominance continues to grow, the book is of significant importance to China scholars, political scientists and especially policy makers who must confront the realities of this new world order.'

Dr Jane Richards, Lecturer in Law at The University of Leeds, UK

'In this highly readable monograph, Andreas Fulda scrutinises, and debunks, some of the most consequential flaws in German academic and policy thinking about the People's Republic. Xi Jinping's unmistakably clear intent to make China the next superpower requires no less than a strategic view on this country, underpinned by serious China expertise. Fulda's account, thus, betrays the power-related frictions that conventional German approaches will need to undergo. The author's research achieves this ambitious goal rather superbly.'

Maximilian Terhalle, Visiting Professor, London School of Economics, UK

'In this accessibly written and meticulously researched book, Andreas Fulda brilliantly dissects Germany's destructive entanglement with China. By systematically documenting the inadequacies in Germany's strategic culture, and how China takes advantage of it, Fulda shows what is at stake in Germany's *Zeitenwende* and what it will take to carry it through. The book carries important lessons for democracies in general. It shows the risks of developing deep economic interdependencies with autocratic regimes – how they may lead to highly destructive material and psychological dependencies, opening-up for malign foreign influence. As such, Fulda's new book provides a critical contribution and a must read for European policymakers and business managers at large now struggling with "de-risking" their China relations and developing greater autocracy competence in the wake of Russia's war of aggression in Ukraine.'

Mikael Wigell, Research Director at the Finnish Institute of International Affairs, Finland

'As Germany seeks to draw lessons from its failed Russia policy for its potentially much bigger challenge from China, Andreas Fulda delivers a much-needed in-depth study of Berlin's entanglement with Beijing. This book lays the groundwork for a reassessment of a German (and European) China policy. Fulda discusses the ideas and policy decisions that led to the current level of dependency and vulnerability. It is required reading for anybody who wants to know how we got there, how politicians, scientists, diplomats and lobbyists created the German ideology of "rapprochement through interweaving". Fulda also offers a way out of the policy of voluntary entanglement. His book is a landmark on the way to a new strategic culture vis-à-vis China.'

Jörg Lau, Foreign Affairs Editor at DIE ZEIT

'This book is particularly illuminating for those not only seeking theoretical knowledge and a better understanding of the German policy approach to China and public debates about it, but also knowledge about how this policy approach has manifested itself in Germany. Fulda provides a comprehensive and lively analysis here, ranging from observations related to the business domain to phenomena he himself observed while working for non-governmental institutions in China and finally to academia. This broad spectrum is also revealing. Fulda provides ample evidence that deficits and failures at the political level have an impact on numerous other domains and can thus, in their entirety, turn into a substantial threat to a country's economic sustainability and social cohesion. But Fulda does not stop at simply pointing the finger at failures in his home country. He also makes a number of helpful and constructive suggestions that I hope will receive the attention they deserve.'

Alicia Hennig, Interim Professor for General Business Studies
at the International Institute Zittau, TU Dresden, Germany

'Andreas Fulda's *Germany and China: How Entanglement Undermines Freedom, Prosperity and Security* draws upon a vast literature and primary sources through different policy fields and topics to ask significant questions about Germany's China policies of the last forty years. This monograph is an exciting work that will leave its mark on the work of China scholars, political scientists, and policymakers. Combing his expertise as a consultant in Germany's development agency, a political scientist and China scholar, Andreas Fulda analyses China studies' formation and underlying trends. Analyzing his positionality in these debates and contextualizing the discourses, Fulda makes a significant step for our area to foster our self-reflexivity and need to explore our positionalities for future research and discussions. At a time when the whole academic cooperation with China is adjusted, Fulda's work is required reading for all China scholars.'
Sascha Klotzbücher, Associate Professor, Department of East Asian Studies,
Comenius University in Bratislava, Slovakia

'At a time when a majority in the German academic community was defending closer and allegedly mutually beneficial ties to China, Andreas Fulda has advocated for more conditionality and defended the constrainment theory. In this book he thoroughly deconstructs paradigms which have informed Germany's pro-business China policy for decades. If he receives much praise internationally for his endeavor, he also faces massive criticism in Germany. The reason is that he masterfully unmasks both political and academic tartuffery. Armed with a vast expertise in the history of ideas and International Relations, Andreas Fulda has debunked the myth of the impartiality behind the claim of objectivity in academia by calling out some of his peers and putting them in front of their responsibilities as scientists. No, he argues, Human Rights are not negotiable and yes, it is the role of experts to display clear coordinates. It does not make them lesser scientists. Fulda argues that bowing to Chinese coercion is only displaying provocative weakness which in turn invites more aggressive demands by the Chinese Communist Party. He does not mince his words when it comes to the ones responsible for the self-inflicted foreign policy disaster Germany is in: The same actors who were wrong on Russia are about to repeat the same mistakes on China, he explains. It is the role of the expert community to refrain from delivering commissioned studies justifying government policies and start playing their actual role: issuing clear warnings when necessary. This book will rock the boat but also serve as a very necessary wake up call.'

Nathalie Vogel, Research Fellow at the Center for Intermarium Studies at the Institute of World Politics in Washington DC, USA

'Foreign relations with China are one of Germany's sore spots. Germany is officially committed to democracy and human rights. Yet successive governments have been mostly motivated by economic interests, resulting in increasing entanglement with the Chinese authoritarian regime. Efforts to develop a more principled approach to autocratic China have been unsuccessful. This has resulted in a problematic continuity of German China policy, as Andreas Fulda meticulously shows in his analysis. Hopefully, his book will help break this continuity.'

Heiner Roetz, Professor Emeritus of Sinology at the University of Bochum, Germany

'Andreas Fulda lays bare the flawed logic that has guided the policies of successive German governments towards China over decades. In the case of Russia, the same approach built around "change through trade" proved disastrous. It blinded the political and business elites to the real nature of change taking place in Russia and the increasingly aggressive intent of its leadership. A similarly naïve and over-optimistic approach to dealing with China has created a set of serious vulnerabilities for Germany. This book is a wake-up call for German politicians and business leaders who instinctively want to avoid confrontation with China.'

John Lough, Associate Fellow Russia & Eurasia Programme, Chatham House, UK

'As well as representing an important work on engagement with China in its own right, Andreas Fulda's new book stands up as a valuable and meaningful contribution to a decades-long dialogue about Germany's place in the world. The author's combination of well-chosen thinkers, rich case studies, and razor-sharp analysis ensures that far from being a theoretical exercise, the book feels necessary and immediate. Fulda's book will be particularly useful to those who, like me, have praised Germany's economic prowess without truly grasping the geopolitical compromises that facilitated it. Though it might be an uncomfortable read for those who preside in the corridors of power in Berlin, it contains within it much that could inform policy as Germany assesses the geopolitical landscape. If, as Fulda asserts, Germany's mercantilist China policy prioritised economic gains at the cost of industrial competitiveness and democratic resilience, this book represents a long-overdue reckoning.'

Martin Thorley, Asia Pacific Senior Analyst for the Global Initiative Against Transnational Organized Crime (GI-TOC)

'Andreas Fulda's new work is brilliantly timed, as Germany – and the wider democratic world – casts around, since the Ukraine invasion, for lessons from their "rude awakening" from 20 years' mostly unconditional, economically-driven engagement with the totalitarian powers of Russia and China. He argues persuasively that such engagement risks bestowing legitimacy, especially, on an "official China" – which he differentiates from its people – whose ruling communist party threatens freedom, prosperity and security worldwide. Based on more than 20 years' interdisciplinary research, Fulda's book seeks to provide not a new theory of international relations but more usefully, analytical tools combining theory and practice. It also succinctly proposes replacing Germany's mercantilist China policy – also common worldwide – and its associated, ineffectual, Faustian bargain, with a realistic policy of "constrainment."

> Rowan Callick, who has been China Correspondent for both Australian
> national newspapers, and is an industry fellow at
> Griffith University's Asia Institute, Australia

'Andreas Fulda's new book explores the legacy of failed assumptions in German China policy and hones in on recent public debates challenging these narratives. Based on the political cybernetics of Karl Deutsch, he frames his research in terms of learning capabilities of the German foreign policy system and process. Deutsch made the distinction between creative learning, able for self-reflexion and structural innovation, and pathological learning, in extreme meaning the will of absolute power not to learn. In the first part of the book Fulda dissects the legacy of "change through rapprochement", a foreign policy approach pioneered by Egon Bahr. It has inspired contemporary policy makers in the past twenty years to adopt their own pared down variations of Bahr's *Ostpolitik* such as "rapprochement through interweaving"' or "change through trade". Fulda argues that these foreign policy paradigms had the cumulative effect of normalising autocratic China. In the second part of the book he asks whether constructive or destructive learning has taken place during the last decade. In his case studies, he finds that despite paradigmatic rethinking dominating recent public debates, Germany's China policy has not shifted decisively. He explains that this is due for several reasons: the legacy of the mercantilist dogma being still alive and protected by the veto power of Chancellor Scholz and his closed inner circle firmly believing that the big opportunities of the China market outweigh the risks of autocratic China; the threat of sanctions of the CCP still intimidating the coalition around Scholz; the entanglement of the big German firms deemed "too big to fail"; as well as the loss of steering capacity by the state due to the principal-agent dilemma and the behaviour of acting agents in economy and science. The failures and timidity of German China policy and the recent progress of the debate are well documented, thoroughly researched, dialogically discussed, and presented in a nuanced way.'

Horst Fabian, Civil Society Ambassador Europe – China

CONTENTS

Contents

PREFACE

There is a saying that 'it takes a village to raise a child'. The same could be said about the writing of an academic book, which is rarely the stroke of genius of a solitary writer. To the contrary, as modern academics it is our task to draw on a wide range of ideas and experiences of theoreticians and practitioners alike. In this spirit I would like to thank family members, friends and colleagues for the many learned conversations we have had over the past few years. They have informed my thinking about topics covered in this book. I would like to thank Štefan Auer, Teng Biao, Rowan Callick, Rory Cormac, Horst Fabian, Jo Smith Finley, Joachim, Bernhard, Christian, Mathilde and Gerhard Fulda, Frank Haugwitz, Laura Harth, John Heathershaw, Alicia Hennig, Pascal Jürgens, Peter Kesselburg, Sascha Klotzbücher, Wolfgang Krieger, Jörg Lau, Dimon Liu, John Lough, David Missal, Scott Pacey, Adrian Rauchfleisch, Jane Richards, Heiner Roetz, Timm Rohweder, Erik Schicketanz, Claudia Seitz, Mark Siemons, Jeff Stoff, Didi Kirsten Tatlow, Maximilian Terhalle, Martin Thorley, Steve Tsang, Frank Umbach, Nathalie Vogel, Mikael Wigell and Igor Zarenko. Thank you for offering me your wise counsel and support. I would also like to thank the anonymous reviewers of both my book proposal and first draft of the monograph. The constructive and appreciative feedback they provided has been of great help.

I am also particularly indebted to Horst Fabian, a long-time friend, mentor and frequent co-author. We were colleagues when he worked as Program Coordinator Asia for the Centre for International Migration and Development (CIM). I was an Integrated CIM expert at the China Association for NGO Cooperation from 2004 until 2007. This was a very important period in my life, which provided me with deep insights into the logic and limits of civil society building in authoritarian contexts. Prior to writing my new book Horst Fabian also brought Karl Deutsch and Albert O. Hirschman to my attention. Their scholarship deserves to be rediscovered in the 21st century. I would also like to thank Steve Tsang for suggesting Bloomsbury as a publisher. I also owe a debt of gratitude to David Avital, Editorial Director at Bloomsbury for Politics, International Development and Area Studies for commissioning this book. It has also been my pleasure working with Assistant Editor Olivia Dellow during the production stage of the book. All translations from German to English are mine, apart from few exceptions where English translations were already provided. I am also indebted to Abdus Salam for his very thorough editing of the book. All remaining errors are mine. To my family in Nottingham, I send my love. During the six-month marathon of writing this book, you have endured me with patience and grace.

Andreas Fulda
Nottingham, October 2023

PART 1

GERMANY'S ENTANGLEMENT WITH AUTOCRATIC CHINA

CAUSES, CULPRITS AND CONSEQUENCES

Chapter 1

GERMANY'S RUDE AWAKENING

1.1 Zeitenwende: A 'historic turning point' in German foreign policy

Russia's brazen attack on Ukraine on 24 February 2022, marking a full invasion of the country, has ended decades of German geopolitical complacency. In a landmark speech in the German Bundestag three days later, Chancellor Scholz declared the moment a *Zeitenwende*, a 'historic turning point', after which the world was no longer the same (Bundesregierung, 2022). Starting in the early 2000s, Germany had shed its image as the 'sick man of Europe' and started benefiting from globalization through its export-led economy. After two decades of wealth growth and current account surpluses Germany became an economic powerhouse (Moebert, 2022). But when war returned to Europe, many Germans realized that the country had become increasingly dependent on the United States for security, Russia for gas and China for global supply chains (Röttgen, 2022). Germany's growing dependence on China has sparked a public debate that continues to this day (Fix, 2022).

The political scientist Müller has summarized the dilemma as follows: 'The German model of politics in particular – hard-nosed pursuit of economic advantage combined with high-minded moralising – (. . .) faces a fundamental reckoning' (2022). Russia's war of aggression also falsified a key tenet of German foreign policy: the belief that economic engagement with autocracies would lead to democratic political reforms and promote peace in global affairs. However, Germany's policy failure was more monumental. As National Endowment for Democracy analyst Walker explained aptly '(by) pursuing strictly transactional engagement with the West, China and Russia effectively reverse engineered the logic of "Change Through Trade", exploiting globalization to their advantage' (@Walker_CT, 2022). At the heart of this book thus lies a critical examination of the relationship between Germany and the People's Republic of China (hence China) during the Merkel (2005–2021) and Scholz era (2021–). It addresses a highly significant and challenging research puzzle: Why and how did Germany become entangled with an autocratic China? To what extent has the Chinese Communist Party (CCP) been able to leverage such entanglements? What can Germany do to disentangle itself without hard decoupling? And will the *Zeitenwende* require a new German strategic culture, and if so, what must it entail?

Power, will and destructive learning

In this book I argue that German senior politicians and industrialists have willingly and intentionally intertwined Germany with China for the past thirty years (1993–2023). During an unconditional engagement process with China German elites compromised democratic values, while underestimating the conventional and non-conventional threats posed by an increasingly neo-totalitarian China. As a result of an one-sided foreign trade promotion, Germany became entangled with China and suffered malign foreign interference.

Power and its relationship to *collective learning* are at the heart of this treatise. In this book I draw on the work of Karl Deutsch, a pioneer in applying the principles of cybernetics to political systems (1973). According to Deutsch, *power* is the ability to impose one's *will* on others (1973, 328). People with power can behave in a way that reflects their own memories, preferences and values instead of being constrained by others' expectations (1973). Deutsch points out that 'if "will" was understood as the desire not to learn, "power" is the ability not to having to learn' (1973, 329). Deutsch considers this *pathological learning*, which he defines as a process which reduces a system's *future learning capacity*. Deutsch also warns of *self-destructive learning* where will and power are leading to an overvaluing of the past over the future; relying on experiences acquired in a limited environment over the vastness of the universe; or expecting things to be the same over all possibilities for change, surprises and discoveries (1973). The term *destructive learning* will be used throughout this book to describe phenomena where we can witness a collective inability to engage in *creative learning*.

The German government's failure to anticipate Putin's all-out war against Ukraine can be considered a case of destructive learning. A report by Lau, Sauerbrey and Thumann indicates that Scholz was advised by four Russia experts in January 2022. Not troop deployments on Ukraine's border but Russian colonialism, Putin's understanding of history and Russian fascism were the topics of the consultations (Lau et al., 2022). Participating experts were surprised at the sudden interest in Russia's darker side: hadn't they warned about these developments for years? It appeared that senior German politicians and their advisors had ignored or overlooked key insights from academic and expert discourses. In my view, the German government's learning deficits regarding Russia raise questions about its ability to initiate collective learning processes in time to adequately address the challenges posed by China's Xi regime.

Creative learning, feedback loops and adaptive complex systems

In contrast, *creative learning* is the capacity of a political system to 'extend the possible range of its information intake from the outside world and the possible range of its internal reordering processes' (Deutsch, 1973, 241). By applying Deutsch's political cybernetics to Germany's political economy, we can view it as a collection of agents who continuously interact with one another and their environment. In this analytical vignette, we focus on communication and steering processes in a complex system (1973, 126). The importance of feedback loops in communication processes cannot be overstated. It is important to realize that feedback loops can either contribute to the survival and growth of a system or lead to its demise and ultimately destruction (1973, 331). Whether feedback loops allow continuous learning depends on how key agents process the feedback. What is the perception of gain from responding to new information and is there a possible lag between impulse and response? In order to explain this phenomenon, Deutsch uses the analogy of an unskilled driver drifting towards a ditch. Does the driver recognize the benefits of course correction, such as avoiding an accident (gain)? Will the driver be able to respond in time (lag)?

With regard to Germany's relationship with autocratic China, this scenario raises several questions: Can Scholz and his advisors develop strategies and policies to carefully disentangle Germany from China? What are German elites going to do differently this time around, or will they repeat the mistakes they made in their misguided approach to Putin's Russia? Knoepfel, Kissling-Näf and Marek have emphasized the importance of a 'local theory' in public policy, the set of shared assumptions about problems and potential solutions that determines how individuals deal with contradictions (1997, 20). In complex systems, creative policy-based learning requires high levels of self-reflexivity among the agents. In this book I argue that routine answers no longer yield desired results in Germany's commercially driven China engagement. It is imperative for agents in Germany's political economy to recognize contradictions that reveal flaws in their paradigmatic foreign policy thinking. Otherwise creative learning is unlikely to take place. I will demonstrate that critical introspection as part of an ongoing self-reflection is severely lacking. I hope to provide the academic community, practitioners and the public with an opportunity to recognize destructive learning in German China policy. This is not done in a revanchist spirit, but rather in an effort to avoid repeating past mistakes. And should mistakes be repeated in the future, this book can serve as a proverbial time capsule which captures an important moment in time.

My own learning journey

In writing this monograph, I had the opportunity to revisit a long-standing research area. Between 2003 and 2007 I wrote my PhD thesis on the promotion of participatory development in Sino-German development cooperation (Fulda, 2009). My field research was conducted while I worked for German and Chinese development organizations during the same time. Having supported Chinese civil society organizations for many years, I had hoped for the development of a more open and free China. As a China practitioner, I described my work in *The Struggle for Democracy* (2020) with reference to He Baogang as 'thoughtful wishing'. In my role as a social development practitioner, I also facilitated grassroots democracy experiments in urban and rural Chinese communities, such as Future Search Conferences (展望未来论坛) (Sina, 2007). In the early 2000s I shared the illusions of many engaged with China that the country would gradually move away from authoritarianism. Contrary to US neo-conservatives advocating abrupt regime change, I advocated greater German support for incremental political reforms led by China's nascent civil society. However, this vision never came to fruition. I remember discussing China's future in 2014 with a colleague from the Central Party School. When meeting for the first time we were surprised to discover that we had worked with the same Chinese civil society practitioners in the past. When we discussed the situation in China, my Chinese colleague asked me a personal question: Did I seem dejected whenever we talked about China's future? As I recall, I answered that this was indeed the case. I expressed my disappointment with China's political trajectory under Xi Jinping. In hindsight it has become clear to me that throughout 2014 I mourned a China *that might have been*. Although theoretically possible, it was no longer likely that a civil society-led process of liberalization and democratization would take place. I had detected early signs of China's growing security state following the 2008 uprising in Tibet, the ethnic violence between Han Chinese and Uyghurs in 2009, and the leak of Document No 9 in 2013. After learning about the internment camps in Xinjiang in 2018 it became clear to me that I could not longer justify my previous work of working within the confines of China's political system (体制内改革). My subsequent focus was on the Chinese party-state's dark underbelly. Additionally, I examined the maturing democracy movements in mainland China in my last monograph. A cyber bullying campaign began in 2019 after I spoke publicly about my research findings. My journey over the past twenty years thus has included phases of hope, frustration, acceptance of new political realities, unlearning, and renewed resolve and resilience.

1.2 Premise of the book

In this book I argue that the CCP threatens freedom, prosperity and security worldwide. This is not to say that our problem lies with the Chinese people, who have no meaningful influence over the way China is governed. I take issue with the view that the CCP can represent the diversity of China's society. Former *Global Times* editor Hu Xijin exemplifies this mindset. According to him, the party and the Chinese people have the same interests (党和政府与人民的利益是一致的) (Tiao tiao hu, 2020). Yet such an extent of 'coordination' (*Gleichschaltung*) remains an ambition of CCP hardliners, not a reality. A less deterministic but fairly similar reading of state–society relations in China has been offered by Brown. He argues against drawing too much of a clear line between the party and the Chinese population. Brown considers the large membership of the CCP to be 'broadly representative of Chinese society' (2020). While his viewpoint is mirrored in the scholarship on corporatist state–society relations (Migdal et al., 1994; Howell and Pearce, 2001; Hildebrandt, 2013), it is also largely ignorant of the widening reach and impact of China's maturing democracy movements (Fulda, 2020).

The assumption of a strong overlap between the interests of the party-state and China's population writ large is also problematic since it can serve as a justification for highly exclusive and elite-driven western China engagement. I furthermore argue that any unconditional engagement with China runs the danger of bestowing legitimacy on an increasingly neo-totalitarian party-state. To remedy such shortcomings I suggest a distinction between 'official China', which is constituted of party-state-controlled individuals and organs, and 'unofficial China', composed of academics, doctors, entrepreneurs, citizen journalists, public interest lawyers and young students who seek greater autonomy from the party-state (Yang, 2020). Early in the Covid-19 outbreak we saw many free speech conflicts in China. Proponents of 'unofficial China' such as citizen journalist Chen Qiushi (BBC, 2020), the public intellectual Xu Zhangrun (Feng, 2020) and democracy activist Xu Zhiyong (Yu, 2020) fiercely criticized the party-state's inability to prevent another global pandemic. Although these courageous individuals' voices were silenced, we should never forget that 'unofficial China' still exists, even when it is severely suppressed. While Western politicians and foreign policymakers will struggle to establish communication and collaboration with representatives of 'unofficial China', western China policy should attempt to pressure 'official China' to open up more space for legitimate political participation and contestation.

Pre-scientific value orientations and the need to overcome anti-praxeological traditions in academia

In the interest of reflexivity and researcher positionality (Corlett and Mavin, 2018), I would like to briefly discuss pre-scientific value orientations which inform this study. By making implicit assumptions explicit, they are more transparent and easier to scrutinize. This book is informed by more than twenty years of interdisciplinary research on China. In recent years I have come to realize that the field of contemporary China studies should be considered as post-normal studies, as it '[involves] risk' and is marked by an environment 'where facts are uncertain, values in dispute, stakes high and decisions urgent' (Funtowicz and Ravetz, 1993, 744). In my scholarship I have criticized 'rule-stabilizing, culturally relativistic and culturally essentialist as well as anti-praxeological traditions' in contemporary China studies (Fulda, 2022a, 225).

In a landmark essay Klotzbücher has pointed out that in stark contrast to anthropology, the methodological debate about positionality and resonance in Western Sinology remains underdeveloped (2023, 333). Whereas anthropology had its 'reflexive turn' Klotzbücher argues that 'Sinology is traditionally equated with understanding from within' (2023, 334). This has meant that the (self-)critical reflection about researcher positionality was 'unheard of' and that 'the perception of others and self-perception seem to become irrelevant' (2023). I contend that treating China as a mere perception problem (Schmidt-Glintzer, 2022, 21–33) is insufficient, as such a paradigm does not account for the integration and interactions of a given China scholar within the community of research subjects they are studying. We also need to bear in mind that after China conditionally opened up to the outside world in 1978, not only Sinologists but also German diplomats, businesspeople and technical experts had the opportunity to experience the PRC on a *practical* level.

I agree with Klotzbücher who has argued that instead of conceiving Sinology as philology it should be seen as a 'relational science, which is based on a certain relationship between research subject and object that is to be examined' (2023, 336). Other China scholars have similarly called for the embrace of a new paradigm in contemporary China studies, which hones in on our multifaceted *relationships with China*, for example, on the political, economic and socio-cultural level. An example of this is the scholarship by Franceschini and Loubere, who have convincingly argued that China as a 'country and its people are intimately enmeshed in the global capitalist system' and that we should do more to investigate what could be termed 'global China' (2022, 8). When assessing the impact of *global China* we therefore need to analyse the various political, economic and socio-cultural *interfaces* between China and other countries such as Germany. Doing so is a highly challenging task, as it not only requires a high degree of self-reflexivity but also autocracy competence (more about this in Chapter 11). As this book will show Sino–German relations not only comprise dialogue and cooperation, but have also been marked by competing ideologies, censorship and self-censorship, and highly fluid power dynamics. It is my contention that a comprehensive understanding of Sino–German relations is not possible without a substantial (re-) appraisal of the *German* side.

Limitations of the existing literature on Germany–China relations

Heilmann has pointed out that German–Chinese relations have been extensively written about (2004, 277). Even so, the sum of its parts hasn't provided a better understanding of why Germany could become so deeply entangled with autocratic China. This is due to a variety of factors. As I mentioned earlier, the perception paradigm in Sinology has meant that experiential learning during western China engagement over the past four decades was largely ignored. Furthermore, scholars have often been preoccupied with studying 'official China' and its respective business relationships rather than engaging in a more comprehensive analysis which also examines Germany's (non-)engagement with 'unofficial China'. This can be seen in Albers' work on the early years of German–Chinese economic relations. Albers' historical account of the rapprochement between West Germany and China during the early 1970s demonstrates how the Eastern Committee, the East Asia Association (*Ostasiatischer Verein*) and the German industrialist Otto Wolff von Amerongen lobbied Bonn to establish formal diplomatic relations early in the decade (2016, 52–8).

As Western academia has become increasingly overspecialized (Colagrossi, 2018), research results have also become highly compartmentalized. Miller has made the compelling argument that 'the China-watching community suffers from a contemporary variety of what Chairman Mao might have described as "mountaintopism" (山头主义): analysts have command over their parochial base area of interest but lose track of the overall picture' (2018, 5). This is also evident from literature which focuses on very specific issues in Germany–China relations. There is no shortage of commentary on Sino-German trade and investment (Schüller, 1994, 2000, 2010; Stumbaum, 2009; Bauer and Flach, 2022), development aid (Wolff, 2006; Fulda, 2009; Zajak and Kaplan, 2021), cultural relations (Hu, Triebel, and Zimmer, 2023) or academic cooperation (Thelen, Obendiek, and Bai, 2022), among others. While such research is valuable in its own right, thus far no efforts have been undertaken to inquire whether Germany's geopolitical timidity and increasingly geoeconomic entanglements with autocratic China have impacted all of these policy subfields, and if so, how.

To complicate matters even further, the *risks* inherent in unconditional western China engagement have until very recently not been sufficiently addressed in the academic literature. A key example is Bösch's over-optimistic account of VW's evergrowing investments in China. In his account of Germany's economic engagement with China since the late 1970s and early 1980s he describes VW in China as a 'flagship project' and suggests that its China business 'secured the success of VW AG in the long-term: at least one sixth of its cars are being sold in China' (2019, 180). As I will show in the empirical part of this book, such a rosy account of VW's China business which only emphasizes *opportunities* is hardly warranted. It is encouraging that more recent publications have started to see Germany–China relations as a two-way street, in which risks in the relationship need to be better managed. A prominent example is the book *Hidden Hand* by Hamilton and Ohlberg, which includes a critique of German ex-politicians cultivated by Beijing (2020). In the edited volume *China's Quest for Foreign Technology* Tatlow, Feldwisch-Drentrup and Fedasiuk have also critically assessed technology transfers from Germany to China (2021, 130–48). Stoff has furthermore published a case study which is highly critical of Germany's research collaboration with China (2023). With their different disciplinary foci these novel research contributions have unearthed major challenges in Germany's relationship with China. Yet there currently is no book that brings these different strands together and which analyses how Germany's increasing entanglement with China has impacted industry policy, technology policy, development aid, security policy and science policy. This monograph fills this niche.

It is heartening that following mostly descriptive (Albers, 2016) or archival approaches to the study of history of Germany's rapprochement with China (Leutner, 1995) there is now also a growing willingness to engage in a more (self-) critical introspection of the German side of the equation. Ziesemer has offered a fascinating account of the life of Gerhard Ludwig Flatow, a German industrialist and communist who in the late 1950s and early 1960s became Beijing's most important influence agent (2023). Ziesemer's landmark book suggests that a proto-China lobby already emerged in West Germany shortly after WWII. Yet Ziesemer's study has the limitation of not covering further developments since the 1980s. After all it was Kohl's Asia policy from 1993 which ushered in Germany's increasingly close relationship with China (Leutner, 1995, 372–76; Heilmann, 2004, 277; Stumbaum, 2009, 84). Ziesemer's focus on the past is understandable, given the challenges of studying recent history, especially when it involves living individuals. I would argue that it is much harder to engage in (self-)critical introspection when addressing more recent developments in the Germany–China relationship. In her German-language book *Ende der China-Illusion* Oertel has stated that 'in German foreign policy research, it has long been good practice to maintain a certain distance from politics, in fact from current affairs in general. Even in the field of policy-related research in the Berlin think tanks, it was customary, with a few exceptions, to refrain from assessing the performance of decision-makers and to concentrate on either the broad lines or the smallest details' (2023, 11). This book departs from this norm and sheds light on the *causes, culprits* and *consequences* of Germany's failed China policy.

Limited explanatory power of existing International Relations theories

I agree with Terhalle (2016), who has criticized the German community of International Relations (IR) scholars for failing to bridge the theory to practice gap. I contend that existing IR theories have thus far failed to capture key dynamics in the interplay between liberal democracies and autocracies under the conditions of political censorship and self-censorship. I agree with proponents of *neorealism* that international relations are marked by anarchy and that in order to ensure their survival, states seek either absolute or relative gains. However I also consider neorealism to be overly reductionist. According to this IR theory states are thought of as unitary actors with given preferences (Powell, 1994, 317). Yet ideology, the strategic culture of political elites and non-state actors arguably all play an important role in setting the foreign policy objectives of a given state. These factors, however, are ignored by neorealism. And while a sub-branch of neorealism, known as *neoclassical realism*, has attempted to remedy many of such shortcomings, it still has its limitations. According to this IR theory the international system heavily influences a nation's foreign and security policies. In addition to such external factors, a state's response to them is also determined by internal factors, such as the nature of the given political system, its state–society relations, its strategic culture and its leaders' perceptions (Ripsman, 2017). While this theoretical innovation helps to address the 'inside-out' link between domestic politics and international relations, a key problem remains: after all 'domestic interests are themselves conditioned by the international system, just as international threats and opportunities must be interpreted through the lenses of domestic interests' (2017). More importantly, neoclassical realism also does not account for potential manipulations of domestic preferences, for example, in the case of malign foreign interference.

Though not without its own shortcomings, Keohane and Nye's classic concept of *complex interdependence* addresses some of the phenomena I will explore in this book. The two authors defined it as 'a situation among a number of countries in which multiple channels of contact connect societies (that is, states do not monopolize these contacts); there is no hierarchy of issues; and military force is not used by governments towards one another' (1987, 731). Mindful of the continued relevance of military power and danger of coercion in inter-state relations,

Keohane and Nye emphasized the importance of asymmetrical bargaining (1987, 730), where 'less dependent actors will be able to make bargaining concessions at lower cost than more dependent actors' (1987, 734). This insight corresponds with my own experiential learning during more than fifteen years of consultancy-based research in and on China. I could witness first-hand how Germany's intertwining with China led to entanglement and a great reduction of both organizational and strategic autonomy on the German side. This book explains why the promised benefits of economic interdependence were not only not realized, but also led to both material and psychological dependencies.

I contend that due to epistemological limitations in the field of contemporary China and IR studies, a historically informed interdisciplinary approach is required. Upon reviewing the available academic literature, I have found that no 'off-the-shelf' academic theory addresses the whole research puzzle. As a result, I will have to engage in what can be described as theoretical bricolage. For this book, this means integrating insights from history, strategic studies, comparative politics, cognitive psychology, political cybernetics and public policy analysis. Critics may object that this book does not offer a new theory of international relations, but they should keep in mind that this is not its goal. The goal of theoretical bricolage is to identify the best analytical tools that can help to resolve both the research puzzle and the related research questions.

It is also important for critics to recognize the limits to what an individual researcher can realistically accomplish. As Deutsch has pointed out 'understanding and describing the politics of a single country in all its details is already a life's work. To attempt the same for several countries is to multiply the facts that may be sought and the questions that may need to be raised' (1973, 40). As a German national who has lived and worked in China for more than seven years and researched China for more than twenty-five years I consider myself well prepared for this task. If my paradigm-shifting book enhanced practitioner reflexivity, contributed to epistemic learning in various academic fields and subsequently led to theoretical innovations, I would consider it a success.

1.3 Positionality

It is my contention that modern academics should strive to combine theory and practice. Working as a *pracademic* (Murphy and Fulda, 2011), however, has not been a risk-free endeavour. In our coauthored article Murphy and I pointed out that '(maintaining) academic integrity and scholarly independence may be tough when conducting service in a field that is often intensely partisan . . . For issues such as poverty alleviation, the risk may be small. For more controversial issues on which passions run high . . . publicly taking sides may lead others to question the integrity of your scholarship, which can have potentially deleterious consequences both on and off campus. In particular, opponents may examine your scholarship closely to uncover flaws or try to discredit a scholar's work for spurious but politically significant reasons' (2011, 283). A case in point is the

German Sinology debate, which began in Spring 2022 (Fulda, 2022b). It was marked by 'ad hominem allegations' (H-Asia, 2022) against me and other expert critics, something 'rarely seen in German academic contexts' (2022). As one of the reviewers of my proposal for this book pointed out, I am 'unafraid of inviting controversy in the current scholarship of German-Chinese relations as well as in Germany's current strategic debates'. Such willingness to accept risks is informed by my political philosophy. I agree with Dahrendorf, who was highly critical of 'German yearning for harmony' (1985, 238) and who considered conflicts in society as a productive force (Dahrendorf Forum, 2023). While I am acutely aware of the downsides of overly agonistic discourses in academia (Tannen, 2002), the problem in German academic and public discourses is not so much an excess of contrarian thinking, but its rather striking absence. The author Bernhard Schlink has aptly observed that 'Germans . . . tend to avoid conflict and crave harmony' (Deutsche Welle, 2018).

My scepticism towards consensual politics is not unique. During the 2017 election campaign, SPD candidate Schulz called Merkel's refusal to debate the country's future 'an attack on democracy' (Galaktionow, 2017). Although he later relativized his critique (Süddeutsche Zeitung, 2017), he still made a valid point. Auer has criticized the 'suppression of political contestation engendered by German elites' commitment to consensual politics' (2021, 4). Similarly, former Foreign Minister Gabriel (2017–18) has criticized Merkel's leadership style, which after sixteen years of continuous rule 'left the Germans unprepared for a world that has changed completely. She treats the country like her children, whom she wants to protect from the evil of the world, so to speak' (Moody, 2021, 31). Terhalle refers to cognitive biases and the 'black elephant' phenomenon, a term coined by Ho, to explain this disconnect (cited by Terhalle, 2020, 6). Combining the metaphors of a 'black swan' and 'elephant in the room' Ho suggests that '(the) black elephant is a problem that is actually visible to everyone, but no one wants to deal with it, and so they pretend it is not there' (Ho, 2017). This book aims to discern possible black elephants in German China policy, which will hopefully stimulate long overdue debates about Germany's entanglement with an autocratic China. I would like to briefly mention the following three firmly held political beliefs about Germany, Europe and international relations which also inform this study:

(1) To preserve the sovereignty of nation states, one does not have to be an ethnonationalist. I opposed Brexit and sympathized with the European project. At the same time I also consider myself a Eurosceptic.
(2) Transatlantic approaches to China were emphasized in my PhD thesis (Fulda, 2009, 239). This does not mean giving the US government as the sole remaining superpower a blank cheque. But as Russia's war of aggression against the Ukraine has shown European leaders are currently not in a position to guarantee security from conventional threats on their own. From my vantage point this means that there is a need to strengthen the transatlantic partnership aimed at countering the threat of autocracies.

(3) Together with the independent researcher Fabian I have argued that 'rather than continuing a policy of appeasement, Western liberal democracies would be well advised to adopt a policy of China constrainment . . . Constrainment is more than containment with an "s" and an "r" thrown in for good measure. In the words of security expert Gerald Segal, it means to "tell China that the outside world has interests that will be defended by means of incentives for good behaviour, deterrence of bad behaviour, and punishment when deterrence fails"' (Fabian and Fulda, 2022). I also agree with Benner and Fix, who suggest that 'Germany—in conjunction with other Western partners—will need to employ a "peace through strength" approach to dealing with Russia and China' (2022).

In sum, my positionality indicates a preference for combining theory and practice in academic inquiry. It is also my hope that my applied scholarship can inform a more realistic German and European foreign policy towards autocratic China. What follows is an overview of the structure of the book.

1.4 *The book at a glance*

Throughout this book I argue that Germany's current approach to autocracies such as Russia and China is inadequate in addressing *both* conventional *and* non-conventional threats. I provide new insights into the cognitive processes involved in foreign policymaking and implementation. In Chapter 2 I dissect Germany's inadequate strategic culture vis-à-vis autocracies. I deconstruct the Steinmeier doctrine 'Rapprochement through interweaving' (*Annäherung durch Verflechtung*) and discuss the puzzle of German power.

Chapter 3 centres around China's strategic culture and how it is linked to the CCP's quest for political legitimacy and regime stability. I argue that Germany's entanglement with China is already being exploited by the CCP. This chapter will show how the Chinese party-state employs a 'wedge strategy' of hybrid interference (Wigell, 2019) when interfering in Western liberal democracies. More specifically, the CCP has used the three bundles of hybrid interference, namely (1) clandestine diplomacy; (2) power trading, predatory technology transfers and geoeconomic coercion; and (3) mis- and disinformation to undermine Germany's public institutions, hollow out the country's industrial base and weaken public trust in liberal democracy.

Chapter 4 provides a longitudinal analysis of the leadership roles by German Chancellors Kohl, Schröder, Merkel and Scholz. I describe how their unconditional China engagement had the cumulative effect of normalizing autocratic China.

In Chapter 5 I develop my research approach for the empirical part of the book. This book's empirical research is informed by a highly innovative conceptual framework that allows readers to trace cognitive continuity and change in policymaking and implementation. Drawing on the *Punctuated Equilibrium Theory* by Baumgartner and Jones (1993/2009), I detect challenges to Germany's mercantilist China policy at the dawn of the Merkel era (2018–21). The empirical second part of the book is informed by a close reading of more than 300 German-language media reports in *TAZ, SZ, FAZ, Handelsblatt, WirtschaftsWoche* and *NZZ*. At the heart of my analysis are *policy images* comprising a 'mixture of empirical information and emotive appeals' (Baumgartner and Jones, 1993, 26) used to explain issues and justify preferred policy responses. They either reflect key assumptions of the *old paradigm* (e.g. Rapprochement through interweaving, Change through trade, etc.) or belong to the *emergent paradigm* of a more conflict-capable German China policy (e.g. Dialogue and strength, China constrainment, etc.). The second part of the book contains a critical analysis of the extent of constructive or destructive learning on the German side.

Chapters 6 to 10 tell the story of Germany's hidden liabilities in its complex relationship with China. I provide five case studies – dubbed *unforeseen policy failures (UPF)* – which describe the damage that has already been caused by entanglement with authoritarian China. They range from the collapse of the German solar industry (Chapter 6), the takeover of the robotics company Kuka Roboter GmbH by Chinese investors (Chapter 7), the cooptation of German state and non-state development agencies in China (Chapter 8), Europe's patchy arms embargo and the problem of dual-use exports to China (Chapter 9) and Germany's half-hearted defence of academic freedom (Chapter 10).

In the empirical part I answer four research questions: How does the Policy Equilibrium Theory explain punctuation during the final years of the Merkel era (2018–21) and the beginning of the Scholz administration (2021–)? What types of policy images challenge Germany's mercantilist China policy? Has Germany's China policy shifted as a result? In terms of Scholz' *Zeitenwende*, what has already been accomplished?

I analyse whether a paradigmatic rethinking has already begun in Germany's public China discourse. In five additional case studies – called *policy punctuation analysis (PPA)* – I compare and contrast competing policy images based on my media analysis described in Chapter 5. Punctuation is described with reference to VW's entanglement with China (Chapter 6), Berlin's Huawei dilemma (Chapter 7), the closing space for dialogue and cooperation with China (Chapter 8), Germany's dangerous indifference towards Taiwan (Chapter 9) and the fallacy of tactical compromises in academic cooperation with China (Chapter 10).

In summary the empirical part of this book presents a collection of ten original and insightful qualitative case studies that provide novel insights into the role of cognitive biases and mental models in policymaking and implementation. All ten case studies reveal the need for enhanced critical self-reflection. The findings of this book have important implications for policymakers, highlighting the need for a more honest public debate about the root causes of policy failure.

This book reveals how German Chancellors, foreign ministers and German industrialists had a lasting impact on how the German state, business and civil society engage with China. Following a long period of stasis, Germany's mercantilist China policy is now firmly contested. In the empirical part of the book I will show that despite ample evidence of policy punctuation there has not yet been a decisive shift in German China policy. The research findings suggest that only some of the legwork for Olaf Scholz' *Zeitenwende* has been done. I conclude the book in Chapter 11 by answering the research questions, revisiting the initial research puzzle, providing eight recommendations and making the case for a German version of a Foreign Agent Registration Act (FARA).

References for Chapter 1

@Walker_CT (2022), '…By Pursuing Strictly Transactional Engagement with the West, China and Russia Effectively Reverse Engineered the Logic of "Change Through Trade," Exploiting Globalization to their advantage #WandeldurchHandel', *Twitter*, 10 November. Available online: https://archive.is/3XPbg (accessed 10 July 2023).

Albers, M. (2016), *Britain, France, West Germany and the People's Republic of China, 1969–1982*, London: Palgrave Macmillan.

Auer, S. (2021), 'Merkel's Germany and the European Union: Between Emergency and the Rule of Rules', *Government & Opposition*, 56: 1–19.

Bauer, A. and L. Flach (2022), 'Deutsch-chinesische Handelsbeziehungen: Wie abhängig ist Deutschland vom Reich der Mitte?', *ifo Schnelldienst*, 4/2022 vorab 31 März 2022. Available online: https://web.archive.org/web/20221223180507/https://www.ifo.de /DocDL/sd-2022-04-baur-flach-deutsch-chinesische-handelsbeziehungen_0.pdf (accessed 27 October 2023).

Baumgartner, F. and B. Jones (1993/2009), *Agendas and Instability in American Politics*, 2nd edn, Chicago and London: The University of Chicago Press.

BBC (2020), 'Chen Qiushi: Chinese Journalist Missing Since February "Under State Supervision"', 24 September. Available online: https://archive.is/JX9F8 (accessed 11 November 2020).

Benner, T. and L. Fix (2022), 'Germany's Unlearned Lessons', *GPPi*, 15 December. Available online: https://archive.is/dNmra (accessed 10 July 2023).

Bösch, F. (2019), *Zeitenwende 1979. Als die Welt von heute begann*, 6. Auflage, München: C.H.Beck.

Brown, K. (2020), '[China Series #1] The Communist Party of China and the Idea of "Evil"', Oxford Political Review, 24 April. Available online: https://archive.is/tyeQC (accessed 10 July 2023).

Bundesregierung (2022), 'Regierungserklärung von Bundeskanzler Olaf Scholz am 27. Februar 2022', 27 February. Available online: https://archive.is/yhxI6 (accessed 10 July 2023).

Colagrossi, M. (2018), 'The Dangers of Overspecialization in Academia', *Big Think*. Available online: https://archive.ph/6zUrq (accessed 27 October 2023).

Corlett, S. and S. Mavin (2018), 'Reflexivity and Researcher Positionality', in C. Cassell, A. Cunliffe, and G. Grandy (eds), *The Sage Handbook of Qualitative Business and Management Research Methods*, 377–89, London: Sage. Available online: https://eprints .ncl.ac.uk/file_store/production/242880/44F33FAF-5A18-44BD-90F7-C741D77B03ED .pdf (accessed 10 July 2023).

Dahrendorf Forum (2023), 'The Dahrendorf Legacy', Available online: https://archive.is/ hL6jx (accessed 10 July 2023).

Dahrendorf, R. (1985), 'Soziale Klassen und Klassenkonflikt: Zur Entwicklung und Wirkung eines Theoriestücks', *Zeitschrift für Soziologie*, Jg. 14, Heft 3, Juni 1985: 236–40.

Deutsch, K. (1973), *Politische Kybernetik. Modelle und Perspektiven*, Freiburg im Breisgau: Verlag Rombach.

Deutsche Welle (2018), '"Konfliktscheu und harmoniesüchtig"', 23 April. Available online: https://archive.is/47Vl1 (accessed 10 July 2023).

Fabian, H. and A. Fulda (2022), 'The End of the China Illusion', *RUSI*, 7 November. Available online: https://archive.is/RKZoY (accessed 10 July 2023).

Feng, C. (2020), '"The Rot Goes Right Up to Beijing": Why Detained Professor Xu Zhangrun Is Such a Threat to China's Leadership', *The Conversation*, 7 July 2020. Available online: https://archive.is/P0Q0K (accessed 11 November 2020).

Fix, L. (2022), 'Germany's China Policy: Has It Learned From Its Dependency on Russia?', *Council on Foreign Relations*, 14 November. Available online: https://archive.is/blSrf (accessed 10 July 2023).

Franceschini, I. and N. Loubere (2022), *Global China as a Method*, Cambridge: Cambridge University Press.

Fulda, A. (2009), *Förderung partizipativer Entwicklung in der VR China. Möglichkeiten und Grenzen politischer Einflussnahme durch Akteure der deutsch-chinesischen Entwicklungszusammenarbeit*, Wiesbaden: VS Verlag für Sozialwissenschaften.

Fulda, A. (2020), *The Struggle for Democracy in Mainland China, Taiwan and Hong Kong. Sharp Power and its Discontents*, London and New York: Routledge.

Fulda, A. (2022a), 'The Chinese Communist Party's Hybrid Interference and Germany's Increasingly Contentious China Debate (2018–21)', *The Journal of the European Association for Chinese Studies*, 2: 205–34.

Fulda, A. (2022b), 'Researching China: How Germany Tackles the Issues', *HEPI*, 5 April. Available online: https://archive.is/sRWtO (acccessed 10 July 2023).

Funtowicz, S. and J. Ravetz (1993), 'Science for the Post-normal Age', *Futures: The Journal of Policy, Planning and Futures Studies*, 25 (7): 739–55.

Galaktionow, B. (2017), 'Schulz wirft Merkel einen "Anschlag auf die Demokratie" vor', *Süddeutsche Zeitung*, 25 June. Available online: https://archive.is/8oobJ (accessed 10 July 2023).

H-Asia (2022), 'Germany's Contentious China Debate', 17 March. Available online: https://archive.is/rZ49o (accessed 10 July 2023).

Hamilton, C. and M. Ohlberg (2020), *Hidden Hand: Exposing How the Chinese Communist Party is Reshaping the World*, London: Oneworld Publications.

Heilmann, S. (2004), *Das politische System der Volksrepublik China, 2., aktualisierte Auflage*, Wiesbaden: VS Verlag für Sozialwissenschaften.

Hildebrandt, T. (2013), *Social Organizations and the Authoritarian State in China*, Cambridge: Cambridge University Press.

Ho, P. (2017), 'The Black Elephant Challenge for Governments', *The Straits Times*, 7 April. https://archive.is/tK2AD.

Howell, J. and J. Pearce, eds (2001), *Civil Society and Development: A Critical Exploration*, Boulder: Lynne Rienner Publishers.

Hu, C., O. Triebel, and T. Zimmer, eds (2023), *Im Spannungsverhältnis zwischen Selbst- und Fremdverstehen. Globale Herausforderungen und deutsch-chinesische Kulturbeziehungen*, Wiesbaden: Springer VS.

Joel, M., A. Kohli, and V. Shue, eds (1994), *State Power and Social Forces: Domination and Transformation in the Third World*, Cambridge: Cambridge University Press.

Keohane, R. and J. Nye, Jr (1987), 'Power and Interdependence Revisited', *International Organization*, 41 (Autumn): 725–53.

Klotzbücher, S. (2023), 'Die Zukunft der Chinastudien, aus der Geschichte einer Verführung betrachtet', in D. Fuchs, S. Klotzbücher, A. Riemenschnitter, L. Springer, and F. Wemheuer (eds), *Die Zukunft mit China denken*, 331–53, Vienna and Berlin: mandelbaum verlag.

Knoepfel, P., I. Kissling-Näf, and D. Marek (1997), *Lernen in öffentlichen Politiken*, Basel and Frankfurt am Main: Helbing & Lichtenhahn.

Lau, J., A. Sauerbrey, and M. Thumann (2022), 'Jens Plötner: Why is Chancellor Scholz Wavering?', *Zeit Online*, 22 April. Available online: https://archive.is/yvQnr (accessed 10 July 2023).

Leutner, M. (1995), *Bundesrepublik Deutschland und China 1949 bis 1995. Politik – Wirtschaft – Wissenschaft – Kultur. Eine Quellensammlung*, Berlin: Akademie Verlag.

Migdal, J. S., A. Kohli, and V. Shue (1994), *State Power and Social Forces : Domination and Transformation in the Third World*, Cambridge: Cambridge University Press.

Miller, A. (2018), 'Valedictory: Analyzing the Chinese Leadership in an Era of Sex, Money, and Power', *China Leadership Monitor*. Available online: https://www.hoover .org/sites/default/files/research/docs/clm57-am-final.pdf (accessed 27 October 2023).

Moebert, J. (2022), 'Germany's Current Account: The End of Criticism', *Deutsche Bank*, 21 July. Available online: https://archive.is/NkLWm.

Moody, O. (2021), 'I Might Try Gardening', *Sunday Times Magazine*, 5 September, 22–31.

Müller, J.-W. (2022), 'Germany Inc. Jan-Werner Müller on Europe after the Invasion', *London Review of Books*, 26 May. Available online: https://archive.is/Yc8nD (accessed 10 July 2023).

Murphy, A. and A. Fulda (2011), 'Bridging the Gap: Pracademics in Foreign Policy', *PS: Political Science & Politics*, 44 (2): 279–83. Available online: https://core.ac.uk/ download/33563322.pdf (accessed 10 July 2023).

Oertel, J. (2023), *Ende der China-Illusion. Wie wir mit Pekings Machtanspruch umgehen müssen*, München: Piper Verlag.

Powell, R. (1994), 'Anarchy in International Relations Theory: The Neorealist-Neoliberal Debate', *International Organization*, 48 (2) (Spring): 313–44.

Ripsman, N. (2017), 'Neoclassical Realism', *International Studies*, 22 December. Available online: https://bit.ly/3lSwK1U (accessed 10 July 2023).

Röttgen, N. (2022), *Nie wieder hilflos! Ein Manifest in Zeiten des Krieges*, Munich: dtv.

Schmidt-Glintzer, H. (2022), 'Zur China-Wahrnehmung', in G. Thelen, H. Obendiek, and Y. Bai (eds), *Handbuch China-Kompetenzen. Best-Practice-Beispiele aus deutschen Hochschulen*, 21–35, Bielefeld: transcript Verlag.

Schüller, M. (1994), 'China-Boom in Deutschland: Entwicklungen und Perspektiven der deutsch-chinesischen Wirtschaftskooperation', *China aktuell*, Juni 1994. Available online: https://hasp.ub.uni-heidelberg.de/journals/chakt/article/view/9782/9628 (accessed 27 October 2023).

Schüller, M. (2000), 'Überblick über die deutsch-chinesischen Wirtschaftsbeziehungen zu Beginn des 21. Jahrhunderts', *China aktuell*, Dezember 2000. Available online: https:// hasp.ub.uni-heidelberg.de/journals/chakt/article/view/11538/11296 (accessed 27 October 2023).

Schüller, M. (2010), 'Chinas Aufstieg zum wichtigsten deutschen Wirtschaftspartner in Asien', *Note du Cerfa 71, ifri*, January 2010. Available online: https://www.ifri.org/sites/ default/files/atoms/files/ndc71schullerde_1_0.pdf (accessed 27 July 2023).

Sina (2007), 'Deguoren tuidong zhongguo shequ zizhi: Rang meiguo zoujin shequ', 15 June. Available online: https://archive.is/pSC0l (accessed 10 July 2023).

Stoff, J. (2023), *Should Democracies Draw Redlines Around Research Collaboration with China? A Case Study of Germany, CRSI*. Available online: https://researchsecurity.org/wp-content/uploads/2023/01/Click-here-to-download-the-full-publication.-Stoff-DrawingRedlinesFINAL.pdf (accessed 20 July 2023).

Stumbaum, M-B. (2009), *The European Union and China. Decision-Making in EU Foreign and Security Policy Towards the People's Republic of China*, Baden-Baden: Nomos.

Süddeutsche Zeitung (2017), '"Anschlag auf Demokratie": Schulz relativiert Vorwurf', 3 September. Available online: https://archive.is/qRzjR (accessed 10 July 2023).

Tannen, D. (2002), 'Agonism in Academic Discourse', *Journal of Pragmatics*, 34 (2002): 1651–69.

Tatlow, Feldwisch-Drentrup and Fedasiuk (2021), 'Technology Transfer from Germany', in W. Hannas and D. Tatlow (eds), *China's Quest for Foreign Technology. Beyond Espionage*, 130–48, London and New York: Routledge.

Terhalle, M. (2016), 'IB-Professionalität als Praxisferne? Ein Plädoyer für Wandel', *Zeitschrift für Außen- und Sicherheitspolitik*, 9: 121–38.

Terhalle, M. (2020), *Strategie als Beruf*, Baden-Baden: Tectum bei Nomos.

Thelen, G., H. Obendiek, and Y. Bai (2022), *Handbuch China-Kompetenzen. Best-Practice-Beispiele aus deutschen Hochschulen*, Bielefeld: transcript Verlag.

Tiao tiao hu (2020), '因为党和政府与人民的利益是一致的', YouTube. Available online: https://archive.is/qdCSw (accessed 10 July 2023).

Wigell, M. (2019), 'Hybrid Interference as a Wedge Strategy: A Theory of External Interference in Liberal Democracy', *International Affairs*, 95 (2): 255–75.

Wolff, P. (2006), 'Entwicklungszusammenarbeit im Gesamtkontext der Deutsch-Chineseischen Kooperation: Eine Portfolioanalyse', *Deutsches Institut für Entwicklungspolitik*, Discussion Paper, November 2006. Available online: https://www.idos-research.de/uploads/media/Internetfassung_DiscPaper_11.2006.pdf (accessed 18 July 2023).

Yang, W. (2020), 'China's COVID19 Mishandling Is its "Chernobyl Moment," Said Its International Critics', *Medium*, 17 April. Available online: https://archive.is/YZmH6 (accessed 10 July 2023).

Yu, V. (2020), 'Chinese Activist Detained After Calling Xi Jinping "Clueless" on Coronavirus Crisis', *The Guardian*, 17 February. Available online: https://archive.is/5SSfP (accessed 10 July 2023).

Zajac, K. and L. Kaplan (2021), 'Why Germany Should Continue Its Development Cooperation with China', Kiel Policy Brief, No 159, November 2021. Available online: https://www.ifw-kiel.de/fileadmin/Dateiverwaltung/IfW-Publications/-ifw/Kiel_Policy_Brief/2021/KPB_159.pdf (accessed 18 July 2023).

Ziesemer, B. (2023), *Maos deutscher Topagent. Wie China die Bundesrepublik eroberte*, Frankfurt and New York: Campus Verlag.

Chapter 2

STRATEGIC CULTURE, THE STEINMEIER DOCTRINE AND THE PUZZLE OF GERMAN POWER

2.1 Does Germany have a strategic culture?

From afar, Germany can seem like an exemplary mixed economy. Sir Paul Lever, former British ambassador to Berlin, has praised Germany's manufacturing prowess, export-led economy, solid public finances and functioning social welfare system in *Berlin Rules* (2018, 30). In *Why the Germans Do it Better* (2020) Kampfner complimented Germany as a 'grown-up country'. Fletcher lauded Germany for being governed by centrist politicians and characterized by civil discourse (2021). In the following I argue that such charitable assessments of Germany's political economy overlook idiosyncrasies of *Germany Inc* (Streeck and Höpner, 2003), which traditionally consists of mutually dependent managers, union representatives and politicians (Daub, 2021).

Germanophile observers also often ignore that German governments have benefited greatly from the US-led Western world order, but have not done much to sustain and defend it (Giegerich and Terhalle, 2021). With regard to autocracies such as Russia and China, short-term economic gains have long been prioritized over strengthening the EU and NATO (2021). Few foreign observers would agree that Germany excels at international strategic challenges (2021, 23–4). Germany's approach to security policy is viewed by them as 'immature' (2021, 24). They suggest that Germany is unable to deal with 'the rise or resurgence of revisionist, repressive and authoritarian powers in China and Russia' (2021, 8).

At the heart of their critique lies strategic culture. Snyder described it as 'the sum total of ideas, conditioned emotional responses, and patterns of habitual behavior that members of a national strategic community have acquired through instruction or imitation and share with each other with regard to nuclear strategy' (1977, 8). Whereas Snyder concerned himself primarily with differences between Soviet and US nuclear strategies during the Cold War, present-day studies of strategic culture include a much wider range of security and defence policy issues.

Chapter at a glance

This book chapter consists of four parts. Following a discussion of Germany's strategic culture during the Merkel era (2005–2021) I provide an in-depth critique of the key assumptions that shaped the culture of Germany's foreign policy behaviour under Schröder (1998–2005) and Merkel (2005–21). At the heart of this book chapter lies a deconstruction of former German foreign minister Frank-Walter Steinmeier's concept of 'Rapprochement through interweaving' (*Annäherung durch Verflechtung*). It is followed by a discussion of the underlying historical reason which can help explain Germany's reluctance to project power. It ends with reflections about the tendency of leading German politicians to hide behind Brussels.

2.2 Germany's strategic culture during the Merkel era (2005–2021)

When Chancellor Angela Merkel entered her second grand coalition with the Social Democratic Party (SPD) in 2013 three security experts attempted to analyse strategic cultures across Europe. Based on Snyder's first-generation scholarship Biel, Giegerich and Jonas conceptualized strategic culture as 'a number of shared beliefs, norms and ideas within a given society that generate specific expectations about the respective community's preferences and actions in security and defence policy' (2013, 12). In their studies of strategic culture elites play a key role. This assertion mirrors a finding by Foot, who has pointed out that 'foreign policy-making in European capitals . . . unlike in Washington, tends to be a more élitist affair, and generally less confrontational' (2000, 265). In order to unpack a nation's strategic culture Biel, Giegerich and Jonas distinguished between 'the level of ambition in international security policy', 'the scope of action for the executive in decision-making', 'foreign policy orientation' and 'the willingness to use military force' (2013, 13).

Applying this framework to the case study of Germany Junk and Daase found 'German foreign and security policy to be reactive, passive, and reluctant' (2013, 149). Berlin's ambitions 'remain moderate and are communicated primarily in multilateral forums' and 'the government remains constrained by the strong role of the parliament, by public opinion, by a strong constitutional court, and by a consensus-driven political system' (2013). Junk and Daase point out that 'German strategic culture can only be understood if one considers a deep societal, administrative, and political reluctance to the use of force outside its boundaries' (2013). Their scholarship exposes weaknesses in Germany's capability to counter traditional threats. But due to its primary focus on military affairs Biel, Giegerich and Jonas's analytical framework for analysing strategic culture also exhibits a few blind spots. In the case of Germany, Berlin's level of ambition arguably must be understood in relation to other policies, for example, foreign trade promotion, energy policy or industry policy. It is also necessary to discuss domestic corporate lobbying and foreign interference when discussing limits to the scope of executive action. How national power is imagined and what this means for the division of labour between Germany, the EU and NATO are key questions in terms of foreign policy orientation. And while the willingness to use military force is one key aspect, it does not fully capture other psychological factors which could explain German elites' incapacity to address non-conventional threats in other policy arenas.

Terhalle, on the other hand, has questioned whether Germany has a strategic culture after all. In *Strategie als Beruf* (Strategy as vocation) he criticizes Germany for its limited understanding of world politics, which he explains in relation to the country's post-WWII culture of restraint, its comprehensive prosperity and reliance on the US security umbrella (2020, 5). Terhalle bemoans that 'what Germany lacks, criticised abroad by many strong allies (and secretly approved of by others), is therefore a strategic culture' (2020). He defines strategic culture as 'the ability to think strategically and act accordingly to ensure [Germany's] security' (2020, 6). Terhalle calls for 'a strategic, power-political reading of international politics' (2020, 8). He is highly critical of Chancellor Merkel's view of practical politics as 'problem solving' (2020). Thorny security-related issues such as Nord Stream 2 or Huawei should not be treated as 'unpolitical, economic problems' (2020, 8–9).

How experts think lies at the heart of Terhalle's analysis. He argues that we need to understand their 'style of reasoning' (2020, 9). Terhalle stresses the importance to better understand the cognition among heads of states and their advisors (2020, 10). Drawing on the psychology of decision-making (Kahneman, 2011), Terhalle argues that political decisions are based on dual logic systems. System 1 is based on deep-seated stereotypes and a relatively fixed world view. System 2, on the other hand, could act as a corrective by introducing a more 'rational element of strategy selection' (Terhalle, 2020, 25). In reality, however, the second system is limited by cognitive limitations of the decision-maker and thus may struggle to revise perceptions shaped by the first. Terhalle emphasizes that while 'logic systems 1 and 2 interact . . . the first is clearly the stronger element, precisely because it can prevail without and against the advice of system 2. The key is therefore to think from the decision-maker's point of view, i.e. to know the system 1 of the respective decision-maker in detail' (2020). In this book I argue that Terhalle's emphasis on the cognition and style of reasoning among senior foreign policy decision-makers and their advisors is indeed key to a better understanding of German foreign policy behaviour. Furthermore, I posit that the intellectual and political leadership (or lack thereof) of senior politicians such as Chancellors or Foreign Ministers directly influences the conduct of Germany's foreign policy and will be key to developing a new strategic culture.

It should be pointed out that Terhalle is mindful that pacifism is one among several foreign policy identities (2020, 10). Malici has emphasized the importance of understanding deep-seated beliefs of German decision-makers (2006, 37). He argues that German foreign policy behaviour is characterized by a culture of reticence and accommodation rooted in the traumatic experiences of the two World Wars (2006, 38). Yet Biel, Giegerich and Jonas have argued that while strategic culture was expected to persist it should not be considered as static (2013, 12). During times of crisis – Russia's war of aggression against Ukraine springs to mind – a given countries' strategic cultures can lose some rigidity and become more malleable (2013, 12–13). During a widely noted keynote at the Munich Security Conference in 2014 then German president Joachim Gauck reminded his audience that in order '(to) find its proper course in these difficult times, Germany needs resources, above all intellectual resources. It needs minds, institutions and forums' (Der Bundespräsident, 2014). In light of the challenges which Russia and China pose Giegerich and Terhalle argue persuasively for the development of a new 'strategic mindset', which Germany's leaders should embrace (2021, 16).

German Chancellor Scholz appears to be in agreement with the two authors when writing in *Foreign Affairs* that 'Germany's new role will require a new strategic culture' (2023). Yet the proof will be in the pudding. Scholz also writes that much will depend on the traffic light coalition's new National Security Strategy (2023). The latter was unveiled in June 2023 but did not reveal a major paradigmatic shift in the way the German government imagines Germany's role in a changing world. It is also highly unlikely that a single strategy document will be able to significantly influence the development of a new strategic culture. A new strategic mindset will require the unlearning of flawed assumptions in German foreign and security policy. As a start, a no-holds-barred introspection of the style of reasoning by Frank-Walter Steinmeier, one of Germany's most prominent foreign policy entrepreneurs, is in order.

2.2 The Steinmeier doctrine of 'Rapprochement through interweaving'

Steinmeier joined the Social Democratic Party (SPD) in 1975 while serving in the military. In the following years, he studied law and political science. While completing his PhD, he worked as a research assistant at Gießen University. For more than two decades, Steinmeier has shaped German foreign and security policy. He was Chief of Staff of the Chancellery under Schröder (1999–2005). His relationship with Schröder dates back to 1991, when he started working for him at the State Chancellery of Lower Saxony (Lütjen, 2009, 39). Citing Schröder's close ties with Putin and his work for Russian energy companies the *New York Times* reporter Bennhold described him as a 'pariah in his own country' (2022). In light of such damning public criticism of his former political mentor, Steinmeier has tried to distance himself from Schröder, claiming that starting from 2005 he went his own way. Yet he also had to acknowledge that he was Schröder's right-hand man for fifteen years (ZDF heute, 2022). Two times, Merkel appointed him Foreign Minister (2005–09 and 2013–17). In 2017, Steinmeier was elected as the German president, and in 2022 he was re-elected. For eight years under the grand coalition, Merkel relied on his support as the SPD's Foreign Minister. While coalitions between two major political parties are unheard of in the British and American political context, Germany has had its fair share of grand coalition governments between the Christian Democratic Union (CDU) and the Social Democratic Party (SPD) (1966–1969; 2005–2009; 2013–2017; 2017–2021). Giegerich and Terhalle correctly note that 'even a weaker political partner can force its will by threatening to dissolve the coalition' (2021, 34). With regard to the Foreign Office, Merkel (CDU) never exercised her *Richtlinienkompetenz* to overrule Steinmeier (SPD). Instead, Russia policy became his remit (Hacke, 2006).

We need to learn more about Steinmeier if we want to understand key assumptions that shaped the culture of Germany's foreign behaviour under Schröder

(1998–2005) and Merkel (2005–2021). Steinmeier's essay titled 'Interweaving and integration' (*Verflechtung und Integration*) comes closest to describing Germany's misguided approach towards autocracies (2007). This foreign policy approach was reportedly developed by Markus Ederer, then acting as the Foreign Office's Head of Policy Planning division. Ederer was an energy expert just like Steinmeier (Wehner, 2022). In his article, Steinmeier describes EU integration as a success story and portrayed it as a model for the world. The 'intertwining or interlocking of interests' (Steinmeier, 2007) was believed to be the key to achieving a 'peaceful balance between interests, economic prosperity, and social justice' (2007). As Steinmeier saw it, the 'interweaving and networking of business and society [is] a model for success' (2007). The past integration experience of Europe was projected onto its future relations with Russia.

For two reasons such a projection is highly problematic. First, Steinmeier overlooked the fact that Germany and France reestablished their political ties as liberal democracies after WWII. Second, the positive spin he placed on interweaving in politics contradicted his own learning when seeking to establish a consensus about labour market reform in Germany. In the early 2000s, Steinmeier was tasked by Schröder to convene what was then known as the *Bündnis für Arbeit* (Alliance for Work). It was an effort by the German government to address high unemployment and challenges in the labour market. Steinmeier did not succeed in persuading trade unions and employee associations of the need for reform. In response, Schröder opted for state regulation under the controversial Hartz IV policy, which massively curtailed the German welfare system.

In an op-ed for *Die Zeit* Steinmeier reflected on his frustration with political consensus seeking in liberal democracies (2001). In it he referred to the 'joint decision trap' (*Politikverflechtungsfalle*), an idea developed by German political scientist Fritz Scharpf. In 1988 Scharpf had found that both in the case of a highly federalist West Germany as well as in the European Community (as the EU was referred to prior to the Maastricht treaty) higher-level government decisions were hampered by dependence on lower-level constituent governments. Due to the need for unanimous agreements a 'bargaining' style of decision-making would lead to suboptimal policy outcomes (1988, 254–65). Steinmeier, therefore, was acutely aware that the intertwining of politics in a highly federal Germany and at the supranational EU level often resulted in a gridlock and a lack of progress. It is thus surprising that he was optimistic about the prospect of socializing autocracies through interweaving. And in spite of the differences in political systems, he used the experience of European integration to inform his views on the EU–Russia relationship. In his opinion 'the correct assessment seems to dominate among the Russian elite that only a close partnership with the EU will enable Russia to take advantage of the benefits that globalisation offers' (Steinmeier, 2007). He hoped that Russia would become more prosperous and democratic through interweaving. Steinmeier correctly assumed that such a foreign policy approach could produce short-term economic gains, for example, the import of cheap Russian gas. However, in the long run, he should have foreseen that interweaving under the conditions of authoritarianism would result in entanglement. In order to placate authoritarian partners interweaving requires the tacit acceptance of censorship and other red lines, for example, in terms of politically circumscribed dialogue topics, cooperation partners and collaboration methods. Furthermore, taking part in commercial engagements with autocracies – where there is no transparency and the elite is largely in charge – also exposes one to illiberal world views and kleptocratic practices.

While Steinmeier mentioned the need to also engage with Russia's civil society, his primary concern was Europe's energy partnership with Russia. Germany's growing dependence on Russian gas was evident to Steinmeier in 2007. Since Russia was also increasingly dependent on exporting gas to Europe, he didn't seem concerned. In Steinmeier's view it resulted in 'mutual dependency' which he rationalized as 'shared interest' (2007). It is surprising that Steinmeier, who argues that 'no market participant should be able to pursue his own energy interests at the expense of others' (2007), did not anticipate that the eventual completion of the controversial Nord Stream 1 pipeline only four years after the publication of his essay would undermine Russian–Ukranian economic interdependence (Umland, 2021, 79). Based on the premises of 'Rapprochement through interweaving' Steinmeier should have anticipated that Nord Stream 1 would increase the likelihood of military conflict. Instead, in 2007 he invoked the Energy Charter Treaty and called for 'mutual trust in contract compliance and delivery reliability' (Steinmeier, 2007).

In 2022, Russia's war against Ukraine and the destruction of both the Nord Stream 1 and 2 pipelines (Vakulenko, 2022) reveal that Steinmeier's vision of interweaving for peace and stability has not come to pass. His strategy towards Russia has failed in spectacular ways. With Russia's war of aggression against Ukraine Steinmeier had to learn the hard way that Russian imperialism seeks to solve conflicts through violence rather than settling them through EU-style committees and negotiations (Auer, 2022, 119). Since Steinmeier also applied his foreign policy approach to Germany's relationship with autocratic China, this policy failure is particularly concerning. During a speech at Sichuan University in December 2018 Steinmeier acknowledged that the interweaving between Germany and China had revealed 'differences' and that 'our interweaving was not always straightforward, nor without conflict' (Der Bundespräsident, 2018). Yet Steinmeier doubled down on key premises of 'Rapprochement through interweaving' by emphasizing that 'we live in a time of interconnectedness and mutual dependence', and that 'we must neither weaken nor abandon what we have agreed together' (2018).

Steinmeier's speech in China demonstrates his long-held conviction that interweaving promotes peace. According to Tempel '(if) there were a Steinmeier doctrine, it would have to be: infinite patience for talks under the most difficult conditions and an almost inexhaustible belief in the power of dialogue' (IPG, 2016). The source of his thinking needs to be investigated here. Steinmeier justified his doctrine (hence Steinmeier doctrine) with a reference to 'Change through Rapprochement' (*Wandel durch Annäherung*) by Egon Bahr. In 1963 Bahr had described his theory of change as follows: 'Trusting that our world is the better one, the stronger one in a peaceful sense, the one that will prevail, makes it conceivable to try to open up oneself and the other side and to put aside previous ideas of liberation' (DHI, 2023). Based on this insight Bahr argued that 'changes and alterations are now achievable starting from the regime currently in place there' (2023). With his landmark speech in Tutzing in 1963 Bahr opted for an exclusively state-centric engagement approach. Bahr's political patron Brandt admitted two years before his death that he underestimated Eastern European civil society's power to transform. Polish dissident Geremek recalls Brandt as saying in 1990 that 'I thought that the Soviet Union was a power that simply could not be crushed today. I thought the dissident movement was hopeless . . . Today I know what I didn't know then, that you can break the power of an empire with non-political methods' (Hofmann, 2011, 294). Geremek's recollection seems credible since Brandt will have been acutely aware of the criticism levelled against his *Ostpolitik*. According to Behrends the SPD leadership had prioritized Germany's relations with Moscow through back channels, which came at the expense of closer people-to-people exchanges with Eastern European civil society (Berliner Republik, 2016).

At the same time Steinmeier's 'neo-Ostpolitik' (Lough, 2021, 134) also deviated from Bahr's original in other ways. In actual foreign policy implementation the German Eastern Business Association (*Ost-Ausschuss*) played a key role. Similar to the 1950s and 1960s economic diplomacy was supposed to bring about 'change through trade' (Rezková, 2015, 62). Surprisingly, Steinmeier never explained his theory of change in greater detail. How exactly was closer cooperation between German and Russian companies expected to nurture the growth of Russia's civil society and promote democratization? (Lütjen, 2009, 116) Such conceptual blind spots suggest that Steinmeier's actual concern was a different one. Lough has suggested that Steinmeier was keen to ensure that Russia remained a constructive global stakeholder and would not form an anti-Western axis with China (2021, 135). Such a feat was supposed to be accomplished by 'promoting closer relations between the EU and Russia while de-emphasising the broader goal of supporting political and social modernisation in Russia' (2021, 134). Steinmeier's foreign policy approach thus was not geared towards liberalizing and democratizing autocracies. His preferred approach can instead be considered one of 'stabilitocracy'. This term was coined by Pavlović and describes 'a regime where undemocratic practices persist' and where the 'West has . . . turned a blind eye to this while simultaneously preaching the virtues of democracy and the rule of law' (BiEPAG, 2017). Pavlović critique echoes Youngs' observation of European security and defence policy in the early 2000s. Youngs lamented that in their dealings with conflict states European governments had departed from liberal approaches. While the latter paid lip service to '(balancing) state capacity and accountability' (2010, 87) he observed that '(in) practice, the latter is still a blind spot' (2010).

In addition, Steinmeier's neo-Ostpolitik ignored the importance of 'speaking softly and carrying a big stick'. Both carrots and sticks arguably helped the West win the Cold War. Both Brandt and Bahrs' policy of 'Change through Rapprochement' and the Helsiniki Accords from 1975 contributed to building trust between former enemies. On its own, the efficacy of Germany's *Ostpolitik* however should not be overstated. Krause has instead pointed out the transformational leadership of Mikhail Gorbachev. He argues that it was Gorbachev's realization that the USSR could neither keep up economically nor militarily, which changed the dynamics of the bloc confrontation. Krause argues that NATO rearmament with medium-range missiles and the rapid modernization of the US military was of pivotal importance (2022). In stark contrast, the Steinmeier doctrine of the early 21st century almost exclusively relied on carrots. Steinmeier's claim that 'a pan-European peace order and a lasting solution to important security problems . . . can only be achieved with Russia, not without it or even against it' (2007) is a case in point. The criticism he levelled at Merkel for championing sanctions against Russia following the annexation of Crimea should also not be forgotten (Joffe, 2016).

In the case of China, too, Germany cannot rely on the principle of hope and allow 'optimism to override realism' (Lough, 2021, 148), as has been the case with its Russia policy. By the late 1990s Buzan had already warned Western foreign policymakers and business people of blind optimism. Buzan pointed out that as Asia and the West trade and invest with China, they face the dilemma of wanting to maximize profits while having to simultaneously minimize the influence of a revisionist, authoritarian government. Anticipating rapid economic development in the early 2000s Buzan asked 'whether the liberal mechanisms of peace-making economic-entanglement work faster or slower than the realist ones of military and political power increasing on the back of an expanding economy?' (1998, 83) In light of Beijing's increasingly hostile posture towards Taiwan we are fast approaching the time when Buzan's question can be answered.

Since Steinmeier's neo-Ostpolitik failed, one must ask why domestic criticism was ignored earlier. Though Steinmeier admitted that his 'adherence to Nord Stream 2 was clearly a mistake' he also suggested that 'we continued to believe in bridges that Russia no longer believed in and against which our partners had been warning us' (Deutsche Welle, 2022). However, Germany's Eastern European partners had not been the only ones to warn him. As early as February 2006, Umbach had pointed out that in light of the Russian-Ukrainian gas conflict of 2005–2006 core assumptions in Germany's energy and foreign policy had already been demystified. He warned against the prevalent view that growing German energy imports and Russia's desire to export would lead to 'mutual dependency' (2006, 6). He warned that following the collapse of the Soviet Union, 'Moscow has used its energy exports and pipeline monopolies for intimidation and blackmail of its neighboring states' (2006). Steinmeier was not amused. In an op-ed in *Handelsblatt* titled 'Foreign energy policy is peace policy' published a month later he criticized Umbach's article 'Europe's next Cold War' as alarmist. Steinmeier wrote that 'confrontation would be the wrong way and stems from old thinking' (2006). Instead of addressing Umbach's warning of weaponized interdependence head on, Steinmeier doubled down on his preferred 'cooperative energy security strategy' (2006). In an interview in 2022 Umbach has complained that 'critics were not listened to' (Malzahn et al., 2022). Another documented case of Steinmeier's unwillingness to learn is from 2014. Steinmeier had invited the German security expert Joachim Krause to comment on the Foreign Office's Global Review. In his submission Krause pointed out that 'Russia has burned many bridges behind it' and that following the annexation of Crimea NATO would need to initiate a 'new deterrence policy towards Russia' (Sirius, 2022). This kind of warning, however apt, was also not well received. His assessment was not documented alongside other expert opinions on the Foreign Office's website. Krause subsequently learned through third parties that he was branded a 'cold warrior' (2022). This comes to show that the German institutional diplomacy is not immune to groupthink. According to Janis foreign policy ingroups often suffer from an overly consensual approach in their deliberations. Pressure on contrarian thinkers to fall in line with other group members not only promotes self-censorship. A flawed group consensus also contributes to an 'illusion of invulnerability', which in turn encourages extraordinary risk-taking (1971, 85).

Duelling open letters published in the wake of Russia's annexation of Crimea further illustrate the gulf in understanding between senior decision-makers and Eastern Europe experts. On 5 December 2014 sixty senior politicians, lobbyists and celebrities signed an open letter which called for continued dialogue with Russia, a new détente policy and continued intertwining (Tagesspiegel, 2014a). The signatories also cautioned journalists against supposedly 'demonizing entire peoples without sufficiently appreciating their history' (2014a). It prompted more than 100 Eastern Europe experts from the fields of academia, politics and media to publish their own open letter in which they bemoaned that 'German policy on Eastern Europe should be based on experience, factual knowledge and analytical results, and not on pathos, forgetfulness of history and sweeping judgments' (Tagesspiegel, 2014b). In hindsight we can see clearly that domestic critics weren't listened to. This undermines Steinmeier's claims of engaging in frank discussions about German foreign policy in a changing world without 'self-pity' (Federal Foreign Office, 2014). Furthermore, it raises questions whether the Steinmeier doctrine was designed in a way to inoculate the German government against legitimate criticism. Schneckener has raised the question: 'How can more openness and reflection for contradictory or deviating signals be achieved in politics and the ministerial bureaucracy, especially when they shake one's own traditional guidelines?' (2022) Which reference to Deutsch I distinguished two types of political learning from each other in the first chapter: *creative learning*, which allows systems to grow, expand and restructure; and *destructive learning*, which blocks constructive developments and promotes self-destructive tendencies (1973, 329). Germany's political economy, which is highly corporatist, made possible the development and continued defense of the Steinmeier doctrine, even when it had passed its shelf-life. The division of labour between the Foreign Office and private sector organizations involved in Russia and China policy, such as the German Eastern Business Association (OA) or the Asia-Pacific Committee of German Business (APA), is crucial to understanding destructive learning among German political and economic elites.

Organizational sociology can help us better understand the dynamics at play. Routine games refer to daily routines and practices that maintain the status quo.

In 2017, the key intellectual force behind the Steinmeier doctrine Ederer, who had by then risen to the rank of State Secretary in the Foreign Office, said about the *Ost-Ausschuss*: 'We do not want closed spaces, but opening and networking . . . We know that the German Eastern Business Association will continue to be at our side in the future' (Auswärtiges Amt, 2017). During his time as German president, Steinmeier thanked the German Eastern Business Association and its member companies for building bridges to the East through many projects and partnerships (Ost-Ausschuss, 2021). Using Luttwak as a reference, Kundnani (2011, 41) has described the relationship between politicians and businesses as 'reciprocal manipulation'. The problem here is that when German foreign policy objectives are too closely aligned with those of the private sector, conflicts of interest multiply, democratic accountability is reduced, mutual dependencies are developed and transparency is compromised. Chapter 4 will demonstrate that APA, the *Ost-Ausschuss* equivalent for China and the Asia-Pacific region, also vigorously defended Germany's pro-business approach to China. For lobby organizations such as the OA and APA, alignment with the Steinmeier doctrine has always made good business sense.

Steinmeier's thinking about governing under the conditions of 'complexity' and the need for 'consensus' was grounded in the belief that modern statecraft requires the government to seek solutions beyond the political arena. In his view the government should invite economic or societal stakeholders to participate in policy deliberations (Lütjen, 2009, 63). During his time as Chief of Staff of the Chancellery under Schröder (1999–2005) Steinmeier repeatedly sidelined the SPD and its parliamentary caucus in favour of 'active exchange with experts and interest representatives' (2009, 65). And while the Chancellery used its convening power to facilitate stakeholder interaction, it was not always clear what the Schröder administration hoped to achieve through its various commissions and consensual politics. Steinmeier biographer Lütjen suggests that during stakeholder consultation and consensus building the red-green government often failed to provide political leadership and policy guidance (2009, 66).

Innovation games, on the other hand, introduce new ideas and encourage change. Umbach and Krause, both contrarians who questioned the conventional wisdom of Germany's Russia policy, could be seen as undermining both Steinmeier's personal authority as well as profitable relations between German conglomerates and Moscow. In light of the lack of clarity regarding who would benefit from a successful innovation game, the latter are particularly hard fought for (Bogumil and Schmid, 2001, 68). Despite Umbach and Krause's right critique of German Russia policy, Steinmeier failed to grasp the problem. Bingener and Wehner are spot on when highlighting '(in) the creed of the German Social Democrats, the policy of détente is regarded as the cornerstone of Social Democratic foreign policy – and criticism of it as an attack on the party's holy of holies' (2023). As of 2022, Steinmeier has publicly declared he is no longer convinced that trade can bring about change (Spiegel, 2022). He has also stated that '(for) the future, we must learn lessons, and learning lessons means that we must reduce unilateral dependencies wherever possible, especially vis-à-vis China' (Der Spiegel, 2022).

However, the damage done to Germany by his doctrine of intertwining it with autocracies like Russia and China is already done. In spite of this, it is important to point out that Steinmeier's core beliefs were not developed in a vacuum of history, space or politics. As the following discussion will show it appears that Steinmeier's failure is indicative of a much broader malaise.

2.3 Germany's reluctance to project power

In its fundamentals, the Steinmeier doctrine consisted of (1) a selective reading of Europe's integration experiences; (2) a highly problematic projection of the principles and practices of interest negotiations in liberal democracies onto Europe's relationship with autocracies; (3) an unfounded scepticism about civil society's transformative power in non-democratic countries; (4) a romanticisation of Bahr's Ostpolitik and a disregard for the importance of military power in international relations; (5) an overly close relationship between German foreign policymakers and corporate lobbying groups; and (6) a propensity for groupthink among German diplomats and an intolerance for contrarian foreign and security advice. However, Steinmeier's claim that 'we have failed on many points' (Der Bundespräsident, 2022) still merits a closer inspection. The idea that Germans – both at the elite and mass level – were collectively wrong on Russia policy is persuasive if we consider the Steinmeier doctrine as representing a 'post-heroic society' that opposes 'power projection' (Kundnani, 2015, 4).

Scholars have repeatedly pointed to the 'paradox' (Kundnani, 2015) or 'puzzle' (Maull, 2018) of German power. In the aftermath of WWII and under US tutelage, Germany relinquished autonomous security policies (Maull, 1990/1991). While constraining Germany's ability to project military power, this limitation allowed successive governments to develop its statecraft in the field of economics and foreign trade promotion. In light of this, it is not surprising that West German foreign and security policy developed slowly after WWII. Bulmer and Paterson aptly described post-war Germany 'as an economic giant but political dwarf' (2013, 1388). Alternative descriptions in the literature have ranged from 'semi-sovereign' to 'semi-Gulliver': 'a shackled giant' (2013, 1388). According to Wittlinger and Larose West Germany's semi-sovereign status and the weight of the country's collective memory resulted in foreign policy behaviour 'characterised by self-limitation, a strong commitment to multilateralism and a civilian foreign policy culture' (2007). Such historically shaped foreign policy restraint gradually changed under the red-green government under Schröder (1998–05) (2007). Staun has pointed out that under Schröder (1998–2005) a major change occurred in the justification of use of military force. Whereas prior to unification the national consensus was '*nie wieder Krieg* (never again war)' (2020, 94), after 1991 limited participation in military operations abroad was justified on the basis of '*nie wieder Auschwitz* (never again Auschwitz)' (2020). In light of the Srebrenica massacre, then Foreign Minister Joschka Fischer had invoked memories of the Holocaust to justify NATO intervention. A subsequent paint attack on Fischer is testament of the highly controversial nature of this decision (Nagorski, 1999). Despite such piecemeal changes to Germany's approach to military affairs Maull has argued that 'the old, originally West German role concept of "civilian power" still corresponds rather well to the foreign policies that Germany has pursued since 2013 under its grand coalition government' (2018, 474).

As a result, the Steinmeier doctrine needs to be viewed in the context of post-unification Germany, which has yet to learn the language of power (for an in-depth discussion of *leverage* as power see Chapter 8). I agree with Bulmer and Paterson who claim that 'Germany is intrinsically a reluctant hegemon' (2013, 1392). I also concur with Auer who has observed that in foreign affairs German elites have a tendency to hide behind Brussels (Auer, 2022, 108). This is also evident from the way leading German politicians have argued their case in public. Chancellor Merkel has considered 'the European Union as our life insurance. Germany is far too small to exert geo-political influence on its own' (Kampfner, 2020, 75). Former Foreign Minister Heiko Maas (2018–2021) has similarly argued that 'we as Germany are also too small to stand up to the Chinese. [China] will become the new superpower. For this we need a European strategy' (Maischberger, 2020).

What neither Maas nor Merkel sufficiently explained to the German public is that it is very hard to seek consensus on foreign policy issues among twenty-seven member states, not least since they all exhibit 'hugely different foreign policy traditions, capabilities and interests' (Fraser, 2021, 3). Auer is right in questioning whether the European Union has the ability to act as a unitary foreign policy actor (2022, 104–5). He has also accused EU member states for shirking from their responsibilities to develop a more muscular foreign policy by hiding 'behind the EU's weakness and disunity' (2022, 108).

2.4 Brussels to the rescue?

Streeck reminds us that 'the benefits of large size political rule tend to be oversold while its costs, including the political capital that has to be spent on instituting encompassing and centralised institutions of governance in the first place, are typically downplayed' (2019, 14). At the European level, the relationship with China remains ambiguous. As of Spring 2019, EU–China relations are described as follows: 'China is, simultaneously, in different policy areas, a cooperation partner with whom the EU has closely aligned objectives, a negotiating partner with whom the EU needs to find a balance of interests, an economic competitor in the pursuit of technological leadership, and a systemic rival promoting alternative models of governance' (European Commission, 2019, 1). As might be expected, Beijing has reacted with irritation to this position. Foreign Minister Wang Yi has noted that the 'EU's triple positioning for China is mutually contradictory and cancels itself out' (Lau, 2021). He was not wrong, since an approach based on partnership takes advantage of opportunities in Western engagement with China, whereas a systemic rivalry is more concerned with economic and political risks. The space for cooperative approaches is greatly reduced, however, when risk mitigation is implemented.

The European Commission has reiterated that 'finding the right balance of policy approaches is a political judgement, requiring the attention of the European Council' (2019, 2). In foreign policy decision-making, the European Council, headed by Charles Michel, is considered a key arbiter (Maurer and Wright, 2021). It is clear from this that the development of a more unified European China strategy cannot happen by itself, but requires the leadership of individual EU member states. A clearer understanding of what systemic rivalry with China means will also be necessary. It was reported that in Spring 2020 that the European External Action Service's StratCom division prepared a report, which was highly critical of Russian and Chinese disinformation regarding Covid-19 (Eder, 2020). It later transpired that the published report had been watered down (von der Burchard, 2020). While a EEAS spokesperson denied bowing to Beijing's pressure (Stolton, 2020), this saga illustrates how difficult it is to counter non-conventional threats emanating from China. Calling out nefarious actions of state or non-state agents acting on behalf of the Chinese party-state requires a willingness to assert oneself vis-à-vis the CCP. Taylor's scholarship has shown that the EU has thus far failed to 'rise to this normative challenge and defend the rules-based world order' (2021).

Beijing's divide-and-conquer tactics vis-à-vis Europe

In an interview Merics director Huotari has pointed out that '(everyone) who knows the European Union knows that there is no united position on anything really. But there is a zone of consensus that creates the possibility to act. And on certain matters, including trade and investment policy, you see a lot of consensus on the question of sharpening our defensive toolbox' (Peaple, 2022). A case in point has been European Commission president von der Leyen, who during a speech at the Berlin-based think tank made the case for 'de-risking' (European Commission, 2023). This new approach was to include measures to restrict 'trade in highly sensitive technologies where military use cannot be excluded or where there are human rights implications' (Kynge, 2023). De-risking was also mean to include a mechanism for outbound investment screening of European firms which could contribute to the build up of military capabilities of rivals (2023).

von der Leyen's policy entrepreneurship has in part been a reaction to Beijing's efforts to drive a wedge between European member states. As Jiroš has rightly pointed out since 2012 Beijing has initiated a 'China-centric initiative incorporating 16 Central and Eastern European (CEE) countries. In 2019, Greece – which is heavily indebted to China – joined, and the platform was briefly renamed 17+1. While it is officially described as an economic cooperation platform, its real achievements and the PRC's approach to it show that trade and investment were never its true focus. Rather, the PRC used it as a propaganda and influence tool, wasting CEE diplomatic capacity on activities that only benefited Beijing' (Jiroš, 2022). While Estonia and Latvia have now quit the 16+1 format (2022) the Chinese party-state has not given up on trying to influence Europe as much as possible. In a recent comment Huoatari has commented on Beijing's ambition to 'keep the Europeans as far away from the Americans as possible' (Solomon and Hong, 2023), suggesting that in order to do so 'Germany plays a huge role in that' (2023).

But why would the Chinese Communist Party try to drive a wedge between Germany, Europe and NATO ally United States? In Chapter 3 I will shed light on China's strategic culture, including its irredentist and revisionist tendencies. I argue that a better understanding of senior leaders of the Chinese Communist Party such as General Secretary Xi is essential for a better grasp of the China's increasingly aggressive foreign policy.

References for Chapter 2

Auer, S. (2021), 'Merkel's Germany and the European Union: Between Emergency and the Rule of Rules', *Government & Opposition*, 56: 1–19.

Auer, S. (2022), *European Disunion*, London: Hurst.

Auswärtiges Amt (2017), 'Rede von Staatssekretär Markus Ederer beim Jahresempfang des Ost-Ausschusses der Deutschen Wirtschaft: „Eurasien – Brennpunkt der Interessen oder Raum der Kooperation?"', 12 July. Available online: https://web.archive.org/ web/20221108085144/https://www.auswaertiges-amt.de/de/newsroom/170712-sts-e -ostausschuss/291376 (accessed 10 July 2023).

Bennhold, K. (2022), 'The Former Chancellor Who Became Putin's Man in Germany', *New York Times*, 23 April. Available online: https://archive.is/xKksM#selection-365.0-365 .55 (accessed 10 July 2023).

Berliner Republik (2016), '»Heute haben wir es mit einem anderen Russland zu tun«', May. Available online: https://archive.is/Pp9ro (accessed 10 July 2023).

Biel, H., B. Giegerich, and A. Jonas (2013), 'Introduction', in H. Biel, B. Giegerich, and A. Jonas (eds), *Strategic Cultures in Europe: Security and Defence Policies Across the Continent*, 7–17, Wiesbaden: Springer Fachmedien Wiesbaden GmbH.

BiEPAG (2017), 'What Is a Stabilitocracy?', 5 May. Available online: https://archive.is/ HA05g (accessed 10 July 2023).

Bingener, R. and M. Wehner, (2023), 'Die Moskau-Connection', *Frankfurter Allgemeine Zeitung*, 13 March, 6.

Bogumil, J. and J. Schmid (2001), *Politik in Organisationen. Organisationstheoretische Ansätze und praxisbezogene Anwendungsbeispiele*, Opladen: Leske + Budrich.

Bulmer, S. and W. E. Paterson (2013), 'Germany as the EU's Reluctant Hegemon? Of Economic Strength and Political Constraints', *Journal of European Public Policy*, 20 (10): 1387–405.

Buzan, B. (1998), 'The Asia-Pacific: What Sort of Region in What Sort of World?', in A. McGrew and C. Brook (Hrsg), *Asia-Pacific in the New World Order*, 68–87, London: Routledge.

Daub, A. (2021), 'The Weird, Extremely German Origins of the Wirecard Scandal', *The New Republic*, 21 April. Available online: https://archive.is/RAuzv (accessed 10 July 2023).

Der Bundespräsident (2014), 'Speech to Open 50th Munich Security Conference', 31 January. Available online: https://archive.is/BeThk (accessed 10 July 2023).

Der Bundespräsident (2018), 'Besuch der Sichuan-Universität in China', 7 December. Available online: https://archive.is/kkjQp (accessed 10 July 2023).

Der Bundespräsident (2022), 'Interview mit dem ZDF-Morgenmagazin', 5 April. Available online: https://archive.is/DYnvi (accessed 10 July 2023).

Der Spiegel (2022), 'Steinmeier warnt vor Abhängigkeit von China', 26 October. Available online: https://archive.is/jKtE5 (accessed 10 July 2023).

Deutsch, K. (1973), *Politische Kybernetik. Modelle und Perspektiven*, Freiburg im Breisgau: Verlag Rombach.

Deutsche Welle (2022), 'German President Steinmeier Admits Mistakes Over Russia', 4 May. Available online: https://archive.is/as2Re (accessed 10 July 2023).

DHI (2023), 'Wandel durch Annäherung (15. Juli 1963)', Available online: https://archive.is/l49kl (accessed 10 July 2023).

Eder, F. (2020), 'Russia and China Promote Coronavirus "Conspiracy Narratives" Online, Says EU Agency', *Politico*, 21 April. Available online: https://archive.is/MqaSb (accessed 10 July 2023).

European Commission (2019), 'EU-China – A Strategic Outlook', 12 March. Available online: https://commission.europa.eu/system/files/2019-03/communication-eu-china-a-strategic-outlook.pdf (accessed 10 July 2023).

European Commission (2023), 'Speech by President von der Leyen on EU-China relations to the Mercator Institute for China Studies and the European Policy Centre', 30 March. Available online: https://archive.is/SKYcu (accessed 10 July 2023).

Federal Foreign Office (2014), '"Review 2014 – A Fresh Look at German Foreign Policy" - Closing Remarks by Foreign Minister Frank-Walter Steinmeier', 20 May. Available online: https://web.archive.org/web/20220325105017/https://www.auswaertiges-amt.de/en/newsroom/news/140520-bm-review2014-abschlussrede/262346 (accessed 10 July 2023).

Fletcher, M. (2021), 'From Germany, the UK Appears Ever More Dysfunctional and Absurd', *The New Statesman*, 11 October. Available online: https://archive.is/UsKEa (accessed 10 July 2023).

Foot, R. (2000), *Rights Beyond Borders: The Global Community and the Struggle Over Human Rights in China*, Oxford: Oxford University Press.

Fraser, C. (2021), 'Give Lisbon a Chance: How to Improve EU Foreign Policy', *European Policy Centre*, Policy Brief, Europe in the World Programme, 8 January. Available online: https://www.epc.eu/content/PDF/2021/Foreign_Policy_v3.pdf (accessed 10 July 2023).

Giegerich, B. and M. Terhalle (2021), *The Responsibility to Defend: Rethinking Germany's Strategic Culture*, Oxon: Routledge.

Hacke, C. (2006), 'Deutsche Außenpolitik unter Bundeskanzlerin Angela Merkel', *Aus Politik und Zeitgeschichte*, B43, 13 October. Available online: https://archive.is/PquZf (accessed 10 July 2023).

Hofmann, G. (2011), *Polen und Deutsche. Der Weg zur europäischen Revolution 1989/90*, Berlin: Suhrkamp.

IPG (2016), 'Steinbeißermeier', 28 November. Available online: https://archive.is/rsHEx (accessed 10 July 2023).

Janis, I. (1971), 'Groupthink', *Psychology Today*, November, 43–6: 84–90. Available online: https://agcommtheory.pbworks.com/f/GroupThink.pdf (accessed 10 July 2023).

Jirouš, F. (2022), 'Time to Leave China's "16+1" Influence Trap, August 2022', *ICDS*. Available online: https://icds.ee/wp-content/uploads/dlm_uploads/2022/08/ICDS

_EFPI_Brief_Time_to_Leave_China%C2%B4s_161_Influence_Trap_Filip_Jirous _August_2022.pdf (accessed 10 July 2023).

Joffe, J. (2016), 'Putins Freunde', *Zeit Online*, 30 June. Available online: https://archive.is/ jz7L4 (accessed 10 July 2023).

Junk, J. and C. Daase (2013), 'Germany', in H. Biel, B. Giegerich, and A. Jonas (eds), *Strategic Cultures in Europe. Security and Defence Policies Across the Continent*, 139–52, Wiesbaden: Springer Fachmedien Wiesbaden GmbH.

Kahneman, D. (2011), *Thinking, Fast and Slow*, London: Allen Lane.

Kampfner, J. (2020), *Why the Germans Do it Better*, London: Atlantic Books.

Krause, J. (2022), 'Der deutsche Beitrag zur Ostpolitik bleibt bescheiden. Es wird Zeit, dass SPD und Union endlich eine kritische Bewertung ihrer Fehler machen', *Neue Züricher Zeitung*, 12 December. Available online: https://archive.is/jRP2p#selection-495.0-499 .333 (accessed 10 July 2023).

Kundnani, H. (2011), 'Germany as a Geo-Economic Power', *The Washington Quarterly*, 34 (3): 31–45.

Kundnani, H. (2015), *The Paradox of German Power*, New York: Oxford University Press.

Kynge, J. (2023), 'Von der Leyen's "De-Risking" Is a Tougher Stance on China', *Financial Times*, 30 March. Available online: https://archive.is/Atqwv (accessed 10 July 2023).

Lau, S. (2021), 'Chinese Foreign Minister: EU Diplomacy Is "Contradictory"', *Politico*, 24 July. Available online: https://archive.is/4I9Qm (accessed 10 July 2023).

Lever, P. (2018), *Berlin Rules*, London: I.B. Tauris.

Lough, J. (2021), *Germany's Russia Problem: The Struggle for Balance in Europe*, Manchester: Manchester University Press.

Lütjen, T. (2009), *Frank-Walter Steinmeier - Die Biografie*, Freiburg im Breisgau: Herder.

Maischberger (2020), 'Bundesaußenminister Heiko Maas bei maischberger. die woche 03.06.2020', 3 June. Available online: https://www.youtube.com/watch?v=pheTUqvY2sI &t=666s (accessed 10 July 2023).

Malici, A. (2006, January), 'Germans as Venutians: The Culture of German Foreign Policy Behavior', *Foreign Policy Analysis*, 2 (1): 37–62.

Malzahn, C., N. Doll, H.-M. Tillack, and S. Lehnartz (2022), 'Die vielen Irrtümer des Frank-Walter Steinmeier', *Welt*, 10 April 2022. Available online: https://archive.is/ W2DSj (accessed 10 July 2023).

Maull, H. (1990–91), 'Germany and Japan: The New Civilian Powers', *Foreign Affairs*. Available online: https://archive.is/njjo5 (accessed 10 July 2023).

Maull, H. (2018), 'Reflective, Hegemonic, Geo-economic, Civilian … ? The Puzzle of German Power', *German Politics*, 27 (4): 460–78.

Maurer, H. and N. Wright (2021), 'Still Governing in the Shadows? Member States and the Political and Security Committee in the Post-Lisbon EU Foreign Policy Architecture', *Journal of Common Market Studies*, 59 (4): 856–72.

Nagorski, A. (1999), 'The Paint Attack', *Newsweek*, 23 May. Available online: https://archive .is/zBhUy (accessed 10 July 2023).

Ost-Ausschuss (2021), 'Virtueller Jahresauftakt mit Bundespräsident Steinmeier und 350 Gästen', 26 February. Available online: https://web.archive.org/web/20210420124437/ https://www.ost-ausschuss.de/de/Jahresauftakt%20OA (accessed 10 July 2023).

Peaple, A. (2022), 'Mikko Huotari on Germany's "Capacity to Act"', *The Wire*, 5 June. Available online: https://archive.is/VK510 (accessed 10 July 2023).

Rezková, E. (2015), 'Wandel durch Handel. Die Wegbereiter der Ostpolitik in den 50-er und 60-er Jahren', Diplomarbeit, Philosophische Fakultät, Institut für Wirtschafts- und Sozialgeschichte, Karls-Universität in Prag. Available online: https://dspace.cuni.cz

/bitstream/handle/20.500.11956/74420/120197118.pdf?sequence=1&isAllowed=y (accessed 10 July 2023).

Scharpf, F. (1988), 'The Joint-Decision Trap: Lessons from German Federalism and European Integration', *Public Administration*, 66 (3): 239–78.

Schneckener, U. (2022), 'Gestörter Empfang: Putins Kriegsnarrative und die deutsche Russlandpolitik', Zeitschrift für Friedens- und Konfliktforschung, 29 December, 279–93. Available online: https://doi.org/10.1007/s42597-022-00086-4 (accessed 10 July 2023).

Scholz, O. (2023), 'The Global Zeitenwende. How to Avoid a New Cold War in a Multipolar Era', *Foreign Affairs*, January/February. Available online: https://archive.is/y6WLU#selection-1461.0-1465.47 (accessed 10 July 2023).

Sirius (2022), 'Global Review 2014: Warnungen vor Russland gab es zu genüge, sie wurden nur nicht beachtet', Available online: https://archive.is/Ff9nR (accessed 10 July 2023).

Snyder, J. (1977), 'The Soviet Strategic Culture: Implications for Limited Nuclear Operations', *The Rand Corporation*, Santa Monica: RAND.

Solomon, E. and N. Hong (2023), 'Germany and China Try to Reset Relations for a Changed World', *New York Times*, 19 June. Available online: https://archive.is/l2q75#selection-469.0-469.60 (accessed 10 July 2023).

Staun, J. (2020), 'The Slow Path Towards "Normality": German Strategic Culture and the Holocaust', *Scandinavian Journal of Military Studies*, 3 (1): 84–99.

Steinmeier, F.-W. (2001), 'Abschied von den Machern', *Zeit Online*, 7 September. Available online: https://archive.is/WmfpA (accessed 10 July 2023).

Steinmeier, F.-W. (2006), '„Energie-Außenpolitik ist Friedenspolitik"', *Handelsblatt*, 22 March. Available online: https://archive.is/LAAVU (accessed 10 July 2023).

Steinmeier, F.-W. (2007), 'Verflechtung und Integration', *Internationale Politik*, 1 March. Available online: https://archive.is/DA9V5 (accessed 10 July 2023).

Stolton, S. (2020), 'EEAS Denies Toning Down China Disinformation Report Under Pressure', *Euractiv*, 27 April. Available online: https://archive.is/Be3v6 (accessed 10 July 2023).

Streeck, W. (2019), 'Reflections on Political Scale', *Jurisprudence*, 10 (1): 1–14.

Streeck, W. and M. Höpner (2003), *Alle Macht dem Markt? Fallstudien zur Abwicklung der Deutschland AG*, Frankfurt and New York: Campus Verlag.

Tagesspiegel (2014a), 'Aufruf für eine andere Russland-Politik: "Nicht in unserem Namen"', 5 December. Available online: https://archive.is/TwUZ7 (accessed 10 July 2023).

Tagesspiegel (2014b), '"Gegen-Aufruf" im Ukraine-Konflikt: Osteuropa-Experten sehen Russland als Aggressor', Available online: https://archive.is/qsSuk (accessed 10 July 2023).

Taylor, M. (2021), 'Assessing the Practical Implementation of the EU's Values in EU–China Dialogues', *Asia Europe Journal*, 19: 227–44.

Terhalle, M. (2016), 'IB-Professionalität als Praxisferne? Ein Plädoyer für Wandel', *Zeitschrift für Außen- und Sicherheitspolitik*, 9: 121–38.

Terhalle, M. (2020), *Strategie als Beruf*, Baden-Baden: Tectum bei Nomos.

Umbach, F. (2006), 'Europas nächster Kalter Krieg', *Internationale Politik*, 1 February. Available online: https://archive.is/HFXWH (accessed 10 July 2023).

Umland, A. (2021), 'Germany's Russia Policy in Light of the Ukraine Conflict: Interdependence Theory and Ostpolitik', *Orbis*, 66 (1): 78–94.

Vakulenko, S. (2022), 'Shock and Awe: Who Attacked the Nord Stream Pipelines?', Carnegie Endowment for International Peace, 30 September. Available online: https://archive.is/7XBm9 (accessed 10 July 2023).

von der Burchard, H. (2020), 'EU's Diplomatic Service Launches Probe Over China
      Disinformation Leak', *Politico*, 27 May. Available online: https://archive.is/PVHNY
      (accessed 10 July 2023).

Wehner, M. (2022), 'Rechtfertigt Steinmeiers Russland-Politik die Ausladung?',
      Frankfurter Allgemeine Zeitung, 13 April. Available online: https://archive.is/kMjP6
      (accessed 10 July 2023).

Wittlinger, R. and M. Larose (2007), 'No Future for Germany's Past? Collective Memory
      and German Foreign Policy', *German Politics*, 16 (4): 481–95.

Youngs, R. (2010), *The EU's Role in World Politics*, Milton Park: Routledge.

ZDF heute (2022), 'Steinmeier distanziert sich von Schröder', 12 June. Available online:
      https://archive.is/U6MnN (accessed 10 July 2023).

Chapter 3

WHY THE CCP STRUGGLES AGAINST ITS OPPONENTS, AT HOME AND ABROAD

3.1 The rise of plutocracy

For more than two decades Germany's 'change through trade' mantra has implied a causal relationship between commercial engagement with China and political reform. Yet despite the Chinese middle class' exponential growth, it has not played the role attributed to it by modernization theory. Thus far China's middle class has not pushed the party-state to liberalize and democratize (Fewsmith, 2007; Ekman, 2015; Goodman, 2018). In recent years China's middle class may have grown impatient with 'intrusive social monitoring and censorship' (French, 2022), but whether it will play a decisive role in shaping China's political future remains anyone's guess.

The social question in China remains unresolved as well. Since the early 2000s China's Gini coefficient – which measures income inequality – has consistently hovered above 0.4 and appears to be increasing (Mazzocco, 2022). Such scores are associated with political instability and social unrest. In 1995, the bottom 50 per cent of China's population owned 16 per cent of personal wealth, but only 6 per cent in 2021 (Mo, 2022, 1). Due to the party-state's unwillingness to reform the *hukou* system (Jaramillo, 2022), rural Chinese are still treated as second-class citizens. As a result of this Maoist institution from 1958, Chinese citizens' chances at success are still largely determined by where they were born. In contrast, Chinese billionaires have fared much better. As the poor became poorer, China's uber rich increased their wealth by 70 per cent, from under 6 per cent in 2016 to nearly 10 per cent in 2021 (Mo, 2022, 1). Consequently, China's economic boom has not resulted in democracy but in plutocracy.

While there is a correlation between Germany's mercantilist China policy and rapid economic development in China, China's GDP growth has also empowered the party-state, which remains 'a major source of both wealth and class position' (Goodman, 2018, 207). If we want to better understand the downsides of Steinmeier's preferred approach of 'stabilitocracy' (BiEPAG, 2017) we need to familiarize ourselves with Chinese elite culture. I argue that understanding China's strategic culture, including its irredentist and revisionist tendencies, is also essential for a better grasp of the CCP's increasingly aggressive foreign policy.

Chapter at a glance

This book chapter provides a historically informed overview of the CCP's ongoing struggle against opponents, at home and abroad. It begins with a discussion on China's strategic culture and the CCP's quest for political legitimacy. It then proceeds by comparing and contrasting China's so-called 'reform and opening up' period (1978–2012) with the subsequent hard authoritarian turn under Xi Jinping (2012–). The discussion then moves to sharp power projection, concepts of struggle and the principles and practices behind the CCP's foreign interference in liberal democracies.

3.2 China's strategic culture and the CCP's quest for political legitimacy

This next section will explain how China's strategic culture is infused with references to pre-modern history, exhibits pre-political concepts of Chinese identity, reveals a willingness to project hard power and glorifies the role of the People's Liberation Army (PLA). In Chapter 2, I discussed Biel, Giegerich and Jonas comparative study of European strategic cultures from 2013. A few years on Tellis invited ten experts to analyse the strategic cultures of national elites in China, Russia, Japan, South Korea, India, Indonesia and the United States. The resulting edited volume *Understanding strategic cultures in the Asia-Pacific* (Tellis et al., 2016) explored the world views of national security decision-makers. Tellis argues that these outlooks are shaped by ideas inherited from one generation to another, contested and reproduced in social settings (2016, 7). Although he acknowledges the importance of material capabilities in international politics, Tellis suggests that observers of the physical world need a priori concepts to make sense of what they see (2016, 7–8). He argues that a strategic culture provides decision-makers with a methodologically preexistent frame of mind, but not necessarily an unchanging one (2016, 8–9).

Ford's contribution to the volume explains how China's strategic culture relates to the CCP's quest for legitimacy (2016, 54). The official narrative of China's strategic culture portrays Beijing as having 'a uniquely ancient history and political-cultural continuity' (2016, 29), which validates Beijing's status as a supposedly peace-loving power at the centre of world civilization (2016). Rather than calling them virtues, Ford dismisses such self-perceptions 'virtuocratic' storylines, conceits or pretensions (2016, 29–37). He argues that the CCP is primarily driven by realpolitik. A major challenge in international relations is its obsession with 'ideological grievances' while wanting to reclaim 'its perceived birthright and expunging past humiliation at foreign hands by returning itself to first-rank global status' (2016, 30). In Ford's view, this leads to 'exacerbated realism' (2016) and a willingness to use hard power to achieve party objectives. According to him, the CCP is using 'narratives about China's strategic culture in a complex process of appropriation, manipulation, and selective remembering' (2016, 31). A key point that Ford repeatedly makes is that the lack of democratic legitimacy has led to the party-state to distort or invent historical information to shore up public support (2016).

Such reflections about the CCP's strategic use of China's history is consistent with Tatlow's observation that the 'party is taking older norms of imperial power and statecraft and reworking them in the modernist crucible of the CCP' (2018). Tatlow argues that China's policymaking is influenced both by imperial thought and Marxist ideology. She highlights three pre-modern Chinese tenets that still have bearing on China today. To begin with, she refers to 天下 ('All under heaven'), which connotes a unified world with the emperor and China in the middle. Another point which she emphasizes is 天朝 ('Heavenly court'). By this she refers to the imperial state ruled by the emperor, who was considered a 'son of heaven'. Her view is that the heavenly court is the predecessor of the one-party state we have today. Finally, she accentuates the importance of 羈縻 ('Bridling and feeding'). Here she refers to this as '(a) method used to pacify non-Chinese territories and create vassal states by reward and threat', something she calls 'an earlier version of today's "carrot and stick"' (Tatlow, 2018, 3). Thus tradition is embedded in a dialectic process whereby Xi Jinping reads the works of emperors Yao and Shun and 'takes notes' but also is a determined communist, Tatlow believes.

But how seriously should we take it when the CCP selectively highlights aspects of Chinese imperial rule to justify its own autocracy? Ford argues that notions of 'Chineseness' play an important role in the official narrative (2016, 32). He contends that the CCP presents itself as a custodian of Chinese civilization through 'self-Orientalizing essentialism' (2016). The regime's use of 'special Chinese values' is meant to legitimize its autocratic political system, promote the CCP's leadership and discredit 'Western' democratic values (2016). Ford's findings echo Roetz critique of the CCP appealing to 'the peculiarity of Chinese culture', a form of 'identity management' aimed at curtailing "Western" liberalism' (2022, 41). Roetz argues that by manufacturing a 'pre-political identity' of Chinese culture, the CCP seeks to pre-empt demands for greater political participation (2022). Roetz has warned against treating such a cultural identity as 'static or monolithic' (1997, 41). He is also highly critical of senior German politicians, who have uncritically embraced notions of a supposedly monolithic and never-changing Chinese 'Confucian culture' (2007, 48–9). He is highly critical of such generalizations, as they can inform 'assertions that collaboration with China, a dictatorship, after all, is legitimate since there would be no reason to invoke and respect norms of freedom which have never been shared by or even known to 'the Chinese' themselves' (215). He further points out that such cultural relativism is 'driven by economic interests and used as a simple pretext to get rid of moral misgivings' (2019).

Studying China's *strategic* culture, on the other hand, requires us to analyse what kind of *political* culture informs Chinese elites' thinking. While research on the latter has been sparse, the following insights from the academic literature can shed light about the subject matter. Gold has summarized Chinese political culture 'as revealed in centuries of practice, [which] takes a zero-sum, moralistic view of political disagreements, in which the ultimate objective is the elimination of rivals as well as their followers, families, and even names' (1997, 167). A similar claim has been made by Fewsmith. He argues that the emperor system in mainland China contributed to the tendency for political matters to be resolved by dominance (1999, 49). This approach to politics was exacerbated by the end of the dynastic system in 1911, the humiliation China suffered under foreigners, internal conflict, the revolutionary ideologies of the Kuomintang (KMT) and the CCP (with their privileged claims to truth), and the civil war, during which those two political parties struggled for power. According to Fewsmith a 'winner-take-all conception of politics has been a hallmark of CCP politics' (1999, 49) ever since. It should not come to anyone's surprise, therefore, that since the early 2000s, the political thinking of the German Nazi philosopher Carl Schmitt has been enthusiastically received by party ideologues and Chinese establishment intellectuals alike. Sapio has pointed out that '(the) related concepts of "friend and enemy", "state of exception" and "decisionism" are simple and usable. Policy advisors and policy-makers can easily apply these concepts in their analysis of situations' (2015). Such a winner-takes-all conception of politics is problematic, as it does not allow for peaceful contestation of political power.

Ford suggests that in order to better understand China's strategic culture we need to go beyond words and pay attention to deeds as well. In both past and present, he calls this 'actual Chinese practice', which highlights the party's willingness to use or project hard power when necessary. His examples include China's invasion of Vietnam in 1979, its disregard for the South China Sea Arbitration ruling in favour of the Philippines and its belligerent attitude towards Taiwan (2016, 44–54). As such, we must also consider the role of the People's Liberation Army (PLA) in the study of China's strategic culture. General Secretary Xi Jinping, like his predecessors Jiang Zemin and Hu Jintao, is the 'first in command' (一把手) for China's party, state and military (党政军) (BBC, 2013). As far as party–military relations are concerned, the PLA ought not to be considered as a conventional national army, but rather as the armed wing of the CCP (Mattis, 2018). Mattis emphasizes that 'the Chinese military's purpose is to create political power for the party' (2018). Chinese citizens have long been told to take lessons from the PLA. The mid-1960s 'Learn from the PLA' movement is a good example of the elevated status of the Chinese military. Immediately following China's disastrous Great Leap Forward (1958–1962) and shortly before the Cultural Revolution (1966–1976), this national campaign emphasized the PLA's 'firm grip on political-ideological work' (Powell, 1965, 128). During the campaign, citizens were tasked with learning from the PLA's grasp of the *four firsts*: human factor, ideology, political work and the integration of theory and practice (1965). Powell notes that this campaign was motivated 'by the long military experiences of the Party leaders, by their ideological convictions and especially their emphasis on the "mass line"' (1965, 125). In this context and if we want to better understand China's strategic culture it is important to take into account some of the rather peculiar lessons the PLA learned from history.

As described in Kaufman and Mackenzie's 2009 study *The Culture of the Chinese People's Liberation Army*, the PLA promotes six beliefs about Chinese history after

1840. The first narrative, which is centred on the exaggeration of China's 'century of humiliation', describes Western nations as 'fundamentally rapacious, greedy, and aggressive' (2009, 25). Contrary to that, China is presented as a nation striving for peace. Military confrontations are rationalized as 'defensive actions against invaders' (2009, 26). It should be noted that the PLA has also been authorized to strike first against 'strategic threats' based on the Maoist principle of 'active defence'. These threats extend beyond those against China's military and also include threats against 'China's sovereignty, the Chinese people, or CCP political control' (2009). A second belief emphasizes the link between China's external sovereignty and domestic stability. The PLA has a 'rather paranoid attitude toward other nations' intentions' (2009). In particular, the United States is suspected of wanting to foment unrest at home. Third, the CCP and PLA are credited with liberating the country from foreign aggression and domestic oppression. A fourth narrative emphasizes the PLA's unwavering loyalty to the party. In a fifth motif, the PLA is shown to be capable of defeating stronger adversaries. Lastly, a sixth trope states that the PLA has always won.

The PLA's historiography infuses China's strategic culture with a strong sense of self-righteousness. China is portrayed as a victim of foreign powers. In this retelling of China's contemporary history, the heroic role of the CCP and PLA against foreign threats is being emphasized. It should not surprise that such a highly selective reading of China's military history omits war crimes committed by the PLA during the siege of Changchun (1948). Based on interviews with PLA soldiers Lung estimates that around 100,000 to 650,000 people died of starvation during the blockade (SCMP, 2009). The glorification of the Chinese military role also ignores that during the Korean War (1950–1953) China had to mourn between 100,000 and 400,000 lost lives (Choe, 2014). Such narratives also fail to mention the PLA's defeat in the war against Vietnam in 1979 (Nguyen, 2017). Whereas Germany's lessons from military defeat was an aversion to military power, the CCP's selective reading of history portrays China's past military actions in an airbrushed manner. This shows that German and Chinese foreign policy elites approach geopolitical conflict in vastly different ways. In this segment I have argued that China's strategic culture is rooted in pre-modern history, emphasizes a peculiar form of Chinese identity which bestows legitimacy on the CCP's authoritarian rule and projects hard power through a glorified role of the PLA. As the following discussion of political development since 1978 will show such a strategic culture does not bode well for a peaceful resolution of conflicts, both at home and abroad.

3.3 The end of the China illusion

During the 20th Party Congress in Autumn 2022, a press photo captured global attention. It showed former General Secretary Hu Jintao being removed from the stage. China's so-called 'reform and opening up era', which lasted from 1978 to 2012, was repudiated in this incident. Why was Hu walked off the stage, and what happened before that? A video recording showed that he attempted to access a red folder in front of him (CNA, 2022). Li Zhanshu, the outgoing Chairman of the Standing Committee of the National People's Congress, prevented Hu from doing so. The folder included a list of the newly selected Politburo members (Davidson, 2022). Upon reading it, Hu would have realized that his once-powerful China's Communist Youth League had been completely marginalized. It is likely that Xi removed Hu because he anticipated Hu would publicly express his frustration.

The Hu incident demonstrates that communist regimes are subject to their own political calendars, except for the Soviet Union's downfall in 1991. Every spring thaw is followed by a political winter: Brezhnev replaced Khrushchev, Husák succeeded Dubcek. With the exception of Eastern European and Soviet communist regimes, Leninist systems tend to follow a hydraulic principle of power retention. Controlled openings serve the stability of the regime by lowering pressure. The same can be said for China. During the 1980s, there were some political reforms aimed at institutionalizing a dialogue between the state and society (The Gate of Heavenly Peace, 1995). The national movement for democracy and against corruption was repressed in 1989, resulting in a political winter. In the early days of Hu Jintao's administration (2003–07), there was a brief political spring. The CCP's adaptability to changing environments has been called 'authoritarian resilience' by Nathan (2003). Three basic assumptions informed this concept: First, the CCP was adaptive and open to innovation. Second, China's authoritarian resilience was largely a result of its ability to implement gradual reforms under one-party control. Finally, it was also crucial that the CCP encouraged or tolerated local policy experiments in addition to opening up the economy to innovation. It was emphasized here how the central government can learn from successful pilot projects (Heilmann, 2008). As a result of this supposedly experimental style of government, the economy was stimulated and living standards were raised. A form of 'consultative Leninism' (Tsang, 2009) consolidated the 'Communist Party's gains in confidence and competence' (2009, 879).

Western China experts have long been interested in 'authoritarian resilience' since it offered a good explanation why the Chinese party-state has not (yet) imploded like the Soviet Union's CPSU. Its conceptual Achilles' heel, however, was that it assumed the CCP had perfectly learned from the collapse of socialism in Eastern Europe. As a result, the question of whether regressive dynamics can be observed alongside creative learning was no longer considered important. Authoritarian resilience has the problem of not addressing the limits, contradictions and logic of domination of adjustment reforms conceptually or empirically. However, Nathan's optimistic description of the party's adaptability was not universally endorsed. Pei noted above all institutional erosion, systemic and endemic corruption, and signs of regime collapse in *China's Crony Capitalism (2016)*. Shambaugh developed a similar counter-position in the polarized debate. A simultaneous process of atrophy and adaptation was observed by him (2008). However, he added an important caveat: the steady erosion of China's political institutions could be slowed or reversed through short-term adaptive measures. In an interview with the *New York Times* Shambaugh later revised this optimistic assessment. Commenting on the hard authoritarian turn under General Secretary Xi Jinping he argued that 'no China watcher can remain wed to arguments that have lost their empirical basis' (Buckley, 2015). His change of heart is significant, since Shambaugh had criticized Pei in 2008 for being too pessimistic about China's future.

It is evident in retrospect that Pei's pessimistic outlook was justified. The CCP tightened the reins as soon as its power was threatened. At the end of the Hu era, CCP leaders began viewing the Arab Spring, other colour revolutions and China's maturing pro-democracy movements as potential threats (Fulda, 2020). After 2012, Xi radicalized the party's prevention and defence strategy. There was a loss of semi-autonomy in many social systems, such as academia, culture, the economy, civil society and the law. Patronage, re-centralized control, hierarchical control and preventive repression were the answers. As Xi Jinping sought to defend the party's power, he began using quasi-Stalinist methods, including anti-corruption campaigns. Garnaut (2019) emphasizes that neither Mao nor Xi repudiated Stalin. In 2013, Xi said that '(to) dismiss the history of the Soviet Union and the Soviet Communist Party, to dismiss Lenin and Stalin, and to dismiss everything else is to engage in historic nihilism, and it confuses our thoughts and undermines the Party's organizations on all levels' (Beach, 2013). In Garnaut's view, Maoism and Stalinism are based on 'perpetual struggle' (2019). The Maoist friend/enemy dichotomy (Klotzbücher, 2019, 185) promotes ideological partisanship, prevents collaborative problem-solving and results in party policies which only benefit the CCP as opposed to the (global) public good.

Odell has argued that the principle and practice of struggle (斗争) is not limited to domestic politics but also informs China's evolving foreign policy doctrine in the Xi era (2023). In 2019, Xi used the term struggle close to sixty times in a speech to young and middle-age cadres attending the opening ceremony of a training programme. They were tasked to struggle to protect the leadership of the CCP, China's governance system and sovereignty, and to never make concessions over 'core interests and major principles' (Zhou and Zheng, 2019). The term struggle has also featured prominently in numerous of Xi's speeches between 2017 and 2021 (Dangjianwang, 2022). The call to 'perservere in the spirit of struggle' (坚持发扬斗争精神) was also the final of five major principles (五条重大原则) outlined by Xi during his major speech at the 20th party congress of 2022. Under Xi's instruction to 'persistently enhance strategic self-confidence (坚持增强战略自信)' (Odell, 59), Chinese diplomats and CCP cadres are constantly pressured to 'signal fealty to the CCP, with Xi at its core' (2023, 62). This has resulted in what is now commonly referred to as a particularly aggressive form of 'wolf warrior diplomacy' (NBR, 2021). A striking example of this phenomenon is a tweet from 24 June 2021 by Zhang Heqing, cultural counsellor at the Chinese embassy to Pakistan. In the two pictures attached to the tweet, China's 'friends' receive a thumbs up, while its 'enemies' are given the middle finger.

A second example of hateful political rhetoric would be the language used by China's Ambassador to Sweden, Gui Congyou. He gained notoriety for his particularly aggressive stance against journalists and dissidents critical of the

Chinese party-state during his secondment to Stockholm (2017–2021). During a two-year period, the Swedish foreign ministry called him over forty times to explain himself (The Economist, 2020). Gui, undeterred, said in a radio interview in November 2020 that 'we treat our friends with fine wine, but for our enemies we have shotguns' (The Economist, 2020). As a third and last example, we can take the case of China's consul general Zheng Xiyuan. A pro-Hong Kong democracy protest took place in front of Manchester's Chinese consulate in Autumn 2022. One protester was assaulted by Zheng and five other Chinese diplomats. As shown in video footage, Zheng dragged him onto the grounds of the consulate by the hair. Asked about the assault, Zheng replied that 'any diplomat' would have responded the same way to a public protest including banners mocking Xi (Yeung, 2022). In order to avoid police questioning, he and the other five Chinese diplomats were subsequently recalled to China (Wintour, 2022). How can such counterproductive behaviour be interpreted? After briefly considering the possibility that Xi may no longer receive accurate information from below due to power overconcentration, Odell dismisses it and suggests a different dynamic. She argues that the concept of struggle itself may explain the lack of a more constructive feedback loop, which in turn makes destructive learning more likely. When resistance to CCP coercion is viewed as being caused by structural contradictions, CCP leaders might risk doubling down and struggling even harder (Odell, 2023, 63).

Maintaining power is justified by the party-state's self-image as the quasi-sacral 'saviour' of the Chinese nation. In order to ensure the party's survival, it has developed a technological surveillance state, detects problems early, resolves them and struggles against political opposition both at home and abroad. During both the so-called 'reform and opening up era' from 1978 until 2012 and the Xi era (2012–), the CCP's monopoly on power and ideology has remained untouchable. Levitsky and Way explain the durability of dictatorships born out of revolution in *Revolution and Dictatorship (2022)*. In China enforced party unity, control of the military and the elimination of dissenting power centres all played a key role. Because of the CCP's willingness to employ ruthless violence in 1989, it has managed to protect its monopoly on power. However, Xi's regime also marks a political regression as it employs quasi-Stalinist methods to defend its power, including purges of opponents within the party and anti-corruption campaigns. In critical phases, Leninist party-states tend to personalize power. Eventually, a personality cult develops as a central aspect of institutional decay.

Xi's decivilization of elite politics, suppression of intra-party democracy and abolition of succession rules have led to a personalized dictatorship. The political and institutional weaknesses and risks of strongman rule cannot be disguised: a shrinking power base in elite politics; toxic nationalism; an ideologically driven overestimation of Chinese citizens' willingness to sacrifice for the nation; an economic crisis due to a failed Covid policy; and political subjugation of Chinese tech firms. In Chapter 2, I discussed constructive and destructive learning with reference to the Steinmeier doctrine. In the case of autocratic China, however, the scope to engage in creative learning is even more limited. According to Chinese public intellectual Xu the CCP under Xi's leadership has become 'a self-deconstructing structure that constantly undermines normal governance while tending towards systemic atrophy' (2020). He describes the Xi regime as 'an evolving form of military tyranny' (2020). According to Xu, the Xi regime's ideology draws on a strict interpretation of Legalism, a Leninist-Stalinist interpretation of Marxism and a 'Germano-Aryan' form of Fascism (2020). Predictably, such outspoken criticism of the party-state cost Xu his job as professor at Tsinghua University, earned him house arrest and led to a brief arrest in 2020 (BBC, 2020). And while it is debatable how much Sino-Marxism after 1949 is actually shaped by the school of thought of Legalism, Roetz has argued that both 'share the notion of a strong state and the accompanying willingness for repression' (2016, 98).

No matter what one thinks about China's 'reform and opening up era', it was infinitely more open, both at home and abroad, than the current Xi era. Still, China wasn't fully open during that time. According to Hoffman, CCP authoritarianism uses both 'hard' and 'soft' authoritarian methods continuously (2017a). Hoffman reminds us that coercion does not stop to allow for cooptation, but instead the two operate together in unison (2017b, 14). Fewsmith has highlighted the contradiction between a Leninist system, which only offered reconciliation without abandoning exclusivity during the reform and opening up era, and a society that sought to limit the party's power (2021, 112). This tension is most evident when we look at the CCP's strict curbs on China's internet. There has never been a full coupling between China and the outside world as evidenced by the Great Firewall. Yet people-to-people exchanges on political, economic and social levels were frequent. In terms of the CCP's power strategy, we witnessed an uneasy coexistence between openness and isolation between 1978 and 2012. With the arrival of Xi, the blockade of the nerve tracts of government however has greatly intensified. Document No. 9 (2013) codified Xi's rejection of the foundations of any open society: constitutional democracy, universal values, civil society, neoliberalism, independent journalism, critical historical research and regime criticism were made taboo. This has led to anti-liberal laws including China's National Security Law (2015), National Intelligence Law (2017) and Hong Kong's National Security Law (2020).

It is clear that Xi is motivated to be a charismatic leader like Mao Zedong. It has a thoroughly egomaniacal component, like Vladimir Putin. Carrico speaks of 'Putinism with Chinese Characteristics' (2017). Xi Jinping is supposed to prove his supernatural abilities through risky and strategic undertakings. The CCP's zero-Covid strategy and brutal repression of Uyghurs come to mind, as well as the threat of military annexation of Taiwan. The cult of personality and propaganda from the unified party exaggerate his real or alleged successes. The party's historiography has helped Xi Jinping consolidate his power. Neither Mao nor Deng Xiaoping reappraised Stalinism critically. The lack of any significant reappraisal of Stalinism, Maoism and the Cultural Revolution has contributed to the hard authoritarian turn under Xi. International ramifications of this development will be discussed below. I contend that a hard authoritarian China under an unreformed Stalinist Xi poses a threat to peace, at home and abroad. In 1978, Deng still told his compatriots to 'bide our time and build up our capabilities' (Ford, 2016). Ford, however, suggests that this posture wasn't really pacifism (2016). Instead, it was merely a strategy to avoid confrontation when China was viewed as weak. In the early 2000s Nye still gave credibility to China's 'new diplomacy, coupled with the slogan of "China's peaceful rise"' (Nye, 2005), which he suggested 'helps to alleviate fears and reduce the likelihood of other countries allying to balance a rising power' (2005).

Former CCP Central Party School professor Cai Xia however has cautioned against reading the CCP's global intentions in this way (2021). Cai reveals that in the early 2000s, Xiong Guangkai, the CCP's top military intelligence officer, made a big deal over the English translation of Deng's strategy to hide the CCP's true strategic intentions. In Cai's view, China's 'peaceful rise' should not be taken literally. She quotes Zhao Qizheng, a former director of the Information Office of the State Council, explaining that '(the) "peaceful" is for foreigners, and the "rise" is for us Chinese' (2021, 13). CCP officials are not the only ones guilty of such duplicity. During a 2009 trip to Mexico, Xi let his carefully cultivated mask of a prudent leader-in-waiting slip. Xi complained that '(there) are a few foreigners, with full bellies, who have nothing better to do than try to point fingers at our country' (Mitchell, 2017). He also claimed that 'China does not export revolution, hunger or poverty. Nor does China cause you headaches. Just what else do you want?' (2017) As I will argue in the following, it is the CCP's approach to power which should worry us all. Since 2012 the CCP has consistently moved from soft power to sharp power projection.

3.4 *Sharp power, struggle and hybrid interference*

Sharp power was first described in a pioneering report by the National Endowment for Democracy (NED). Published on 5 December 2017, NED's study *Sharp Power. Rising Authoritarian Influence* marked a turning point in research on autocracies like Russia and China. According to its authors 'authoritarian influence is not principally about attraction or even persuasion; instead, it centers on distraction and manipulation' (NED, 2017, 6). In contrast to the analytical frame of 'soft power', the authors propose 'sharp power', which 'pierces, penetrates, or perforates political and information environments in targeted countries' (2017, 6). In his contribution to the debate Nye has argued that sharp power is 'a type of hard power' grounded in 'threats and inducements' (2018), whereas soft power is marked by 'voluntarism and indirection' (2017, 6). It is important to note that Nye's definition is not without its problems, since hard power is a term which refers to the overt use of force to achieve political goals. By contrast, sharp power refers to influencing governments, societies and populations more covertly and indirectly.

The concept of sharp power must also be distinguished from competing terms such as political warfare. It is Mattis's belief that many threats to the CCP and its political system come from ideas (2018). A thorough understanding of political warfare is essential, he says. In addition to protecting territorial integrity, Mattis points out that the PLA is also responsible for building political power for the party through the 'Three Warfares'. According to a political instruction issued in

2003, the PLA was to conduct 'public opinion warfare, psychological warfare, and legal warfare' (2018). 'Public opinion warfare' includes convincing the Chinese public that the CCP maintains a strong military and defence position. There is also 'psychological warfare', which involves influencing decision-makers and the way they approach China policy (2018). 'Legal warfare', however, provides legal cover for the party's actions at the same time as it signals its resolve to potential adversaries. As a result, political warfare aims not only to protect China's sovereignty, but also to protect the party's sovereignty. In other words, this implies absolute sovereignty for the party-center, which contradicts Westphalian principles of national sovereignty (Pottinger et al., 2022). The concept of political warfare can be helpful for emphasizing the extent to which the CCP is willing to go to maintain control. At the same time all three kinds of warfare Mattis mentions in his article are in fact non-kinetic. Although non-kinetic warfare exists, Wigell has cautioned against 'unnecessarily militarizing the language of international politics' (2019, 256).

It is Wigell's position that we should distinguish between military and non-military means in the 'grey zone' between war and peace (2019). When Odell speaks of the CCP's 'nonconventional tools for deterring or coercing other states and non-state actors' (2023, 45) she cites information operations, political influence operations, controversial legislation and paramilitary maritime presence operations as part of Beijing's non-conventional deterrence (2023, 64–5). In Wigell's logic Oddell's overly broad approach can be seen as problematic since 'practices that rely exclusively on non-military means need to be differentiated from those that involve military means, as they may require different counter-measures' (2019, 256). Braw has similarly noted that non-military grey zone aggression can give the 'attacking side the benefits it seeks, which may be industrial prowess rather than territorial gains' (2022, 3). Wigell has developed the concept of 'hybrid interference', which should be understood as a 'wedge strategy' (2019). As a policy it is aimed at 'dividing a target country or coalition, thereby weakening its counterbalancing potential' (2019). At the heart of hybrid interference are 'a panoply of state-controlled, non-kinetic means that are concealed in order to provide the divider with official deniability and manipulate targeted actors without elevating their threat perceptions' (2019). I adopt Wigell's concept since it not only captures the non-military dimensions of CCP foreign interference, but also illuminates what Xi refers to as 'struggle' and what the authors of the NED study call 'sharp power'.

More specifically, Wigell draws our attention to 'three bundles of means' (2019), which, he claims, are central to hybrid interference: (1) clandestine diplomacy, (2) geoeconomics and (3) disinformation. The aim of clandestine diplomacy is to exacerbate tensions within a target country (2019, 263). Geoeconomics, on the other hand, aims to weaken the resolve of a target country by dividing it (2019, 264). Disinformation aims to 'foment public discontent and distrust' (2019, 266). According to Wigell, 'hybrid interference is a strategy for the mostly covert manipulation of other states' strategic interests' (2019, 262). Wigell argues that 'drawing on an enhanced toolkit of state-controlled non-kinetic capabilities and reflexive control techniques, the hybrid agent interferes in domestic politics by seeking to shape perceptions in order, ideally, to incline targets to voluntarily take steps that further the agent's agenda, or, failing that, to paralyse its decision-making capacity' (2019, 262). In this book Wigell's concept of hybrid interference will be adjusted in order to better analyse the CCP's strategic practice of struggle. Specifically, I differentiate between (1) clandestine diplomacy *conducted through the CCP's united front system*; (2) *power trading, predatory technology transfers and geoeconomic coercion*; and (3) *attempts at global speech control and* disinformation *campaigns*. Further adding to Wigell's original concept, I suggest that hybrid interference involves a combination of carrots and sticks, what I have previously called the CCP's 'rule by bribery' and 'rule by fear' (Fulda, 2020, 84–7). In the following, I will elaborate on how the CCP has already conducted hybrid interference in Germany by manipulating the Chinese diaspora in Germany as well as various actors in German politics, economics and society.

3.5 Clandestine diplomacy conducted through the CCP's united front system

We need to familiarize ourselves with the origins of the CCP's united front *approach* in order to better understand the first means of hybrid interference, clandestine diplomacy. Developed during China's civil war, it identifies the CCP and its supporters as the political avant-garde. An even larger group of waverers exists in the middle, who may either support or oppose the CCP. The third group consists of the party's enemies. The practice of united front *work*, on the other hand, aims to win over the uncommitted and neutralize those who might side with the enemy (van Slyke, 128). Xi spoke about the importance of the party's united front work in September 2014 (CPC, 2015). He called it one of the CCP's 'magic weapons', along with party building and military operations (Brady, 2017, 7). This activity is carried out by the United Front Work Department (UFWD), which has been tasked with both combating potential political opposition to the CCP at home and engaging in foreign interference abroad (Bowe, 2018). As Joske notes, united front work should be imagined as an entire united front *system* consisting of various 'bureaucratic grouping of agencies and leadership bodies' (Jichang Lulu, 2020). Overseas united front work has been prioritized by Xi, as evidenced by substantial increases in its budget. On the basis of official budget documents, Fedasiuk calculated that in 2019, '$600 million' was set aside for offices designed to influence foreigners and overseas Chinese communities (2020). Hamilton and Ohlberg have pointed out that CCP interference abroad is mostly covert, making it hard to detect (2020).

Political influence operations of the Xi era fall into four categories, according to Brady (2017). Such efforts seek to (1) instrumentalize Chinese overseas communities with the goal of advancing the party-state's foreign policy objectives; (2) leverage of 'people-to-people, party-to-party, plus PRC enterprise-to-foreign enterprise relations with the aim of co-opting foreigners to support and promote

CCP's foreign policy goals' (2017, 7); (3) establish an international communication strategy; and (4) build an economic and strategic bloc centred on China (2017). It is important to note that Brady's trailblazing work on united front work in New Zealand came at a high personal price. Her home and office were burgled after her widely acclaimed paper *Magic Weapons* was published in 2017 (Graham-McLay, 2018). Afterwards, her car was also tampered with (Roy, 2018). For Western researchers, creating transparency about the CCP's overseas united front work thus carries considerable risks. A group of 303 scholars and China experts responded by signing an open letter condemning the harassment campaign (Jichang Lulu, 2018).

Tatlow has conducted pioneering work on united front work in Germany. She was based in Beijing as *New York Times* reporter from 2010 to 2017. Upon her return to Berlin in 2017 she was surprised that '(few) sinologists or even politics experts in Germany seemed aware of the presence, or increasing spread, of the united front in Europe' (2019). Based on her analysis of both German and Chinese sources in which she was aided by a researcher she identified over 190 groups which are directly affiliated with China's United Front bureaucracy (2019). Additionally, she identified a national German organization with thirty-seven affiliates that partners with a key CCP influencing organization belonging to the UFWD in Beijing. Adding approximately eighty Chinese Student and Scholar Associations (CSSAs), about twenty Confucius Institutes (CIs) and roughly a dozen of Chinese-language media with united front links Tatlow found that '(there) are hundreds of groups working in Germany to maintain the CCP's ideology, values, language and goals to varying degrees among a relatively small Chinese diaspora, and, importantly, more broadly in society from the grassroots to the elite' (2019). Thorley has pointed out that organizations such as CSSAs should be considered as 'latent networks', which are 'though not necessarily controlled by the CCP directly in their day-to-day affairs, are dependent on CCP patronage and thus, subject to CCP direction' (2019). Cautioning against viewing China as a 'country of informers' (2019), Thorley has criticized the party-state's 'attempted weaponization of informal Chinese social networks' (2019).

An investigation by the Spanish NGO Safeguard Defenders has revealed that members of the Chinese diaspora are not safe from the long arm of Beijing. The report found that China's security apparatus operates 'at least 102 "Chinese Overseas Police Service Centers" in 53 countries' (Safeguard Defenders, 2022a). As highlighted in *Patrol and Persuade*, some overseas Chinese associations offer valuable assistance to Chinese residents and tourists, while others play a nefarious role and are affiliated with the Chinese Communist Party's UFWD (Safeguard Defenders, 2022b). According to a report by Tatlow, Chinese police proxies are found in five German cities: Hamburg, Berlin, Düsseldorf, Frankfurt and Munich (2022). It's particularly concerning that attempts have been made to force Chinese diaspora members to 'voluntarily' return to China for prosecution. According to a German-language investigative report (Stremmel, 2023) political activists of the Chinese diaspora are intimidated in a mafia-like manner. In this

TV report it was revealed how the Chinese security apparatus is using family members living in China to press exiles to cooperate. Jensen, Chair of the Committee on Human Rights and Humanitarian Aid of the German Bundestag, has called for a new government strategy in light of such threats (Zeit Online, 2021).

Interference operations, however, are not limited to the Chinese diaspora living in Germany. Tatlow and Rácz have pointed out that the CCP takes a great interest in German elites, too (2021). They explain how the establishment of the elite networking club 'China-Brücke' in 2019 has provided an entry point 'for Chinese interests among a select, but largely anonymous, group of highly influential people in politics, business, healthcare, digital economy, academia, and industry in Germany' (2021). China-Brücke is led by former Minister of the Interior (2011–2013) and former Vice President of the German Bundestag (2017–2021) Hans-Peter Friedrich, a member of the Christian Social Union (CSU). While the names of board members are listed publicly, the identities of regular members are not revealed. Tatlow and Rácz are critical of China-Brücke's links deep into the heart of the party-state, including its key contact person in China Wang Chen, who was a member of the 19th Politburo when the organization was founded and who also serves as Vice Chairman of the Standing Committee of the National People's Congress. Other senior CCP contacts include former Politburo Standing Committee member Li Zhanshu and deputy director of the CCP's International Department Qian Hongshan. They conclude that the 'China-Brücke represents a classic CCP influence and interference operation – similar to tactics deployed in Asia-Pacific and Australia – reaching deep into Germany's economy and politics' (2021).

Furthermore, events such as the 9th German-Chinese Business Conference in Frankfurt in September 2022 have targeted German economic elites as well. The event was convened by former German Minister of Defence Rudolf Scharping (1998–2002), and his consulting firm was jointly responsible for organizing it with the China Economic Cooperation Center (CECC) (Weber, 2022). It is shown by Weber that CECC is tied to the CCP's International Liaison Department (ILD), which also interferes in foreign affairs according to Joske (2020, 19). Weber reported that ILD sent a current official and a former official to Frankfurt to attend the event. As a participant of an ILD-hosted event in China in 2021, Scharping praised the CCP multiple times (Weber, 2022). Scharping also referred to China's political system as 'a multi-party system' in an interview with *People's Daily* (2022). This kind of close collaboration with political actors in China has been criticized by Weber as always resulting in cooptation (2022). According to him, those who favour a cooperative approach to China must also address the problem of cooptation (2022). In the process of cooperation, Weber suggests, self-censorship plays a significant role, either to placate the Chinese counterpart or perhaps out of self-interest on the German side. Furthermore, he warns German elites against echoing official CCP positions and normalizing them. The acceptance of the CCP's discourse power on the basis of cooperation could instead be seen as complicity (2022).

3.6 Power trading, predatory technology transfers and geoeconomic coercion

In another means of hybrid interference countries exploit globalization to increase their power and weaken the power of their rivals (Braw, 2022). Braw calls this strategy 'subversive economics' (2022), which can be understood as the 'systematic undermining of liberal democracies' open markets by hostile governments, their businesses, or a combination of the two' (2022). She points out that these practices are nothing new (2022, 57). In light of Hirschmann's scholarship, Atkinson argues that Germany was neither a free trader nor a protectionist prior to World War II (2020, 14). Rather it should be considered 'a "power trader" which used trade as a key tool to gain commercial and military advantage over its adversaries' (2020). Atkinson argues that China's current approach to global trade is remarkably similar to Nazi economic statecraft. A brief review of key features of German power trading between 1933 and 1945 can help to better understand what Tobin has described as China's 'brute force economics' (2023).

In his monograph *National Power and the Structure of Foreign Trade* Hirschman identified supply and influence effects as the two main sources of Germany's trade power before WWII (1945, 14–5). As for the *supply effect* the Nazi regime ensured the import of goods which would support the war effort, engaged in stockpiling of strategic materials, redirected trade to countries which were either subject nations or politically close, and attempted to take control of oceanic trade routes (1945, 34). As for the *influence effect* one set of policies were aimed to make it difficult for trading partners to divert from Nazi Germany. This was to be achieved by ensuring the benefits from trade (without reducing the supply effect), inhibit industrialization among trading partners by exploiting monopolistic positions in overseas markets, by trading predominantly with poorer countries and by creating 'vested interests and tie the interests of existing powerful groups to the trade' (1945). Another set of policies was 'designed to make it difficult for the trading partners to *shift* trade each other or to third countries' (1945). This objective could be achieved by directing trade towards smaller countries. Export dependence of trading partners was generated by importing their goods which are not in high demand elsewhere, by monetary manipulation which allowed for paying above world average prices for their exports, and by providing export advantages unrelated to the price of products (1945, 35). At the same time German exports were designed to create 'consumption and production habits' (1945). Hirschman argues that 'practically all the outstanding features of German economic policy since 1933 can be subsumed under this scheme' (1945).

Atkinson argues that allowing China to enter the WTO gave it a pathway to power trader status (2020, 17). In deciding whether or not to extend its Most-Favored-Nation status to China on an annual basis, throughout the 1990s the United States still enjoyed what Anderson calls 'bargaining leverage' (2014, 6). However, such leverage has dissipated since China joined WTO in 2001. The 'complicated and rules-based WTO process for taking action against China' (2020,

17) has been a major obstacle in disciplining China when it uses opaque power trade tactics. Atkinson reminds us that Xi seeks unchecked 'wealth and power' (2020). In political practice this has meant that for the CCP the ends often justify the means. In particular, Atkinson argues that 'China employs its vast array of policy tools to use trade to increase its relative economic power not only over the United States, but over other nations that it seeks to influence as it strives to become the new global hegemon' (2020). China's Belt and Road initiative and the Regional Comprehensive Economic Partnership (RCEP) trade agreement are two prime examples of how it is expanding its economic influence. Atkinson criticizes predatory practices in China, such as subsidized manufacturing. He argues that with the help of 'currency manipulation, free land, tax incentives, cheap loans, and cash grants, China induced the offshoring of critical manufacturing sectors to China' (2020, 54). China also created export dependency among resource-rich countries by importing commodities in large quantities, which risks turning them into vassal states (2020). By manipulating the currency, China has been able to keep exports cheap, which has further contributed to its status as 'the world's manufacturing workshop' (2020). Due to underpriced products, China leapfrogged in multiple industries such as shipbuilding, telecommunications equipment, solar panels and steel (2020). The rapid industrial upgrading of China has accelerated the offshoring of key industries in Western nations and contributed to their deindustrialization. Zhang has noted that while 'Germany's industry has contributed heavily to China's growing competitiveness . . . the price has been its own deindustrialization – in other words, Germany is destroying its own industrial base by fostering its very competitors' (2022). A case in point is the decline of Germany's photovoltaic sector, which is discussed in Chapter 6 as an unforeseen policy failure.

The success of China's power trading is evident when we examine how dependent Germany has become in recent years on China for raw materials such as cobalt, boron, silicon, graphite, magnesium, lithium, niobium, rare earths and titanium. Flach, Teti, Gourevich, Scheckenhofer and Grandum found that China is among the top five exporters of seven of the nine critical raw materials (2022, 4). Similarly, the IFW Kiel Institut für Weltwirtschaft found in early 2023 that laptop computers, mobile phones, textiles, computer units, photographic elements, LEDs and printed circuit boards are input goods that are mainly sourced from China. German industry relies heavily on these intermediate products and they cannot be replaced easily in the event of global supply chain disruptions (2023). A third dependency is the importance of the Chinese market for German companies. In 2021, VW reported 41 per cent of its revenues from China, BMW 32 per cent and BASF 11.4 per cent (Sommer, 2021). In and of themselves, such dependencies of German big corporations on China are problematic for the reasons mentioned above. The fourth problem, however, is that these deep trade and investment ties also provide a means for the party-state to rapidly acquire foreign technology (Sutter, 2021).

In 2015, the State Council published MIC2025, a plan that aims to transform China into a global manufacturing leader by leapfrogging existing industrialized economies. Germany plays a crucial role in the realization of 'Made in China 2025' (MIC2025), according to de La Bruyère and Picarsic (2020, 4). The authors argue that 'MIC2025 targets Germany first as a source of technology, second as a partner through which to export standards favorable to China, and third as a competitor for the lead in the current industrial revolution' (2020). It is important to note that Western-Chinese ventures are often conduits for technology transfers in this context. According to a study by Korteweg, Donninger, Kranenburg, Caberlon and van der Putten of twenty European-Chinese joint ventures, most were involved in MIC2025 technology sectors, and the Chinese party-state sometimes exercised high levels of control. The finding that technology transfer was a 'likely' component of joint venture activity in one-quarter of the cases was more concerning (2022). Hannas and Chang have shown, however, that the challenge extends beyond contractually agreed technology transfers. According to them, there are thirty-two legal, illegal and extralegal methods of technology transfer (2021, 7).

As a result of predatory technology transfers, Germany's industrial base is gradually hollowed out. At the same time there are also concerns about foreign technology being used to strengthen the surveillance state and modernize the PLA. Since 2012 Xi has aggressively promoted Military-Civil Fusion (MCF, 军民融合) (U.S. Department of State, 2020). As Fritz argues, MCF aims at combining military and civilian industries in order to strengthen China's economic, technological and military power (2019). Although entire weapon systems cannot be exported to China under Europe's decade-long arms embargo, which was imposed after Beijing suppressed the nation's pro-democracy and anti-corruption movement in 1989, the key issue here is dual-use technology. Technology such as 'robotics and advanced materials' (Kania and Wood, 2021, 232) raises particular concerns. In accordance with Article 78 of the National Security Law from 2015, Chinese companies are required to 'cooperate as required by national security efforts' (Pearson, Rithmire and Tsai, 2022, 150). Articles 7 and 14 of China's National Intelligence Law from 2017 stipulate that '(organizations) and citizens shall support and cooperate with the state intelligence work' (2022). A creeping securitization of China's party-state capitalism directly affects Germany's economic engagement with the country. Rather than promoting 'change through trade', German commercial engagement thus runs the risk of strengthening the surveillance capacities of an increasingly neo-totalitarian Xi regime, and knowingly or unknowingly assist with the modernization of the PLA.

At the end of the 'Reform and Opening Up era' and during the final years of Hu Jintao's rule, economic coercion by the CCP had become increasingly common. Several examples are provided by Odell to illustrate this point, including the ban on rare earth exports to Japan, the temporary restriction on salmon exports from Norway following Liu Xiaobo's Nobel Peace Prize award by the Oslo Nobel Committee and the ban on Chinese tourism after Seoul agreed to deploy a theatre missile defence system, which China resisted (Odell 2023, 47). Recent examples of this trend during the Xi era include the initiation of a trade conflict with Australia in response to Canberra's demand for an independent inquiry into Covid-19's origins. In another example, Lithuania was sanctioned for setting up a Taiwanese representative office that called itself 'Taiwanese' rather than 'Taipei'. As a third example, Taiwanese farmers and individuals have been targeted for activities perceived by Beijing as promoting 'secession' (2023, 48).

Germany has also already been subjected to geoeconomic coercion. China's Ambassador to Germany Wu Ken issued a blunt warning to the German government in December 2019. According to him, excluding Huawei from 5G infrastructure building in Germany could have dire consequences for German automobile companies in China. During a Handelsblatt event he stated that '(the) Chinese government will not stand idly by' (Czuczka and Arons, 2019). Such threats should not be considered as empty words. When Lithuania upgraded its diplomatic relations with Taiwan by opening 'The Taiwanese Representative Office in Lithuania' in November 2022, this had immediate consequences for German businesses. A dozen German companies, mostly from the agricultural and automotive sectors, were put under pressure by the party-state (Sytas and O'Donnell, 2021). Chinese officials allegedly pushed Continental to stop using components manufactured in Lithuania for cars exported to other countries, including China (Fukao, 2021). A letter sent to Lithuania's foreign and economy ministers by the German-Baltic Chamber of Commerce demonstrates how effective such arm-twisting has been. The letter warned that 'imports of Chinese machinery and parts and the sale of Lithuanian products to China had ground to a halt and that some firms may have to leave' (Sytas and O'Donnell, 2022). The incident has accelerated efforts in Brussels to develop an anti-coercion instrument (Patey, 2022). It also serves as a stark reminder that German companies, many of which have heavy investments in China, can be forced to comply with Beijing's demands in times of geopolitical crisis.

3.7 Attempts at global speech control and disinformation campaigns

The CCP's third hybrid interference means is to influence global discourse about China and to engage in disinformation campaigns. Chinese censorship has been a hallmark of Chinese politics since 1949, but during the more liberal Hu Jintao era, some more independent-minded news outlets still existed, such as Southern Weekend (南方周末). Nevertheless, we have witnessed a steady march towards ever-greater political censorship since 2012. Document No 9 and the oral directive 7 Don't Speak (Bandurski, 2013) indicate this trend. They were both issued just a year after Xi took power. Tsang aptly explains the consequences of strictly enforced censorship. During a TV debate recorded at the Oxford Union he said: 'The Communist Party of China has a monopoly of the truth and a monopoly of history in China. Therefore what they say must be true, by definition. And what anybody else has to say that does not coincide with what the party says are false news' (@AMFChina, 2020). Globalization was supposed to open China. Instead, the CCP has expanded speech restrictions beyond its borders.

Ford and Grant have examined the CCP's internationalization of its censorship system to control how outsiders speak about China (2022). According to them, the CCP seeks to control global narratives about China by instilling fear among discourse participants, leading to self-censorship (2022, 2–3). In the CCP's intimidation toolkit, extraterritorial legal instruments, official complaints and professional punishment all play a role. In retaliation for the EU's sanctions against Chinese officials implicated in crimes against humanity in Xinjiang, countersanctions were imposed on the Berlin-based think tank Merics (Merics, 2021). Charon and Vilmer have suggested that the CCP's drive to assert its discursive power (话语权) is based on a superficially understood Foucauldian view of a *conditioned* discursive space. According to the two authors CCP ideologues assume that in order '(to) seize a voice is to seize power, and to seize power is to exclude the others' voice. This is how the Party represents itself on the international stage: incapable of asserting its interests for lack of a sufficiently audible voice' (2021, 32). This would explain the why 'the Party seeks to dominate [the world] by imposing its voice and its narratives' (2021). Here again, we can see how an anti-liberal mindset among CCP hardliners leads to a zero-sum view of the world, this time in the discursive space.

Aside from coercion, financial incentives play an important role in CCP propaganda export. Shen and Lai have argued that media and academia should be considered Germany's 'Achilles' heel' (2022). They criticize the practice of paid media tours in China and paid supplements by China's state media in newspapers like *Handelsblatt* and *FAZ*. Such partnership agreements do not tell the whole story, however. According to Kurlantzick, the CCP manipulates information environments overseas in three ways (Scott, 2022). While foreign journalists have been hired and major investments have been made, the efforts to internationalize Chinese state media have mostly failed, he argues. In addition, he is sceptical about the CCP's ability to expand control by building telecommunication infrastructure, such as 5G infrastructure in North America, Europe and Africa. Despite this, Kurlantzick notes an increase in sophisticated disinformation (2022). An example of this is the Russian and Chinese governments' efforts to spread disinformation about Covid-19. In a public statement the German Ministry of the Interior complained that both governments had 'spread false and misleading information about the different vaccines developed in Germany, the United States and the United Kingdom' (2023). Democracies and open societies have also been discredited by both the Russian and Chinese governments for their initial problems handling Covid-19. An analysis by European Values and Konrad Adenauer Stiftung found that China's interference tactics are increasingly similar to those used by Russia (2019). Chinese diplomacy is increasingly aggressive and unafraid of 'losing face'; economic interdependence is weaponized for political purposes; anti-Americanism is instrumentalized as a means of prodding European states into staying neutral in geopolitical conflicts; and the 16+1 format is used to split Eastern Europe from the rest of Europe (2019, 12). Only three weeks before Russia's war of aggression against Ukraine, Putin and Xi signed a joint statement stating that '(friendship) between the two States has no limits, there are no "forbidden" areas of cooperation' (President of Russia, 2022). China's party-state has also helped spread Russian disinformation regarding its war of aggression against Ukraine. An ASPI study by Niblock, Hoffman and Knight revealed that Chinese diplomats have used social media exclusively to blame the United States, NATO and the West (2022). Its authors have pointed out that Chinese diplomats 'repeated Russian conspiracy theories about US biological weapon labs in Ukraine with gusto and linked the alleged activities to conspiracy theories about the origin of Covid-19' (2022). Furthermore, the non-profit Great Translation Movement has pointed to Chinese official media such as the People's Daily Overseas Edition spreading disinformation about US biological laboratories in Ukraine (@TGTM_Official, 2022).

German academia is the other proverbial 'Achilles' heel' which Shen and Lai identified. The CCP has used its considerable financial resources to buy access. In my scholarship and public commentary I have been very critical of Western universities accepting party-state funding for Confucius Institutes, something I have called a form of reputation laundering (Sharma, 2021). I will elaborate on Germany's failure to protect academic freedom from the CCP's globalising censorship regime in greater detail in Chapter 10.

It should have become clear from the numerous examples cited in this book chapter that the CCP has a strong willingness and operational ability to fight its opponents on both home and foreign soil. It should also be noted that the means of clandestine diplomacy, geoeconomic coercion, and mis- and disinformation can also be combined, thus leading to a force multiplication effect. Here it is important to remind readers that foreign interference occurs in the grey zone between peace and war. Due to the clandestine nature of interference operations, the CCP enjoys plausible deniability for its actions. Such plausible deniability also allows CCP officials and their proxies to adopt seemingly contradictory measures, which in combination contribute to what Wigell refers to as the 'manipulation of other states' strategic interests' (2019, 262). This chapter has shown that in hybrid interference operations state and non-state agents acting on behalf of the Chinese party-state are able to simultaneously *charm* senior German politicians (e.g. by signalling that China could potentially play a role in bringing Putin to the negotiation table), *coerce* German industrialists with a large China portfolio (e.g. by suggesting that a tougher stance by the German government towards China on the issue of Taiwan could put their assets at risk and jeopardise their market opportunities) and *confuse* the German public through mis- and disinformation (e.g. by claiming that it is NATO and the Western alliance which is endangering world peace in Europe and East Asia). Since much of the CCP's hybrid interference happens covertly rather than overtly, Western liberal democracies have struggled to develop adequate countermeasures.

References for Chapter 3

@AMFChina (2020), "'The Communist Party of China has a Monopoly of the Truth and a Monopoly of History in China. Therefore What They Say Must Be True, by Definition.

And What Anybody Else Has to Say that Does Not Coincide with What the Party Says Are False News." - Steve Tsang, 15 March 2019/1', Twitter, 6 March. Available online: https://twitter.com/AMFChina/status/1235912674262818816?s=20 (accessed 11 July 2023).

@TGTM_Official (2022), 'Me: Where Is Xuzhou Chained Woman? When Will Shanghai Lockdown End? Why Do Chinese Apps Now Display My IP? CCP: MIND YOUR OWN BUSINESS. AMERICA HAS BIOLABS IN UKRAINE SPREADING PNEUMONIA. #ChinaIsWithRussia #RussiaUkraineWar #TheGreatTranslationMovement #大翻译运动 @SolomonYue', Twitter, 2 May. Available online: https://twitter.com/TGTM_Official/status/1520975365669335040?s=20 (accessed 11 July 2023).

Atkinson, R. (2020), 'A Remarkable Resemblance', *The International Economy*, Fall. Available online: https://www2.itif.org/2020-Fall-TIE-Remarkable-Resemblance.pdf (accessed 11 July 2023).

Bandurski, D. (2013), 'Control, on the Shores of China's Dream', *China Media Project*, 22 May. Available online: https://archive.is/wkOoR (accessed 11 July 2023).

BBC (2013), '习近平：集党政军大权于一身的领导人', Available online: https://www.bbc.com/zhongwen/simp/china/2013/03/130313_xi_jinping_profile_update.

BBC (2020), 'Xu Zhangrun: Outspoken Professor Freed After Six Days', Available online: https://archive.is/A7H9G (accessed 11 July 2023).

Beach, S. (2013), 'Leaked Speech Shows Xi Jinping's Opposition to Reform', *China Digital Times*, 27 January. Available online: https://archive.is/iVmpm (accessed 11 July 2023).

BiEPAG (2017), 'What Is a Stabilitocracy?', 5 May. Available online: https://archive.is/HA05g (accessed 10 July 2023).

Bowe, A. (2018), 'China's Overseas United Front Work', U.S.-China Economic and Security Review Commission, 24 August. Available online: https://www.uscc.gov/sites/default/files/Research/China%27s%20Overseas%20United%20Front%20Work%20-%20Background%20and%20Implications%20for%20US_final_0.pdf (accessed 11 July 2023).

Brady, A.-M. (2017), 'Magic Weapons: China's Political Influence Activities Under Xi Jinping', Wilson Center. Available online: https://www.wilsoncenter.org/sites/default/files/media/documents/article/magic_weapons.pdf (accessed 11 July 2023).

Braw, E. (2022), *The Defender's Dilemma. Identifying and Deterring Gray-Zone Aggression*, Washington, DC: American Enterprise Institute.

Buckley, C. (2015), 'The Coming Chinese Crackup (9)', *MCLC Resource Center*, 17 March. Available online: https://u.osu.edu/mclc/2015/03/17/the-coming-chinese-crackup-9/ (accessed 11 July 2023).

Cai, X. (2021), 'China-US Relations in the Eyes of the Chinese Communist Party: An Insider's Perspective', June. Available online: https://www.hoover.org/sites/default/files/research/docs/xia_chinausrelations_web-ready_v2.pdf (accessed 11 July 2023).

Carrico, K. (2017), 'Putinism with Chinese Characteristics: The Foreign Origins of Xi Jinping's Cult of Personality', *The Jamestown Foundation*, China Brief, 22 December. Available online: https://archive.is/NQBbL (accessed 11 July 2023).

Charon, P. and J.-B. Jeangène Vilmer (2021), *Chinese Influence Operations: A Machiavellian Moment*, Institute for Strategic Research, Paris: Ministry for the Armed Forces.

Choe, S-H. (2014), 'After Six Decades, Chinese Soldiers Killed in South Korea Head Home', *New York Times*, 28 March. Available online: https://archive.is/e6E3m (accessed 11 July 2023).

CNA (2022), 'Rare look: Moments Before Former Chinese President Hu Jintao was Escorted Out of Party Congress | Video', Available online: https://www .channelnewsasia.com/watch/rare-look-moments-former-chinese-president-hu-jintao -was-escorted-out-party-congress-video-3023206 (accessed 11 July 2023).

CNN (2022), 'Exclusive: China Operating Over 100 Police Stations Across the World with the Help of Some Host Nations, Report Claims', Available online: https://edition.cnn .com/2022/12/04/world/china-overseas-police-stations-intl-cmd/index.html.

CPC (2015), Available online: http://cpc.people.com.cn/xuexi/n/2015/0731/c385474 -27391395.html.

Czuczka, T. and S. Arons (2019), 'China Threatens Retaliation Should Germany Ban Huawei 5G', Bloomberg, 14 December. Available online: https://archive.is/I19X3 #selection-3447.0-3447.56 (accessed 11 July 2023).

Dangjianwang (2022), '学习语 | 坚持发扬斗争精神', Available online: https://web.archive .org/web/20230227133623/http://www.dangjian.com/shouye/dangjianyaowen/202212/ t20221202_6523247.shtml (accessed 11 July 2023).

Davidson, H. (2022), 'Was Hu Jintao's Removal from China's 20th Party Congress Suspicious Or Not?', *The Guardian*, 27 October. Available online: https://archive.is/ BNHnD (accessed 11 July 2023).

de La Bruyère, E. and N. Picarsic (2020), 'Made in Germany, Co-opted by China', Foundation for Defense of Democracies, October. Available online: https://www.fdd .org/wp-content/uploads/2020/10/fdd-monograph-made-in-germany-co-opted-by -china.pdf (accessed 11 July 2023).

Ekman, A. (2015), 'China's Emerging Middle Class: What Political Impact?', *IFRI Center for Asian Studies*, Asie, Visions 76, June. Available online: https://www.ifri.org/sites/ default/files/atoms/files/av76_ekman_middle_classes2.pdf (accessed 11 July 2023).

European Values and Konrad Adenauer Stiftung (2019), 'Handbook on Countering Russian and Chinese Interference in Europe', Available online: https://www .europeanvalues.cz/wp-content/uploads/2020/10/Handbook-on-Countering-Russian -and-Chinese-Interference-in-Europe.pdf (accessed 11 July 2023).

Fedasiuk, R. (2020), 'Putting Money in the Party's Mouth: How China Mobilizes Funding for United Front Work', *China Brief*, 20 (16). Available online: https://archive.is/TOD08 (accessed 11 July 2023).

Federal Ministry of the Interior and Community (2023), 'Disinformation Related to the Coronavirus Pandemic', Available online: https://archive.is/33b1l (accessed 11 July 2023).

Fewsmith, J. (1999), 'Elite Politics', in M. Goldman and R. Mac-Farquhar (eds), *The Paradox of China's Post-Mao Reforms*, 47–75, Cambridge: Harvard University Press.

Fewsmith, J. (2007), 'The Political Implications of China's Growing Middle Class', *China Leadership Monitor*, No 21, July. Available online: https://www.hoover.org/sites/default/ files/uploads/documents/CLM21JF.pdf (accessed 11 July 2023).

Fewsmith, J. (2021), *Rethinking Chinese Politics*, Cambridge: Cambridge University Press.

Flach, L., F. Teti, I. Gourevich, L. Scheckenofer, and L. Grandum (2022), 'Wie abhängig ist Deutschland von Rohstoffimporten?', *IFO Institut*, June. Available online: https://www .ifo.de/en/publications/2022/monograph-authorship/wie-abhangig-ist-deutschland -von-rohstoffimporten-eine (accessed 11 July 2023).

Ford, C. (2016), 'Realpolitik with Chinese Characteristics: Chinese Strategic Culture and the Modern Communist Party-State', in A. Tellis, A. Szalwinski, and M. Wills (eds), *Understanding Strategic Cultures in the Asia-Pacific*, 29–60, Seattle and Washington, DC: The National Bureau of Asian Research.

Ford, C. and T. D. Grant (2022), 'Exporting Censorship: The Chinese Communist Party Tries to Control Global Speech about China', *The National Security Institute*, March. Available online: https://nationalsecurity.gmu.edu/wp-content/uploads/2022/04/ Exporting-Censorship-FINAL-WEB-2.pdf (accessed 11 July 2023).

French, H. (2022), 'China's Restive Middle Class Will Be Xi's Greatest Test Yet', *Foreign Policy*, 6 December. Available online: https://archive.is/qGLAH (accessed 11 July 2023).

Fritz, A. (2019), 'China's Evolving Conception of Civil-Military Collaboration', *CSIS*, 2 August. Available online: https://archive.is/VTUMj (accessed 11 July 2023).

Fukao, K. (2021), 'China Said to Arm-twist Continental on Lithuania Business', *Nikkei Asia*, 18 December. Available online: https://archive.is/kVqCF (accessed 11 July 2023).

Fulda, A. (2020), *The Struggle for Democracy in Mainland China, Taiwan and Hong Kong*, Oxon and New York: Routledge.

Garnaut, J. (2019), 'John Garnaut Takes a Deep Look at What Drives China and "What Australia Needs to Know About Ideology in Xi Jinping's China"', interest.co.nz, 20 January. Available online: https://archive.is/IIV5r (accessed 11 July 2023).

Gold, T. (1997), 'Taiwan: Still Defying the Odds', in L. Diamond, M. Plattner, Y.-H. Chu, and H.-M. Tien (eds), *Consolidating the Third Wave Democracies: Regional Challenges*, 162–91, Baltimore: John Hopkins University Press.

Goodman, D. (2018), 'Social Mobility in China: Class and Stratification in the Reform Era', *Current History*, 117 (800): 203–8.

Graham-McLay, C. (2018), 'Fingers Point to China After Break-Ins Target New Zealand Professor', *New York Times*, 21 September. Available online: https://archive.is/Q8zWM (accessed 11 July 2023).

Hamilton, C. and M. Ohlberg (2020), *Hidden Hand: Exposing How the Chinese Communist Party is Reshaping the World*, London: Oneworld Publications.

Hannas, W. and H.-M. Chang (2021), 'Chinese Technnology Transfer: An introduction', in W. Hannas and D. Tatlow (eds), *China's Quest for Foreign Technology: Beyond Espionage*, 3–20, Oxon: Routledge.

Heilmann, S. (2008), 'From Local Experiments to National Policy: The Origins of China's Distinctive Policy Process', *The China Journal*, 59 (January): 1–30.

Hirschman, A. (1945), *National Power and the Structure of Foreign Trade*, Berkely, Los Angeles and London: University of California Press.

Hoffman, S. (2017a), 'Programming China: The Communist Party's Autonomic Approach to Managing State Security', *MERICS*, Merics China Monitor, 12 December. Available online: https://merics.org/en/report/programming-china (accessed 22 October 2018).

Hoffman, S. (2017b), *Programming China: The Communist Party's Autonomic Approach to Managing State Security*, PhD thesis, University of Nottingham, School of Politics and International Relations. Available online: https://eprints.nottingham.ac.uk/48547 /1/Hoffman%2C%20Samantha%20Student%20ID%204208393%20PHD%20THESIS %20Post%20Viva%20copy.pdf (accessed 11 July 2023).

IFW Kiel Institut für Weltwirtschaft (2023), 'Abhängigkeit der deutschen Wirtschaft von China: Bei einzelnen Produkten kritisch', 15 February. Available online: https://archive .is/lKD6U (accessed 11 July 2023).

Jaramillo, E. (2022), 'China's Hukou Reform in 2022: Do They Mean it this Time?', *CSIS*, 20 April. Available online: https://archive.is/D9Uii (accessed 11 July 2023).

Jichang Lulu (2018), 'Open Letter on Harassment Campaign against Anne-Marie Brady', *Sinopsis*, 5 December. Available online: https://archive.is/WriZU (accessed 11 July 2023).

Jichang Lulu (2020), 'Decoding United Front Work from Australia to Europe', *Sinopsis*, 15
    June. Available online: https://archive.is/jrMbU (accessed 11 July 2023).
Joske, A. (2020), 'The Party Speaks for You: Foreign Interference and the Chinese
    Communist Party's United Front System', Australian Strategic Policy Institute. Available
    online: https://s3-ap-southeast-2.amazonaws.com/ad-aspi/2020-06/The%20party
    %20speaks%20for%20you_0.pdf?gFHuXyYMR0XuDQOs_6JSmrdyk7MralcN=
    (accessed 18 January 2024).
Kania, E. and P. Wood (2021), 'The People's Liberation Army and Foreign Technology',
    in W. Hannas and D. Tatlow (eds), *China's Quest for Foreign Technology: Beyond
    Espionage*, 225–40, Oxon: Routledge.
Kaufman, A. and P. Mackenzie (2009), *The Culture of the Chinese People's Liberation Army*,
    Quantico, Virginia: Marine Corps Intelligence Activity. Available online: https://info
    .publicintelligence.net/MCIA-ChinaPLA.pdf (accessed 11 July 2023).
Klotzbücher, S. (2019), *Lange Schatten der Kulturrevolution. Eine transgenerationale Sicht
    auf Politik und Emotion in der Volksrepublik China*, Gießen: Psychosozial-Verlag.
Korteweg, R., D. Donninger, V. Kranenburg, C. Caberlon, and F.-P. van der Putten
    (2022), 'Sino-European Joint Ventures and the Risk of Technology Transfers',
    Clingendael China Centre and datenna, Clingendael Alert. Available online: https://
    www.clingendael.org/sites/default/files/2022-08/CA_Datenna_0.pdf (accessed 11 July
    2023).
Levitsky, S. and L. Way (2022), *Revolution and Dictatorship: The Violent Origins of Durable
    Authoritarianism*, Princeton: Princeton University Press.
Mattis, P. (2018), 'China's "Three Warfares" in Perspective', *Texas National Security Review*,
    War on the Rocks, 30 January. Available online: https://archive.is/7BqGH (accessed 11
    July 2023).
Mazzocco, I. (2022), 'How Inequality Is Undermining China's Prosperity', *CSIS*, 26 May.
    Available online: https://archive.is/cuLMN (accessed 11 July 2023).
MERICS (2021), 'Statement on the Sanctions Imposed by China that Also Affect MERICS',
    22 March. Available online: https://archive.is/56A7I (accessed 11 July 2023).
Mitchell, T. (2017), 'Xi Jinping, China's New Revolutionary Hero', *Financial Times*, 20
    October. Available online: https://archive.is/3X2uz (accessed 11 July 2023).
Mo, Z. (2022), 'Is East Asia Becoming Plutocratic?', *Wold Inequality Lab*, Issue Brief 2022–
    11, November. Available online: https://wid.world/document/is-east-asia-becoming
    -plutocratic-world-inequality-lab-issue-brief-2022-05/ (accessed 11 July 2023).
Nathan, A. (2003), 'China's Changing of the Guard: Authoritarian Resilience', *Journal of
    Democracy*, 1: 6–17.
NBR (2021), 'Understanding Chinese "Wolf Warrior Diplomacy"', *The National Bureau
    of Asian Research*, 22 October. Available online: https://archive.is/nkQFv (accessed 11
    July 2023).
NED (2017), 'Sharp Power: Rising Authoritarian Influence', National Endowment for
    Democracy, December. Available online: https://www.ned.org/wp-content/uploads
    /2017/12/Sharp-Power-Rising-Authoritarian-Influence-Full-Report.pdf (accessed 11
    July 2023).
Nguyen, M. (2017), 'The Bitter Legacy of the 1979 China-Vietnam War', *The Diplomat*, 23
    February. Available online: https://archive.is/0y097 (accessed 11 July 2023).
Niblock, I., S. Hoffman, and M. Knight (2022), 'China's Messaging on the Ukraine
    Conflict', *ASPI*, May. Available online: https://ad-aspi.s3.ap-southeast-2.amazonaws
    .com/2022-05/Chinas%20messaging%20on%20the%20Ukraine%20conflict.pdf
    ?VersionId=NTxOLMJgwYuHxr8nflwxovIBCkkt3U.c (accessed 11 July 2023).

Nye, J. (2005), 'The Rise of China's Soft Power', *Belfer Center for Science and International Affairs*, 29 December. Available online: https://www.belfercenter.org/publication/rise -chinas-soft-power (accessed 11 July 2023).

Nye, J. (2018), 'China's Soft and Sharp Power', Available online: https://archive.is/K6ahF.

Odell, R. (2023), '"Struggle" as Coercion with Chinese Characteristics: The PRC's Approach to Nonconventional Deterrence', in R. Kamphausen (ed), *Modernizing Deterrence: How China Coerces, Compels, and Deters*, 45–64, Seattle and Washington, DC: The National Bureau of Asian Research.

Patey, L. (2022), 'Hope for the Best, Prepare for the Worst: How the European Union Can Address China's Economic Coercion', *Danish Institute for International Studies*, 19 December. Available online: https://archive.is/ OPKZ5 (accessed 11 July 2023).

Pearson, M., M. Rithmire, and K. Tsai (2022), 'China's Party-State Capitalism and International Backlash', *International Security*, 47 (2) (Fall): 135–76.

Pei, M. (2016), *China's Crony Capitalism*, Cambridge: Harvard University Press.

Pottinger, M., M. Johnson, and D. Feith (2022), 'Xi Jinping in His Own Words', *Foreign Affairs*, 30 November. Available online: https://archive.is/X3JFs#selection-1465.0 -1468.0 (accessed 11 July 2023).

Powell, R. (1965), 'Commissars in the Economy: "Learn from the PLA" Movement in China', *Asian Survey*, 5 (3): 125–38.

President of Russia (2022), 'Joint Statement of the Russian Federation and the People's Republic of China on the International Relations Entering a New Era and the Global Sustainable Development', 4 February. Available online: https://archive.is/vLs4F (accessed 11 July 2023).

Roetz, H. (1997), 'China und die Menschenrechte: Die Bedeutung der Tradition und die Stellung des Konfuzianismus', in G. Paul and C. Robertson-Wensauer (eds), *Traditionelle chinesische Kultur und Menschenrechtsfrage*, 36–55, Baden-Baden: Nomos Verlagsgesellschaft.

Roetz, H. (2007), 'China und die Standards einer künftigen Weltordnung: Eine kulturelle Herausforderung?', in D. Döring and E. Kroker (eds), *An der Schwelle zu einem „Asiatischen Jahrhundert"?*, 37–56, Frankfurt am Main: Societäts-Verlag.

Roetz, H. (2016), 'Der antike Legismus - Eine Quelle des modernen chinesischen Totalitarismus?', in H. von Senger and M. Senn (eds), *Maoismus oder Sinomarxismus?*, 75–99, Stuttgart: Franz Steiner Verlag.

Roetz, H. (2019), 'On Political Dissent in Warring States China', in K. Kellermann, A. Plassmann, and C. Schwermann (eds), *Criticising the Ruler in Pre-Modern Societies - Possibilities, Chances, and Methods*, 211–36, Göttingen: V&R unipress / Bonn University Press.

Roetz, H. (2022), 'Unterdrückung als kulturelle Besonderheit: Autoritarismus und Identitätsmanagement in China', *polylog*, 48 (Winter): 41–54.

Roy, E. (2018), 'NZ Police Investigate after Prominent China Critic's Car "sabotaged"', *The Guardian*, 16 November. Available online: https://archive.is/4UvKN (accessed 11 July 2023).

Safeguard Defenders (2022a), 'Patrol and Persuade - A Follow up on 110 Overseas Investigation', 5 December. Available online: https://archive.is/TkjZh (accessed 11 July 2023).

Safeguard Defenders (2022b), 'Chinese Overseas Police Service Stations Tied to Illegal Policing in Madrid and Belgrade', 15 September. Available online: https://archive.is/ e3EhG (accessed 11 July 2023).

Sapio, F. (2015), 'Carl Schmitt in China', *The China Story*, 7 October. Available online: https://web.archive.org/web/20151020142101/http:/www.thechinastory.org/2015/10/carl-schmitt-in-china/ (accessed 11 July 2023).

SCMP (2009), '1949: The Untold Story', 21 September. Available online: https://archive.is/i00mv (accessed 23 October 2018).

Scott, L. (2022), 'How China Became a Global Disinformation Superpower', *Coda*, 6 December. Available online: https://archive.is/iUUee (accessed 11 July 2023).

Shambaugh, D. (2008), *China's Communist Party: Atrophy and Adaptation*, Washington, DC: Woodrow Wilson Center Press.

Sharma, Y. (2021), 'New Row Over Confucius Institutes' Role on Campuses', *University World News*, 29 October. Available online: https://archive.is/7v1fq (accessed 11 July 2023).

Shen, P. and Y.-F. Lai (2022), 'Chinas Einfluss in Deutschland: Wissenschaft und Medien sind die Achillesferse', Friedrich Naumann Stiftung, 3 August. Available online: https://archive.is/VBSNF (accessed 11 July 2023).

Sommer, U. (2021), 'Der riskante China-Boom der Dax-Konzerne', *Handelsblatt*, 18 February. Available online: https://archive.is/w4Zu3#selection-1433.0-1440.0 (accessed 11 July 2023).

Stremmel, J. (2023), '"Morgen bist Du tot!"', *Süddeutsche Zeitung*, 12 January. Available online: https://archive.is/cuqfS (accessed 11 July 2023).

Sutter, K. (2021), 'Foreign Technology Transfer Through Commerce', in W. Hannas and D. Tatlow (eds), *China's Quest for Foreign Technology: Beyond Espionage*, 57–73, Oxon: Routledge.

Sytas, A. and J. O'Donnell (2021), 'Exclusive China Pressures Germany's Continental to Cut Out Lithuania – Sources', *Reuters*, 17 December. Available online: https://archive.is/ACYCI (accessed 11 July 2023).

Sytas, A. and J. O'Donnell (2022), 'Analysis: German Big Business Piles Pressure on Lithuania in China Row', *Reuters*, 21 January. Available online: https://archive.is/fRHLd (accessed 11 July 2023).

Tatlow, D. (2018), 'China's Cosmological Communism: A Challenge to Liberal Democracies', MERICS, Report, 18 July. Available online: https://archive.is/WSgxD (accessed 11 July 2023).

Tatlow, D. (2019), 'Mapping China-in-Germany', *Sinopsis*, 2 October. Available online: https://archive.is/6tJ6z (accessed 11 July 2023).

Tatlow, D. (2022), 'Xi Jinping Ramps Up China's Surveillance, Harassment Deep in America', *Newsweek*, 12 March. Available online: https://archive.is/15kyQ (accessed 11 July 2023).

Tatlow, D. and A. Rácz (2021), 'Assessing China and Russia's Influence on the German Parliamentary Elections', *DGAP*, DGAP Kommentar. Available online: https://web.archive.org/web/20221208051421/https://dgap.org/de/node/35613 (accessed 11 July 2023).

Tellis, A., A. Szalwinski, and M. Wills (2016), *Understanding Strategic Cultures in the Asia-Pacific*, Seattle and Washington, DC: The National Bureau of Asian Research.

Teon, A. (2021), 'Chinese Diplomat Gives Middle Finger to China's "Enemies"', *The Greater China Journal*, 25 June. Available online: https://web.archive.org/web/20221001112709/https://china-journal.org/2021/06/25/chinese-diplomat-gives-middle-finger-to-chinas-enemies/ (accessed 11 July 2023).

The Economist (2020), 'How Sweden Copes with Chinese Bullying', 20 February. Available online: https://archive.is/s1xwd#selection-575.0-575.38 (accessed 11 July 2023).

The Gate of Heavenly Peace (1995), 'May 4', Available online: http://www.tsquare.tv/film/transmay4.html (accessed 11 July 2023).

Thorley, M. (2019), 'Huawei, the CSSA and Beyond: "Latent Networks" and Party Influence Within Chinese Institutions', *The Asia Dialogue*, 5 July. Available online: https://archive.is/gWV4D (accessed 11 July 2023).

Tobin, L. (2023), 'China's Brute Force Economics: Waking Up from the Dream of a Level Playing Field', *Texas National Security Review*, 6 (1) (Winter 2022/2023): 82–98. Available online: https://tnsr.org/wp-content/uploads/2022/12/TNSR-Journal-Vol-6-Issue-1-Tobin.pdf (accessed 11 July 2023).

Tsang, S. (2009, November), 'Consultative Leninism: China's New Political Framework', *Journal of Contemporary China*, 18 (62): 865–80.

U.S. Department of State (2020), 'Military-Civil Fusion and the People's Republic of China', Available online: https://www.state.gov/wp-content/uploads/2020/05/What-is-MCF-One-Pager.pdf (accessed 11 July 2023).

van Slyke, L. (1970), 'The United Front in China', *Journal of Contemporary History*, 5 (3): 119–35.

Weber, R. (2022), 'At What Point Does Cooperation Lead to Complicity?', *China.Table*, 20 September. Available online: https://archive.is/CJeK8 (accessed 11 July 2023).

Wigell, M. (2019), 'Hybrid Interference as a Wedge Strategy: A Theory of External Interference in Liberal Democracy', *International Affairs*, 95 (2): 255–75.

Wintour, P. (2022), 'Chinese Diplomats at Centre of Manchester Consulate Row Return Home', *The Guardian*, 14 December. Available online: https://archive.is/EIbLx (accessed 11 July 2023).

Xu, Z. (2020), 'Viral Alarm: When Fury Overcomes Fear', *ChinaFile*, 10 February. Available online: https://archive.is/HYUcH (accessed 11 July 2023).

Yeung, J. (2022), 'Chinese Diplomat Says Pulling Hair of Hong Kong Protester was his "Duty"', *CNN*, 21 October. Available online: https://archive.is/mSefd (accessed 11 July 2023).

Zeit Online (2021), 'China übt Druck auf Hongkonger Bürger in Deutschland aus', 19 February. Available online: https://archive.is/S5LUR (accessed 11 July 2023).

Zhang, J. (2022), 'Where are China-Germany Relations Headed?', *GIS*, 1 November. Available online: https://archive.is/U8bC3 (accessed 11 July 2023).

Zhou, X. and S. Zheng (2019), 'Xi Jinping Rallies China for Decades-Long "Struggle" to Rise in Global Order, Amid Escalating US Trade War', *South China Morning Post*, 5 September. Available online: https://archive.is/6Dx1O (accessed 11 July 2023).

Chapter 4

HOW KOHL, SCHRÖDER, MERKEL AND SCHOLZ NORMALIZED AUTOCRATIC CHINA

4.1 Logic and limits of an overly pragmatic foreign policy approach

If we want to understand how Germany could become entangled with autocratic China we need to adopt a longitudinal perspective. In Chapter 2 I already critiqued Steinmeier's doctrine of 'Rapprochement through interweaving' for facilitating entanglement. Yet he was not solely responsible for this outcome. In Germany's parliamentary democracy, it is the Chancellor who has the greatest political power. This requires us to review the leadership role of Chancellors Kohl (1982–1998), Schröder (1998–2005), Merkel (2005–2021) and Scholz (2021–). My following critique distinguishes between two types of political leadership: principled and pragmatic. According to Boin and Lodge principled leadership prioritizes guiding responses to political challenges by communicating core values and adhering to them in a consistent manner (2021). A pragmatic approach to leadership, on the other hand, can be viewed as one that rejects one core value or set of values, and recommends responding to changing circumstances in a situational manner (2021).

Chapter at a glance

In this chapter I argue that all four Chancellors followed a pragmatic approach, which prioritized short-term economic gains over long-term industrial competitiveness and democratic resilience. A brief exception were the first years of Merkel's Chancellorship (2005–2008), when she tried to forge a more principled German China policy. But she soon abandoned it due to domestic opposition and geoeconomic challenges. I also explain that from the mid-1990s onwards China policy was de facto outsourced to the private sector. Successive chairmen of the Asia-Pacific Committee of German Business (APA) not only lobbied for greater commercial engagement with China but at times also discredited public concerns about China's lack of democracy and human rights. I also highlight the problematic role of former Chancellor Schmidt (1974–1982). In his role as elder statesman and through his public interventions in the early 2000s he did the CCP's bidding. I contend that the five Chancellors, in concert with industrialists, helped cement the primacy of trade and investment over the primacy of politics.

4.2 *Money over morals: Kohl's visit to the PLA 196 Infantry Division*

Chancellor Kohl is best known for his role in Germany's reunification. In 1990 he won the first election in a reunified Germany for the Christian Democratic Union (CDU) by a landslide. His governing coalition with the Free Democratic Party (FDP) was confirmed by a slightly smaller majority four years later. This allowed Kohl to govern Germany for sixteen years (1982–1998). Kohl played a pivotal role in Germany's relationship with China. By 1992 Foreign Minister Kinkel (FDP) signalled that Germany was ready to move on from the economic sanctions imposed after the 1989 Tiananmen massacre (UPI, 1992). Yet it was Kohl who helped normalize the CCP in 1995 by becoming the 'first Western leader to visit a Chinese military base' (Kinzer, 1995). Kohl's visit to the PLA 196 Infantry Division outside Tianjin sent a clear signal that the atrocities of 1989 were no longer an obstacle to Western business engagement with China (SCMP, 1995). Kohl's economic rapprochement with China came at a time when Germany was struggling with the very high costs of reunification. By 1992 economic growth in western Germany was stalling whilst inflation was rising. Public borrowing for infrastructure building in eastern Germany and unemployment payments was at record high (Kiefer, 1992).

Karnitschnig has argued that Kohl helped to '[convince] a generation of German political and business elites that China held the key to Germany's long-term prosperity' (2020). Kohl, he writes, opened the door to China only to throw away the key and then let Beijing use it to bind them to an economic relationship they could not escape (2020). Despite Karnitschnig's hyperbole, his critique is not completely unfounded. Metaphorically speaking Kohl of course did not throw the key away. But if we stick to the analogy it can be said that he handed it over to the Asia-Pacific Committee of German Business (APA). This umbrella organization was formed on 24 September 1993 in order to 'encourage German companies to become more involved in the Asia-Pacific region and, at the same time, to improve the political and economic framework conditions for such involvement both in the Federal Republic of Germany and in the Asia-Pacific countries' (ASIEN, 1994). In 2023 APA comprised five heavyweight business associations: the Federation of German Industries (BDI), the German Chamber of Commerce and Industry (DIHK), the German Asia-Pacific Business Association (OAV), the Federation of German Wholesale, Foreign Trade and Services (BGA) and the Association of German Banks (Bankenverband). APA describes itself as an 'agenda-setter for crucial economic issues regarding the future of our cooperation with the Asia-Pacific region' (APA, 2023).

APA's modest self-description considerably underplays its importance to German China policy. The Kohl administration unveiled its first Asia concept at the end of 1993, emphasizing economic opportunities (Deutscher Bundestag,

1993). Priority was given to the economy. Foreign and security policy were listed at the end and under item six and seven, respectively. The Kohl administration 'welcomed the founding of the Asia-Pacific Committe of German Business' (1993), which was expected to 'coordinate and support specific initiatives of the private sector towards Asia' (1993). As a result of APA's establishment an influential player emerged which started to dominate German China policy for years to come. As Schultes points out in his PhD thesis, the German government allowed the private sector lead foreign trade promotion (2003, 53). Schultes highlighted the Germany-specific 'transfer of sovereign tasks to private economic entities that fulfil them on behalf of the state' (2003). Foreign policy formulation was no longer a political prerogative, but was co-determined by the commercial interests of Germany's export-oriented industries. In Chapter 2 I already outlined the role which the German Eastern Business Association (*Ost-Ausschuss*) played as an intermediary between Germany and the Soviet Union and its successor state, the Russian Federation. Since it was founded APA has played a similar role in the Asia-Pacific in general and China in particular. APA regularly hosts 'high-level economic talks during visits of Asian government representatives to Germany and during visits of the German Federal Government to Asia' (2023). Meetings have taken the form of bi-annual Asia-Pacific Conferences of German Business (APK). Seventeen APKs have been conducted by 2023, with the most recent in Singapore in 2022.

A review of APA's leadership over time reveals its elevated position in Germany's political economy. Apart from the Chairmanship of Voith CEO Lienhard (2014–2019), APA was led either by a Siemens CEO (von Pierer, 1993–2006; Löscher, 2010–2014; Kaeser, 2019–2021; Busch, 2021–) or a BASF CEO (Hambrecht, 2006–2010). Both Siemens and BASF are industrial behemoths which enjoy direct access to the top echelons of German politics. The prominence of its chairmen has arguably allowed APA to punch above its weight. But as I will show in the following, successive APA chairmen have also played a problematic role by either hyping the Chinese market, by downplaying the political dimension of Germany's China engagement or by doing both. In Chancellor Schröder (1998–2005) from the Social Democratic Party (SPD) they found a political patron who was widely nicknamed 'comrade of the bosses' (*Genosse der Bosse*) for his pro-business views. Schröder is widely associated with Germany's 'Change through trade' mantra, which in recent years has alternatively been described as a 'fairy tale' (Groitl, 2021) or a 'life lie' (Büschemann, 2021).

4.3 Genosse der Bosse: Schröder's attempt to lift Europe's arms embargo

German industrialists saw Schröder as a 'door opener' who during his visits to China enabled CEOs to engage in direct communication with senior CCP officials (Deutsche Welle, 2003). In his dual role as Siemens CEO and APA Chairman von Pierer frequently accompanied Schröder on his official visits to China. In an op-ed published in 2001 von Pierer praised the speed of change in China as 'breathtaking' and suggested that 'the size of the internal market and the interest and receptiveness to cutting-edge technology and innovation of all kinds will further increase the pull on companies from all over the world' (2001). von Pierer also coined the memorable one-liner of 'the risk of not being in Asia-Pacific is greater than the risk of being in' (Bovensiepen, 2004). In 2004 he announced that Siemens would invest about 1 billion euro in China (Busse, 2004). In the period 2003–2004 Siemens commitment to the Chinese market paid off, leading to a plus of 34 per cent in new contracts and a rise of 28 per cent in revenues (Süddeutsche Zeitung, 2005a). And while the Chinese leadership showed an interest in Siemens Transrapid technology and agreed to build a link between Shanghai and its airport (Süddeutsche Zeitung, 2001), von Pierer's dream of securing a contract for building a high-speed monorail connection between Beijing and Shanghai did not materialize (Süddeutsche Zeitung, 2004).

Schröder's preoccupation with China's growing market and his close proximity to leading German industrialists came at the expense of other German enlightened interests. During an early visit to China Schröder reportedly showed no interest in raising the issue of human rights with his counterparts. In 2001 he was asked whether he had submitted a list of political prisoners. He negated the question and dismissed such acts as 'rituals', which according to Schröder belonged to the past (Lorenz, 2001). In 2000 the Schröder administration had relegated the topics of democracy and human rights to the status of a bilateral rule of law dialogue. The latter was sold to the public as a more constructive venue to seek improvements to China's human rights situation (Blume, 2000). In fact, however, the rule of law dialogue primarily sought to improve the legal framework conditions for German businesses. von Hein has rightly pointed out that 'the high-level symposia and conferences are more concerned with patent protection and procedural security than, for example, the right to freedom of expression' (2003). Yet even more concerning was Schröder's attempt to lift Europe's arms embargo, which Schröder called 'outdated' and 'superfluous', since 'the China of today isn't the China of 1989' (Phalnikar, 2005).

A lifting of the embargo, according to Schröder, would only serve as a symbolic act that would not lead to actual arms trade (Bernstein, 2005). Schröder neglected to mention that despite a European Code of Conduct, arms sales from the EU to China had already increased significantly. As a result of the lack of specificity in the 1989 arms embargo, EU member states were able to exploit 'exemptions' that allowed dual-use products to be exported. They included Rolls Royce engines, which were used in Chinese fighter jets, as well as Italian and Spanish helicopter technology, which found their way into Chinese military helicopters (Riegert, 2005). Schröder's proposal, as Wernicke has rightly pointed out, 'sounds as if someone, in their drive for the Chinese market, first wants to remove all the hurdles they have built up themselves – in order to then allegedly chase lucrative business more slowly and cautiously than ever' (2005a).

For what allegedly would be a symbolic act, Schröder was willing to risk a major conflict, not only in Germany but also at the European level and across the Atlantic. Parliamentarians across the political divide where incensed by Schröder's suggestion that the German Bundestag might be sidelined in the decision-making process (Spiegel International, 2005). Schröder led the effort to lift the arms embargo alongside French President Chirac. In the case of a vote by the European Council, he suggested he would vote yes (Fried, 2005a). Neither the UK government nor numerous Eastern European states were convinced (Kornelius, 2005). The European Parliament opposed the planned lifting of the arms embargo in February 2005 (Süddeutsche Zeitung, 2005b). The US Congress was particularly hostile to Schröder's proposal (Fried, 2005b).

In light of this, one has to wonder why Schröder was so insistent on pushing an unpopular proposal. Strittmatter has criticized Schröder and Chirac for wanting 'to lift the EU arms embargo . . . without demanding anything in advance: not on human rights, not on China's aggressive Taiwan policy' (Strittmatter, 2005). Kornelius however suggests that Schröder hoped to gain China's support for Germany's permanent seat in the UN Security Council (2005). As a result of massive political pressure from the United States, European foreign ministers shelved the plan in Spring 2005 (Wernicke, 2005b). Even though Schröder's plan ultimately failed, much of the attention on China during 2004 and 2005 focused on his proposal. A strong message was sent to the German public: anything was on the table for profit-making, even a decision that would likely assist the CCP in modernising their military. But as the following discussion will show Schröder was not the first German Social Democrat to display surprising closeness to China's autocrats.

4.4 Admirer of authoritarians: Schmidt's normalization of the CCP in public debates

Former Chancellor Helmut Schmidt (1974–1982) was Schröder's political role model (Spiegel, 2017). Though Schmidt retired from frontline politics in the early 1980s, he exercised a very problematic intellectual leadership role during the early years of the Merkel era. Schmidt repeatedly argued against Western countries helping China democratize. In his book *Nachbar China*, Schmidt argued on the basis of cultural essentialist views that 'China lacks all the prerequisites for democracy, and there have been no democratic traditions in Chinese history' (Ziesemer, 2006). Schmidt discredited the idea of promoting democracy in China in his conversation with Sieren. Schmidt said that in order 'to introduce democracy in a developing country, I would not give a cent out of my hand' (Schmidt and Sieren, 2006, 288). During a public debate in 2012 reiterated this point. Schmidt brushed off audience questions regarding a possible export of democracy to China as 'arrogant' or 'foolish'. In an absurd role reversal Schmidt dismissed the idea that democracy would suit China, while his dialogue partner on the stage, Gu Xuewu – a Chinese political scientist living and working in Germany – had to remind the audience that 'a free system was always a better option than the naked exercise of power' (von Hein, 2012).

During this infamous 2012 public debate with Gu Schmidt parroted CCP talking points such as the 'humiliation of the Chinese by Western powers' (Podcampus, 2014). He argued that one cannot 'put oneself in the shoes of today's Chinese leaders' without a basic understanding of China's history (2014). Schmidt's praise for Xi Jinping's book *The Governance of China* further demonstrated his empathy for China's autocratic rulers. In late 2014 Schmidt published an op-ed in which he lauded Xi's book with which 'the world can get to know and understand China's development and in particular China's domestic and foreign policy better' (Renminwang, 2014). Why did Schmidt normalize the CCP? Schmidt, according to the German journalist Erling, was part of Germany's 'sceptic generation': a product of the Third Reich, disillusioned, cynical, rejecting political visions and advocating pragmatism (2014). According to Erling Schmidt was an 'authoritarian character dressed in the cloak of the sceptic. And therefore an admirer of all authoritarians in this world as long as they have power; and a despiser of anti-authoritarian democracy' (2014). Erling explains that sceptics like Schmidt thought that the dichotomy between democracy and autocracy could be overcome by 'system convergence' and 'change through rapprochement' (2014).

During the talk Schmidt also downplayed the PLA's military posture. Asked about China's raw material needs, Schmidt responded that 'there is no indication so far that China would try to get access to raw materials by military means. There aren't any. Maybe with the exception of two archipelagos in the South China Sea – maybe. But there, too, this hasn't led to military imbroglio so far' (Podcampus, 2014). He did not mention Taiwan as a potential flashpoint in East Asia. We can better understand Schmidt's disregard for Taiwan's security when we examine his view of the self-governing island. According to Schmidt 'even today, Taiwan democracy has little to do with a Western democracy. Taiwan democracy was nurtured by the Western media and politicians. First and foremost by the House of Representatives and the Senate; the aim was to damage the communists in Beijing' (Schmidt and Sieren, 2006, 143). He also pointed out that 'Taiwan has become dependent on the interconnectedness of the mainland Chinese economy to an unusual but – given its geographical situation – understandable extent. This serves the cause of peace' (2006, 147). The idea that economic interdependence would create peace has already been deconstructed in Chapter 2. Yet Schmidt's comments are also striking in the way he uncritically reproduced Beijing's imperialist perspective on Taiwan. In his 2006 book he stated that the 'Taiwan question' was inextricably linked with China's relationship with America (2006). Schmidt lamented that Taiwan 'should indeed be a domestic matter for China, but it isn't' (2006).

Sieren argued that Germans should consider how to address Schmidt's legacy when he passed away in 2015 (2015). While he correctly noted that Schmidt has always shown an interest in China (2015), he did not mention that Schmidt's portrayal of China was culturally essentialist. Throughout his publications and public appearances, Schmidt sought to better understand 'official China'. His seemingly limitless empathy for autocratic rulers led Germany's former Chancellor to disregard the plight of 'unofficial China'. It is impossible to estimate the harm

Schmidt has done to German public discourse. However, as Erling rightly noted in 2014, 'many Germans regard Schmidt as a particularly independent authority – as a liberal among the Socialists, defender of the democratic constitutional state against the RAF, saviour of the West before the peace movement' (2014). Schmidt's public commentary about China is likely to have resonated with Germans reminiscent of his Chancellorship in the 1970s and early 1980s. Schmidt's legacy also extended to his follower, as Schröder's lack of interest in the issue of democracy and human rights in China has shown. Merkel thus became Chancellor of Germany in 2005 amid a public debate on China led by two senior Social Democrats who were strongly opposed to a value-based approach to German China policy.

4.5 A chastened reformer: how Merkel ended up as a servant of Germany Inc.

When Merkel first ran for office in 2005, she was compared to Thatcher (Taylor, 2005). During her time as opposition leader, Merkel advocated radical tax reforms and promised to take a tougher line with Beijing (Moody, 2022). However, her reform ideas were unpopular with the electorate and nearly cost her the election. In the 2005 federal election, the CDU/CSU garnered 35.2 per cent of the votes, followed closely by Schröder's SPD with 34.2 per cent. Merkel had no option other than to form a Grand Coalition with the Social Democrats to govern. To her credit, Merkel announced publicly shortly after she had been sworn in as the new Chancellor that, 'no matter how hopeful they are as trading partners and how important they are for stability and security' (Handelsblatt, 2005), the new government would always address human rights violations openly. But although she began with such political rhetoric, Merkel soon became a chastened reformer who had her wings clipped. It may have been one of her most important lessons from her narrow election victory that being principled on certain policies carries the risk of not bringing her electoral success. Müller highlights that 'she started out as a politician stressing her first-hand experience of living under totalitarianism, ready to confront Russia and China on human rights' (2022). But according to Müller 'she ended as a servant of Germany Inc., fuelled by cheap energy from one autocracy and profiting from high-end exports to another' (2022).

What led to Merkel's change of heart? Since Merkel was dependent on the SPD she never used her *Richtlinienkompetenz* to overrule Foreign Minister Steinmeier (SPD). As a result Steinmeier was able to dominate Russia policy and develop his doctrine of 'Rapprochement through interweaving' (*Annäherung durch Verflechtung*) largely unopposed. Yet Merkel did initially try to develop a more principled approach in Germany's relationship with China. To underscore her value-based approach she met with the Dalai Lama at the Bundeskanzleramt in Berlin (Handelsblatt, 2007). It was Sandschneider, Director of the German Council on Foreign Relations (DGAP, 2003–2016), who criticized Merkel's meeting with the Dalai Lama. He said that 'domestically, she has received a positive reception, but in terms of foreign policy, German-Chinese relations have suffered damage' (Hansen, 2007). Following Beijing's temporary cancellation of a planned dialogue on rule of law and human rights, Sandschneider also warned that Germany could suffer long-term economic consequences (Roloff, 2007). Additionally, BASF CEO and APA Chairman Hambrecht (2006–2010), who succeeded SIEMENS CEO von Pierer as head of the influential lobby group APA, reiterated this warning.

Hambrecht had advocated a more 'positive' German China engagement in a radio interview in 2007. He said German exports are growing because of Asia's strong economy (Deutschlandfunk Kultur, 2007). On 16 April 2008, Hambrecht gave a TV interview in which he expressed concern about possible reprisals as a result of Germany's Tibet debate. Without providing any evidence Hambrecht claimed that addressing human rights silently behind closed doors 'was particularly effective' (FAZ, 2008). It was an indirect criticism of Merkel, who had just spoken to the Parliamentary Assembly of the Council of Europe. She had argued that 'trade should not outweigh human rights: economic issues and human rights issues were not in opposition' (Parliamentary Assembly, 2008). In an op-ed for *Süddeutsche Zeitung*, Oldag criticized Hambrecht's position by pointing out that 'the supposedly more efficient diplomacy behind closed doors has so far shown above all: China does not care. Beijing's rulers are practising strong-arm tactics, while the West grovels' (Oldag, 2008). Unfazed, in an interview with the economic magazine *WirtschaftsWoche*, Hambrecht argued that China had to feed a billion people and provide 300 to 400 million people with employment opportunities. He argued that it took Germany centuries to achieve democracy. Hambrecht also called for 'respect for the performance and the market opening of the Chinese since 1989' (WirtschaftsWoche, 2007). Citing Bahr's Ostpolitik Hambrecht argued that 'it was not constant criticism but constant dialogue that brought us reunification' (2007).

Merkel's subsequent pivot away from a value-based approach to China can be explained by a number of factors. In the public debate on China, she faced a trio of senior SPD politicians, former Chancellors Schröder and Schmidt as well as Foreign Minister Steinmeier, who either argued for 'Change through trade' (*Wandel durch Handel*) or 'Rapprochement through interweaving' (*Annäherung durch Verflechtung*). She also had to face criticism from German industrialists. According to Büscheman and Kuhr, a manager complained that Merkel's new approach 'should not harm German companies' (2008). In his dual role as CEO of BASF and Chairman of APA, Hambrecht added weight to critics of Merkel's attempt to develop a more principled German China policy. Aside from such domestic opposition, Merkel's failed attempt to change course was also due to the short-term success of Schröder's mercantilist approach to China. According to Tooze, German exports to China in fact helped boost Germany's economy. He has pointed out that 'Germany is the rare Western economy that since 2009 has run a trade surplus with China' (2022). Moody has similarly noted that 'the initial economic dividend was enormous' (Moody, 2022) and that 'China overtook the US as Berlin's biggest trading partner, trebling its share of German exports in the course of 15 years' (2022).

Such economic gains, however, need to be put in historical perspective. Setser has illustrated that 'German exports (measured by Chinese imports) have been basically flat since mid 2012' (@Brad_Setser, 2022). He has also highlighted the fact that '(the) growth impulse was all from 05 through 11' (2022). In addition, Tooze noted that since 2012 exports to China as a share of German GDP have plateaued between 2.5 and 2.75 per cent (2022). This has led Tooze to argue that exports to China after 2012 can no longer be seen as a current 'driver' of growth (2022). Setser and Tooze have emphasized this period in Sino-German relations in order to support their overall argument that China's influence on Germany in 2022 should not be overestimated. Nevertheless, their insight is also highly relevant to show that Germany had benefited greatly from China's economic growth during the first six years of Merkel's Chancellorship (2005–2011). Merkel's re-election chances arguably increased as a result of rapid GDP growth in Germany during that time. Merkel consequently won the 2009 Federal Election (33.7%) comfortably, putting the SPD (23%) into opposition.

Brattberg has called the 2008 global financial crisis a turning point. According to him it marked the beginning of an 'economics-driven approach – a kind of Germany First strategy – [which] prioritized strong trade and investment with Beijing over concerns regarding human rights and values issues' (2021). During the Eurozone crisis, Beijing bought about $50 billion of IMF bonds (Spiegel, 2009). As part of its financial diplomacy, the Chinese government also pledged to buy Portuguese and Spanish government bonds. Although such interventions captured headlines (Reuters, 2011), they were insufficient to lower rising yields in crisis-hit Southern European countries. Only when the European Central Bank started buying bonds in August 2011 did this desired effect occur (Financial Times, 2011) Merkel's experience of the role of China during the Eurozone crisis, however, was strikingly different. According to Barkin, a German diplomat who worked closely with Merkel had observed that the former Chancellor greatly appreciated that 'China bought the bonds of ailing eurozone member states and provided a market in which German firms could continue to thrive' (2020). It should also be noted that as soon as the EU reached an agreement on its Fiscal Compact in early 2012, Merkel visited China 'to assure Chinese risk-averse leaders that Europe is back on track' (Parello-Plesner, 2012). This coincided with the EU-China Summit in February 2012, where the European Commission was authorized to work on an investment agreement (European Commission, 2014). While Merkel would continue meeting Chinese activists during her subsequent visits to China (Mudie, 2015), the CCP no longer had to worry about her paying lip service to human rights. In the words of Müller, by that time, she had already transformed into a servant of Germany Inc.

A case in point is Merkel's attempt to pass the EU-China Comprehensive Investment Agreement (CAI) during her final months as Chancellor. According to Wettach, Beijing offered German Telekom a side deal as part of CAI to enter China's lucrative mobile market (2021). It had been reported in the previous months that Merkel had linked Huawei's role in building Germany's 5G infrastructure to Telekom's market access in China (Wettach, 2020). It had been seven years since 2014 when the negotiations for CAI began. China, however, had undergone a dramatic change by 2021. An open letter signed in January 2021 by more than 100 experts called for the suspension of the deal. In the opinion of signatories, the agreement ignored Europe's increasing dependence on China and was based on an overly optimistic view of the Chinese Communist Party. Signatories considered even the current level of European economic dependence on China concerning. Furthermore, they noted that Chinese state-owned companies bought significant stakes in European infrastructure following the financial crisis of 2008 (Baumgärtner and Müller, 2021). In December 2020, the European leaders concluded the agreement in principle, but it was subsequently put on ice. According to the European Parliament, it cannot be ratified as long as European lawmakers are subject to Chinese sanctions imposed by the Xi regime as retaliation for European sanctions on Chinese officials implicated in crimes against humanity in Xinjiang (European Parliament, 2021).

In 2021 German FDP politician Vogel described Merkel's conundrum of overseeing German China policy for sixteen years in an interview. Due to its centrality to my argument, I would like to quote his answer in its entirety. Vogel notes that '(one) must first acknowledge here that the Merkel governments had to deal with two different Chinas. China was never a democracy in the last decades, but the regime has changed in nature once again with the change of the leadership generation from Hu Jintao to Xi Jinping. There were definitely different factions in the CP before and the further development of the CP was open; there were also a variety of ideas for the country within the party' (China.Table, 2021). Vogel goes on to say that 'under Xi Jinping, on the other hand, a completely new systemic challenge has emerged. And that happened during the Merkel era. Since then, we have had a strategy deficit: the West is stuck with a China strategy from the time before Xi' (2021). In light of Merkel's abandoning of a principled approach to China three years into her first administration, Vogel's observation is especially compelling. In a rather ironic turn of events, Merkel's embrace of a pragmatic approach vis-à-vis China coincided with Xi's authoritarian turn since 2012. In 2021 Merkel rode out her fourth term without changing course, did not stand for re-election and thus left unfinished business to her successor.

4.6 Merkel's tribute act: Scholz's unwillingness to face up to new geopolitical realities

Germany's Federal Election of 2021 resulted in six political parties entering the Bundestag. The CDU/CSU (26.8%) and SPD (20.5%) suffered at the polls. Smaller parties such as the Free Democratic Party (10.7%) and Alliance 90/The Greens (8.7%) became kingmakers as a result. As a result of parliamentary arithmetic, a 'traffic light' coalition was formed with the SPD (red), FDP (yellow) and Alliance 90/The Greens (green). Scholz was elected Chancellor of Germany with 395 votes on 8 December 2021 (The Federal Government, 2021). It was a remarkable journey for a Social Democrat who, when he was a youth member of the SPD, wrote articles

criticizing an supposedly 'aggressive-imperialist NATO' and describing Germany
as a 'European stronghold of big business' (Schröm and Hollenstein, 2022, 43).
Scholz told Spiegel that he now views what he believed then as largely incorrect
(Hickmann and Medick, 2019). After a brief hiatus from politics, he reinvented
himself as a pragmatic technocrat with pro-business views. His notable positions
in public life include Mayor of Hamburg from 2011 to 2018 and Vice-Chancellor
under Merkel from 2018 to 2021.

In his capacity as mayor, Scholz became embroiled in the CumEx scandal.
As part of a tax fraud scheme, Hamburg-based MM Warburg bank shifted share
packages with ('cum') and without ('ex') dividend entitlement around the dividend
record date (Handelsblatt, 2022). This widespread fraudulent practice in Germany's
banking sector led to large-scale refunds of capital gains taxes. The German state
lost approximately 31.8 billion euros (Blickle et al., 2017). A surprising decision
was made by Hamburg's finance authorities not to recover 47 million euros from
MM Warburg bank at the end of 2016 (2017). There were allegations that Scholz,
who had met the bank's co-owner several times before the tax demand was waived,
had influenced the decision. Scholz has always denied all allegations and claims he
does not remember any of the talks with the banker Olearius (Burghardt, Ott and
Schmitt, 2020). And during the Wirecard scandal, Scholz's role as Finance Minister
was also criticized. Germany's financial regulators responded with disbelief when
Financial Times reported dubious accounting practices at the German financial
giant. The German Securities and Exchange Commission, BaFin, which is
subordinate to Germany's Ministry of Finance, initially suspected that short
sellers were attempting to manipulate Wirecard's share price (Daub, 2021). When
Wirecard went insolvent in 2021 due to unethical business practices and financial
misstatements opposition politicians pinned political responsibility on Scholz for
economic damage to the tune of 30 billion euros (Süddeutsche Zeitung, 2021).

Scholz was described as an 'accidental Chancellor' by David-Wilp, who made
his way into the job as a result of a conservative rival's gaffes (Luyken, 2022). Scholz
had emulated Merkel's style of politics during the election campaign. A SPIEGEL
editorial noted that '(never) before has a candidate in Germany sought to present
themselves as a clone of their predecessor' (von Hammerstein et al., 2021). Scholz
political communication style earned him the nickname 'Scholzomat' in the early
2000s, which blends the words 'Scholz' and 'automat'. This term was used to describe
Scholz's ability to 'express himself in public in a polished way, but often with little
content' (Scherschun, 2011). In spite of his *Zeitenwende* speech in the German
Bundestag on 27 January 2022, Scholz has thus far failed to make any major changes
to German mercantilist China policy. Most of the rhetorical changes so far have
involved rather timid calls for German companies to diversify their global supply
chains. In terms of geopolitics, Scholz remains firmly committed to intertwining.
As Scholz wrote in a *FAZ* op-ed, he hopes to avoid a bloc confrontation and
decoupling from China (2022a). In a subsequent op-ed Scholz argued that 'in a
multipolar world, dialogue and cooperation must extend beyond the democratic
comfort zone' (2022b). To engage autocracies, Scholz suggested, one must possess
'pragmatism and humility' (2022b). The question how pragmatism and humility,

on its own, can help during Western engagement with an unreformed Stalinist like Xi Jinping was not answered in either of his two op-eds.

With regard to Germany's economic entanglement with China, Scholz has exhibited a surprising tendency to ignore advice. A good example is the controversy surrounding the Chinese state-owned shipping company Cosco's growing ownership of container terminals in the EU. Based on a think tank report, Beijing currently controls about 10 per cent of European throughput (Mardell, 2021). A growing Chinese presence in critical European infrastructure poses 'risks to the strategic autonomy of European policymakers and their ability to control supply chains' (2021). The US government, six German ministries and Scholz's two coalition partners warned Scholz not to green-light a Chinese investment in a shipping terminal of the port of Hamburg (Pamuk, 2022; Yang, 2022). An open letter warning of the geopolitical risks of the deal was published by Sinologists (Vogelsang, 2022). More than 250,000 signatures were collected by Campact against the Cosco investment (2022). A political compromise was reached as a result of such resistance. It was decided that Cosco could only own a stake below 25 per cent in HHLA Container Terminal Tollerort GmbH (BMWK, 2022). Scholz claimed later that Cosco's 24.9 per cent stake would not lead to 'strategic dependence' on China, nor that this decision had anything to do with his upcoming trip to China (Tagesschau, 2022).

In early November 2022, Scholz visited Beijing with twelve managers from BASF, Merck, Volkswagen, BMW, Hipp, Biontech, Bayer, Siemens, Deutsche Bank, Wacker, Adidas and Geo Clima (Jensen and Osterholt, 2022). Following Scholz's visit to China eight industrialists wrote an op-ed in *Frankfurter Allgemeine Zeitung* (FAZ, 2022). They advocated greater technological leadership, reduced dependency and continued dialogue with China. Arguing that China engagement had been a success story the coauthors highlighted the continued 'great potential of the Chinese market' (2022). Moreover, they emphasized economic competition with China over systemic rivalry. In the aftermath of the trip, Scholz claimed that his Beijing visit had succeeded in securing Xi's warning against Russia using nuclear weapons in Ukraine (t-online, 2022). Critics of Scholz were unconvinced, arguing that his trip 'contravened German government strategy and endangered EU unity' (Yang, 2022). In choosing pragmatism over principles, Scholz continued the China approach taken by his predecessors Kohl, Schröder and Merkel. In light of this, it is important to ask who is advising Scholz on foreign policy matters. Following Russia's war of aggression against Ukraine, Scholz's foreign policy advisor Plötner spoke at Berlin's German Council on Foreign Relations (DGAP) in an effort to dispel concerns. Since German special advisors to Chancellors usually avoid publicity, this was seen as a highly unusual act.

During his talk, Plötner warned that equating Russia with China might lead to a self-fulfilling prophecy. He also expressed scepticism regarding the EU's distinction between China as partner, competitor and rival. Plötner pointed out that '(the) stronger the dimension 'systemic rival' becomes, the more it radiates into the others' (Schneider, 2022). According to him, German foreign policy should aim 'to reduce systemic rivalry as far as possible in international dealings with each other' (Greive and Koch, 2022). Senior Advisor at Rhodium Group Barkin has suggested that Plötner's public comments shed light on Scholz's thinking about geopolitics. According to Barkin it exposed 'an old SPD vision of the world that some had dared to hope was dying out. It is alive' (Hollstein, 2022). It should be noted that as a member of Steinmeier's inner circle since 2014, Plötner was integral to the development of Ederer's 'Rapprochement through interweaving' policy towards Russia. According to Hollstein, a former colleague of Plötner's claims that he does not oppose his bosses' convictions, but rather supports them in implementing them. If such reports accurately reflect Plötner's role as Scholz's key foreign policy adviser, it seems unlikely that Germany's China policy will undergo any significant change. In the empirical part of the book, I will demonstrate that while some work has been accomplished for the *Zeitenwende*, it occurred *despite* Scholz's pragmatic approach to China, not *because* of his principled leadership.

References for Chapter 4

@Brad_Setser (2022), 'German Exports to China Really Did Provide a Positive Impulse to Germany's Economy in the Years Immediately After the Global Crisis. But German Exports (Measured by Chinese Imports) Have Been Basically Flat Since Mid 2012. The Growth Impulse Was All from 05 Through 11', Twitter, 29 October. Available online: https://archive.is/8OtAx (accessed 12 July 2023).

APA (2023), 'About APA', Asien-Pazifik-Ausschuss der Deutschen Wirtschaft. Available online: https://archive.is/QH8Sx (accessed 12 July 2023).

ASIEN (1994), 'Asien-Pazifik Ausschuss der Deutschen Wirtschaft (APA)', Nr. 51. Available online: https://hasp.ub.uni-heidelberg.de/journals/asien/article/view/15609/15185 (accessed 12 July 2023).

Barkin, N. (2020), 'What Merkel Really Thinks About China—And the World', *Foreign Policy*, 31 December. Available online: https://archive.is/krrwp (accessed 12 July 2023).

Baumgärtner, M. und A.-K. Müller (2021), 'Experts Demand Suspension of EU-China Investment Deal', *Spiegel International*, 25 January. Available online: https://archive.is/S3TGO (accessed 12 July 2023).

Bernstein, R. (2005), 'Schröder Asserts His Authority On Ending China Arms Embargo', *New York Times*, 1 April. Available online: https://archive.is/zViAT (accessed 12 July 2023).

Blickle, P., P. Faigle, K. Polke-Majewski, N. Rausch, and F. Rohrbeck (2017), 'The Multibillion Euro Theft', *Zeit Online*, 8 June. Available online: https://archive.is/B91q9 (acccessed 12 July 2023).

Blume, G. (2000), 'Keine Frage des Stolzes', *Zeit Online*, 18 May. Available online: https://web.archive.org/web/20161116220629/https://www.zeit.de/2000/21/200021.china2_.xml (accessed 12 July 2023).

BMWK (2022), 'Bundeskabinett verabschiedet Teiluntersagung im Investitionsprüfverfahren Hamburger Hafen', 26 October. Available online: https://archive.is/XXpaY (accessed 12 July 2023).

Boin, A. and M. Lodge (2021), 'Principled or Pragmatic? The Two Approaches Leaders Can Take During a Drawn-out Crisis', *LSE Blog*, 2 August. Available online: https://archive.is/wXbxR (accessed 12 July 2023).

Bovensiepen, N. (2004), „Wir müssen aufpassen", *Süddeutsche Zeitung*, 20–21 November 2004. Nr. 270, 20.

Brattberg, E. (2021), 'Merkel's Mixed Legacy on China', *Carnegie Endowment for International Peace*, 30 September. Available online: https://archive.is/6Z7ap (accessed 12 July 2023).

Burghardt, P., K. Ott, and J. Schmitt (2020), 'Tagebuch bringt Scholz in Erklärungsnot', *Süddeutsche Zeitung*, 3 September. Available online: https://archive.is/pEPQc (accessed 12 July 2023).

Büscheman, K.-H. and D. Kuhr (2008), 'Wirtschaft besorgt über Tibet-Debatte', *Süddeutsche Zeitung*, 17 April. Nr. 90, 20.

Büschemann, K.-H. (2021), 'Kein Wandel durch Handel', *Süddeutsche Zeitung*, 14–15 August. Nr. 186. 22.

Busse, C. (2004), 'Siemens will China-Geschäft ankurbeln', *Handelsblatt*, 18 May. Available online: https://archiv.handelsblatt.com/document/HBON__475185 (accessed 12 July 2023).

Campact (2022), 'Hamburger Hafen: Kein Ausverkauf an China', Available online: https://archive.is/oZi3I (accessed 12 July 2023).

China.Table (2021), '„Peter Altmaiers Pseudo-Industriepolitik bringt uns nicht voran"', 24 September. Available online: https://table.media/china/analyse/johannes-vogel-fdp -interview-china/ (accessed 12 July 2023).

Daub, A. (2021), 'The Weird, Extremely German Origins of the Wirecard Scandal', *The New Republic*, 21 April. Available online: https://archive.is/RAuzv (accessed 12 July 2023).

Deutsche Welle (2003), 'Der Kanzler ist ein Türöffner', 1 December. Available online: https://archive.is/GnYuA (accessed 12 July 2023).

Deutsche Welle (2022), 'Scholz Criticized Over China's Cosco Bid in Hamburg Port', 20 October. Available onine: https://archive.is/rYKOw (accessed 12 July 2023).

Deutscher Bundestag (1993), 'Asien-Konzept der Bundesregierung', *DocPlayer*. Available online: https://docplayer.org/194582841-Unterrichtung-deutscher-bundestag-12 -wahlperiode-drucksache-12-6151-durch-die-bundesregierung-asien-konzept-der -bundesregierung.html (accessed 12 July 2023).

Deutschlandfunk Kultur (2007), 'Hambrecht fordert Korrektur des China-Bildes', 24 August. Available online: https://archive.is/sV6k7 (accessed 12 July 2023).

Erling, J. (2014), 'Helmut Schmidt erklärt den Chinesen ihre Diktatur', *Welt*, 5 December. Available online: https://archive.is/kMP4c (accessed 12 July 2023).

European Commission (2014), 'EU and China Begin Investment Talks', 20 January. Available online: https://archive.is/8hYjg (accessed 12 July 2023).

European Parliament (2021), 'MEPs Refuse Any Agreement with China Whilst Sanctions Are in Place', 20 May. Available online: https://archive.is/VQTFk (accessed 12 July 2023).

FAZ (2008), '„Wir setzen auf Dialog mit China"', 16 April. Available online: https://archive .is/c3kAp (accessed 12 July 2023).

FAZ (2022), '„Ein Rückzug aus China schneidet uns ab"', 10 November. Available online: https://archive.is/vqQLm#selection-1415.0-1415.40 (accessed 12 July 2023).

Financial Times (2011), 'Good News from China Is Not All It Seems for Bonds', 13 September. Available online: https://archive.is/HTK3S (accessed 12 July 2023).

Fried, N. (2005a), '„Ich werde mit Ja stimmen"', *Süddeutsche Zeitung*, 4 May 2005. Nr. 102, 6.

Fried, N. (2005b), 'Schweigen ist Gold', *Süddeutsche Zeitung*, 24 February. Nr. 45, 2.

Greive, M. and M. Koch (2022), 'Ein Herz für Putin und andere Autokraten? Wie ein Scholz-Berater mit umstrittenen Äußerungen Kritik auslöst', *Handelsblatt*, 21 June. Available online: https://archive.is/K1y9x (accessed 12 July 2023).

Groitl, G. (2021), 'Das Märchen vom Wandel durch Handel – Wenn seine Logik je funktioniert hat, dann umgekehrt: China führt mit seiner Wirtschaftsmacht die westlichen Demokratien vor', *Neue Züricher Zeitung*, 15 June. Available online: https://archive.is/36emA#selection-255.0-255.162 (accessed 12 July 2023).

Handelsblatt (2005), 'Berlin arbeitet an einer Balance in der künftigen Ostpolitik', 2 December. Available online: https://archiv.handelsblatt.com/document/HBON__HB _1149986 (accessed 12 July 2023).

Handelsblatt (2007), 'Merkel hält Druck aus Peking stand', 24 September. Available online: https://archive.is/iu8Gk#selection-1269.0-1276.0 (accessed 12 July 2023).

Handelsblatt (2022), 'Redeverbot über frühere Scholz-Aussagen soll fallen - Protokolle werden einsehbar', *Handelsblatt*, 14 December. Available online: https://archive.is /5VmSA (accessed 12 July 2023).

Hansen, S. (2007), "'China vorzuführen, nutzt gar nichts'", *TAZ*, 20 November. Available online: https://archive.is/F1KdR (accessed 12 July 2023).

Hickmann, C. and V. Medick (2019), "'Ich habe mich entgiftet'", *Spiegel Politik*, 21 June. Available online: https://archive.is/HzkqO (accessed 12 July 2023).

Hollstein, M. (2022), 'Ist der wichtigste Scholz-Berater "Putins Mann im Kanzleramt"?', *t-online*, 5 July. Available online: https://archive.is/MqA69#selection-1459.7-1459.16 (accessed 12 July 2023).

Jensen, M. and S. Osterholt (2022), 'Fliegen ein Kanzler und zwölf Topmanager nach China', *manager magazin*, 3 November. Available online: https://archive.is /20221103064402/https://www.manager-magazin.de/politik/deutschland/olaf-scholz -reise-nach-peking-diese-12-manager-fliegen-mit-nach-china-a-880f0f38-2d15-4443 -8701-df949934beea (accessed 12 July 2023).

Karnitschnig, M. (2020), 'How Germany opened the door to China — And threw away the key', *Politico*, 9 October. Available online: https://archive.is/AmKN7 (accessed 12 July 2023).

Kiefer, F. (1992), 'Costs of German Reunification Slow Europe's Economic Engine', *The Christian Science Monitor*, 21 April. Available online: https://archive.is/j3dVT (accessed 12 July 2023).

Kinzer, S. (1995), 'Kohl to Visit China; To Woo Trade, He Braves Rights Protests', *New York Times*, 9 November. Available online: https://archive.is/MEZKs (accessed 12 July 2023).

Kornelius, S. (2005), 'Chinesische Unweisheiten', *Süddeutsche Zeitung*, 7 April 2005. Nr. 79, 4.

Lorenz, A. (2001), 'Business statt Menschenrechte', *Spiegel Ausland*, 2 November. Available online: https://archive.is/Au8gH (accessed 12 July 2023).

Luyken, J. (2022), 'Accidental Chancellor' Olaf Scholz Heckled As He Tours Germany in Search of Support', *The Telegraph*, 29 August. Available online: https://archive.is/pxQ5B (accessed 12 July 2023).

Mardell, J. (2021), 'COSCO takes stake in Hamburg Port terminal', *MERICS*. Available online: https://archive.is/j3i9m (accessed 12 July 2023).

Moody, O. (2022), 'Why Is Germany Now Brutally Re-evaluating Angela Merkel's Legacy?', *The Times*, 16 July. Available online: https://archive.is/ym6QE#selection-805.0 -805.65 (accessed 12 July 2023).

Mudie, L. (2015), 'Germany's Angela Merkel Meets With Rights Activists, Dissidents During China Trip', *Radio Free Asia*, 30 October. Available online: (accessed 12 July 2023).

Müller, J-W. (2022), 'Germany Inc. Jan-Werner Müller on Europe After the Invasion', *London Review of Books*, 26 May. Available online: https://archive.is/Yc8nD (accessed 12 July 2023).

Oldag, A. (2008), 'Mehr als Geschäfte', *Süddeutsche Zeitung*, 19–20 April 2008. Nr. 92, 23.

Pamuk, H. (2022), 'U.S. Cautioned Germany Against a Chinese Controlling Stake in Hamburg Port', *Reuters*, 2 November. Available online: https://archive.is/ZltiF (accessed 12 July 2023).

Parello-Plesner, J. (2012), 'Grading the Voice of Europe – Merkel in China', *European Council on Foreign Relations*, 10 February. Available online: https://archive.is/Llp30 (accessed 12 July 2023).

Parliamentary Assembly (2008), 'Angela Merkel. Chancellor of the Federal Republic of Germany. Speech Made to the Assembly, Tuesday, 15 April 2008', Available online: https://web.archive.org/web/20181101040524/http://www.assembly.coe.int/nw/xml/Speeches/Speech-XML2HTML-EN.asp?SpeechID=149 (accessed 12 July 2023).

Phalnikar, S. (2005), 'Choosing Markets Over Morals', *Deutsche Welle*, 5 February. Available online: https://archive.is/qoRG1 (accessed 12 July 2023).

Podcampus (2014), 'Magnet China!', Available online: https://www.podcampus.de/nodes/ReZjG (accessed 12 July 2023).

Renminwang (2014), 'Xi Jinping: China regieren - Rezension von Helmut Schmidt (4)', Available online: http://german.people.com.cn/n/2014/1204/c209052-8817818-4.html.

Reuters (2011), 'China to Buy 6 Billion Euros of Spanish Debt: Report', 6 January. Available online: https://archive.is/ajYee#selection-325.0-325.52 (accessed 12 July 2023).

Riegert, B. (2005), 'China Weapons Embargo Full of Holes', *Deutsche Welle*, 16 March. Available online: https://archive.is/pLD5d (accessed 12 July 2023).

Roloff, E. (2007), 'Ehre für den Dalai Lama zum Ärger der Chinesen', *Tagesspiegel*, 18 October. Available online: https://archive.is/jXBIz (accessed 12 July 2023).

Scherschun, N. (2011), 'Der Scholzomat', *Deutsche Welle*, 20 February. Available online: https://archive.is/EX4jq (accessed 12 July 2023).

Schmidt, H. and F. Sieren (2006), *Nachbar China*, Berlin: Econ.

Schneider, S. (2022), 'Was der Kanzlerberater über Russland zu sagen hat', *n-tv*, 22 June. Available online: https://archive.is/TmYbs (accessed 12 July 2023).

Scholz, O. (2022a), 'Darum geht es bei meiner Reise nach China', *Der Bundeskanzler*, 3 November. Available online: https://archive.is/kEbMK (accessed 12 July 2023).

Scholz, O. (2022b), 'The Global Zeitenwende', *Foreign Affairs*, January/February. Available online: https://archive.is/y6WLU (accessed 12 July 2023).

Schröm, O. and O. Hollenstein (2022), *Die Akte Scholz. Der Kanzler, das Geld, und die Macht*, Berlin: Ch. Links Verlag.

Schultes, N. (2003), *Deutsche Außenwirtschaftsförderung. Ökonomische Analyse unter Berücksichtigung der Aktivitäten und Programme in Japan*, München: VVF-Verlag. Available online: https://edoc.ub.uni-muenchen.de/9049/1/Schultes_Norbert.pdf (accessed 12 July 2023).

SCMP (1995), 'Kohl to Make Rare PLA Visit', 9 November. Available online: https://archive.is/X0QTH (accessed 12 July 2023).

Sieren, F. (2015), 'Sieren's China', *Deutsche Welle*, 13 November. Available online: https://archive.is/VlwoF (accessed 12 July 2023).

Spiegel (2009), 'China kauft Anleihen für 50 Milliarden Dollar', 3 September. Available online: https://archive.is/DlXir (accessed 12 July 2023).

Spiegel (2017), 'Schröder ersteigert Schmidt-Porträt - Für 18.000 Euro', 15 September. Available online: https://archive.is/5qd2U (accessed 12 July 2023).

Spiegel International (2005), 'Schroeder Sparks Outrage with China Embargo Comments', 31 March. Available online: https://archive.is/YA3CR (accessed 12 July 2023).

Strittmatter, K. (2005), 'Im Reich der Wölfe', *Süddeutsche Zeitung*, 6 December 2004. Nr. 283, 4.

Süddeutsche Zeitung (2001), 'China kauft den Transrapid', 22 January 2001, 25.

Süddeutsche Zeitung (2004), 'Siemens hofft nicht mehr auf China', 23 January. Nr. 18, R2.

Süddeutsche Zeitung (2005a), 'Auftragsboom für Siemens in China', 7 January 2005. Nr. 4, 20.

Süddeutsche Zeitung (2005b), 'Gegen Waffen für China', *Süddeutsche Zeitung*, 25 February 2005. Nr. 49, 9.

Süddeutsche Zeitung (2021), '"Die politische Verantwortung trägt Olaf Scholz"', 22 June. Available online: https://archive.is/mMT7X (accessed 12 July 2023).

t-online (2022), 'Scholz: "Alleine dafür hat sich die ganze Reise gelohnt"', 5 November. Available online: https://archive.is/vrhRH (accessed 12 July 2023).

Tagesschau (2022), 'Scholz verteidigt Cosco-Entscheidung', 26 October. Available online: https://archive.is/OKMgd (accessed 12 July 2023).

Taylor, F. (2005), 'Is Germany Desperate Enough?', *Spiegel International*, 13 September. Available online: https://archive.is/R3E0D (accessed 12 July 2023).

The Federal Government (2021), 'New Federal Government in Office', 8 December. Available online: https://archive.is/FiUoJ (accessed 12 July 2023).

Tooze, A. (2022), 'Chartbook #168: Germany's Economic Entanglement with China', *Substack*, 6 November. Available online: https://archive.is/DeWnf (accessed 12 July 2023).

UPI (1992), 'Three Years After Tiananmen, Germany Restores Ties with China', 2 November. Available online: https://archive.is/FpbXW (accessed 12 July 2023).

Vogelsang, K. (2022), 'Der Cosco-Deal beschädigt die Glaubwürdigkeit der deutschen Politik', *Zeit Online*, 25 October. Available online: https://archive.is/lelxL (accessed 12 July 2023).

von Hammerstein, K., C. Hoffmann, D. Kurbjuweit, T. Lehmann, C. Reiermann, J. Schaible, C. Schult, A. Siemens, C. Teevs, and S. Weiland (2021), 'Olaf Scholz Aims to Succeed Merkel by Emulating Her', *Spiegel International*, 3 September. Available online: https://archive.is/wEsoJ (accessed 12 July 2023).

von Hein, M. (2003), 'Wirtschaft contra Menschenrechte?', *Deutsche Welle*, 1 December. Available online: https://archive.is/XOuB1 (accessed 12 July 2023).

von Hein, M. (2012), 'Rising Power', *Deutsche Welle*, 2 February. Available online: https://archive.is/jXXgq (accessed 12 July 2023).

von Pierer, H. (2001), 'China wird in die Spitzengruppe der Volkswirtschaften aufsteigen', *Welt*, 12 November. Available online: https://archive.is/7DEAf (accessed 12 July 2023).

Welt (2022), '„Das müsste die deutsche Politik auch nachträglich noch schamrot werden lassen"', Available online: https://archive.is/knYnW.

Wernicke, C. (2005a), 'Macht, Moral und Moneten', *Süddeutsche Zeitung*, 23 March. Nr. 68, 4.

Wernicke, C. (2005b), 'EU gibt amerikanischen Druck nach', *Süddeutsche Zeitung*, 16–17 April 2005. Nr. 87, 6.

Wettach, S. (2020), 'Merkel macht sich für Marktzugang in China stark', *WirtschaftsWoche*, 25 September. Available online: https://archive.is/iymTi (accessed 12 July 2023).

Wettach, S. (2021), 'Guter Geheimdeal – oder gefährliches Spiel', *WirtschaftsWoche*, 12 January. Available online: https://archive.is/ZnLc8 (accessed 12 July 2023).

WirtschaftsWoche (2007), '"Jetzt reicht's!"', 3 May. Available online: https://archive.is/vinXL#selection-1739.150-1739.258 (accessed 12 July 2023).

Yang, W. (2022), 'Scholz's China Trip Raised More Doubts than Congratulations', *Deutsche Welle*, 11 May. Available online: https://archive.is/RsiSZ (accessed 12 July 2023).

Ziesemer, B. (2006), 'Die Konfuzius-Konfusion', *Handelsblatt*, 31 October. Available online: https://archive.is/jyvRx (accessed 12 July 2023).

Chapter 5

CHALLENGES TO GERMANY'S CHINA POLICY AT THE DAWN OF THE MERKEL ERA (2018–21)

5.1 Change through trade: what did it mean?

In a press conference in Lisbon on 13 October 2022, former Chancellor Merkel said that 'I never believed that there was such a thing as change through trade but certainly connection through trade' (Reuters, 2022a). Her stance on Germany's overdependence on Russian gas was defended by the fact that 'you always act in the time in which one is' (Reuters, 2022b), which she saw as unavoidable from Germany's decision to eliminate nuclear energy and coal. The attempt by Merkel to explain away her administration's failures in the Russia and energy policy is just one of several (Boyse, 2023). Adding to that, Merkel retroactively moved the goal posts of Germany's policy towards autocracies by using 'connection' in place of 'change'. According to Hamilton and Ohlberg, *change through trade* has been used for decades as a quasi-religious mantra to justify Germany's relationship with China (2020). As Strittmatter wrote, 'in China business, the saying [change through trade] has always been a prophecy and a promise' (2012). But what did politicians and industry leaders promise when they uttered the words 'change through trade' in public speeches, interviews and press conferences?

German Economy Minister Altmaier still argued that 'change can be achieved through trade' when the CCP was already cracking down on Hong Kong's democracy movement (Karnitschnig and Vela, 2020). His experience as Merkel's former chief of staff will have given him an understanding of how she viewed the issue. Altmaier cautioned against adopting a more assertive stance towards Beijing (2020). In Chapter 2 I argued that two-time German foreign minister Steinmeier promoted 'stabilitocracy' in China by his 'Rapprochement through interweaving' strategy. Fischer has offered a similar perspective, arguing that German China policy was designed to promote 'stability through trade' (2022). To substantiate her claim she has referred to recollections by Peter Christian Hauswedell, former *Asienbeauftragter* of the German Federal Government. It is of course possible that Merkel and Steinmeier were privately sceptics who never believed that promoting economic liberalization and market opening with China would lead to political liberalization as well. But as the following discussion will demonstrate, this is not how the political slogan 'Change through trade' was widely interpreted.

Chapter at a glance

Two parts make up this book chapter. To begin with, I discuss how perceptions, slogans and paradigms have shaped German foreign policy behaviour over the past thirty years. I will analyse how politicians, industrialists, journalists and academics have conceptualized the slogan 'Change through trade'. I discuss the vast gulf between interpretations with reference to philosophy of science. German foreign policy disagreements will be revealed in duelling op-eds by a German journalist and China expert from 2013. As part of the discussion about 'Change through trade', a tension is revealed between passive and active perspectives on German engagement with China. Many pundits now believe that CCP-led China has influenced Germany more than the other way around, as will be revealed in the discussion. Based on a comprehensive review of the public discourse, I identify twelve conceptual flaws in 'Change through trade', 'Rapprochement through interweaving', as well as their historical predecessor, 'Change through rapprochement' (see Chapter 2 for my critique of Steinmeier's doctrine). Despite the fact that many pundits consider 'Change through trade' a policy failure, there are discourse participants in Germany who still suggest that it is too early to draw such conclusions.

The second part of my book chapter explains how public policy analysis can shed light on outdated axioms influencing German foreign policy. I explain how the Punctuated Equilibrium Theory (PET) by Baumgartner and Jones helps make sense of long periods of policy stasis and sudden punctuation. After discussing its building blocks, I explain how PET can shed light on the contested goals and means of German China policy. Using PET can help us trace challenges to the old policy consensus and provide the necessary tools to measure progress in any future policy shift. I also outline the research approach for Part 2 of the book in the second part of the fifth chapter. A reflection on my role both in public and academic discourse is included. In addition, I outline four research questions. Through ten case studies, I will discuss both problems and possible solutions in the five subfields of industry policy, technology policy, development aid, security policy and science policy. I argue that a case study approach has several advantages, however, there are some important caveats related to the problem of potential attribution as well as hindsight and selection bias. Finally, I conclude the book chapter with observations about a supposed 'polarized' German public debate. It is my contention that duelling interpretations actually occupy a middle ground where consensus and in-between solutions to pressing policy issues may be reached.

5.2 *Perceptions, political slogans and paradigms*

According to Schneckener '(for) decades, the parameters of Russia policy served as a cognitive framing that acted like a filter of perception through which only those messages penetrated that could be brought halfway into line with one's own premises and ideas' (2022). The selective perception of Putin's 'master narrative', Schneckener argues, had the effect of amplifying uncritical assumptions about German Russia policy and resulting in a lack of a 'Plan B' should German dialogical and cooperative efforts fail. My argument is that such an analytical lens underestimates the agency of German political and economic elites, even though 'perception filters' (*Wahrnehmungsfilter*) may have played a role. As well as being victims of Russian or Chinese propaganda, they were also actors in their own right. 'Change through trade' can be considered shrewd political messaging. This German slogan doesn't just uses alliteration, but also rhymes (*Wandel durch Handel*). It is worth pointing out that a well-crafted and highly memorable three-word slogan such as 'Take back control' or 'Get Brexit done' can even be decisive in winning an election, as British politics have shown. Although less catchy, Steinmeier's doctrine of 'Rapprochement through interweaving' was compelling thanks to its reference to Bahr's famed Ostpolitik of 'Change through rapprochement'.

'Change through rapprochement', 'change through trade' and 'rapprochement through interweaving' were three key paradigms which guided Germany's relationship with autocratic countries. According to Patton, a paradigm is 'a world view, a general perspective, a way of breaking down the complexity of the real world. As such, paradigms are deeply embedded in the socialization of adherents and practitioners: paradigms tell them what is important, legitimate, and reasonable. Paradigms are also normative, telling the practitioner what to do without the necessity of long existential and epistemological considerations. But it is this aspect of paradigms that constitutes both their strength and weakness – their strength in that it makes action possible, their weakness in that the very reason for action is hidden in the unquestioned assumptions of the paradigm' (cited in Sparke, 1989). The purpose of the three paradigms was to accommodate incompatible political systems, interests and values in Germany's foreign relations. Rather than emphasising Germany's partner countries' autocratic nature, they downplayed it. Their key axiom was that cooperative approaches were more productive than confrontational ones. As a consequence, German politicians and industrialists claimed that cooperation with Russia and China was preferable to more assertive measures.

Borrowing from the philosophy of science: the importance of thought styles

Microbiologist Ludwik Fleck (1896–1961) sheds more light on the importance of paradigms in his pioneering research. It was Fleck's scholarship that helped lay the foundations for the sociology of science. I contend that there are important parallels between paradigms in academia and politics. We can better understand cognitive development challenges by studying the philosophy of science. In Fleck's view, scientific knowledge can neither be objective nor universal, rather it depends on culture, history and society. In Fleck's view, cognitive development is a result of people exchanging ideas and forming *thought collectives*. It is through the accumulation of misunderstandings and understandings that people develop a distinct *thought style*, which Fleck sees as part of a *mood*. Fleck believes that when a thought style becomes sufficiently sophisticated, it splits into esoteric and exoteric groups. These terms are used to describe professionals and laypeople, respectively. The *active elements* of a thought style determine how professionals perceive and think about the world, whereas the *passive elements* are considered as objective truth. As only what is true to culture is true to nature, what is called a fact is actually a social construct. It also means that thought styles may be incommensurable, as what is true for one group may be false for another (Stanford Encyclopedia of Philosophy, 2012).

We can better understand the vast gulf in understanding between different types of thought styles by studying Fleck. As I mentioned previously, the lessons from the Shoah and German militarism resulting in WWII were widespread aversions to military power among German elites. Only after the war in Ukraine started in February 2022 has this thought style been more widely questioned. However, leading CCP officials have derived different conclusions from past military disasters. It was learned that building a strong and assertive PLA is key to restoring China's great power status. By measuring attitudes towards the military, we can see that there is a stark difference in thought styles between thought collectives from both countries. However, Fleck's concept of thought styles can also be used to understand the vast gap in understanding of Germany's China policy among *domestic* discourse participants. In terms of information processing in public policy, I argue we are over-supplied with information not under-supplied (Jones and Baumgartner, 2005, 9). Paradigms such as 'Change through trade' have helped reduce complexity and distinguish between signal and noise in foreign policy. It is important to ask how German elites used it to interpret Germany's complex relations with autocratic China. Did it primarily serve as a perception filter or was it also used to justify a particular course of action (or inaction)?

The Lau versus Sandschneider dispute in 2013

Passionate debates have taken place over what role values and interests should play in Germany's engagement with China. A good example of competing thought styles is the public debate between Lau and Sandschneider in 2013. In a widely noted op-ed Lau argued that Germany had become intertwined with many kleptocrats, theocrats and autocrats (2013). The direction of German foreign policy was the subject of a battle of interpretation, wrote Lau. Moreover, he criticized those who 'advocate silence in the face of tyrants' and who claim that a value-oriented foreign policy hampers German progress. In contrast to 'brute pragmatism', Lau advocated a 'realistic, but not cynical attitude' (2013). Particularly, he objected to an essay Sandschneider had written one year earlier. Lau criticized him for his assertion that 'the actual risk for German foreign policy is that it could be incapable of reacting quickly and efficiently to new challenges due to too strong an orientation towards historical continuity and an overloaded discourse of values' (Sandschneider, 2012). Sandschneider was criticized by Lau for supposedly considering human rights policy a 'weakness – Western self-restraint in an amoral world full of hard interest politics' (Lau, 2013).

Lau disagreed with Sandschneider's claim that any criticism of the Chinese government amounts to 'post-colonialist arrogance towards the rest of the world'.

In Lau's view this argument ignored the role of 'dissidents who are much tougher on their leadership than the German government dares to be' (2013). Lau criticized figures of speech (*Redefigur*) where 'tyrants are declared untouchable', as they 'stand for stability'. He pointed out that German critics of autocratic regimes are often accused of 'gambling away influence and market access', are told they endanger 'cooperation for the solution of global problems' and are being instructed that 'German history (colonialism or any other occidental guilt) urges us to exercise restraint and respect'. He regarded such arguments as excuses for doing nothing. In his view 'historical guilt obliges at least as much to stand up for what is right as to exercise moderation in doing so' (2013). Lau's critique prompted Sandschneider to double down on what he called a 'pragmatic foreign policy' (2013). He argued that 'there is no alternative to dealing with dictators. You don't have to love them, but you do have to cooperate with them' (2013). Using Hosni Mubarak as an example, Sandschneider argued that cooperation with his regime secured 'fragile stability in the Middle East', which was supposed to be in the European interest (2013). In this way, Sandschneider supported the concept of 'stabilitocracy'.

Moving the goal posts: stability promotion instead of political change?

In his reply to Lau Sandschneider also asserted that while values and interests should not be separated a 'credible and effective foreign policy is based on what is feasible and not on dogmatism' (2013). Sandschneider, while using a language of pragmatism, assumed a highly dogmatic position himself by asserting that there is 'no alternative' to cooperating with dictators. He failed to state how German values and interests can realistically be maintained through dialogue and cooperation with autocratic regimes. Sandschneider also attacked Lau when he wrote that 'insinuations and feelings of moral superiority' would limit the scope of 'contentious discourse' (2013). It is important to note that Sandschneider also spoke of the importance of an open public debate about German foreign policy. However, such statements should not be taken at face value. As Sandschneider claimed that his approach to dealing with autocracies was the only feasible solution, he displayed an illiberal attitude which made no allowance for any other alternative policy options. It is noteworthy that Lau and Sandschneider's public conflict reinforces Fleck's belief that there are times when different thought styles are incompatible, rendering it impossible to reach a compromise or an in-between position. Sandschneider disagreed with what Lau believed to be self-evident or true. As the following examples illustrate, Sandschneider was far from being an outlier with his position in the dispute.

In an interview with *Süddeutsche Zeitung* in June 2022 former Siemens CEO Kaeser, who was also APA Chairman between 2019 and 2021, said that '(the) principle of "change through trade" was formulated by some as a system-changing claim. This has never really worked' (Busse and Fromm, 2022). As a result of trade, he argued, millions of people had emerged from poverty in developing countries. Trade had also created and maintained prosperity in industrialized countries (2022). Kaeser's comments support Emcke's contention that 'talk of "change through trade" was all too often rhetorical carnival, meant to mask the fact that hardly anyone believed in changing or influencing the Chinese system anymore' (2022). His statements also echoes Fischer's view that 'no one should seriously be under the illusion that Germany or the activities of individual German companies could change the political system in China' (2022). The post-facto rationalizations of former Siemens CEO Kaeser and China expert Fischer are useful, since they show how 'Change through trade' could be interpreted as a passive strategy that, contrary to the rhetorical connotation of the political slogan itself, could be seen as a transactional commercial relationship with the aim of promoting China's political stability.

Unheeded calls for a deepening of Germany's China engagement

It is important to note that not all discourse participants adhered to such a narrow interpretations. At a roundtable with then Foreign Minister Steinmeier at the German Embassy in Beijing in Spring 2006, I suggested more German funding support for Chinese civil society organizations. A rapidly growing civil society sector developed in China during the semi-liberal Hu Jintao years. Steinmeier's immediate response to my proposal was positive, but the Ministry for Economic Cooperation and Development (BMZ) balked at the idea of providing greater financial support for China's civil society (Fulda, 2009, 220–31). In my PhD thesis, published as a book in 2009, I criticized the German government for not leveraging its development aid to China. I pointed out that 'instead of using the considerable German financial commitment to implement a strategy of maximum China engagement, it became clear from various case studies that German governmental and non-governmental external actors have adapted to Chinese structures and conditions rather than the other way around' (2009, 262).

In calling for a more comprehensive German-Chinese engagement, I was not alone. In a 2014 op-ed for *Süddeutsche Zeitung* German China expert Heilmann argued that 'China will not simply allow itself to be reshaped from the outside. But German and European policy towards China should aim to stabilise relations across the entire spectrum – from diplomacy to economics and the environment to education. Such a China policy by no means unilaterally follows the interest in economic exchange; it goes beyond the formula of "change through trade". Only through such a broad-based and consistent engagement can those forces be strengthened that are working in China itself towards a more open society – and towards an internationally integrated, responsible government' (2014).

A similar value-oriented foreign policy was advocated by Westerwelle only two years earlier, when he served as Foreign Minister under Merkel from 2009 to 2013. During a radio interview he expressed hope that 'Change through trade' would work, 'that is, with economic exchange comes liberal ideas in a country, with growing prosperity comes more education, and with education comes enlightenment' (Deutschlandfunk, 2012). A more active interpretation of this paradigm can be seen in his statement. However, both passive and active perspectives of German China engagement overestimated Germany's leverage relative to China, while simultaneously underestimating the CCP's agency.

Who actually changed whom?

The CCP's secret party edict Document No 9 served as an important initial indicator of China's hard authoritarian turn under General Secretary Xi. As soon as it was leaked in 2013, it should have caused alarm bells to ring in Berlin and prompted a reassessment of German China policy. Unlike its highly critical reception in the United States (ChinaFile, 2013), Document No 9 was misinterpreted in Germany (Spross, 2014). Nevertheless, there were critical voices as well. Among the journalists who have consistently criticized the German government is Strittmatter. Many of his op-eds have pointed out that 'Change through trade' had run its course. In 2017 Strittmatter wrote that '(the) West must now say goodbye to the wishful thinking that a wise author exposed years ago as a "China fantasy": the idea that economic opening and growing prosperity would automatically bring about a political liberalisation of China' (2017). A year on he wrote another op-ed in which he argued that 'weren't we recently led to believe that China was becoming more and more like us? . . . It was called "change through trade"' (2018). Strittmatter went on to note that 'all of a sudden China is turning the tables? Who is now transforming whom once again?' (2018)

The former Vice President of the European Chamber of Commerce in Shanghai, Sack, similarly argued in April 2022 that 'the principle of change through trade has come to fruition. But not in the way we had anticipated, but the other way around. Through trade with China, we Germans in particular have also begun to change' (China.Table, 2022). Sack critiqued that '(the) confidence of the West in its own strength, which apparently grew immeasurably after the Cold War, seems to have blinded many' (2022). By now Beijing was in a position to use growing German dependencies on the Chinese market to 'divide and conquer'. Sack bemoaned the fact that 'we now adapt our behavior to Chinese sensitivities' (2022). Those commenting on current Chinese affairs on social media had already self-censored for fear of reprisals. Attempts would be made by executives to avoid public criticism. He also noted that 'even our government is extremely careful not to give Hong Kong human rights activists, exiled dissidents, or even the Dalai Lama too much of a stage, if any' (2022). Considering what Strittmatter and Sack have said about 'Change through trade', it would seem the evolving power dynamics in Sino-German relations were obfuscated rather than illuminated by the paradigm. But why was the paradigm not questioned by more professionals sooner?

A life lie?

Lau has noted in a recent essay that 'Change through change', as a figure of speech, stems from Bahr's Ostpolitik of 'Change through rapprochement' (2021). Lau has questioned the underlying premise of this paradigm, calling it a paled down version (*Schwundform*) of Bahr's Ostpolitik. Lau pointed out that 'the Chinese example has been disproving this simple belief for years: Never has there been more exchange and yet never more repression' (2021). A critique similar to Lau's has been echoed by SPD politician Sigmar Gabriel, who served as German foreign minister for two years (2017–2018) under Merkel. He said that 'change through trade' is actually a perversion of the original idea. It all started back in the 60s and 70s under former SPD chancellor Willy Brandt and his senior diplomatic advisor Egon Bahr. Their formula was "change through rapprochement" . . . It wasn't until later that the slogan became "change through trade. . ." The success of Germany's economy and society is founded on successful economic integration and the conviction that the closer the economic ties are, the safer the world will be. That was obviously a gross misjudgment' (Gabriel, 2022).

Some commentators have been even less charitable. In *Neue Zürcher Zeitung* Groitl writes that '(like) a grail, the West has carried before it the motto of change through trade. The rules of economics, so the idea goes, promote democracy, freedom and the rule of law worldwide. A fairy tale and a life lie, as a look at China shows' (2021). In *Süddeutsche Zeitung* Büschemann argues that '(the) 'change through trade' model is now seen as a life lie in the case of China' (2022). And in an interview with *Tagesspiegel* Thome stated that '(the) life lie of "change through trade" has been exposed, the German autosuggestion of win-win – we make a lot of money and contribute to China's opening up at the same time – is done' (Dieckmann and Tartler, 2023). It is significant that pundits are beginning to discuss Germany's foreign policy failure with the term *Lebenslüge*, because it suggests a no-holds-barred introspection. Alfred Adler, an Austrian psychotherapist, described a life lie as the false conviction that an individual's life plans are bound to fail because of other people or circumstances out of their control (APA, 2023). A false belief such as this would serve as an escape route from responsibility (Oxford Reference). Adler regarded life lies as forms of neurosis or psychosis (1925, 235–45). As Henderson summarizes Adler's concept of life lies, they aim to 'blame others; escape personal responsibility; a last-ditch attempt to protect their social image ("it's not my fault"); obtain advantage over others; who now walk on eggshells; seek security in helplessness' (@robkhenderson, 2021).

Conceptual weaknesses of the three paradigms

In the introduction of this chapter I quoted Strittmatter as stating that 'Change through trade' was a 'prophecy and promise' (2012). In his clear-eyed op-ed he argued that it also served as a 'shield' for Western politicians and industrialists to justify their commercial relationship with dictatorships (2012). My contention is that 'Change through trade', its contemporary twin brother 'Rapprochement through interweaving' and their historical antecedent 'Change through rapprochement' have twelve conceptual weaknesses in common:

(1) By default, the tyrannical nature of autocratic regimes was de-emphasized to overcome bloc confrontation; (2) An implicit bias towards modernization theory led to an unrealistic assumption that autocratic political regimes would willingly cede power to an economically empowered society; (3) Germany's normative power towards autocracies was overestimated: it was never able to

undermine or stabilize their political systems in any significant way; (4) German enlightened interests and values related to democracy and human rights were sacrificed in order to promote foreign trade; (5) Those with commercial interests in Russia and China could exploit a mythical SPD *Ostpolitik*; (6) Opportunities in cooperation with autocracies were overstated, risks underestimated; (7) Germany's China engagement was unconditional: dialogue and cooperation became an end in themselves; (8) Partnership models were not sufficiently scrutinized: the key question of whether organizational autonomy was still sufficiently protected was not asked; (9) There were neither benchmarks nor periodic reviews that could inform a critical introspection of the paradigms; (10) Eventually, the paradigms evolved into dogmas, which inhibited the development of a more realistic German strategic culture; (11) It was not uncommon for domestic critics of Germany's mercantilist foreign policy to be perceived as moralizers and sometimes dismissed as 'cold warriors'; (12) Intertwining led to entanglement: due to widespread self-censorship growing material dependencies on China were overlooked.

I argue that for Germany to disentangle itself from an autocratic China, the flawed premises which informed such paradigms will need to be unsparingly critiqued. Yet it is far from a foregone conclusion that German elites will abandon outdated foreign policy paradigms, as we shall see in the following sections. In order for German China policy to become more realistic, elites will need to acknowledge their failure in the first place.

A policy failure?

According to Giesen, 'Change through trade' has failed as a strategy (2019). In addition, Weidenfeld has said that it has reached its end and that what Germany needs now is 'security through independence' (2022). Does mounting public criticism of Germany's China policy offer any hope for a shift in policy anytime soon? A healthy dose of scepticism is necessary. The previous discussion has shown that pundits have already criticized it as a life lie, an unwillingness to face the harsh realities of autocratic regimes. It is important not to forget that a majority of German elites in politics, business, academia and society, particularly those in positions of power, were socialized under the 'change through trade' paradigm. It will be difficult for individuals who have internalized this paradigm to critically reflect on its flawed premises. We can see that economists and industrialists are already leading the charge against a swift paradigm shift.

As an example, Fischer argues that 'attaching a concrete time horizon to ["Change through trade"] – according to the motto: if it has not worked by 2022, then the endeavour has failed' would even surpass the 'wishful thinking . . . that Germany or the activities of individual German companies could change the political system in China' in terms of 'naivety' (2022). A similar argument to Fischer's is developed by Hank, in which he considers 'the polemic against "change through trade" not only clearly premature, but misguided and in the end even dangerous. . . . [There is] . . . evidence that trade of non-democratic countries with democratic countries at least leads to bringing democratic values into view and to building up a country's "democratic capital"' (2022). A comparable opinion has been expressed by Felbermayer, who has argued that '(to) pretend that the concept of "change through trade" has failed, I think is completely over the top. Without economic globalisation, who knows what would have happened to world security, to the frequency and intensity of warlike events' (De Gruyter, 2022). Likewise, former VW CEO Diess has argued that Germany should not abandon 'Change through trade' (Menzel, 2022). Economic connections would ensure 'that we talk to each other' (2022). While Fischer, Hank, Felbermermayer and Diess use different arguments to warn against abandoning 'Change through trade', their underlying conviction appears to be similar: Germany's close trade ties with China, both in the past and now, was a force for good and should continue in the future. The arguments they make are defensible, but uncritically viewing the shortcomings of 'Change through trade' could lead to a repeat of past mistakes.

5.3 Punctuated Equilibrium Theory: explaining continuity and change in German China policy

Baumgartner and Jones' Punctuated Equilibrium Theory (PET) is an apt tool for analysing the dynamics of policy change. Their theory can explain 'long periods of stability and domination of important policy areas by privileged groups of elites, and for rapid change in political outcomes, where apparently entrenched economic interests find themselves on the losing side of the political battle' (1993/2009, 3). *Complex system thinking* underpins PET. According to Quarmby 'complex systems involve feedback mechanisms, so that the results of actions (the outputs) are not commensurate to the original actions (the inputs)' (2018). When an intervention is made within a complex system, there can be system-wide repercussions. This phenomenon is known as non-linearity. Emergent behaviour, based on the interaction between actors and their environment, can lead to sudden and unexpected changes in a complex system as it relies on self-organization instead of central control. Baumgartner and Jones developed this theory in the context of US politics, but I argue that it can also be applied to Germany's China policy during the Merkel era. In this study, PET is particularly useful, since it can help explain Germany's long period of stasis in China policy, which was followed by increasingly frequent challenges to Germany's China policy during the Merkel era (2018–21) (see Figure 1).

Policymakers' *rationality* and how they *process information* are key building blocks of PET. Many policy issues cannot be addressed simultaneously by senior politicians. Therefore, few policy matters make it to the top of their agenda. As policymakers have limited time, cognitive abilities and information available when making decisions, their rationality is bounded. As a result, decision-makers prefer satisfactory solutions as opposed to ideal ones (Stanford Encyclopedia of Philosophy, 2018). As one of many competing policy matters requiring consideration, an acting German Chancellor will only have limited time to consider Germany's China policy in depth. Cairney suggests that 'this lack of

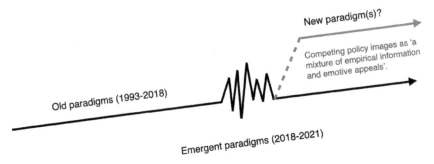

Figure 1 Policy punctuation in the final years of the Merkel era (2018–21).

attention to most issues help explain why most policies may not change, while intense periods of attention to some issues may prompt new ways to frame and solve policy problems' (2011/2020, 147). Governments tend to either under- or overreact based on how they interpret signals. Jones and Baumgartner argue that 'disproportionate information-processing leads to a pattern of extreme stability and occasional punctuations, rather than either smooth adjustment processes or endless gridlock' (2005, 5).

PET distinguishes between *policy communities* and *issue networks*, and how they either defend or challenge *policy monopolies* through the use of *policy images*. Policy communities can be understood as small groups of decision-makers who consult frequently, participate in relatively stable interactions and share a common understanding of the policy problem (Cairney, 2011/2020, 151). As Baumgartner and Jones put it (1993/2009, 6), they naturally strive to establish monopolies so that they can define the policy problem authoritatively and determine the best solution. In order to defend a policy monopoly, policy images are imperative. Policy images can be understood as 'a mixture of empirical information and emotive appeals' (1993/2009, 26). As Pal further explains 'since these images are shorthand, they convey more than information; they give a sense of the tone of the issue in positive or negative terms' (2006, 105–8). As part of securing a policy monopoly, all actors opposed to it must be excluded. Within the context of PET excluded critics are subsumed under the category of issue network. The latter is characterized by a low threshold for participation, variable frequency and quality of consultations, unstable and fluctuating interactions, and where 'a measure of agreement may be reached but conflict and opposition is more likely' (Cairney, 2011/2020, 151). Baumgartner and Jones have highlighted that '(participation) in a policy monopoly is structured by two things: the formal or informal rules of access discourage the participation of "outsiders," and the prevalent understanding of the policy are so positive that they evoke only support or indifference by those not involved' (1993/2009, 7).

In the case of Germany, a close-knit policy community of senior politicians and industry officials could capitalize on 'Change through trade'. They could employ the paradigm to establish a positive policy image in the public debate, which supposedly clarified how to handle autocratic nations. It appears that the repeated repetition of the 'Change through trade' mantra created what cognitive psychologists have called the 'illusory truth effect'. As Hassan and Barber explain '(people) tend to perceive claims as truer if they have been exposed to them before' (2021). As a result, a policy monopoly was established. Even so, the three paradigms were occasionally challenged. Increasing the scope of political conflict was an outcome of critics highlighting new or unresolved issues in Germany's relationship with China. The Lau/Sandschneider dispute comes to mind in this context. According to Lau, it was a battle over German foreign policy's direction (2013). There have been a wide range of critics of Germany's China policy, such as politicians (often when in opposition), think tankers, journalists and academics. Although they formed a loose issue network, their influence over Germany's China policy was limited.

Is a paradigm shift possible?

We are reminded by Cairney that 'the privileged status of a paradigmatic set of ideas ensures that most ideas are ignored or rejected, revisited only in rare case of third-order change following policy failure' (2011/2020, 195). In his description of third-order change, he compares it to Kuhn, another founding father of philosophy of science. Kuhn's primary interests were paradigm shifts, drawing heavily on Fleck's earlier work on thought styles and thought collectives. In Kuhn's view, existing paradigms started to decline when practitioners began to realize they weren't sufficiently addressing anomalies. In times of crisis, they lost faith in the established paradigm and sought alternatives. In the event that a new paradigm managed to attract a large enough following, this would amount to a Kuhnian revolution (Stanford Encyclopedia of Philosophy, 2013). Earlier discussions on the rise and demise of 'Change through trade' appear to follow Kuhn's trajectory. Nevertheless, the pushback against seeing it as a policy failure indicates there is no imminent shift in Germany's China policy. Several recent publications on the subject have overestimated the amount of third-order change in Germany.

As Damm suggests '(the) varied and deeply polarized along "ideological" fault lines discussions among Germany's sinologists and policy analysts are having a deep influence on the new China policy of the German government under Chancellor Scholz and Foreign Minister Annalena Baerbock' (2023, 179). A similar argument is made by Meijer who argues that '(since) the 2010s, Germany has responded to Beijing's rising assertiveness in Europe by hardening its "China policy" and by promoting the formulation of a common EU policy towards Beijing' (2022, 193). I contend that it is too early to tell whether public criticism of Germany's China policy will change policy. I agree with Barkin who has articulated his scepticism as follows: 'Indeed, with nothing to replace "Wandel durch Handel," Germany finds itself in a strategic gray zone with China, aware that its largest trading partner is evolving into a bigger and brasher threat, but unwilling to test the relationship in any serious way' (2020). The second part of the book aims to demonstrate that Germany has not yet achieved the cognitive change needed to inform a genuinely new paradigm (or paradigms) in China policy. Despite the abundance of evidence that punctuation is occurring – new policy images which challenge outdated paradigms of the aforementioned three paradigms – I will show that the contours of a new emerging paradigm are still sketchy and much work remains to be done before Scholz's *Zeitenwende* becomes a reality.

For Germany to achieve decisive foreign policy reform could prove challenging because of its corporatist political economy. Structural factors can lead to resistance to paradigm change and an unwillingness to unlearn on the elite level. It is important not to lose sight of the fact that the three paradigms have been effective in serving Germany's big corporations. A geoeconomic foreign policy has also powered Germany's political economy and contributed to its persistent current account surplus for decades. A mercantilist China policy, favouring big corporations, has benefited German conglomerates like Volkswagen, Siemens and BASF disproportionally. Felbermayer recently stated in an interview that BASF and Volkswagen are 'too big to fail' (De Gruyter, 2022). It has been argued by Schneier (2012) that large corporations have the ability to deliberately manipulate societal pressure. Among the problems a government and society may face are corporate lobbying, jurisdictional arbitrage and excessive risk-taking. With both BASF and VW heavily invested in China, this bodes ill for establishing the primacy of politics over trade and investment.

In 2021 the foreign policy spokesperson for the Social Democratic Party Schmid had told journalists that '(we) need a real foreign policy for China – not just a business-oriented policy . . . We need to decouple our foreign policy from the commercial interests of big business' (Solomon and Chazan, 2021). Still, Scholz visited China with a large business delegation nine months after being appointed Chancellor. According to my argument in Chapter 4, Scholz has failed to provide intellectual leadership that could help turn his much vaunted *Zeitenwende* into reality. Despite the possibility of a policy shift, I do not believe that it is inevitable.

If a shift in policy occurs in the future, it will likely be the result of numerous factors and actors. To ensure greater transparency, I would like to briefly explain my theory of change (TOC). Policy change will need to be driven from the outside-in and from the bottom-up. International criticism will play a crucial role in pressing the German government to assume greater geopolitical responsibilities. German civil society will also need to provide an important impetus for reform. This will require political and intellectual leadership by independent-minded academics, journalists and civil society practitioners. Lastly, the private sector will have to play an important role as well. I am thinking here of industry associations like the BDI, which published a highly critical account of Germany's China policy in 2019. The discussion of a reformed Germany's China policy will also require the participation of industrialists representing German SMEs. As described in Chapter 3, German SMEs face a long-term existential risk from the CCP's power trading.

5.4 *Research approach*

As I explained in the introductory chapter, there is no 'off-the-shelf' academic theory that can help resolve the book's research puzzle. This problem is compounded in the case of Germany, where for historical reasons there has been an almost complete neglect of the academic discipline of strategic studies (Giegerich and Terhalle, 2021, 35–9). My argument in Chapter 2 was that German strategic culture – if it exists at all – is inadequate to deal with conventional and unconventional threats emanating from autocratic regimes. Furthermore, I maintained that Germany still needs to learn the language of power. Conversely, the discussion on strategic culture in the Chinese context reveals that the CCP prefers to settle political conflicts through dominance. Both at home and abroad, the CCP has applied its united front approach based on a zero-sum view of the political process. As a result of Xi's emphasis on struggle (斗争), the CCP has increased its hybrid interference in liberal democracies. When it comes to CCP-led China we not only face a (geo-)political but also an intellectual challenge. As it is rare for Western elites to have a comprehensive understanding of both German and Chinese history, strategic culture and the political economies of the two countries, it has become much clearer to me why senior policymakers will have found foreign policy paradigms which greatly reduce complexity very helpful. A German politician uttering words to the effect of 'change through trade' or 'rapprochement through interweaving' in response to a journalist's question about democracy and human rights abuses in China arguably greatly simplifies things. Such shorthands can be used to cut short any lengthy debate which would require in-depth country expertise. And although I can now better understand why German Chancellors, Foreign Ministers and their advisors have adopted a pragmatic approach in the past, I believe their unconditional engagement approach has also contributed to Germany's entanglement with autocratic China.

Some of my critics may argue that my own involvement in the German China debate makes me biased. To those critics, I would like to respond with a quote from Biden. It was during the mid-term elections of 2022 that he pointed out that governments are capable of multitasking and engaging in situational leadership. Biden responded to a journalist's question by saying '(we) oughta be able to walk and chew gum at the same time' (Glasser, 2022). The same principle can also be applied to a modern-day academic. It is perfectly possible to be a *passionate* participant in a fast-paced and high-stakes public debate while simultaneously adopting the role of a *dispassionate* researcher who conducts a fairly slow-paced book project. Sceptical readers may still remain unconvinced. As an op-ed author, haven't I already taken sides in this debate by writing op-eds criticizing the 'Change through trade' paradigm (Fulda, 2020a), former Chancellor Merkel (Fulda, 2020b), Sandschneider's views on Sino-German relations (Fulda, 2021a) as well as German Sinology (Fulda, 2021b, 2021c; Fulda et al., 2022; Fulda and Klotzbücher, 2022)?

While I have publicly argued for a paradigm shift in German China policy (Fulda, 2021a), writing this book has provided me with an opportunity to engage in what Schön calls 'reflection-in-action'. I have had the opportunity to reflect on my own pre-scientific value orientations, tacit norms, approaches and theories, as well as my perceptions of situations that led me to choose particular approaches. My reflections also include the ways in which I have framed problems and the role I have played within a larger institutional framework (Schoen, 1983, 62). It is also important to emphasize that this book does not propose a new paradigm that should be blindly followed. Instead, I aim to raise awareness about the central role paradigms have played in German China policy. It is my hope that by documenting and deconstructing underlying premises of competing paradigms my book will contribute to greater reflexivity among politicians, industrialists, journalists and academics.

The second empirical part of this book addresses four research questions: How does the Policy Equilibrium Theory explain punctuation during the final years of the Merkel era (2018–21) and the beginning of the Scholz administration (2021–23)? What types of policy images have challenged Germany's mercantilist China policy? To what extent has Germany's China policy shifted as a result? In terms of Scholz's *Zeitenwende*, what has already been accomplished? I discussed paradigms at the meta level in the first part of the book. 'Rapprochement through interweaving' and 'Change through trade' were discussed in Chapter 2 and Chapter 4, respectively. In the second part of the book, I will examine whether these three paradigms also informed public debate in specific policy subfields. A second analytical step is necessary, since it is possible that policymakers and practitioners defended their respective policy monopolies with policy images which are distinct from the axiomatic beliefs and orientations to action of the aforementioned three paradigms. Additionally, policy communities and issue networks can vary considerably depending on the specific sub-policy and the policy venue (Cairney, 2011/2020, 149). My own advocacy efforts over the last twenty years taught me that most German development aid to China is debated without much participation from the general public. When it came to this policy issue, there was no public lobby, as a former colleague once said. As evident from the Sinology debate (Fulda, 2022), science policy has been a policy venue that has received much more public attention.

Unforeseen policy failures (UPF)

Chapters 6 to 10 will tell the story of Germany's hidden liabilities in its complex relationship with China. I provide five case studies dubbed *unforeseen policy failures (UPF)*. They range from the decline of the German solar industry (Chapter 6), the takeover of the robotics company Kuka by Chinese investors (Chapter 7), the squandering of German leverage in development cooperation with China (Chapter 8), the misuse of German dual-use technology for the purpose of modernization the People's Liberation Army (Chapter 9) and the undermining of academic freedom in Germany through hybrid interference (Chapter 10). If readers are concerned about selection bias they should note that the topics of these five case studies were widely covered in the German-language media at the dawn of the Merkel era (2018–2021) and thus need to be discussed in greater detail. Through the five UPF, I aim to achieve three interrelated goals. The first thing I want to do is describe what in the introductory chapter I called the contours of Germany as a proverbial 'black elephant'. In addition, I want to illustrate the material and psychological damage already caused by Germany's entanglement with autocratic China. It is not my intention here to judge individual actors for their actions or inactions in the past. Lessons learned from mistakes of the past, however, can be used to inform Germany's future China policy. Three leading questions (LQ) guide the five UPF:

UPF LQ 1 What were the unforeseen consequences of the policy failure?
UPF LQ 2 What factors contributed to the entanglement with China, and who benefited from it?
UPF LQ 3 To what extent are we witnessing either creative or destructive learning?

I am aware of the problem of attribution when discussing the UPF. Decisions made by individuals and organizations at one point in time may lead to policy failures later. However, it is often difficult or impossible to establish direct causation. The phenomenon of non-linearity in dynamic complex systems further complicates post-facto rationalizations. Additionally, hindsight bias will present a challenge. The scholarship of Koselleck reminds us that individual actors make decisions based on their 'space of experience' and their 'horizon of expectation' at the time (Koselleck, 2004). In addition, I will have to select primary and secondary sources carefully in order to inform the UPF. In addition to reviewing both authors' and publishers' political affiliations, I will triangulate to minimize potential bias.

Policy punctuation analysis (PPA)

As part of the second part of the book, I examine whether Germany's discourse on China has already undergone a paradigmatic change. Rivaling policy images will be compared and contrasted in five *policy punctuation analyses (PPAs)*. I will map Germany's evolving China debate with reference to VW's possible involvement in forced labour in Xinjiang (Chapter 6), Deutsche Telekom's embrace of Huawei (Chapter 7), the closing space for dialogue and cooperation with China under the conditions of the draconian Overseas NGO Law (Chapter 8), the question how Germany can upgrade its relationship with Taiwan (Chapter 9) and public controversies around German academic cooperation with China (Chapter 10). Since all of these five topics featured prominently in the German China debate again there is no selection bias. All five PPAs are key to a better understanding of the difficulties Germany faces in recalibrating its formerly mercantilist China policy.

There are two main objectives of the PPA. I am interested in learning to what extent the three aforementioned paradigms have influenced the policy-specific public discourse. As part of the PPA, I will also document the extent (or lack of) the legwork that has already been done with regard to Zeitenwende. More specifically I will analyse whether new policy images indicate an increasing willingness to speak the 'language of power' (for an in-depth discussion of *leverage* as power see Chapter 8). There are several leading questions (LQ) that inform the PPA. The first LQ is the same for all PPAs (PPA LQ1 What kind of domestic or geopolitical developments led to policy punctuation?). The second leading question will always be specific to the policy subfield:

PPA LQ2a How does VW monitor and evaluate its supply chains in Xinjiang? (Chapter 6)

PPA LQ2b How to mitigate risks in Germany's 5G infrastructure? (Chapter 7)

PPA LQ2c Why does Germany still provide official development assistance to China? (Chapter 8)

PPA LQ2d How can Germany upgrade its diplomatic relationship with Taiwan? (Chapter 9)

PPA LQ2e Are compromises are permissible in academic cooperation with China, and if so, what could they entail? (Chapter 10)

The subsequent third leading question is the same for all five PPAs (PPA LQ3 Who were the disruptors and what were their achievements?). Like the case studies about unforeseen policy failures (UPF), I will have to address attribution and hindsight issues in my presentation of the PPA. In addition, I am aware that in terms of sources informing the PPAs I need to avoid selection bias. The German-language newspapers *TAZ, Süddeutsche Zeitung, Frankfurter Allgemeine Zeitung, Handelsblatt, WirtschaftsWoche* and *NZZ* will be reviewed to capture relevant policy images supporting both the old and the emergent paradigm(s). They represent all sides of the political spectrum from the left, center-left to the center-right. For my analysis of policy images, I will disregard news outlets on the hard left or the hard right. When it comes to the public discourse on German China policy I have noticed that participants often speak of a 'polarized' discussion. Damm's previously mentioned comment on 'deeply polarized . . . fault lines' in the China debate illustrates this point. His assessment must be understood within the context of a highly consensus-oriented political culture in Germany. It is also important to note that adherents of both the old and emergent paradigms occupy a middle ground (see Illustration 2).

While the German China debate is often viewed as deeply entrenched, it is actually a public dispute between two perfectly legitimate political positions. Neither side advocates extreme viewpoints, for example, arguing that Germany should become

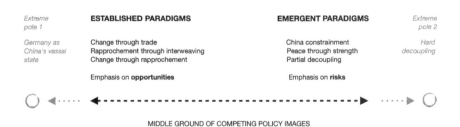

Figure 2 Towards a paradigm shift in German China policy?.

a vassal state of China (Extreme pole 1) or advocating hard decoupling (Extreme pole 2). It is also entirely possible that discourse participants neither fully identify with the old or the emergent paradigm. Figure 2 does not represent an either/or situation but should be seen as a continuum, where in-between positions in the public debate are both possible and desirable. An example of a policy image supporting the established paradigms is von Pierer's assertion that 'the risk of not being in Asia-Pacific is greater than the risk of being in' (Bovensiepen, 2004). Using this catchy phrase, the former Siemens CEO and former APA Chairman addressed concerns among German industrialists about the risks of trade and investment overseas while emphasizing that if they failed to engage with the Asia-Pacific region, they would lose out on profits. A BDI report from 2019 offers a very different policy image supporting emergent paradigms. It combines empirical information and emotional appeals in different ways: 'German industry continues to be interested in close economic exchange with China and rejects targeted and politically forced economic de-coupling. Nevertheless, German industry generally believes that it makes sense to maintain diversified trade relations and investment decisions. Excessive dependence on a single market is always associated with political and economic risks that must be minimized' (BDI, 2019, 20).

The two examples of policy images were developed at very different times: in the late 1990s von Pierer highlighted opportunities in order to persuade sceptical German industrialists to strengthen their overseas engagement. About twenty years later the BDI had critically examined Germany's commercial relationship with China and found shortcomings. In their 2019 report, the employed policy image was unequivocal: while opportunities remained, there were also risks. It is evident from both policy images that Germany can benefit from trade with China. Their emotive appeals, however, are very different and assess risks related to Germany's commercial China engagement from very different vantage points. Despite such differences in emphasis, the policy images are not completely incompatible and suggest a degree of constructive political learning among the authors of the BDI study.

Like Emcke I believe that liberal democracies have a 'reflective capacity that makes democratic societies more rational and resilient in the long run' (2022). Nevertheless, for reflection to occur, discourse participants must accept that robust public debates and disagreements are integral parts of the democratic process. If our democratic values are indeed our interests, we should be able to come to an agreement on how best to protect them from CCP-led China. This question will be revisited in the concluding eleventh chapter, which will address Germany's China policy going forward.

Chapter 5 References

@robkhenderson (2021), 'Alfred Adler Wrote that the "Life-Lie" Is a Way to •Blame Others •Escape Personal Responsibility •A Last-Ditch Attempt to Protect Their Social Image ("It's Not My Fault") •Obtain Advantage Over Others, Who Now Walk on Eggshells

•Seek Security in helplessness', *Twitter*, 7 August. Available online: https://archive.is/
O7WJG (accessed 13 July 2023).

Adler, A. (1925), *The Practice and Theory of Individual Psychology*, London: Kegan Paul,
Trench, Trubner & Co., Ltd.

APA (2023), 'Life Lie', *American Psychological Association*. Available online: https://archive
.is/YcApM (accessed 13 July 2023).

Barkin, N. (2020), 'Germany's Strategic Gray Zone with China', *Carnegie Endowment
for International Peace*, 25 March 2020. Available online: https://archive.is/XsU1c
(accessed 13 July 2023).

Baumgartner, F. and B. Jones (1993/2009), *Agendas and Instability in American Politics*,
2nd edn, Chicago and London: The University of Chicago Press.

BDI (2019), 'Partner and Systemic Competitor – How Do We Deal with China's State-
Controlled Economy?', Available online: https://www.wita.org/wp-content/uploads
/2019/01/201901_Policy_Paper_BDI_China.pdf (accessed 13 July 2023).

Bovensiepen, N. (2004), „Wir müssen aufpassen", *Süddeutsche Zeitung*, 20–21 November.
Nr. 270, 20.

Boyse, M. (2023), 'Germany Remains in Denial over Its Russia Policy', *Hudson Institute*, 1
February. Available online: https://archive.is/kORbH (accessed 13 July 2023).

Büschemann, K.-H. (2021), 'Kein Wandel durch Handel', *Süddeutsche Zeitung*, 14–15
August. Nr. 186, 22.

Busse, C. and T. Fromm (2022), '"Wir brauchen eine neue Ehrlichkeit"', *Süddeutsche
Zeitung*, 29 June. Nr. 147, 15.

Cairney, P. (2011/2020), *Understanding Public Policy. Theories and Issues*, 2nd edn,
London: Macmillan Education Limited.

China.Table (2022), 'Stefan Sack: "Change Through Trade" was a Successful Strategy for
China', 26 April. Available online: https://archive.is/Q95mJ (accessed 13 July 2023).

ChinaFile (2013), 'Document 9: A ChinaFile Translation', 8 November. Available online:
https://archive.is/DtRYA (accessed 13 July 2023).

Damm, J. (2023), 'China and Germany After the 2021 Election: Between Continuity and
Increasing Confrontation', in S. Grano and D. Huang (eds), *China-US Competition
Impact on Small and Middle Powers' Strategic Choices*, 159–90, Cham: Palgrave
Macmillan.

De Gruyter (2022), '„Wandel durch Handel funktioniert durchaus"', *De Gruyter*, 29 June.
Available online: https://archive.is/DsESe (accessed 13 July 2023).

Deutschlandfunk (2012), '„Wir machen eine werteorientierte Außenpolitik"', 2 September.
Available online: https://archive.is/hHWw0 (accessed 13 July 2023).

Dieckmann, C. and J. Tartler (2023), 'Die Deutschen und Taiwan: „Es gibt
Widersprüche zwischen unseren Wirtschaftsinteressen und unseren Werten"',
Tagesspiegel, 19 March. Available online: https://archive.is/tBz8z (accessed 13 July
2023).

Emcke, C. (2022), '"Huch"', *Süddeutsche Zeitung*, 4–6 June. Nr. 128, 6.

Fischer, D. (2022), 'Gibt es eine Zukunft ohne China?', *+49security*, 16 November.
Available online: https://web.archive.org/web/20221117102105/https://
fourninesecurity.de/2022/11/16/gibt-es-eine-zukunft-ohne-china (accessed 13 July
2023).

Fulda, A. (2009), *Förderung partizipativer Entwicklung in der VR China. Möglichkeiten
und Grenzen politischer Einflussnahme durch Akteure der deutsch-chinesischen
Entwicklungszusammenarbeit (2003–2006)*, Wiesbaden: VS Verlag für
Sozialwissenschaften.

Fulda, A. (2020a), 'Germany's China Policy of "Change Through Trade" Has Failed', *RUSI*, 1 June. Available online: https://archive.is/9TQOr (accessed 13 July 2023).

Fulda, A. (2020b), 'China Is Merkel's Biggest Failure in Office', *Foreign Policy*, 15 September. Available online: https://archive.is/3xjby (accessed 13 July 2023).

Fulda, A. (2021a), 'The Case for a Paradigm Shift in German China Policy', *China.Table*, 6 April. Available online: https://archive.is/ZiZqM (accessed 13 July 2023).

Fulda, A. (2021b), 'Rote Linien längst überschritten', *Forschung & Lehre*, 13 September. Available online: https://archive.is/n74tV (accessed 13 July 2023).

Fulda, A. (2021c), 'German Academic Freedom Is Now Decided in Beijing', *Foreign Policy*, 28 October. Available online: https://archive.is/YoC7H (accessed 13 July 2023).

Fulda, A. (2022), 'Researching China: How Germany Tackles the Issues', *HEPI*, 5 April. Available online: https://archive.is/sRWtO (accessed 13 July 2023).

Fulda, A. and S. Klotzbücher (2022), 'Kooperation mit Autokratien: Still und heimlich schließen sich die Türen', *Tagesspiegel*, 7 October. Available online: https://archive.is/sdsrt#selection-1493.0-1505.43 (accessed 13 July 2023).

Fulda, A., M. Ohlberg, D. Missal, H. Fabian, and S. Klotzbücher (2022), 'Grenzenlos kompromissbereit?', *Frankfurter Allgemeine Zeitung*, 16 März. Available online: https://archive.is/xVZhQ (accessed 13 July 2023).

Gabriel, S. (2022), 'Nord Stream 2 was a Mistake. We Simply Didn't Listen to the Eastern Europeans', *Atlantik-Brücke*, 18 May. Available online: https://web.archive.org/web/20220518150510/https://www.atlantik-bruecke.org/en/nord-stream-2-was-a-mistake/ (accessed 13 July 2023).

Giegerich, B. and M. Terhalle (2021), *The Responsibility to Defend. Rethinking Germany's Strategic Culture*, Oxon: Routledge.

Giesen, C. (2019), 'Überfällige Strategie', *Süddeutsche Zeitung*, 18 March. Nr. 65, 4.

Glasser, S. (2022), 'Joe Biden's Walk-and-Chew-Gum Campaign', *The New Yorker*, 20 October. Available online: https://archive.is/NEPb1 (accessed 13 July 2023).

Groitl, G. (2021), 'Das Märchen vom Wandel durch Handel – Wenn seine Logik je funktioniert hat, dann umgekehrt: China führt mit seiner Wirtschaftsmacht die westlichen Demokratien vor', *Neue Züricher Zeitung*, 15 June. Available online: https://archive.is/36emA#selection-255.0-255.162 (accessed 12 July 2023).

Hamilton, C. and M. Ohlberg (2020), *Hidden Hand: Exposing How the Chinese Communist Party is Reshaping the World*, London: Oneworld Publications.

Hank, R. (2022), 'Gefährliche Polemik am „Wandel durch Handel"', *Frankfurter Allgemeine Zeitung*, 20 June. Available online: https://web.archive.org/web/20220623140740/https://www.faz.net/aktuell/wirtschaft/wandel-durch-handel-ehrenrettung-einer-leitidee-18109718.html (accessed 13 July 2023).

Hassan, A. and S. Barber (2021, December), 'The Effects of Repetition Frequency on the Illusory Truth Effect', *Cognitive Research: Principles and Implications*, 6: 38. Available online: https://archive.is/E1vma (accessed 13 July 2023).

Heilmann, S. (2014), 'Peking öffnet seine Türen', *Süddeutsche Zeitung*, 24 March. Nr. 69, 2.

Jones, B. and F. Baumgartner (2005), *The Politics of Attention: How Governments Prioritizes Problems*, Chicago and London: University of Chicago Press.

Karnitschnig, M. and J. Vela (2020), 'Germany's Altmaier Defends Berlin's Muted Response to China's Crackdown in Hong Kong', *Politico*, 15 July. Available online: https://archive.is/Unchm (accessed 13 July 2023).

Koselleck, R. (2004), *Futures Past: On the Semantics of Historical Time*, trans. Keith Tribe, New York: Columbia University Press.

Lau, J. (2013), 'Die deutsche Liebe zu den Diktatoren', *Zeit Online*, 21 February. Available online: https://web.archive.org/web/20130224084420/http://blog.zeit.de/joerglau/2013/02/21/schurken-die-wir-brauchen_5889 (accessed 13 July 2023).

Lau, J. (2021), '„Wandel durch Handel"', *Internationale Politik*, 1 September. Available online: https://archive.is/VE5t7 (accessed 13 July 2023).

Meijer, H. (2022), *Awakening to China's Rise: European Foreign and Security Policies toward the People's Republic of China*, Oxford: Oxford University Press.

Menzel, S. (2022), 'Volkswagen: Teile aus der Ukraine kommen wieder zuverlässig', *Handelsblatt*, 12 May. Available online: https://archive.is/DA8FR (accessed 13 July 2023).

Pal, L. (2006), *Beyond Policy Analysis: Public Issue Management in Turbulent Times*, 3rd edn, Scarborough: Thomson/Nelson.

Quarmby, S. (2018), 'What Are the Implications of Complex Systems Thinking for Policymaking?', LSE Blog, 12 October. Available online: https://archive.is/4DR73 (accessed 13 July 2023).

Reuters (2022a), 'Merkel - Habe nie an "Wandel durch Handel" geglaubt', Available online: https://www.reuters.com/video/watch/idOV211713102022RP1 (accessed 13 July 2023).

Reuters (2022b), 'Merkel: No Regrets on Energy Policy with Russia', 13 October. Available online: https://archive.is/GcQ41#selection-423.0-423.47 (accessed 13 July 2023).

Sandschneider, E. (2012), 'Deutsche Außenpolitik: Eine Gestaltungsmacht in der Kontinuitätsfalle - Essay', *Aus Politik und Zeitgeschichte*, 1 March. Available online: https://archive.is/bHdQk (accessed 13 July 2023).

Sandschneider, E. (2013), 'Raus aus der Moralecke!', *Zeit Online*, 27 February. Available online: https://archive.is/gaTfZ (accessed 13 July 2023).

Schneckener, U. (2022), 'Gestörter Empfang: Putins Kriegsnarrative und die deutsche Russlandpolitik', Zeitschrift für Friedens- und Konfliktforschung, 29 December, 279–93. Available online: https://doi.org/10.1007/s42597-022-00086-4 (accessed 10 July 2023).

Schneier, B. (2012), *Liars & Outliers: Enabling the Trust that Society Needs to Thrive*, Indianapolis: John Wiley & Sons, Inc.

Schoen, D. (1983), *The Reflective Practitioner: How Professionals Think in Action*, London: Ashgate.

Solomon, E. and G. Chazan (2021), '"We Need a Real Policy for China": Germany Ponders Post-Merkel Shift', *Financial Times*, 5 January. Available online: https://archive.is/epKGQ#selection-1619.0-1623.10 (accessed 13 July 2023).

Sparkes, A. C. (1989), 'Paradigmatic Confusions and the Evasion of Critical Issues in Naturalistic Research', *Journal of Teaching in Physical Education*, 8 (2): 131–51.

Spross, H. (2014), 'Parteilinie und Zensur unter Xi Jinping', *Deutsche Welle*, 14 June. Available online: https://archive.is/C1Nx6 (accessed 13 July 2023).

Stanford Encyclopedia of Philosophy (2012), 'Ludwik Fleck', Available online: https://archive.is/8HfkJ (accessed 13 July 2023).

Stanford Encyclopedia of Philosophy (2013), 'Scientific Revolutions', Available online: https://archive.is/s2IcC (accessed 13 July 2023).

Stanford Encyclopedia of Philosophy (2018), 'Bounded Rationality', Available online: https://archive.is/wa4qW (accessed 13 July 2023).

Strittmatter, K. (2012), 'Die Diktatur lebt', *Süddeutsche Zeitung*, 20–21 October 2012. Nr. 243, 25.

Strittmatter, K. (2017), 'Totale Kontrolle', *Süddeutsche Zeitung*, 21–22 October. Nr. 243, 4.

Strittmatter, K. (2018), 'Das Reich der Mittel', *Süddeutsche Zeitung*, 17–18 February. Nr. 40, 49.

Weidenfeld, U. (2022), '„Wandel durch Handel"? Dieser epochale Irrtum trifft Deutschland besonders hart', *Welt*, 18 April. Available online: https://archive.is /20221119224713/https://www.welt.de/wirtschaft/plus237781839/Wandel-durch -Handel-Wie-Deutschland-der-epochale-Irrtum-trifft.html (accessed 13 July 2023).

PART 2

POLICY FAILURES AND COMPETING POLICY IMAGES

GERMANY'S PROTRACTED PARADIGM SHIFT

Chapter 6

THE DEMISE OF GERMANY'S SOLAR INDUSTRY
AND VOLKSWAGEN'S CHINA CONUNDRUM

6.1 Doubling down on China despite existing dependencies?

Germany has been governed by Chancellor Scholz since December 2021 with the help of two smaller coalition partners. Chancellor Scholz (SPD) and Foreign Minister Baerbock (Alliance 90/The Greens) thus far have failed to develop a joint approach to an increasingly assertive China. Amid arguments within the traffic light coalition, German conglomerates have continued to increase their direct investments in China to more than ten billion euros in the first half of 2022 alone (Patey, 2022). Such direct investments cast doubt on the ability of the new government to alter Germany's decade-long mercantilist approach to China. The dangers of increased economic dependence on China seem to escape German industrialists. In Chapter 3, I outlined how the Chinese Communist Party engages in what could be termed 'power trading'. In my argument, which is based on Hirschman's scholarship, I argued that the Chinese party-state would make it difficult for existing trade partners to divert from China.

Chapter at a glance

The chapter begins by analysing the unforeseen policy failure (UPF 1) of Germany's solar industry. It is my objective to examine the factors that led to its collapse and dissect the long-term costs of Germany's entanglement with autocratic China. I illustrate how competing interests in the private sector complicated the search for a satisfactory solution. I discuss VW's entanglement with China in the second part of the book chapter. As part of the book's first policy punctuation analysis (PPA 1), I examine Volkswagen's controversial factory in Urumqi and China's forced labour problem. VW faces a fundamentally changed regulatory landscape following Germany's new supply chain act, as well as strong headwinds in the public debate about its corporate behaviour in China. In addition, I analyse how key stakeholders have positioned themselves in the ongoing debate about decoupling, diversification and dependence on China. The chapter concludes with reflections on what can be learned from my analysis of policy failure and policy punctuation.

6.2 Unforeseen policy failure 1 | The rise and demise of Germany's solar industry

The first unforeseen policy failure (UPF 1) provides a cautionary tale about the dangers of relying on a single policy and a globalized market to drive the development of an emerging industry. Germany's photovoltaic energy production was jump-started in the early 2000s with the help of a state-backed Feed-in Tariff (FiT). The German government's Erneuerbare Energie-Gesetz (EEG) came into effect in 2000. The EEG incentivized the installation of solar panels by individual and corporate investors. The EED act guaranteed priority access to the power grid and fixed the price per kilowatt hour for up to twenty years (FuturePolicy.org, 2023). A surcharge imposed on all consumers procuring electricity from the grid ensured the financial viability of the EEG act for more than a decade (European Commission, 2017). The FiT helped increase the production of solar energy, which climbed from a mere 0.3 gigawatt power generation capacity in 2002 to 33 gigawatt in 2012 (Appunn and Wehrmann, 2019). This boom in installed photovoltaic panels however was short-lived. Germany's solar industry started collapsing after 2012. By 2014 the number of employees working in the photovoltaic sector shrunk to 56,000 from 100,000 in the previous year (Zeit Online, 2014). In Spring 2018, the once world-leading German photovoltaic company SolarWorld filed for insolvency (Enkhardt, 2018).

In 2022 Conte published a visualization of China's growing dominance in the global solar panel supply chain. It revealed that in terms of its manufacturing capacity China not only dominated the world market in terms of the primary material polysilicion (79.4%), but also when it comes to wafer production (96.8%), solar cells (85.1%) and solar panel modules (74.7%) (2022). Whereas 'China made up 55% of global solar panel manufacturing capacity in 2010' by 2021 this share had risen to 84 per cent in 2021 (2022). As Rooks has noted, China has rapidly developed into one of the world's leading photovoltaic producers. State subsidies and investments played a key role, he argues. Due to this trend, all ten of the world's top solar panel manufacturers are now based in China, which accounts for over 80 per cent of the world market. Due to China's economies of scale, solar components are now 35 per cent cheaper in China than in Europe (2022). Witsch has described the resulting dependency of Germany's solar industry on China as 'absolute' (2023). In early February 2023 news broke that the Chinese party-state was weighing the option of restricting the export of technology used to make solar panels (Jucca, 2023). Such export restrictions could considerably slow down the recovery process of Germany's once mighty solar industry.

What led to the collapse?

As we proceed, I will examine how leading German politicians have rationalized the collapse of the country's solar industry. I seek to identify domestic and international circumstances that may have contributed to the sector's sudden demise. My argument is that a number of interrelated variables contributed to this outcome, not all of which could be foreseen *ex ante* by policymakers. When we compare and contrast alternative *post facto* rationalizations, however, we can gauge whether *creative learning* has taken place in recent years, or if an unproductive blame game has contributed to *destructive learning*.

The photovoltaic company Solarwatt has suggested that the decline of the photovoltaic sector in Germany was in large part a result of sudden policy changes that reduced the profitability of solar panels (Solarwatt, 2023). The Federal Association of the Solar Industry (BSW) had warned the German government in 2015 that its 'breathing cap' aimed at preventing that the rapid expansion of renewable energy was driving up electricity prices was no longer functioning. It also bemoaned that increasing red tape related to consultation and planning processes was increasing 'investment risk and make investment decisions considerably more difficult' (BSW, 2015). In an interview with Der Spiegel SolarWorld founder Asbeck has similarly argued that 'five years of badmouthing have taken their toll on solar energy. This was compounded by falling remuneration, expansion limits and the levy on own consumption' (Dohmen and Klawitter, 2017). Haugwitz has noted that China's national R&D expenditure increased from US$11 billion to US$154 billion between 1995 and 2009, at an average annual rate of 21 per cent. In contrast, Germany's public investment in technological innovation only increased by an average of 5 per cent per year over the same period (Aecea, 2012). This suggests that successive German governments appear to have overestimated the private sector's willingness or ability to invest in R&D, including in the photovoltaic sector. Morris has offered a markedly different analysis, suggesting that 'it may have been unwise to expect the country to be home to such an industry; after all, solar panels are about as high-tech as radios, which Germany also no longer makes many of' (2020). Such a view informed by the logic of continuous industrial upgrading arguably overlooks that even relatively low-tech products such as mass-produced solar panels can be key to Germany's energy security, contribute to job retention and even aid technological development, for example, roll-to-roll manufacturing which is now also used in the automotive and aerospace industries. But was the decline of the sector a case of market or government failure, or a combination of both?

Are German private investors to blame?

If we want to better understand China's contribution to the demise of Germany's solar industry the experiential learning of the German politician Altmeier is instructive. During a talk show in Summer 2022 he offered the following policy image to explain the woes of Germany's solar industry during the Merkel era (2005–21). He said that 'when I became Minister of the Environment [in 2012], these jobs [in the German solar industry] were in great jeopardy. Why? Because the Chinese flooded the markets with their cheap solar systems. And the German investors who put solar systems on their roofs, freelancers who secured their pensions with them, said that the returns are much higher if I buy the cheap systems from China. And at that time, 80% of the systems were purchased from China' (ZDF, 2022a). His comment suggests that in fact private investors drove Germany's entanglement with China. Price-sensitive German investors were ideal customers for Chinese PV producers keen to reduce their domestic overcapacity of solar panels. This phenomenon also implies that for a considerable period of time the German government effectively subsidized Chinese producers of solar panels through the EEG, which jeopardized the sustainability of German solar companies.

Altmeier also claimed that he was instrumental in persuading the EU to impose temporary tariffs on imported solar panels, cells and wafers from China. The limited success of the EU's anti-dumping measures, which were lifted in 2018, can partially explained by domestic opposition in Germany. According to Altmaier 'German businesses said that we would now get punitive tariffs from China, because they supply the solar panels, but the polycrystalline silicon with which they are made comes from Wacker-Chemie in Bavaria, the machine tools that are needed to make the panels are Made in Germany, and that is political interference in the free play of the markets. Of course, we could have said that we would ban the import of Chinese panels completely, which would have been a violation of world trade law, and then the Chinese might have said, and we won't buy any more VW Golfs in China, and we'll ban that' (ZDF, 2022a). Altmaier's comment suggests that policymakers were concerned that harsh punitive tariffs for Chinese solar panels could prompt the party-state to retaliate against Germany's automobile industry. In an interview, Trittin, a Green politician who served as Minister of the Environment during the Schröder era (1998–2005), admitted that 'we have a huge problem with the three automobile companies and with BASF. In other words, there are four companies of systemic importance from a German perspective that have an implicit state guarantee in Germany' (China. Table, 2023a).

What were the long-term costs of entanglement?

During an investigation of the European Commission in 2013, it was discovered that Chinese solar panels were being sold far below their market value on the European market, which resulted in an average dumping margin of 88 per cent (2013). As a result, the European Commission imposed relatively moderate anti-dumping duties set at an average of 47.6 per cent (2013), likely in response to Beijing's intense lobbying in Brussels and threats of retaliation (Traynor, 2012). According to Chaffin (2013), the trade dispute resulted in a settlement favourable to Beijing. As long as the price of the solar products was no less than 56 cents per watt, Chinese companies were allowed to export up to 7 gigawatts of solar products to the EU without paying duties. Products sold above the quota or below the minimum price were subject to anti-dumping duties of 47 per cent (2013). Nitzschke, president of EU ProSun, scorned the agreement, saying that it 'is not a solution but a capitulation. Under tremendous Chinese pressure the EU Commission decided to sell the European solar industry to China' (2013). Considering the EU–China trade relationship 'too big to fail' Yu Chen has considered the negotiated settlement a success, at least insofar as it averted a trade war (Chen, 2015).

In retrospect, we can see that the critics of the settlement were right to raise concerns. The overly moderate punitive tariffs did not give German and European photovoltaic producers enough time to out-innovate their Chinese competitors. Additionally, SolarWorld founder Asbeck has claimed that 'Chinese solar companies, apparently with the help of German accomplices, have been circumventing anti-dumping duties for years in order to get rid of their monstrous overcapacities . . . The accusations regarding Chinese imports that German public prosecutors and customs investigators are now investigating. They concern customs evasion, forged loading documents and cash-back payments' (Dohmen and Klawitter, 2017). When Altmaier, the aforementioned former German Economic Minister, stated that punitive tariffs were lifted only when few producers were left in Germany and Europe (ZDF, 2022a), he seems to realize the limited impact of European anti-dumping measures. The leader of the opposition in the Bundestag, Merz, however, blamed German photovoltaic companies: 'Because we have simply become too expensive. And because we paid too high compensation rates . . . so the manufacturers in Germany got too fat for too long and were no longer competitive. Then the Chinese and others showed us how to do it better and suddenly the Chinese were on the market and we saw that we had done it wrong' (ZDF, 2022b).

Competing interests of producers, exporters and investors

Minister-President of North Rhine-Westphalia Laschet (CDU) employed a similar policy image when stating in an interview that 'the reason why solar energy collapsed was that the panels were produced more cheaply in China. That was not a question of subsidies but a question of where do you produce solar panels now, and in the end Germany was too expensive' (Kölner Stadt-Anzeiger, 2019). This explanation, as discussed previously, is far too reductionist and overlooks the role the party-state played in supporting China's photovoltaic industry. Merz's and Laschet's public statements provide insight into the uncritical 'free market' mindset of leading CDU/CSU politicians. A more sensible failure analysis would be to highlight the trade-offs policymakers must make when engaging the private sector. Policymakers faced a similar situation during a textile dispute with China in 2005, when they needed to square the circle of competing private sector interests of European producers, retailers and consumers (Stumbaum, 2009, 146). In hindsight we can see that it proved too difficult for policymakers to come up with a satisfactory solution for the solar industry in Germany because the interests of photovoltaic producers, automobile manufacturers, chemical and mechanical engineering exporters, as well as private investors in renewable energy were too divergent.

Merz and Laschet also ignored the environmental and social impacts of global supply chains. German retailers and consumers should be concerned about the conditions under which solar panels are produced. It has been reported by Giesen and Hecking that approximately 45 per cent of the world's polycrystalline silicon (also called polysilicon), which is used in the production of solar modules, is produced in the Xinjiang Uyghur Autonomous Region (XUAR), the 'Silicon Valley' of the global solar industry (Giesen and Hecking, 2023). They highlight that in addition to solar energy 'masses of subsidized coal-fired electricity are needed to produce crystalline silicon' (2023). Murphy and Elimä have detailed how forced labour in the Uyghur region can permeate an entire supply chain and penetrate deep into international markets (2021, 7). Among the findings of their study, eleven companies were complicit in forced labour transfers, four companies operated in industrial parks that accepted forced labour transfers and ninety Chinese and international companies' supply chains were affected (2021). In addition to being dependent on *raw materials* and *intermediate products*, German importers now also have to contend with human rights abuses in China's supply chains. As we will see in the following discussion, forced labour has also affected German automobile manufacturers who produce in China.

6.3 Policy punctuation analysis 1 | VW's entanglement with China

As the first policy punctuation analysis (PPA 1) will show Volkswagen (VW) has faced mounting challenges in China in recent years. I discuss how domestic and political factors have contributed to its woes. VW's problems in China in recent years have been exacerbated by a flawed decision to build a factory in Urumqi and by a BBC journalist's interview in 2019 with former VW CEO Diess that turned into a public relations catastrophe.

   Political developments in China have also played a key role in addition to such company-specific errors. Chapter 3 described the hard authoritarian turn under Xi Jinping in great detail. Xi, nicknamed 'accelerator in chief' on the Chinese internet, has been criticized for 'his aggressive approach to "stability" [which] has caused more domestic and international conflict' (Su, 2020). As Human Rights Watch has succinctly summarized '(since) Xi Jinping's rise to power in 2013, the Chinese government has aggressively pursued assimilationist policies in ethnic minority regions, increasingly insisting on the "Sinicization" of those communities, driven by nationalism and in many instances Islamophobia inside and outside China' (2021). The German anthropologist Zenz was one of the first experts to alert the world community to China's political re-education campaign in the Xinjiang Uyghur Autonomous Region (XUAR) (2018). Ramzy and Buckley in 2019 documented the campaign against Uyghurs in intricate detail using leaked internal government documents (2019). They included a previously unpublished speech by Xi calling for a 'struggle against terrorism, infiltration, and separatism', in which cadres should show 'absolutely no mercy' (2019). China expert Smith Finley has critiqued the party-state's 'holistic strategy of ethnic cleansing' (2022, 353) in the XUAR.

According to a long-delayed UN report released in 2022, the extent of arbitrary and discriminatory detention in the primarily Uighur-populated region 'may constitute international crimes, in particular crimes against humanity' (Feng and Ruwitch, 2022). Due to the deterioration of human rights in the XUAR, German industrialists have been questioned about their commercial engagement in the region. One example is an interview Diess gave to the BBC in Spring 2019. Upon being pressed to comment on the emergence of re-education camps, Diess said 'I can't judge this' and claimed he didn't know what the BBC journalist was referring to (Deutsche Welle, 2019). Then he stated that he was 'not aware' about re-education camps (BBC, 2019). As a result of the interview, Volkswagen suffered a public relations crisis that has reverberated for years.

Volkswagen's factory in Urumqi

As to how VW monitors and evaluates its XUAR supply chains, there are diametrically opposed answers. To begin, I will review the policy images invoked to defend VW's Chinese commercial engagement in general and in the XUAR in particular. Diess changed course when pretending ignorance of the Uyghurs' human rights situation backfired during the BBC interview. In a subsequent defence of the factory in Urumqi he asserted that neither Volkswagen nor its suppliers employed forced labour, and that the company's values, such as worker representation, respect for minorities and social and labour standards, were also upheld in the XUAR (Süddeutsche Zeitung, 2021). This message was reinforced by Volkswagen's new China boss, Brandstätter. In addition to stating that the company does not engage in forced labour, he also stated that the supply network is carefully monitored and that good working conditions are maintained at the SAIC Volkswagen factory (Ankenbrand and Müßgens, 2023a).

Moreover, Diess explained, before Covid, 600 co-workers were employed at VW's Urumqi plant, of whom 30 per cent belonged to minorities. In the factory, they were able to pray and eat according to their religious beliefs (Rasch and Höltschi, 2022). By providing jobs to all ethnic groups, the company argued in 2019 that the social environment at the Urumqi location had been significantly improved (Handelsblatt, 2019). There were calls to close the Urumqi plant, but they were dismissed. In defence of VW's engagement in the XUAR, Lower Saxony Minister-President Weil (SPD) invoked Mandela. Based on Weil's recollections, Mandela 'thanked the Western companies that stayed despite the sanctions after apartheid ended in South Africa' (FAZ, 2023). In this context, it is important to note that Weil represents a Bundesland that is also VW's second largest shareholder. Brandstätter has argued less prosaically that SAIC, VW's joint venture partner, opposed a retreat (Müßgens, 2023a). Moreover, CAR Center Automotive Research Director Dudenhöffer has suggested that the closing of the factory could threaten VW's entire China business (Sigmund et al., 2022; Giesen, Hage and Obermaier, 2022). The policy images in defence of VW's China engagement can be summarized as follows: there was no forced labour in the factory or its supply chain; VW's joint venture offered good working conditions; and it allegedly contributed to the regional economy. The emotive appeal of these policy images suggested that retreat was neither necessary nor possible. The following discussion will show that such policy images have not gone uncontested.

Volkswagen's China conundrum

VW has come under criticism from prominent European Parliament member Bütikofer (Alliance 90/The Greens) for supporting the Chinese authorities in the XUAR (Koch and Specht, 2020). Additionally, he has argued that Volkswagen's 'size and importance. . . it could well afford to pull out of Xinjiang' (Giesen and Hägler, 2021a). In a similar vein, Hennig has argued that corporations such as Volkswagen or BASF should not undermine liberal values by investing in dictatorships such as China (Feldwisch-Drentrup, 2022). Zenz, who first unveiled the cultural genocide in the XUAR through his pioneering research on internment camps, has suggested that forced labour would likely be more prevalent in low-skilled jobs. However, if former camp inmates were to attend vocational training schools or take part in state-sponsored labour transfers, their chances of finding employment for more complex jobs would increase (Zenz, 2022). As Zenz asserts, VW will be unable to claim that there is no forced labour with them as time advances (Heißler, 2022).

Cavallo, the chair of the VW works council, maintains that 'we have no evidence that anything is happening at our sites that is not in line with our charter' (Krüger and Beucker, 2022). This perspective ignores the fact that government surveillance is widespread in the XUAR, affecting Uyghur life beyond the factory gate. As Drinhausen points out 'much of the surveillance is no longer visible, but takes place digitally in the background' (Heide, 2021). Additionally, she has noted that the Chinese leadership may perceive foreign companies monitoring compliance with human rights standards as an attack (2021). Volkswagen's conundrum is summarized by Deuber, Giesen and Obermaier as follows: 'If the company is too critical of the Chinese action against the Uyghurs, it risks its economic future in the People's Republic. If Volkswagen continues to remain silent, the scandal-ridden company will lose its credibility' (2019). However, such an analysis has not gone unchallenged. Geier has argued 'to claim that VW is losing its credibility as a result is naïve. One should be honest. The VW bosses will hide what is happening in Xinjiang, just as the German government has done for years' (2019). Yet calls for a retreat have not been completely dismissed. Chairman of the influential union IG Metall, Jörg Hofmann, a member of the Supervisory Board of Volkswagen AG, has asked 'what it means for the company's reputation to continue to be invested there' (Menzel, 2022). The following discussion about the role of values in Volkswagen's China engagement will show that this question remains unresolved.

Making human rights negotiable?

Eight German industrialists wrote an opinion piece after Chancellor Scholz's trip to China in Autumn 2022. Their commercial engagement with China was justified by a positive policy image: 'Our locations in China, as well as those around the world, contribute significantly to our competitiveness' (FAZ, 2022), the authors argued. 'At the same time, they are ambassadors of our values and culture and show how German companies all over the world deal responsibly with employees, the environment and supply chains' (2022). According to the CEO of automotive supplier POW Lazzarini, it would be better to follow our own values than abandon the Chinese market (Menzel and Tyborski, 2022). But what values were the industrialists referring to? What are the ways in which a MNC like VW defends our values, which are also our enlightened and material interests?

Opening a factory in Urumqi was a grave error of judgement. Early on Giesen reported that Chinese regulators had made VW's further expansion in China dependent on building a plant in Urumqi (2017). He cited the Managing Director of JSC Automotive Siebert as saying that 'VW was given a choice: Do you want approval for the other planned plants, yes or no? . . . If yes, then build one in Ürümqi as well' (2017). Giesen and Hägler reiterated this point four years later. They pointed out that 'when a factory opens in Urumqi, Volkswagen gets to open half a dozen highly lucrative plants in the east – and this happened' (2021b). China expert Zenglein commented that 'many projects have a lead time of years and have been decided upon partly due to political pressure. Anyone who made an investment decision five, six or seven years ago could not have had any idea of the development of the human rights situation in Xinjiang' (Stratmann, 2019). This rather charitable assessment overlooks the fact that more than 140 people were killed in inter-ethnic violence in 2009 in Urumqi (Branigan, 2009). The new VW plant was operational four years later in 2013. German decision-makers had a choice: they could have rejected building a plant in a region known for ethnic tensions. While this may have made it more difficult for VW to get approval for the Foshan mega plant in Guangdong province (Mattheis, 2013), it would have avoided the current controversy. By building the factory in Urumqi VW accepted a direct link between human rights and its trade opportunities. Human rights thus became negotiable. The investment decision was a sign of VW's confidence in the Chinese government's ability to provide a secure and stable business environment in the XUAR. As a flip-side of the coin, this decision legitimized Chinese party-state claims that it was acting in the best interests of XUAR residents (Xinhua, 2018).

Germany's new supply chain law: will it solve the problem?

The question of how Volkswagen monitors and evaluates its Chinese suppliers has also been a contributing factor to Germany's year-long discussion about a supply chain act that went into effect on 1 January 2023 (European Coalition for Corporate Justice, 2023). This new law requires companies to conduct due diligence on their supply chains and prevent human rights abuses. Aside from fines, victims may pursue legal recourse against companies that violate the law. The challenges that come with increased transparency and accountability have been aptly summarized by Kretschmer: 'Recently, international auditors announced that they would no longer screen Western companies' supply chains for forced labour because of the lack of transparency on the part of Chinese authorities. Critical questions should be asked of VW. How does the company know that its supply chains in China comply with human rights?' (2021)

There has been passionate debate over the supply chain act. Riecke argues that policymakers must convey a clear message regarding what is permissible and what is not (2021). As Brüggmann puts it, a new supply chain law is a first and an important step in a complex matter (Brüggmann and Specht, 2021), while Specht questions whether German companies can screen very long and opaque global supply chains (2021). According to Freytag, however, such a law may make any behaviour of German entrepreneurs or managers in China illegal in the future (2020). In order to address human rights abuses, he says, the German government should collaborate with the EU and Five Eyes instead. Freytag suggests that 'it is not expedient to burden companies with this diplomatic task' (2020). A variant of this argument was developed by VW Sustainability Council Spokesperson Kell. According to him, companies are not suited to replace state power (2022). Despite asserting that human rights are non-negotiable, he also suggested that 'the idea that the West has something like a monopoly on moral superiority is simply wrong' (2022). Kell subsequently decried what he considered 'moral superiority' as an 'expression of the arrogance of our interpretation', calling instead for 'humility and respect' (2022). The policy image Kell projected was highly contradictory. While emphasizing state regulation, his emotive appeal criticized efforts to defend human rights abroad. In my view it was also problematic to bring morality into the discussion. As political pressure played a role in VW's investment decision in the early 2000s, VW's decision-makers would have been morally justified in refusing such political conditions. Yet Kell's op-ed did not contain any critique of VW's past corporate behaviour.

Volkswagen's uncertain future

There has already been a significant impact from increasing public awareness of VW's supply chain dilemma. According to Speich, Head of Sustainability and Corporate Governance at Deka Investment, Volkswagen is no longer an investable company when it comes to sustainable financial products (WirtschaftsWoche, 2023b). There are indications that Union Investment fund company may follow Deka's lead and remove Volkswagen securities from its sustainability segment (China.Table, 2023b). Volkswagen shareholders will likely exert increasing pressure due to increased public awareness and tightening state regulations. Moreover, Widmann and Shaw argue that greater transparency will become mandatory for large corporations once the EU's proposed supply chain legislation is enacted (2022).

The controversy surrounding the Urumqi plant, and the difficulty in monitoring and evaluating supply chains in the XUAR have also informed the debate about the benefits and drawbacks of continuing commercial engagement with China. The following is a brief review of policy images put forth in order to prevent a decoupling from China. In an interview with Der Spiegel, Diess highlighted the contributions of Volkswagen's China business to Germany's growth, prosperity and employment. According to him 'Volkswagen employs 20,000 to 30,000 developers in Germany. Half of them work for customers in China. Four billion euros in profits flow here from the People's Republic every year. I always tell my managers: a large part of your bonus is earned in China' (Hage and Klusmann, 2023). In a separate interview, he discussed how China could assist Germany in modernizing. He said that 'the country must also be seen as a market for the future that will advance the whole world technologically. If you cut yourself off from China, you cut yourself off from growth and technological progress' (Mattheis, 2022). Considering VW only holds a 2.7 per cent market share in China's fast-growing EV market, Diess' claim that Germany can benefit from China's technological progress is questionable (Ankenbrand and Müßgens, 2023b). Also noteworthy is that Diess' opposition to decoupling is similar to Chancellor Scholz's (Reuters, 2022a). According to a VW spokesperson, the company supports Scholz's call for 'diversification to strengthen independence and resilience' (Focus, 2022). According to such policy images, decoupling should be considered self-harm. A strong emotive appeal was made for business as usual to continue. However, as I will demonstrate in the following, the status quo can no longer be maintained and structural adjustments must be made. Rather than decoupling, diversification is now widely cited as a solution to dependencies.

Can diversification solve the problem of one-sided dependencies?

German politicians, industry leaders and journalists have adopted diversification as a buzz word, but its associated policy images remain ambiguous. Despite opposing 'complete decoupling' Höltschi and Rasch have argued that 'unilateral dependencies must be avoided if one does not want to be blackmailed' (2022). A similar argument has been made by Benner who has complained that 'some large German corporations have created a cluster risk in their China business' (Greive et al., 2022f). To address this problem Benner has called for 'sustainable prosperity and security of supply through trade' (2023). As I outlined in Chapter 3, there are three different types of dependencies: on *raw materials*; on *intermediate products* which are required for industry production; and on *revenues* generated in the Chinese market. There is an argument to be made that Volkswagen's China operations exhibit all three types of dependencies.

It is not always clear whether a diversified market or a greater variety of global supply chains is being called for in the public discourse. Globally, Volkswagen already operates 120 production sites and sells vehicles in 153 countries (Volkswagen Group Rus, 2023). My view is that further diversifying markets would not accomplish much. It is possible that the diversification argument becomes a rhetorical device designed to avoid the bigger issue, which is Volkswagen's overexposure to China. By using policy images in this manner, Volkswagen can protect its considerable investments in China and avoid decoupling costs. When it comes to exploring alternative supply chains, the diversification discourse is more relevant. An electric vehicle's battery is built from raw materials such as lithium. According to Höltschi and Rasch, it is primarily sourced from Australia,

Chile, China and Argentina. The report cites industry sources predicting that 'more than two thirds of all battery cells worldwide will still be produced in China in 2031' (2022). Without simultaneous expansion of Gigafactories in Europe (Mihalascu, 2023), diversifying raw material supplies however will not solve one-sided dependencies on China. Additionally, Volkswagen's joint venture with SAIC has already contributed to the success of Made in China 2025 through ongoing technology transfer. Volkswagen is unlikely to play a significant role in China's emerging EV market, which can be considered a major achievement for China's power trading. The German automobile industry could be the next to decline following the photovoltaic industry. And another sword of Damocles hanging over Volkswagen is the possibility of a future military annexation of Taiwan, as the following discussion will show.

Is Volkswagen prepared for a Taiwan shock?

Between 2005 and 2019 (Volkswagen Group, 2023), car sales grew exponentially. They peaked in 2018 and have since declined slightly. In 2022, VW expected to sell 3.3 million cars, mostly due to China's Covid lockdowns and chip shortages (Reuters, 2022b). Volkswagen, despite current headwinds, thus continues to generate significant revenue in the Chinese market. This raises the question of what the company would do if Xi ordered Taiwan's military annexation. According to the policy punctuation analysis 4 in Chapter 8, senior politicians, industrialists and security analysts are increasingly concerned about this worrisome scenario. Brandstätter, VW's China boss, has admitted that a military conflict over Taiwan would cause serious consequences for all of us (Müßgens, 2023b). However, he has also downplayed the geopolitical risks by stating that 'I have the impression that all parties are interested in de-escalation, not escalation' (2023b). Volkswagen has been criticized by Lee for their failure to take the Taiwan scenario seriously and their unwillingness to find substitutes for China (Lee, 2023). This raises the wider question what major conglomerates like Volkswagen are willing to do in terms of managing geopolitical risks. In the late 1990s former APA Chairman von Pierer still argued that 'the risk of not being in Asia-Pacific is greater than the risk of being in' (Bovensiepen, 2004). A revised policy image has been provided by Haerder, Knieps, Maier, Salz, Schnaas, Schlesiger, Seiwert, Petring and Wettach. They contend that 'the risk of staying in China may be greater than the risk of looking for alternatives altogether as soon as possible' (Haerder et al., 2022).

I explained in Chapter 5 how policy communities and issue networks compete with one another through the use of policy images to defend or challenge policy monopolies. There should be no surprise that VW's senior management tried to make the most of a difficult situation. The policy images they presented emphasized continued opportunities to succeed in the Chinese market. Chancellor Scholz's relationship with German industrialists has been more concerning, which is evident from his one-day trip to China in Autumn 2022, which was accompanied by a big business delegation. While Scholz has pledged to 'dismantle one-sided dependencies in the interest of smart diversification, which requires prudence and pragmatism' (2022), he has so far not signalled any resolve to stop skyrocketing German investment in China, including by Volkswagen (Reuters, 2022d). Herrmann has rightly pointed out that Germany does not have a screening mechanism for outbound investments (Lester, 2022).

Who were the disruptors and what were their achievements?

Volkswagen's China engagement, on the other hand, has been criticized by a motley crew of parliamentarians, journalists and academics. Members of this loose issue network deployed policy images that emphasized Volkswagen's commercial liabilities with China. Policy images have raised concerns about ethical issues, commercial problems and geopolitical risks. A number of emotive appeals were made, from terminating the Urumqi plant to calling on Volkswagen to develop a backup plan should Xi decide to wage war on Taiwan. As Volkswagen is neither closing its controversial Urumqi plant nor reducing its footprint in China, it raises the question of whether policy punctuation since 2017 was successful. All things considered, I would argue that real-world impacts are tangible. As a result of punctuation, awareness was raised and the policy agenda set. Also, public criticism contributed to the search for alternative policy instruments, such as the supply chain act or outbound investment screening. In addition, it has influenced Deka Investment's decision to exclude Volkswagen from its sustainable financial products. Moreover, punctuation has revealed an important dimension of dependence on China that is often overlooked. In spite of the Volkswagen Group's high sales revenue of over 250 billion in the year 2021 alone (Volkswagen Group, 2022), the company has not yet terminated a very small factory that has generated negative headlines since 2017. As a result, in addition to the aforementioned three types of dependence, a fourth dependency should be added: psychological dependency.

Volkswagen's former CEO Diess has admitted as much by saying that 'China probably doesn't need VW . . but VW needs China a lot' (Miller, 2022). Due to Volkswagen's and the Chancellery's opposition to decoupling, any divestment from China currently seems highly unlikely. Senior managers at Volkswagen may also believe that the company is 'too large to fail, rightly or wrongly. As a response, the economist Wolff has called for the end of state-backed guarantees for private investments in China' (Koch, 2023). He has also called for a rethink about the Hermes cover, which is an export credit guarantee of the German government (2023). In Spring 2022 the Federal Ministry for Economic Affairs and Climate Action (BMWK) rejected 'four applications from a company over human rights concerns in Xinjiang but declined to name the company. Der Spiegel said, without naming sources, that Volkswagen was the company in question' (Reuters, 2022c). The decision indicates that German foreign trade promotion is now undergoing rapid change. I contend that a decision like this was made possible in part because of Volkswagen's many critics and their continuous policy punctuation.

6.4 What can we learn from past failures and current headwinds?

In hindsight, German solar industry's rise and fall should have served as a wake-up call to politicians and industry leaders. Instead, the first unforeseen policy failure (UPF 1) revealed a blame game, with policymakers, producers and investors calling each other as the main culprits. I found it particularly concerning that senior conservative politicians such as Merz and Laschet reduced the debate to differences in prices between German and Chinese solar panels. The focus on price points neglected other problems, such as Chinese state subsidies, environmental impacts or forced labor in China's supply chains. As we look back, it should have become obvious that China's supposedly 'cheap' solar panels came with a high price tag, as they put German and European photovoltaic companies out of business and imposed varied dependencies on China.

Considering Volkswagen's growing entanglement with China, a refusal to learn lessons from the solar industry fiasco is all the more concerning. Based on the first policy punctuation analysis (PPA 1), VW seems to be doubling down on China rather than reducing its dependence on it. In a desperate attempt to gain a foothold in China's rapidly expanding electric vehicle market, Volkswagen announced in April 2023 a €1 billion ($1.1 billion) investment in an electric car development and business centre in China (Cheng, 2023). As Seiwert argues, such investments may be too late to help Volkswagen succeed in China's EV market (2023). The controversies surrounding VW's factory in Urumqi, the challenge of supply chain monitoring in the XUAR and the prospect of a Taiwan shock have also cast doubt on VW's future in China.

Chancellor Scholz has repeatedly criticized the idea of decoupling and deglobalization. During a speech in November 2022 he asserted that 'Germany and Europe in particular, with their high-tech and export-oriented economies, are dependent on the international division of labour' (Die Bundesregierung, 2022). Increasing corporate investment in China, however, makes lofty rhetoric about diversifying markets and global supply chains insufficient. As a result of Germany's demise in the solar industry and the challenges the German automobile industry faces today, more decisive action will need to be taken. In the concluding Chapter 11 I will argue that some form of decoupling from China and the reshoring of industries will be required to counter China as a 'power trader'. In order to suceed the German government will need to simultaneously develop a new strategy for China and an industry policy that puts economic resilience and national security first.

References for Chapter 6

Aecea (2012), 'March 2012 - Briefing-Paper - China Solar Development', March. Available online: http://www.frankhaugwitz.info/mediapool/134/1345433/data/2012_03_China_Briefing_Paper_Solar_Market_Development_Frank_Haugwitz_AECEA.pdf (accessed 14 July 2023).

Ankenbrand, H. and C. Müßgens (2023a), 'Gefangen im *Xinjiang*-Dilemma', *Frankfurter Allgemeine Zeitung*, 24 February. Nr 47: 24. F.A.Z.-Archiv.

Ankenbrand, H. and C. Müßgens (2023b), 'Vertreibung aus der zweiten Heimat', *Frankfurter Allgemeine Zeitung*, 16 April. Available online: https://archive.is/s2fFQ (accessed 14 July 2023).

Appunn, K. and B. Wehrmann (2019), '20 Years On: German Renewables Pioneers Face End of Guaranteed Payment', *Clean Energy Wire*, 16 September. Available online: https://archive.is/eP6wJ (accessed 14 July 2023).

BBC (2019), 'VW Boss "Not Aware" of China's Detention Camps', 16 April. Available online: https://www.bbc.co.uk/news/av/business-47944767 (accessed 14 July 2023).

Benner, T. (2023), 'Moralische Abrüstung in der Außenwirtschaftspolitik', *WirtschaftsWoche*, 4 February. WirtschaftsWoche Archive.

Bovensiepen, N. (2004), '„Wir müssen aufpassen"', *Süddeutsche Zeitung*, 20–21 November 2004. Nr. 270: 20.

Branigan, T. (2009), 'Ethnic Violence in China Leaves 140 Dead', *The Guardian*, 6 July. Available online: https://archive.is/H0BHC (accessed 14 July 2023).

Brüggmann, M. and F. Specht (2021), 'Ist das Lieferkettengesetzrealitätstauglich?', *Handelsblatt*, 19 May. Handelsblatt Archive.

BSW (2015), 'Stellungnahme des BSW-Solar zur Marktanalyse „Photovoltaik-Dachanlagen"', Available online: https://www.erneuerbare-energien.de/EE/Redaktion/DE/Stellungnahmen_Marktanalysen/bsw.pdf?__blob=publicationFile&v=3 (accessed 14 July 2023).

Chaffin, J. (2013), 'EU and China Settle Trade Fight Over Solar Panels', *Financial Times*, 27 July. Available online: https://archive.is/Qx5KD#selection-1519.0-1519.49 (accessed 14 July 2023).

Chen, Y. (2015), 'EU-China Solar Panels Trade Dispute: Settlement and Challenges to the EU', *EIAS*, June. Available online: https://www.eias.org/wp-content/uploads/2016/02/EU-Asia-at-a-glance-EU-China-Solar-Panels-Dispute-Yu-Chen.pdf (accessed 14 July 2023).

Cheng, E. (2023), 'Volkswagen Takes on China's EV Market with a Higher-End Car and $1 Billion Investment', *CNBC*, 21 April. Available online: https://archive.is/sTioX#selection-1909.0-1909.85 (accessed 14 July 2023).

China.Table (2023a), '"We Need to Rebuild a Solar Industry"', 25 April. Available online: https://table.media/china/en/feature/we-need-to-rebuild-a-solar-industry/ (accessed 14 July 2023).

China.Table (2023b), 'Xinjiang Becomes a Burden for German Carmakers on the Capital Market', 13 April. Available online: https://table.media/china/en/feature/xinjiang-becomes-a-burden-on-the-capital-market-for-german-automakers/ (accessed 14 July 2023).

Conte, N. (2022), 'Visualizing China's Dominance in the Solar Panel Supply Chain', *Visual Capitalist*, 30 August. Available online: https://archive.is/JkFn3 (accessed 14 July 2023).

De Gruyter (2022), „Wandel durch Handel funktioniert durchaus", De Gruyter, 29 June 2022, https://www.degruyter.com/document/doi/10.1515/pwp-2022-0020/html?lang=de

Deuber, L., C. Giesen, and F. Obermaier (2019), 'Pakt mit Peking', *Süddeutsche Zeitung*, 26 November. Nr. 273, 2.

Deutsche Welle (2019), 'Volkswagen CEO Diess "Not Aware" of China's Uighur Camps | DW News', Available online: https://www.youtube.com/watch?v=shlL4sc82l4 (accessed 14 July 2023).

Die Bundesregierung (2022), 'Rede von Bundeskanzler Olaf Scholz beim SZ-Wirtschaftsgipfel 2022 am 22. November 2022 in Berlin', 26 November. Available online: https://archive.is/Nmc4Y#selection-8145.1-8157.63 (accessed 14 July 2023).

Dohmen, F. and N. Klawitter (2017), '"Wir wurden illegal zur Strecke gebracht"', *Spiegel Wirtschaft*, 23 May. Available online: https://archive.is/HZi2P (accessed 14 July 2023).

Enkhardt, S. (2018), 'SolarWorld Files for Insolvency – Again', *PV Magazine*, 28 March. Available online: https://archive.is/SHcy3#selection-1155.0-1162.0 (accessed 14 July 2023).

European Coalition for Corporate Justice (2023), 'German Supply Chain Law Comes into Force', 10 January. Available online: https://archive.is/qmiUI (accessed 14 July 2023).

European Commission (2013), 'Memo: EU Imposes Provisional Anti-Dumping Duties on Chinese Solar Panels', 4 June. Available online: https://archive.is/Uzh58 (accessed 14 July 2023).

European Commission (2017), 'State Aid: Commission Approves Progressive Application of Renewable Energy Surcharge for Certain Self-Suppliers of Electricity in Germany', 19 December. Available online: https://archive.is/XbueO (accessed 14 July 2023).

FAZ (2022), '„Ein Rückzug aus China schneidet uns ab"', 10 November. Available online: https://archive.is/vqQLm#selection-1415.0-1415.40 (accessed 12 July 2023).

FAZ (2023), '„Die Diskussion ist nicht schwarz-weiß, und VW ist alles andere als blauäugig"', 1 April 2023. F.A.Z.-Archiv.

Feldwisch-Drentrup, H. (2022), 'Wie unsere Freiheit mit der Freiheit der Uiguren zusammenhängt', *Frankfurter Allgemeine Zeitung*, 22 November 2022. F.A.Z.-Archiv.

Feng, E. and J. Ruwitch (2022), 'The United Nations Says Crimes Against Humanity May Have Happened in China's Xinjiang', *NPR*, 31 August. Available online: https://archive.is/ISK2v (accessed 14 July 2023).

Focus (2022), 'VW hält an bisheriger China-Strategie fest', 3 November. Available online: https://archive.is/qusUj (accessed 14 July 2023).

Freytag, A. (2020), 'Kann ein Lieferketten-Gesetz die Menschenwürde wahren?', *WirtschaftsWoche*, 17 July. WirtschaftsWoche Archive.

FuturePolicy.org (2023), 'The German Feed-in Tariff', (no date). Available online: https://archive.is/OPC8u (accessed 14 July 2023).

Geier, J. (2019), 'EU und USA gemeinsam gefragt', *Süddeutsche Zeitung*, 14–15 December 2019. Nr. 289: 14.

Giesen, C. (2017), 'Nichts ist gut', *Süddeutsche Zeitung*, 28–29 October. Nr. 249: 34.

Giesen, C. and C. Hecking (2023), 'Wie China den Wiederaufbau der deutschen Solarindustrie torpediert', *Spiegel Wirtschaft*. Available online: https://archive.is/ICRKO (accessed 14 July 2023).

Giesen, C. and M. Hägler (2021a), 'Autos und Moral', *Süddeutsche Zeitung*, 19 April 2021. Nr. 89: 17.

Giesen, C. and M. Hägler (2021b), 'Der Druck auf deutsche Unternehmen steigt', *Süddeutsche Zeitung*, 9 June. Available online: https://archive.is/Y4fSt (accessed 14 July 2023).

Giesen, C., S. Hage, and F. Obermaier (2022), 'VW Under Fire for Ongoing Operations in Xinjiang', *Spiegel International*, 27 May. Available online: https://archive.is/h0mYL (accessed 14 July 2023).

Greive, M., D. Heide, K. Knitterscheidt, M. Koch, J. Münchrath, S. Prange, and C. Schlautmann (2022), '„Hauptverlierer wird Deutschland sein" –So gefährdet ist das Erfolgsmodell der deutschen Wirtschaft', *Handelsblatt*, 18 March. Handelsblatt Archive.

Haerder, M., S. Knieps, A. Maier, J. Salz, D. Schnaas, C. Schlesiger, M. Seiwert, J. Petring, and S. Wettach (2022), 'Raus aus China!?', *WirtschaftsWoche*, 25 August. WirtschaftsWoche Archive.

Hage, S. and S. Klusmann (2022), '»Ohne die Geschäfte mit China würde die Inflation noch weiter explodieren«, *Spiegel Wirtschaft*, 30 June. Available online: https://archive .is/NU2a3 (accessed 14 July 2023).

Handelsblatt (2019), 'VW-Chef wehrt sich gegen Vorwürfe zu Umerziehungslagern', 18 April 2019.

Heide, D. (2021), '„Lässt mich nicht kalt": Wie deutsche Firmen in Chinas unterdrückter Provinz Xinjiang Geschäfte machen', *Handelsblatt*, 15 July. Handelsblatt Archive.

Heißler, J. (2022), '„Chinas Regierung ist paranoid geworden"', *WirtschaftsWoche*, 27 May. WirtschaftsWoche Archive.

Höltschi, R. and M. Rasch (2022), 'Wie abhängig ist die deutsche Wirtschaft von China – Und wie gefährlich ist das?', *Neue Zürcher Zeitung*, 11 May. NZZ Archive.

Human Rights Watch (2021), '"Break Their Lineage, Break Their Roots"', 19 April. Available online: https://archive.is/dH3Qp (accessed 14 July 2023).

Jucca, L. (2023), 'China Ban Would Slow, Not Halt, Western Solar Push', *Reuters*, 3 February. Available online: https://archive.is/owSfM#selection-485.0-485.50 (accessed 14 July 2023).

Kell, G. (2022), 'Deutschland und China: Ein Plädoyer für Zusammenarbeit', *Handelsblatt*, 6 September. Handelsblatt Archive.

Koch, H. (2023), '„Vorstände gehen hohe Risiken ein"', *TAZ*, 23 January. Available online: https://archive.is/HIdmD (accessed 14 July 2023).

Koch, M. and F. Specht (2020), 'Das Lieferkettengesetz kommt – Und wird durch China zum Problem', *Handelsblatt*, 12 August. Handelsblatt Archive.

Kölner Stadt-Anzeiger (2019), 'Klare Kante zeigen! | Ministerpräsident Armin Laschet (CDU) im Interview', Available online: https://www.youtube.com/watch?v =AknKNB35rxk (accessed 14 July 2023).

Kretschmer, F. (2021), 'Empörung reicht nicht', *TAZ*, 16 February. Available online: https:// archive.is/CNDnw (accessed 14 July 2023).

Krüger, A. and P. Beucker (2022), '„Wir haben eine Verantwortung"', *TAZ*, 18 June. Available online: https://archive.is/18eIw (accessed 14 July 2023).

Lee, F. (2023, '„Wenpo, kannst du noch deine Muttersprache?": Wie Volkswagen in die Abhängigkeit mit China rutschte', *Tagesspiegel*, 16 March. Available online: https:// archive.is/0XSAg (accessed 14 July 2023).

Lester, S. (2022), 'German Ministers' Remarks May Suggest Broadening of Chinese Investment Scrutiny', *China Trade Monitor*, 29 May. Available online: https://archive.is /0SuEq (accessed 14 July 2023).

Mattheis, P. (2013), 'Der riskanteste Standort im VW-Imperium', *WirtschaftsWoche*, 22 November. Available online: https://archive.is/AyLUU (accessed 14 July 2023).

Matthes, S. (2022), 'Herbert Diess: „Wir können nicht nur mit Demokratien arbeiten"', *Handelsblatt*, 31 May. Handelsblatt Archive.

Menzel, S. (2022), 'IG Metall fordert Rückzug von VW aus Uiguren-Region Xinjiang', *Handelsblatt*, 17 June. Handelsblatt Archive.

Menzel, S. and R. Tyborski (2022), ' Risiko Lieferkette – Wie der Rohstoffmangel die deutsche Autoindustrie ausbremst', *Handelsblatt*, 8 December. Handelsblatt Archive.

Mihalascu, D. (2023), 'Volkswagen Breaks Ground On Its Second Battery Gigafactory In Europe', *InsideEVs*, 20 March. Available online: https://archive.is/mnFfP (accessed 14 July 2023).

Miller, J. (2022), 'Volkswagen and China: The Risks of Relying on Authoritarian States', *Financial Times*, 15 March. Available online: https://archive.is/gs1hA#selection-1525.0 -1525.66 (accessed 14 July 2023).

Morris, C. (2020), 'Germany's Losing Renewable Jobs', *Energy Transition*, 29 June. Available online: https://archive.is/vZQrX (accessed 14 July 2023).

Murphy, L. and N. Elimä (2021), 'In Broad Daylight: Uyghur Forced Labour and Global Solar Supply Chains', *Sheffield Hallam University and Helena Kennedy Centre for International Justice*, May. Available online: https://www.shu.ac.uk/helena-kennedy -centre-international-justice/research-and-projects/all-projects/in-broad-daylight (accessed 14 July 2023).

Müßgens, C. (2023a), '"*VW* macht sich zum Feigenblatt"', *Frankfurter Allgemeine Zeitung*, 1 March. Nr. 51: 19. F.A.Z.-Archiv.

Müßgens, C. (2023b), 'Autokonzern in der Chinafalle', *Frankfurter Allgemeine Zeitung*, 17 January. Nr. 14: 19.

Patey, L. (2022), 'Germany Can Afford to Spurn China', *Foreign Policy*, 4 November. Available online: https://archive.is/WJf2l#selection-853.0-853.33 (accessed 14 July 2023).

Ramzy, A. and C. Buckley (2019), '"Absolutely No Mercy": Leaked Files Expose How China Organized Mass Detentions of Muslims', *New York Times*, 16 November. Available online: https://archive.is/Ky43r#selection-291.0-291.89 (accessed 14 July 2023).

Rasch, M. and R. Höltschi (2022), 'VW-Rechtsvorstand Manfred Döss: «Ich kann für das Werk inUrumtschi sagen, dass uns keine Hinweise vorliegen, dassZwang auf die Werktätigen ausgeübt wird»', *Neue Zürcher Zeitung*, 30 June. NZZ Archive.

Reuters (2022a), 'Germany's Scholz: It is Clear China, Germany Are No Friends of "Decoupling"', 4 November. Available online: https://archive.is/g1psQ (accessed 14 July 2023).

Reuters (2022b), 'Volkswagen Sees China Sales on Par with 2021 as Lockdown Impact Lingers - Handelsblatt', 22 November. Available online: https://archive.is/WWxvL (accessed 14 July 2023).

Reuters (2022c), 'Germany Denies VW China Investment Guarantees Over Human Rights Concerns - Spiegel', Available online: https://archive.is/1c6cX (accessed 14 July 2023).

Reuters (2022d), 'German Dependence on China Growing "At Tremendous Pace" - IW', Available online: https://archive.is/50n44#selection-269.0-269.60 (accessed 14 July 2023).

Riecke, T. (2021), 'Europas Symbolpolitik ersetzt keine China-Strategie', *Handelsblatt*, 22 March. Handelsblatt Archive.

Rooks, T. (2022), 'Can Germany Regain Its Solar Power Crown?', *Deutsche Welle*, 8 August. Available online: https://archive.is/BYvm0#selection-515.0-515.41 (accessed 14 July 2023).

Scholz, O. (2022), 'We Don't Want to Decouple from China, But Can't be Overreliant', *Politico*, 3 November. Available online: https://archive.is/R58zr (accessed 14 July 2023).

Seiwert, M. (2023), 'Das ist der Anfang vom Ende für Deutschlands Autobauer in China', *WirtschaftsWoche*, 20 April. WirtschaftsWoche Archive.

Sigmund, T., A. Höpner, S. Menzel, D. Neuerer, and B. Fröndhoff (2022), '„Die Bilder aus China sind schockierend" –So reagieren Politik und Konzerne auf dieUiguren-Enthüllungen', *Handelsblatt*, 24 May, Handelsblatt Archive.

Smith Finley, J. (2022), 'Tabula rasa. Han Settler Colonialism and Frontier Genocide in "Re-Educated" Xinjiang', *HAU: Journal of Ethnographic Theory*, 12 (2): 341–56.

Solarwatt (2023), 'Solarenergie einfach erklärt: Nutzen, Kosten, Vor- und Nachteile', 29 March. Available online: https://archive.is/qK7tf#selection-833.0-833.64 (accessed 14 July 2023).

Specht, F. (2021), 'Das Lieferkettengesetz wird die Erwartungen nicht erfüllen', *Handelsblatt*, 14 February 2021. Handelsblatt Archive.

Stratmann, K. (2019), 'Forscher Max Zenglein: „China führt den Westen vor"', *Handelsblatt*, 27 November. Handelsblatt Archive.

Stumbaum, M.-B. (2009), *The European Union and China: Decision-Making in EU Foreign and Security Policy Towards the People's Republic of China*, Baden-Baden: Nomos.

Su, A. (2020), 'Dreams of a Red Emperor: The Relentless Rise of Xi Jinping', *Los Angeles Times*, 22 October. Available online: https://archive.is/yAGcM (accessed 14 July 2023).

Süddeutsche Zeitung (2021), 'VW verteidigt Engagement in chinesischer Provinz Xinjiang', 14 February. Available online: https://archive.is/o3QzB (accessed 14 July 2023).

Traynor, I. (2012), 'Solar Panel Spat Threatens Trade War Between China and Europe', *The Guardian*, 6 September. Available online: https://archive.is/I2t2j (accessed 14 July 2023).

Volkswagen Group (2022), 'Volkswagen Group Achieves Solid Results in 2021 and Drives Forward Its Transformation to NEW AUTO', 11 March. Available online: https://archive.is/W3K4l#selection-2951.0-2951.97 (accessed 14 July 2023).

Volkswagen Group (2023), 'Growth and Change', Available online: https://archive.is/k6UXY (accessed 14 July 2023).

Volkswagen Group Rus (2023), 'Volkswagen Group: Portrait of the Company', Available online: https://archive.is/9KlM1 (accessed 14 July 2023).

Widmann, E. and R. Shaw (2022), 'Ohne Lithium kann kein E-Auto fahren. Doch die Lieferkette ist intransparent', *Neue Zürcher Zeitung*, 8 October. NZZ Archive.

WirtschaftsWoche (2023b), '„Nicht mehr investierbar": Deka wirft VW-Aktie aus nachhaltigen Finanzprodukten', 9 March 2023.

Witsch, K. (2023), 'Deutschlands Solarindustrie muss mühsam aufbauen, was zuvor leichtfertig zerstört wurde', *Handelsblatt*, 16 February. Available online: https://archive.is/BMNjy (accessed 14 July 2023).

Xinhua.net (2018), 'China Focus: Xinjiang's outlook on Silk Road brings in industries', 12 September. Available online: https://archive.is/w8iOG (accessed 14 July 2023).

ZDF (2022a), 'Markus Lanz vom 9. Juni 2022', 9 June. Available online: https://archive.is/fX7v5 (accessed 14 July 2023)

ZDF (2022b), 'Markus Lanz vom 13. September 2022', 13 September. Available online: https://www.youtube.com/watch?v=06JG3qpXNBg (accessed 14 July 2023).

Zeit Online (2014), 'Solarbranche verliert die Hälfte der Beschäftigten', 26 May. Available online: https://archive.is/soS4N (accessed 14 July 2023).

Zenz, A. (2018), '"Thoroughly Reforming them Towards a Healthy Heart Attitude": China's Political Re-education Campaign in Xinjiang', *Central Asian Survey*, 38 (1): 102–28.

Zenz, A. (2022), 'Unemployment Monitoring and Early Warning: New Trends in Xinjiang's Coercive Labor Placement Systems', Jamestown Foundation, China Brief. Available online: https://archive.is/xVOeK.

Chapter 7

GERMANY'S LOST CROWN JEWEL KUKA ROBOTER GMBH AND BERLIN'S HUAWEI DILEMMA

7.1 The European debt crisis, US-China tech rivalry and the question of national security

The European debt crisis (2009–2010) opened up new opportunities for Chinese companies to increase their footprint in Europe. Godement and Parello-Plesner warned that China was using its economic strength to acquire strategic assets in Europe, including companies, government bonds and infrastructure contracts. They argued that China was using the financial crisis to strike bargains and play off member states against one another. Global financial reform, international governance, environmental norms and human rights could be among the issues that Europe may pay the price for in the long-term (Godement and Parello-Plesner, 2011). Europe has long been a favoured destination for Chinese investments, not least since the United States has increasingly closed the door to international mergers and acquisitions (Fromm, 2021). The Trump administration also lobbied European governments to ban Chinese IT company Huawei, concerned that 'allowing Chinese companies to develop Europe's 5G systems could be a Trojan horse . . . and could grant Beijing undue influence over the trans-Atlantic community's critical infrastructure' (Gramer, 2020).

Chapter at a glance

Against this geopolitical backdrop I investigate how the German government has responded to increasing Chinese acquisitions of German companies. A second unforeseen policy failure (UPF 2) occurred when the Midea Group quickly acquired German robotics company Kuka Roboter GmbH in 2016. Several key lessons were learned from the surprise acquisition, which subsequently led to a tightening of Germany's foreign direct investment control law. Berlin's Huawei dilemma is the focus of the second part of the book chapter. Here I probe how German regulatory authorities have investigated existing commercial partnerships which affect critical infrastructure. At the heart of the second policy punctuation analysis (PPA 2) are Deutsche Telekom's secret agreement with Huawei, security concerns regarding Chinese company's involvement in German 5G infrastructure,

Huawei's trustworthiness and the dynamics of destructive learning among key stakeholders.

7.2 Unforeseen policy failure 2 | How Germany lost its crown jewel Kuka Roboter GmbH

Knappich and Keller founded Kuka in 1898. In its early years, the Augsburg-based German manufacturer specialized in welding technology. During the period between 1920 and 1970, the company expanded its product lineup. Prior to WWII the company established itself in Europe as a market leader in municipal vehicles. In addition, the company launched a popular typewriter for travellers. In 1956, Kuka developed the first automatic welding machine for refrigerators and washing machines, marking a major development in automation. In 1973, Kuka introduced Famulus, a six-axis robot that could perform welding and assembly work. The success of this product helped Kuka establish itself as a global leader in the field of robotics (KUKA, 2023).

Following a series of mergers and acquisitions in the 1970s and 1980s KUKA established Kuka Roboter GmbH as a separate division in 1995. Kuka entered the Chinese market in 2000. In 2014 it opened a plant in Shanghai to manufacture robots of the KR QUANTEC series for the Asian market (Kuka, 2014). This was also the year the German conglomerate Voith acquired a minority stake of 25.1 per cent in Kuka Roboter GmbH. Since Voith is one of the leading providers of water turbine technology this investment came as a surprise to industry analysts (Süddeutsche Zeitung, 2014). Voith has a long history of supplying pump-turbines and motor generators for hydropower plants, including to the Beijing-based Shisanling power station in 1992 (Voith, 2023a) and the Guangzhou Pumped Storage Plant in 1994 (Voith, 2023b). Together with GE Hydro Voith-Hydro also supplied six turbines for the controversial Three Gorges Dam (Geinitz, 2010). Voith's stake in Kuka Roboter GmbH was short-lived and only lasted for about two years. Germany's technologically most advanced robotics companies were taken over by the Chinese Midea Group by 2016.

Widely described as a 'crown jewel' of modern German industry in the press (Zand, 2016; Doll and Hegmann, 2018; Stahl, 2018), the rapid takeover of a technologically leading large-scale German enterprise between August 2015 and August 2016 sent shock waves throughout Berlin and Brussels (Chazan, 2016a). Politicians realized that Chinese investors had begun targeting German companies in the field of mechanical engineering (sixty-eight companies), consumer goods (forty-three), automotive industry (thirty-eight) and electrical engineering (thirty-three) (Die Deutsche Wirtschaft, 2023). Such company acquisitions provided investors not only with market access but also with considerable know-how (2023).

Midea's takeover of Kuka Roboter GmbH

Chinese household appliance manufacturer Midea acquired 5.43 per cent of Kuka shares in August 2015. Commenting on this acquisition finance journalist Eich considered it unlikely that the new investors would seek a strategic majority of 75 per cent, not least since Voith was holding a blocking minority of 25.1 per cent (2015). However, Eich's assessment was soon proven wrong. By February 2016 Midea had already increased its stake to 10.2 per cent. In a mandatory announcement the Chinese investors made clear that Midea was pursuing strategic goals (Handelsblatt, 2016a). By May 2016 Midea had increased its stake to 13.5 per cent . That month an offer was made to buy Kuka shares for 115 euro. This offer was 35 per cent higher than the previous average share price, bringing the valuation of Kuka Roboter GmbH to 4.6 billion euros (Dostert, 2016a). An unnamed trader commented that at such a price shareholders could hardly refuse the offer and that a counteroffer from another investor was not to be expected (FAZ, 2016). A Midea spokesperson tried to assuage political concerns in Berlin, stressing that while the Chinese investor would join the supervisory board Midea did not want to conclude domination agreement, that Kuka's management would remain unchanged, and that Kuka would remain independent and listed on the German stock exchange (2016).

At that time it was also rumoured that due to German government pressure Midea would limit its share to 49 per cent (Spiegel Wirtschaft, 2016). Schönell, an analyst at Bankhaus Lampe, was not convinced, stating that '(it) would not be the first time that such promises are broken by the buyer over time' (Sperber, 2016). Another prescient commentator was Giesen, who pointed out that 'this would require the owners of the remaining 51 per cent to promise very firmly never to sell shares to Midea. How can that be done?' (2016) Giesen's scepticism was well-founded and in June 2016 Midea signed an investor agreement with Kuka (Kuka, 2016). By July 2016 Midea had already increased its share to 53 per cent. The same month the two large shareholders Voith and the entrepreneur Friedhelm Loh agreed to sell their shares to Midea (NZZ, 2016). In August 2016, only twelve months after it had bought its first 5.43 per cent share, Midea held 94.5 per cent of Kuka Roboter GmbH shares (Heise online, 2016). Only two years later CEO Till Reuter was prematurely replaced by the company's new Chinese owners (Martin, 2018). In 2019 job cuts in Augsburg and Obernburg were announced (WirtschaftsWoche, 2019). Following a squeeze-out of minority shareholders Kuka was taken off the stock exchange (Kuka, 2022). Kuka had become 100 per cent Chinese.

What lessons can be learned?

Four years after the takeover Bergermann, Petring, Husmann and Finkenzeller have drawn eight lessons from Midea's takeover of Kuka Roboter GmbH: (1) The German company's supervisory board had failed to pick up signals that one of the anchor shareholders had planned to sell its shares to a Chinese investor as early as 2014; (2) due to the party-state's industry policy Made in China 2025, Midea was able to outbid German competitors, (3) while Kuka had presented itself as a poster child of Germany's Industry 4.0, the Chinese investors soon realized that its high-end products were only marginally profitable; (4) neither the Merkel administration nor other potential investors like Daimler were willing to risk a confrontation with Beijing over Kuka; (5) the investor agreement did not stop Midea from taking firm control of the Kuka Roboter GmbH; (6) the new owners cared more about growth rates than investments in R&D; (7) Midea struggled to transfer its experiences with selling refrigerators and washing machines to the robotics market; and (8) fears of large-scale layoffs under Chinese ownership have thus far proven to be unfounded (2020).

To a certain extent Midea itself was simultaneously a short-term beneficiary of party-state patronage as well as a long-term victim of party-state policies. As Giesen pointed out as early as 2016 MIC 2025 provided an incentive for Chinese entrepreneurs to take over technologically advanced German companies. Giesen wrote that 'Chinese companies that are at the forefront of the desired industrial digitalisation are likely to hope for generous subsidies and government contracts. So if Kuka were to go to Midea, the household appliance manufacturer could benefit' (2016). This observation is important since it can help explain the unusually high offer of 115 euros per share by the Chinese investors, which thwarted Voith's reported ambitions to take control of Kuka with the help of a consortium (Handelsblatt, 2016b). But when Midea prematurely terminated the contract with CEO Till Reuter, which was valid until 2022, this decision arguably dented customer confidence. Finkenzeller and Bergermann have highlighted that '(after) all, a robot, for example in a car factory, collects every quantity of sensitive production data. The concern that this could be passed on to Chinese investors has increased rather than decreased among customers' (2020). As Alsabah has pointed out under China's tightened cyber regulations 'International businesses may have to share more data with the state than they want to' (2017). This puts into question whether Kuka Roboter GmbH can survive as a global company or will primarily serve the Chinese market in the future.

Tightening of Germany's foreign direct investment control law

The lawfirm which advised Midea during the acquisition of Kuka has suggested that the 'deal . . . is regarded by many market participants as the blueprint for a successful Chinese outbound acquisition' (Freshfields Bruckhaus Deringer, 2023). If we consider how politicians in Berlin and Brussels perceived Midea's swift acquisition of Kuka Roboter GmbH this upbeat assessment is hardly warranted. Throughout the acquisition process German economics minister Gabriel (2013– 2017) tried to find alternative investors from Germany or Europe (Bauchmüller, Dostert and Giesen, 2016). He was supported by EU's digital commissioner Oettinger, who had also called on European companies to counter Midea's offer, yet to no avail (Chazan, 2016b).

As Bauchmüller, Dostert and Giesen have pointed out Gabriel did not receive sufficient support from German industry. They also cite the President of the Federation of German Industries (BDI) Grillo as saying '(if) the Chinese want to buy something here, it's a good sign' (2016). While such a view is defensible, his comment also raises the broader question whether there is anything Germany should *not* be willing to sell to China. Deputy Chairman of the Supervisory Board Leppek has argued that the German government should have been able to organize a counteroffer with the help of the state bank KfW or the Landesbanken (Dostert, 2016a). Kuka works council member Kolb has similarly expressed his disappointment about the takeover, but more explicitly criticized the anchor shareholders when stating that 'I would have liked to see the major shareholders not give up their strategic stake because of the money' (Dostert, 2016b). The Ministry of Economics tightened the Foreign Trade and Payments Ordinance (AWV) in an attempt to make amends for its failure to prevent the takeover of Kuka by Midea. The threshold for evaluating the security-relevant companies was subsequently lowered from 25 to 10 or 20 per cent, along with the extension of screening periods (Wrage and Kullik, 2022). The Ministry of Economics was also empowered to declare a 'probable' threat to public order or security, whereas previously a 'real' threat was needed (2022). When assessing a 'likely effect on public order or security' the Ministry of Economics could also consider whether or not 'the acquirer is directly or indirectly controlled by the government . . . of a third country' (Federal Ministry of Justice, 2022). The revised AWV now stipulates that a non-EU acquirer who plans to acquire 10 per cent or more voting rights in a German company must notify the government if they are engaged in satellite earth exploration systems; autonomous cars, drones or related products; or industrial robots, to name but a few sectors (Jones Day, 2021).

Increased government scrutiny

On the European level a new framework for the screening of foreign direct investment became operational in October 2020 (European Commission, 2020). It enables the EU Commission and member states to exchange information about investments by third countries, and for the Commission to issue an opinion if it believes the investment poses a security or public order threat to multiple member states (Merics, 2020). The new FDI screening regulation was reviewed a year on. The review revealed that a significant number of transactions were approved without conditions. There were still a third of member states without an individual screening mechanism. Resource constraints, complex multijurisdictional transactions, tight deadlines and a lack of guidelines were identified as shortcomings (Schöning et al., 2021). Zenglein and Sebastian have noted that 'Chinese investments in Europe . . . which had been steadily declining since 2017, bounced back in 2021, increasing by 33 per cent year-on-year, and reaching EUR 10.6 billion' (2022). The two authors highlight that '(despite) this recovery, Chinese FDI in Europe has dropped by 77 per cent compared to the peak in 2016 of EUR 46 billion, and remains on a downward trajectory due to increased scrutiny – including stronger investment screening in Europe as well as ongoing capital controls in China – and an economic slowdown at home' (2022).

In the case of Germany the tightened FDI control law has already led to greater scrutiny of China-related company acquisitions. Berg, Heinrich, Jalinous, Kuhn, Petersen, Wienke and Kueper from the law firm White & Case have provided a comprehensive overview of increased government scrutiny. In 2022 a Chinese takeover of Elmos Semiconductor SE was blocked by the Ministry for Economic Affairs and Climate Action (BMWK) on national security grounds. In addition, the BMWK confidentially blocked a Chinese acquisition of a ERS Electronic GmbH, a semiconductor company in Bavaria. While the German cabinet approved a Chinese investment in HHLA Container Terminal Tollerort GmbH, BMWK restricted Cosco from acquiring more than 25 per cent of the company. As part of its efforts to protect healthcare products during the Covid-19 pandemic, the ministry also blocked a Chinese acquisition of Heyer, a German medical device company (Berg et al., 2022). These examples reveal the German government's ability to adopt assertive countermeasures. But as the next example will show, investment screening does not solve another problem, which is Germany's increasing dependency on Chinese IT suppliers.

7.3 Policy punctuation analysis 2 | Berlin's Huawei dilemma

Huawei's role in Germany's 5G infrastructure has been the subject of contention during the final years of the Merkel administration (2018–2021) and since the beginning of Scholz's traffic light coalition (2021–). Smith, Director of the Asia Programme at the German Marshall Fund, has described the challenge as follows: 'At the heart of the matter is how democratic states protect their societies and economies from the influence of authoritarian states, and from blackmail that may lie far in the future . . . Ultimately, Berlin must make a 5G decision that upholds and protects the values that are important to Germany' (2020). Hua and Scheuer have pointed out that during the final years of Merkel's grand coalition, different ministries pursued their own agendas: whereas the Foreign Office was concerned about security, the Ministry of Economics cared more about progress towards Germany's digitization. The Chancellery was worried about the relationship with Beijing (2019). Despite such different political agendas, Flade and Mascolo have pointed towards a shared belief across German politics, industry and even the security agencies, which is 'that hardly anyone believes the claims of the US side' (2020).

As a further complication, Chinese Ambassador Wu Ken suggested that German automobile manufacturers in China would suffer if Huawei was excluded from 5G in December 2019 (Koch, Scheuer, and Zhang, 2020). In light of the fact that VW sells 40 per cent of its cars in China, Daimler 28 per cent and BMW 25 per cent, security expert Speck has criticized Wu Ken's threat, suggesting that 'Beijing (apparently) believes it can use its economic ties with Germany as leverage to make Germany politically compliant' (Speck, 2019). Berlin thus found itself between a rock and a hard place. According to Soares and Koch 'the Chancellor's Office under Angela Merkel did not want to upset either the Americans or the Chinese' (2023). Scheuer has critiqued Merkel's grand coalition for avoiding a clear position. Since their draft security law would allow future German governments to bar Huawei, network operators who continued to rely on Huawei thereby were at high risk (2020). Such uncertainties have persisted into the Scholz era. Facing the possibility of a Huawei ban following an investigation ordered by the German Ministry of the Interior, a spokesperson of Telefónica suggested that the IT provider may sue the government for damages if they need to rebuild their network (Soares, 2023). An unnamed senior civil servant had previously suggested that the costs of removing components by Huawei or ZTE would have to be covered by IT providers themselves (Soares et al., 2023).

Telekom's secret pact with Huawei

In Spring 2023 Handelsblatt revealed that Deutsche Telekom had forged a secret pact with Huawei (Soares, Koch and Meiritz, 2023). In order to avoid possible US sanctions on Huawei products which include US components it was reported that the two companies had agreed that Huawei would provide and manage spare parts in European storage facilities (2023). Koch has criticized Deutsche Telekom for failing to heed warnings from Berlin, Brussels and Washington. Comparing the secret pact with Germany's Nord Stream 2 disaster he asked the rhetorical question 'is it so hard for the highly paid telecom managers to see the parallel between the energy partnership with Russia and the technology relationship with China? Or do they simply not care because they are only interested in short-term profits and trust the state to bail them out in an emergency? Probably the latter' (Koch, 2023). In 2020 CEO Tim Höttges had gone on the record saying that 'Deutsche Telekom is not dependent on any technological supplier today' (Süddeutsche Zeitung, 2020). In an interview Spokesman of the Deutsche Telekom Management Board Wössner has similarly argued 'we have always pursued a multi-supplier strategy – and will continue to do so. This is how we avoid dependencies' (Bünder and Jansen, 2019). While Höttges and Wössner's claim that the company would always choose from several suppliers can be taken at face value, the positive emotive appeals of their policy images should be questioned.

Drawing on industry estimates Heide, Koch and Neuerer have suggested that 'Telekom has built 65 per cent of its antenna network with technology from the Chinese company' (2023). Husmann has sharply criticized Höttges, arguing that the 'Telekom boss has long looked like a naïve friend of China' (2023a). According to IT expert Entner Deutsche Telekom had 'created facts' and that Höttges had not sufficiently prioritized security and been more concerned with being able to 'buy a good system at low cost' (2023a). A subsequent op-ed by Husmann expanded on her criticism. She criticized IT companies for seeking state bailouts when things went wrong, saying that wrong decisions were part of the entrepreneurial risk. She concluded her op-ed with a call for German mobile phone companies shouldering the costs 'for their Huawei adventure, which they have entered with their eyes wide open' (2023b). It should be noted that the German Federal Government holds about 32 per cent of shares in Deutsche Telekom AG, giving it a blocking minority. Its strong regulatory position raises questions about the governance of Deutsche Telekom. To what extent where German regulators also to blame for the company's predicament?

Security concerns and fears of sabotage

In the public debate over Huawei's role in Germany's 5G network, security concerns have been at the centre. Economics Minister Altmaier signalled early on that he had no objections to Huawei's participation. As long as their products were safe for critical infrastructure, it was up to German network providers to structure their supply chains accordingly (FAZ, 2018). Such a posture, however, also meant that the grand coalition under Merkel effectively left it up to the private sector to manage security risks. Fehr has explained Altmaier's hands-off approach by stating '(if) we hurt Huawei, we hurt ourselves. This also explains why a ruling party and its economy minister are dancing on eggshells when it comes to the issue of sanctions' (Fehr, 2019). Mayer-Kuckuk, on the other hand, offered a more upbeat interpretation. In an op-ed for *TAZ* he wrote that '(the) truth is: German companies and consumers can buy Huawei's products without worry' (Mayer-Kuckuk, 2019). He further explained that '(so) far, there is no proof that the company's devices have built-in backdoors for the secret service. IT experts doubt whether this approach to espionage is at all effective. On the other hand, Huawei offers the most advanced technology at the best price and with short delivery times, which is crucial in the construction phase of the network' (2019).

Mayer-Kuckuk's positive assessment was an outlier in the public debate. Security expert Umbach has pointed out that 'detecting suspicious "backdoors" in digital networks of critical infrastructures often takes months or even years, even if technology companies disclose the source code' (Umbach, 2020). He has further outlined that frequent software updates for 5G networks would make it even harder to detect unauthorized access to data (Umbach, 2020). Bender has similarly pointed out that '(no) operator can check the entire source code of every programme. Even an authority such as the Federal Office for Information Security is not in a position to do so in terms of personnel' (Bender, 2019). Ankenbrand, Finsterbusch and Heeg also cite IT experts who suggest that 'targeted malware can be placed in today's networks or sensitive data can be siphoned off almost unnoticed during maintenance or software updates of the hardware. The possibilities range from espionage and spying to sabotage' (2019). While Mayer-Kuckuk is right in pointing out that security reviews of Huawei technology have not (yet) revealed the equivalent of a 'smoking gun' (2019), Huawei critics arguably have a point when suggesting that one cannot give the Chinese company a 'carte blanche' either. As the following discussion will show, the real problem is not to be found on the technical but on the (geo-)political level.

How trustworthy is Huawei?

The question of Huawei's trustworthiness has been hotly contested in the public debate. Very early in the debate Kurz has summarized the conundrum as follows: 'In the end, it is probably the villainy that the respective manufacturer and its home country are believed to be capable of which will be decisive' (Kurz, 2012). As a result, the public debate has not only focused on technical issues, but also on Huawei's ownership structure. Häberli has disputed claims by Huawei that its employees are owners of the company. Instead, he has pointed out that the only two shareholders are founder Ren Zhengfei and Huawei's trade union. While the latter was holding 99 per cent of Huawei's shares, the employees could only hold 'virtual shares'. He also emphasized that in terms of upward accountability Huawei's trade union was part of the Shenzhen Federation of Trade Unions, which comes under the All-China Federation of Trade Unions (ACFTU). ACFTU, however, was under the command of the CCP (Häberli, 2020a). In an interview the China expert Heilmann has further explained that 'whoever owns shares in Huawei as an employee cannot control the company by any means. The decisions are made by a very small group of people who are probably all members of the Communist Party' (Kamp, 2019). Of particular interest has been the role of Huawei's founder Ren Zhengfei. Finsterbusch, Heeg and von Petersdorff have highlighted Ren's background as 'a trained communications engineer who once worked in one of the development departments of the Chinese People's Army' (2018).

Huawei's close relationship with the party-state is evident from the high level of state support it has received. An investigation of the *Wall Street Journal* revealed that '$75 billion in tax breaks, financing and cheap resources' (Yap, 2019) propelled the swift rise of China's tech champion. Moreover, Koch has emphasized the fact that the Chinese government forces companies to cooperate with security agencies. By doing so, the distinction between state-owned enterprises and private companies would be invalidated (2020). Despite Huawei's avowed desire to pursue purely commercial engagement, Heilmann said the company would be forced to open its doors if state security or military demanded it (Kamp, 2019). And although considering this scenario is highly unlikely, Häberli has similarly argued that '(should) Huawei be "asked" to cause network disruption in a particular country, the group is unlikely to refuse this request' (Häberli, 2020b). In light of China's autocratic system Kuhn has argued that the question of how to deal with Huawei 'is a matter of a fundamental risk assessment that can only be made politically and not technically' (2023).

The dangers of muddling through

Kuhn has also critiqued that despite recent changes to Germany's IT Security Act concerns remain about updates and remote maintenance options that could allow backdoors into systems to be built (2023). During a meeting of Germany's Interior Committee in 2021 experts had severely critiqued a draft of Germany's IT Security Act 2.0. Gärditz, a professor for constitutional law, even referred to it as an 'anti-security law' (Bubrowski, 2021). Following the criticism by IT experts the draft act was adjusted, so that the 'political and the technical audit are now detached from each other' (Christ, 2021). The final version of the act enabled the German Ministry for the Interior (BMI) to exclude deployment of components in critical infrastructure from producers who are controlled by a foreign government. Other possible criteria for exclusion included producers who have been involved in activities that have a detrimental effect on the security of Germany or its allies. The BMI could also judge whether the use of the critical component is in harmony with the security policy objectives of Germany, the EU or NATO (Bundesgesetzblatt, 2021).

The revised IT Security Act 2.0 also provided Germany's Federal Office for Information Security (BSI) with additional powers. Under the new law BSI can inspect premises to certify cybersecurity standards. And while the BSI has had its personnel increased in 2019 (Bubrowski, 2019b), Neuerer has raised doubts about the agency's impartiality. He reported that Germany's Federal Office for Information Security itself relies on Huawei technology in its communication infrastructure. More specifically he highlighted that the German government admitted in an answer to a 'small parliamentary enquiry' (*Kleine Anfrage*) of the opposition party CDU/CSU that in terms of Chinese manufacturers 'BSI uses an LTE router by Huawei for external presentations via an open internet connection' (Neuerer, 2023a). And when asked whether one can separate politics and technology in a meaningful way in an interview with Frankfurter Allgemeine Zeitung BSI President Schönbohm had previously maintained that 'the issue of industrial espionage is controllable' (Freidel, 2019) and suggested that 'sensible risk management' would suffice (2019). Following a scathing TV show Schönbohm was sacked in October 2022 (Litschko, 2022). In his investigative report German *comedian* Böhmermann had exposed the BSI president's close ties to Russian intelligence circles. Such developments have arguably undermined public trust in BSI and raise further questions about the German state's regulatory powers to monitor German IT providers procuring critical components from Chinese suppliers.

Are warnings falling on deaf ears?

Muth has argued that in technical review processes, it is next to impossible for IT providers to guarantee that its components can not be misused by security agencies (2020). The aforementioned security expert Umbach has highlighted that in the British case and according to National Cyber Security Centre (NCSC) the 'risks of using Huawei in 5G technology could never be eliminated, but at best reduced to an "acceptable level"' (Umbach, 2020). It should be noted that some of the strongest criticism of Huawei has not only come from security analysts and journalists but also from parliamentarians and representatives of Germany's security agencies. Chairman of the Parliamentary Control Committee Konstantin von Notz (Alliance 90/The Greens) has bemoaned the lack of political seriousness in dealing with security threats. Commenting on existing technological dependencies he has stated that '(if) an authoritarian and imperialist country can switch off parts of our communication infrastructure through an update, that is a risk we should not take' (Bomke, 2023). Another outspoken critic has been Vice President of the Federal Office for the Protection of the Constitution (BfV) Selen who has stated that 'of course we have a problem there, a sense of interference . . . I always find it difficult when one consciously enters into dependencies with individual companies where one knows that they are connected and integrated by the state' (Neuerer, 2023b). BfV President Haldenwang has warned of situations whereby China 'can have an influence on political events in Germany as well' (Bubrowski, 2022) through infrastructure. Common to these policy images was a highly emotive risk warning.

During a hearing of the Bundestag's parliamentary control committee President of the Federal Intelligence Service (BND) Kahl had already warned in 2019 against involving corporations that cannot be fully trusted with the task of building critical infrastructure (Bubrowski, 2019a). Allied security agencies had also warned about Huawei. Giesen and Mascolo have reported that '(not) only American diplomats have made representations to Germany with this concern, but also the intelligence services of the powerful so-called Five-Eyes network. Canadians, Australians, New Zealanders and Britons warn of far-reaching consequences: in the event of a crisis – such as a Taiwan dispute – China could paralyse parts of the network or threaten to do so. The possibility of backdoors can never be completely ruled out' (Giesen and Mascolo, 2019). The Trump administration even threatened to 'limit intelligence sharing with Berlin if Huawei Technologies Co. is allowed to build Germany's next-generation mobile-internet infrastructure' (Pancevski and Germano, 2019).

European IT suppliers to the rescue?

Fierce criticism has not only been articulated by German security agencies but also by industry associations. von der Hagen, General Manager of Die Familienunternehmer e.V., an association of German family entrepreneurs, has reprimanded the German government for sitting idle whilst 'day after day, hardware is installed by companies from countries that openly want to weaken us' (Soares, Heide, and Koch, 2022a). In light of the German government's calls on the private sector to avoid dependencies on China and to diversify abroad, along with its insistence on high safety standards when using Huawei products in 5G infrastructure von der Hagen has admonished Deutsche Telekom by stating that 'it cannot be true that German state-owned enterprises act completely contrary to what German politics demands of the private sector' (Neuerer, 2023b). According to von der Hagen Deutsche Telekom's secret involvement with Huawei should be considered 'an unbelievable disregard of governmental steering requirements' (2023b). His criticism points to a blind spot in German statecraft, which is the lack of a German industry policy which could provide greater guidance for market actors. In 2018 China expert Heilmann had already warned of China making swift progress in R&D. In an op-ed he wrote that '(the) current innovation leaders must not rest on their laurels. Companies, governments and universities in Europe will have to substantially increase and renew their efforts to promote research, innovation and education in order to maintain an edge over agile Chinese competitors' (2018).

Deputy Director at the Digital Society Institute of ESMT Berlin Schallbruch has also urged policymakers to consider an industry policy which 'only relies on European providers when building the 5G network' (Heide, 2019). Such a decision, the cyber security expert argued, could be justified on grounds of wanting to promote key European technologies from European manufacturers (2019). The German politician

Röttgen has also made the case for procuring services from Huawei competitors Ericsson and Nokia. He said that 'it's important that we stay at the forefront of a strategically crucial technology like 5G and apply it industrially accordingly', adding that 'we are not closing ourselves off, but with 5G we need special market access rules' (Kamp, 2020). Piper, on the other hand, has opposed state interference in the market economy: 'be careful especially in the selection of "Champions", even under the new circumstances' (2019). According to Piper, it is of paramount importance 'to preserve competition in a free society' (2019). But how 'free' and fair can global trade be if one of the Chinese IT suppliers benefits from high levels of state support?

Will Open RAN solve the problem?

The search for a pan-European solution to the 5G impasse has been complicated by the fact that existing 5G technology is not always compatible. While a multi-vendor approach in theory could be a sensible policy solution to minimize risks from an overreliance on one single supplier, in practice technical incompatibilities make it a rather cumbersome solution. Spokesman of the Deutsche Telekom Management Board Wössner has pointed to this problem when explaining that '(unfortunately) technologies from different manufacturers cannot be combined with each other today. In concrete terms: In an area with Huawei antennas, you cannot put Ericsson technology in between and vice versa' (Bünder, 2020).

As part of an economic stimulus package, the German government has started to support the development of Open RAN technology to the tune of 2 billion euro. This new standard will force suppliers to make both hardware and software used in 5G infrastructure interchangeable (Delhaes, Koch, and Scheuer, 2021). Journalists have pointed out that Open RAN, however, will not be a panacea either. Häberli has highlighted that while Open RAN provides IT companies with greater flexibility, it is not exactly a 'ready-made solution', as it will require specialists knowledge or services of a specialized company to make it work (2020c). And Soares, Heide and Koch have cited critics who have called attention to the fact that Chinese companies are part of the Open RAN alliance, even some which are on sanction lists of the United States (2022b).

The challenges of solving the impasse with the help of new technology standards become clearer when we consider who is likely to set the standards for the 5G successor 6G. Husmann cites a 2021 study according to which 'China leads in 6G patent applications with a rate of 40.3 per cent, followed by the USA with 35.2 per cent. Since licence fees will one day be due on every 6G-capable device, this has very far-reaching consequences. The standard will not only play its role in smartphones or cars, but also in millions of chips in the Internet of Things' (2023c). Such findings in the ongoing public debate about Huawei's role in 5G infrastructure building suggest that there are limits to technical solutions: neither will certification processes provide sufficient security nor are new industry standards readily available to support the currently preferred policy solution of a multi-vendor approach. This suggests that the Huawei saga is all but over and is likely to remain firmly on the (geo-)political agenda for some time to come.

Who were the disruptors and what were their achievements?

How to ensure the security of 5G infrastructure and prevent industrial sabotage in Germany has been subject of a heated public debate. Successive US administrations, the Five Eyes, German security agencies such as the BfV and BND, industry associations such as Die Familienunternehmer e.V., non-profit organizations such as the Digital Society Institute of ESMT Berlin, numerous IT and security experts, and scores of journalists have been at the forefront of policy punctuation. While honing in on different aspects of the debate over time, their policy images have one commonality: if in doubt, the German government and industry should err on the side of caution. Emotive appeals have ranged from calls to exclude Huawei on geopolitical grounds to proposals for a more pro-active German and European industry policy and the need for setting new technology standards.

Since by the time of writing Huawei has not (yet) been excluded from German 5G infrastructure, the question must be asked whether policy punctuation has produced *rhetorical* rather than *substantive* wins in terms of policy change. The recent decision by the management of state-owned rail operator Deutsche Bahn (DB) to procure Huawei technology for its IP network has raised concerns among DB's supervisory board as well as among state regulators (Neuerer, 2023c). Foreign policy spokesman Schmid (SPD) has called for extending the IT Security Act to cover other important sectors such as hospitals, energy suppliers or railways (Handelsblatt, 2023). It is perplexing that despite the year-long controversies surrounding Telekom's embrace of Huawei decision-makers at Deutsche Bahn considered it a good idea to entrust the embattled Chinese IT provider for its IP network. Such arguably destructive learning can in part be explained by the relatively low public standing of German security agencies. Whilst GCHQ/MI5 in the UK have had their fair share of scandals, these agencies are still held in relatively high regard by members of the British public (Lomas and Ward, 2022). The comparatively low public standing of both BfV and BND in Germany could explain why their repeated warnings against involving Huawei may have fallen on deaf ears among Deutsche Bahn decision-makers. In Germany, the Federal Office for the Protection of the Constitution (BfV) has long been criticized for its ineffective fight against far-right extremism (Gathmann, Hagen, and Teevs, 2020). It hasn't helped that BfV President Hans-Georg Maaßen (2012–2018) has widely been perceived to be on the far right of the political spectrum (Deutschlandfunk, 2023). And a survey in 2016 revealed that more than two-thirds of the German population have 'little to no trust' in the Federal Intelligence Service BND (Kurz, 2016).

7.4 What can we learn from past failures and current headwinds?

In Chapter 6 I described in unforeseen policy failure (UPF 1) how politicians and industry leaders failed to learn the lessons from the demise of Germany's solar industry and engaged in *destructive* learning. On the other hand, the unforeseen policy failure (UPF 2) with Midea's rapid acquisition of Kuka Roboter GmbH is indicative of some *creative* learning. German stakeholders learned the hard way how swift a Chinese company was able to execute its strategic plan to completely takeover a crown jewel of Germany's industrial companies. It provided the German government a first taste how competition with a state-backed economy looked like in practice. While the government was unable to organize a counter offer to prevent Midea's takeover, it subsequently tightened Germany's FDI control law. Such regulatory changes proved highly consequential when reviewing subsequent acquisitions. Broadening the scope of a 'probable' threat to public order or security also enabled the ministry to justify exclusions based on (geo-)political rather than merely on technical grounds.

The second policy punctuation analysis (PPA 2), however, tells a markedly different story. Álvarez, Goffart, Haerder, Husmann, Kuhn and Petring have pointed out that the Merkel administration could not 'find a line on how to deal with the Chinese network supplier Huawei. The back-and-forth over the expansion of the 5G network is emblematic of Germany's China policy between good business and geopolitical constraints' (2020). It is also worth pointing out that during her final months as Chancellor Merkel invested considerable political capital to pass the EU-China Comprehensive Agreement on Investment (CAI). Wettach reported about a possible CAI side deal which was supposed to secure Telekom's entry into China's lucrative mobile market (2021). Since CAI could still one day be resurrected the traffic light coalition under Chancellor Scholz's leadership thus has an incentive to postpone a decision on excluding Huawei as long as possible. Another possibility is that Wu Ken's threat in 2019 to penalize German automobile manufacturers in response to a possible exclusion of Huawei has been highly effective. In an interview former Minister of the Environment, Nature Conservation and Nuclear Safety Trittin admitted that '(we) have a huge problem with the three automobile companies and with BASF. In other words, there are four companies of systemic importance from a German perspective that have an implicit state guarantee in Germany' (China.Table, 2023). This suggests that the Chinese Communist Party continues to enjoy destructive leverage over Germany's government and industry, both in the past and in the present.

References for Chapter 7

Alsabah, N. (2017), 'China's Cyber Regulations: A Headache for Foreign Companies', *Merics*, 22 March. Available online: https://archive.is/tNMxF (accessed 17 July 2023).

Álvarez, S., D. Goffart, M. Haerder, N. Husmann, T. Kuhn, and J. Petring (2020), 'Die Huawei-Frage spaltet die Bundesregierung', 31 August. WirtschaftsWoche Archive.

Ankenbrand, H., S. Finsterbusch, and T. Heeg (2019), '"Wollen Sie wirklich das Ende von Huawei?"', *Frankfurter Allgemeine Zeitung*, 23 January, Nr. 19: 15. F.A.Z.-Archiv.

Bauchmüller, M., E. Dostert, and C. Giesen (2016), 'Deshalb ringt Gabriel um Roboterbauer Kuka', *Süddeutsche Zeitung*, 1 June. Available online: https://archive.is/FllZq (accessed 17 July 2023).

Bender, J. (2019), 'Hat Peking schon die Kontrolle?', *Frankfurter Allgemeine Zeitung*, 14 December. F.A.Z.-Archiv.

Berg, O., T. Heinrich, F. Jalinous, T. Kuhn, L. Petersen, T.-M. Wienke, and S. Kueper (2022), 'Germany Prohibits Sale of Two Companies to Chinese Investors – FDI Scrutiny in Full Swing', *White & Case*, 16 November. Availalbe online: https://archive.is/flfPZ (accessed 17 July 2023).

Bergermann, M., J. Petring, N. Husmann, and K. Finkenzeller (2020), 'Acht Lehren aus der Kuka-Übernahme', 20 May. WirtschaftsWoche Archive.

Bomke, L. (2023), '„Wir müssen die Spionageabwehr neu und besser aufstellen"', *WirtschaftsWoche*, 9 March 2023. WirtschaftsWoche Archive.

Bubrowski, H. (2019a), 'BND warnt vor Huawei', *Frankfurter Allgemeine Zeitung*, 29 October. Available online: https://archive.is/ObEFc#selection-3403.0-3403.20 (accessed 17 July 2023).

Bubrowski, H. (2019b), 'IT-Sicherheit made in Germany', *Frankfurter Allgemeine Zeitung*, 22 March, Nr. 69: 8. F.A.Z.-Archiv.

Bubrowski, H. (2021), 'Scharfe Kritik am IT-Sicherheitsgesetz', *Frankfurter Allgemeine Zeitung*, 1 March. F.A.Z.-Archiv.

Bubrowski, H. (2022), 'Bundesnachrichtendienst warnt vor Gefahr durch China', *Frankfurter Allgemeine Zeitung*, 17 October. F.A.Z.-Archiv.

Bünder, H. (2020a), '"Ohne Huawei bleiben Funklöcher"', *Frankfurter Allgemeine Zeitung*, 2 May, 22, Nr. 102: 22. F.A.Z.-Archiv.

Bünder, H. and J. Jansen (2019), '"Ohne Huawei wird der 5G-Ausbau länger dauern und teurer"', *Frankfurter Allgemeine Zeitung*, 28 October, Nr. 250: 22. F.A.Z.-Archiv.

Bundesgesetzblatt (2021), 'Zweites Gesetz zur Erhöhung der Sicherheit informationstechnischer Systeme', Available online: https://archive.is/kXqKb (accessed 17 July 2023).

Chazan, G. (2016a), 'Berlin and Brussels Wary of Chinese Robotics Bid', *Financial Times*, 13 June. Available online: https://archive.is/LyZlh (accessed 17 July 2023).

Chazan, G. (2016b), 'German Angst Over Chinese M&A', *Financial Times*, 9 August. Available online: https://archive.is/xro0f#selection-1821.0-1821.29 (accessed 17 July 2023).

China.Table (2023), '"We Need to Rebuild a Solar Industry"', Available online: https://archive.is/eVqFQ (accessed 17 July 2023).

Christ, S. (2021), 'IT-SiG 2.0: Koalition regelt „Causa Huawei" neu', *Basecamp*, 20 April. Available online: https://archive.is/buwMv (accessed 17 July 2023).

Delhaes, D., M. Koch, and S. Scheuer (2021), 'Geheimpapier: Milliarden für neue Mobilfunktechnik sollen Abhängigkeit vonHuawei verringern', *Handelsblatt*, 20 January. Handelsblatt Archive.

Deutschlandfunk (2023), 'Warum Hans-Georg Maaßen politisch hoch umstritten ist', Available online: https://archive.is/wip/2a46o (accessed 17 July 2023).

Die Deutsche Wirtschaft (2023), 'Liste der deutschen Unternehmen in chinesischem Besitz', Available online: https://archive.is/eF6Z8#selection-641.0-641.54 (accessed 17 July 2023).

Doll, N. and G. Hegmann (2018), 'Fall Kuka schürt die Angst vor China', *Welt*, 27 November. Available online: https://archive.is/aHvq0 (accessed 17 July 2023).

Dostert, E. (2016a), 'Die Chinesen sind willkommen', *Süddeutsche Zeitung*, 30 June. Nr. 149: 25.

Dostert, E. (2016b), 'Er kennt sie alle', *Süddeutsche Zeitung*, 3 August. Nr. 178: 16.

Eich, J. (2015), 'Chinesischer Konzern Midea steigt bei Kuka ein', *Finance*, 25 August. Available online: https://archive.is/N8YFo#selection-2059.0-2059.46 (accessed 17 July 2023).

European Commission (2020), 'EU foreign investment screening mechanism becomes fully operational', Available online: https://archive.is/D4KRi (accessed 17 July 2023).

FAZ (2016), 'Was wollen die Chinesen da kaufen?', 18 May. Available online: https://archive.is/mHjzJ (accessed 17 July 2023).

FAZ (2018), 'Altmaier fürchtet Huawei nicht', 14 December. F.A.Z.-Archiv.

Federal Ministry of Justice (2022), 'Foreign Trade and Payments Ordinance', Available online: https://archive.is/9qtoZ (accessed 17 July 2023).

Fehr, M. (2019b), '"Ist Huawei vertrauenswürdig, Herr Altmaier?"', *Frankfurter Allgemeine Zeitung*, 25 November. F.A.Z.-Archiv.

Finkenzeller, K. and M. Bergermann (2020), 'Griff ins Leere', 10 March. WirtschaftsWoche Archive.

Finsterbusch, S., T. Heeg, and W. von Petersdorff (2018), 'Das unheimliche Unternehmen aus China', *Frankfurter Allgemeine Zeitung*, 15 March. Nr. 63, 22. F.A.Z.-Archiv.

Flade, F. and G. Mascolo (2020), '„Das überzeugt uns nicht"', *Süddeutsche Zeitung*, 18 February. Nr. 40: 15.

Freidel, M. (2019), '"Das Thema Wirtschaftsspionage ist kontrollierbar"', *Frankfurter Allgemeine Zeitung*, 7 August. Nr. 181: 4. F.A.Z.-Archiv.

Freshfields Bruckhaus Deringer (2023), 'A Blueprint for Chinese Outbound Investment', Available online: https://archive.is/MTubT#selection-1841.14-1841.57.

Fromm, T. (2021), 'Zum Shoppen nach Europa', *Süddeutsche Zeitung*, 17–18 April. Nr. 88: 25.

Gathmann, F., K. Hagen, and C. Teevs (2020), '"Bedenkliches Verständnis vom Rechtsstaat"', *Spiegel Politik*, 22 May. Available online: https://archive.is/VQROM #selection-3975.1-3991.16 (accessed 17 July 2023).

Geinitz, C. (2010), 'China setzt auf riesige Wasserkraftwerke', *Frankfurter Allgemeine Zeitung*, 18 June. Available online: https://archive.is/0mFao#selection-1183.1-1183.41 (accessed 17 July 2023).

Giesen, C. (2016), 'So will Midea die Roboterfirma Kuka kaufen', *Süddeutsche Zeitung*, 16 June. Available online: https://archive.is/WihKW#selection-691.592-691.737 (accessed 17 July 2023).

Giesen, C. and G. Mascolo (2019a), 'Die Angst vor Chinas Hackern', *Süddeutsche Zeitung*, 21 January. Nr. 17: 17.

Godement, F. and J. Parello-Plesner (2011), 'China's Scramble for Europe', *European Council on Foreign Relations*, 11 July. Available online: https://ecfr.eu/publication/chinas_scramble_for_europe/ (accessed 17 July 2023).

Gramer, R. (2020), 'Trump Turning More Countries in Europe Against Huawei', *Foreign Policy*, 27 October. Available online: https://archive.is/V2YRP#selection-859.0-859.53 (accessed 17 July 2023).

Häberli, S. (2020a), 'Wem gehört Huawei?', *Neue Zürcher Zeitung*, 21 February. NZZ Archive.

Häberli, S. (2020b), 'Kein Huawei-Boykott: Die EU-Kommission hat die richtige Balance gefunden', *Neue Zürcher Zeitung*, 29 January. NZZ Archive.

Häberli, S. (2020c), 'Wer profitiert vom Ausschluss Huaweis aus den 5G-Netzen?', *Neue Zürcher Zeitung*, 7 December. NZZ Archive.

Handelsblatt (2016a), 'Chinesischer Großaktionär will weiter zukaufen', *Handelsblatt*, 26 February. Available online: https://archive.is/2Zrxl (accessed 17 July 2023).

Handelsblatt (2016b), 'Der Kuka-Chef trotzt Berlin', 29 June. Handelsblatt Archive.

Handelsblatt (2023), 'Bahn setzt bei Digitalisierung trotz Bedenken auf Huawei', 10 March. Handelsblatt Archive.

Heide, D. (2019), '„Die Netze sind das Schlachtfeld des Cyberkriegs"', *Handelsblatt*, 17 March. Available online: https://archive.is/cci8y (accessed 17 July 2023).

Heide, D., M. Koch, and D. Neuerer (2023), 'Regierung streitet über Huawei-Verbot', *Handelsblatt*, 3 April. Handelsblatt Archive.

Heilmann, S. (2018), 'Chinas grosse Datenplünderei', *Frankfurter Allgemeine Zeitung*, 11 March. Nr. 10: 22. F.A.Z.-Archiv.

Heise online (2016), 'Midea übernimmt Roboterhersteller Kuka zu 94,5 Prozent', Available online: https://www.heise.de/news/Midea-uebernimmt-Roboterhersteller-Kuka-zu-94 -5-Prozent-3289897.html (accessed 17 July 2023).

Hua, S. and S. Scheuer (2019), 'Wie gefährlich ist Huawei? Einblicke in das Innenleben des umstrittenen Tech-Konzerns', *Handelsblatt*, 15 March. Handelsblatt Archive.

Husmann, N. (2023a), 'Die China-Falle der Telekom', *WirtschaftsWoche*, 23 March. WirtschaftsWoche Archive.

Husmann, N. (2023b), 'Die Mobilfunkbranche soll selbst für ihre Huawei-Verträge geradestehen!', *WirtschaftsWoche*, 31 March. WirtschaftsWoche Archive.

Husmann, N. (2023c), 'Gegen Chinas Mobilfunkriesen hat der Westen keine Chance', *WirtschaftsWoche*, 28 February. WirtschaftsWoche Archive.

Jones Day (2021), 'Germany to Further Tighten its Foreign Direct Investment Control Law', Available online: https://archive.is/ST8uC (accessed 17 July 2023).

Kamp, M. (2019), '«Wenn die Staatssicherheit vor der Tür steht, wird Huawei diese öffnen müssen»', *Neue Zürcher Zeitung*, 28 May. NZZ Archive.

Kamp, M. (2020), 'Erste Konturen einer neuen deutschen Chinapolitik', *Neue Zürcher Zeitung*, 30 October. NZZ Archive.

Koch, M. (2020), '5G-Debatte: Wer Peking misstraut, darf auch Huawei nicht vertrauen', *Handelsblatt*, 30 September. Handelsblatt Archive.

Koch, M. (2023), 'Die China-Abhängigkeit großer deutscher Konzerne schadet der Bundesrepublik', *Handelsblatt*, 23 March. Handelsblatt Archive.

Koch, M., S. Scheuer, and E. Zhang (2020), 'Netzausrüster Huawei sucht die Nähe zum eigenen Staat', *Handelsblatt*, 22 June. Handelsblatt Archive.

Kuhn, T. (2023), 'Höchste Zeit für klare Kante gegen Diktatoren!', *WirtschaftsWoche*, 8 March. WirtschaftsWoche Archive.

KUKA (2014), 'KUKA Opens New Production Site in Shanghai', Available online: https:// archive.is/SJLcL (accessed 17 July 2023).

KUKA (2016), 'KUKA Signs Investor Agreement with Midea and Recommends Acceptance of the Offer', Available online: https://archive.is/9TIKr (accessed 17 July 2023).

KUKA (2022), 'KUKA AG completes Squeeze-out', Available online: https://archive.is/ jX4QP (accessed 17 July 2023).

KUKA (2023), 'Die KUKA Geschichte'. Available online: https://archive.is/YKSGC (accessed 17 July 2023).

Kurz, C (2016), 'Ansehen des BND in der Bevölkerung weiter gesunken', *Netzpolitik.org*, 27 July. Available online: https://archive.is/yD4fw (accessed 17 July 2023).

Kurz, C. (2012), 'Die ganz normale Unterwanderung des Netzes', *Frankfurter Allgemeine Zeitung*, Nr. 286, 33. F.A.Z.-Archiv.

Litschko, K. (2022), 'Schönbohm ist weg', *TAZ*, 18 October. Available online: https:// archive.is/8H6Fg (accessed 17 July 2023).

Lomas, D. W. B. and S. Ward (2022), 'Public Perceptions of UK Intelligence: Still in the Dark?', *The RUSI Journal*, 167 (2): 10–22.

Martin, N. (2018), 'German Robot Maker's CEO to be Fired', *Deutsche Welle*, 24 November. Available online: https://archive.is/h4Lzg (accessed 17 July 2023).

Mayer-Kuckuk, F. (2019), 'Ein Herz für Huawei', *TAZ*, 31 July. Available online: https:// archive.is/j300M (accessed 17 July 2023).

Merics (2020), 'New EU screening framework also targeting Chinese FDI is finally in place', Available online: https://archive.is/TKrdD (accessed 17 July 2023).

Muth, M. (2020), 'Union streitet über möglichen Freibrief für Huawei', *Süddeutsche Zeitung*, 15 May. SZ-Archive.

Neuerer, D. (2023a), 'Deutschlands oberste Cybersicherheitsbehörde setzt Huawei-Technik ein', *Handelsblatt*, 5 April. Handelsblatt Archive.

Neuerer, D. (2023b), 'Verfassungsschutz sieht Huawei-Verbindung zu Telekom und Bahn kritisch', *Handelsblatt*, 24 March. Handelsblatt Archive.

Neuerer, D. (2023c), 'Sicherheitsbedenken – Unruhe im Bahn-Aufsichtsrat wegen Huawei', *Handelsblatt*, 25 March. Handelsblatt Archive.

NZZ (2016), 'Roboterhersteller Kuka wird chinesisch', *Neue Zürcher Zeitung*, 4 July. NZZ Archive.

Pancevski, B. and S. Germano (2019), 'Drop Huawei or See Intelligence Sharing Pared Back, U.S. Tells Germany', *Wall Street Journal*, Available online: https://archive.is/b6c4X#selection-2461.0-2503.12 (accessed 17 July 2023).

Piper, N. (2019), 'Am Wendepunkt', *Süddeutsche Zeitung*, 21 March. Nr. 68: 4.

Scheuer, S. (2020), 'Berlins Entscheidung zu Huawei ist einfauler Kompromiss', *Handelsblatt*, 16 December. Handelsblatt Archive.

Schöning, F., L. Catrain, S. Kirwitzke, and E. Theodoropoulou (2021), 'EU foreign direct investment screening: Lessons learnt after a year in motion', *Hogan Lovells*, 1 December. Available online: https://archive.is/3q7oe (accessed 17 July 2023).

Smith, J. (2020), 'Welche Werte?', *Süddeutsche Zeitung*, 14 February. Nr. 37: 5.

Soares, P. (2023), 'Telekombranche klagt über möglichen Huawei-Bann', *Handelsblatt*, 13 March. Handelsblatt Archive.

Soares, P. and M. Koch (2023), 'Macht die Bundesregierung mit ihrem China-Bann einen Fehler?', *Handelsblatt*, 7 March. Handelsblatt Archive.

Soares, P., D. Heide, and M. Koch (2022a), '„Müssen Naivität dringend ablegen": Das China-Risiko im deutschen 5G-Netz', *Handelsblatt*, 25 October. Handelsblatt Archive.

Soares, P., D. Heide, and M. Koch (2022b), 'Fünf Fragen und Antworten zur 5G-Debatte und zur Rolle von Huawei', *Handelsblatt*, 25 October. Handelsblatt Archive.

Soares, P., D. Heide, M. Koch, and D. Neuerer (2023), 'Regierung plant Verbot von Huawei und ZTE im deutschen Netz', *Handelsblatt*, 7 March. Handelsblatt Archive.

Soares, P., M. Koch, and A. Meiritz (2023), 'Deutsche Telekom sicherte sich gegen US-Sanktionen ab', *Handelsblatt*, 28 March. Handelsblatt Archive.

Speck, U. (2019), 'Deutschland und Huawei: Höchste Zeit, die Reissleine zu ziehen', *Neue Zürcher Zeitung*, 19 December. NZZ Archive.

Sperber, W. (2016), 'KUKA: Darum zahlt Midea soviel', *Der Aktionär*, 23 May. Available online: https://archive.is/cOdMp (accessed 17 July 2023).

Spiegel Wirtschaft (2016), 'Chinesen wollen nur 49 Prozent von Kuka', 14 June. Available online: https://archive.is/lhtA3 (accessed 17 July 2023).

Stahl, S. (2018), 'Chinesen begehen bei Kuka den nächsten großen Fehler', *Augsburger Allgemeine*, 26 November. Available online: https://archive.is/tL8HQ (accessed 17 July 2023).

Süddeutsche Zeitung (2014), 'Voith steigt bei Kuka ein', *Süddeutsche Zeitung*, 4 December. Nr. 279: 24.

Süddeutsche Zeitung (2020), 'Telekom gegen Huawei-Bann', 14–16 August. Nr. 187: 25.

Umbach, F. (2020), 'Huawei ist nur das offensichtlichste Risiko – Das 5G-Netz als solches schafft unzählige neue Cyberangriffspunkte', *Neue Zürcher Zeitung*, 13 February. NZZ Archive.

Voith (2023a), 'Shisanling', Available online: https://archive.is/6yYpb (accessed 17 July 2023).

Voith (2023b), 'Guangzhou', Available online: https://archive.is/lBrqS (accessed 17 July 2023).

Wettach, S. (2021), 'Guter Geheimdeal – oder gefährliches Spiel', *WirtschaftsWoche*, 12 January. WirtschaftsWoche Archive.

WirtschaftsWoche (2019), 'Kuka baut in Augsburg und Franken Stellen ab', 11 December. WirtschaftsWoche Archive.

Wrage, C. and J. Kullik (2022), 'After Kuka – Germany's Lessons Learned from Chinese Takeovers', CHOICE, 21 July. Available online: https://archive.is/F7sqm (accessed 17 July 2023).

Yap, C.-W. (2019), 'State Support Helped Fuel Huawei's Global Rise', *Wall Street Journal*. Available online: https://archive.is/qSZjM#selection-1903.5-1903.51 (accessed 17 July 2023).

Zand, B. (2016), 'Merkel im Land der Maßlosen', *Spiegel Ausland*, 12 June. Available online: https://archive.is/IlEu9 (acccessed 17 July 2023).

Zenglein, M. and G. Sebastian (2022), 'Chinese Foreign Direct Investment in Europe: The Downward Trend Continues', *Industrial Analytics Platform*, December 2022. Available online: https://archive.is/JAMHX (accessed 17 July 2023).

Chapter 8

SQUANDERED GERMAN LEVERAGE AND LIMITS TO DIALOGUE AND COOPERATION WITH CHINA

8.1 *Learning the language of power?*

As I argued in Chapters 2 and 5, Germany must still learn the language of power. The expression intrigued my father, a retired senior German diplomat, when he read an earlier draft of my book manuscript. I should elaborate on this, he suggested. When I refer to power I do not mean the crude exercise of power-over someone but *leverage*. As applied to Germany's relationship with autocratic China, leverage is understood 'as a form of power' (Anderson, 2014, 5) that can be used either *constructively* or *destructively*. It is described by Anderson as a lever and fulcrum that uses a minimum amount of effort to produce a maximum force (2014). He distinguishes between *bargaining, resource* and *investment* leverage (2014, 5–7). For the topic of this book chapter, *bargaining leverage* is most relevant. Anderson cites Shell, a theorist of negotiations who further distinguishes between *threats-based* (e.g. making the other side worse off), *needs-based* (e.g. uncovering what the other side wants) and *normative* (e.g. skillful use of standards and norms) leverage (2014, 6).

Chapter at a glance

My purpose in this chapter is to explore the extent to which Germany has been able to leverage its considerable official development assistance (ODA) to China since the early 1980s to promote socio-economic and political change in the country. The third unforeseen policy failure involves criticism of the Chinese party-state's instrumentalization of Germany's development agency GTZ/GIZ. My goal here is to trace the slow pace of policy-based learning on the German side. Even though early signs of cooptation were evident in 2006, it took sixteen years for the German government to act on this insight. The third policy punctuation analysis explores the public debate surrounding the principles and practices that underlie international cooperation with China in the second part of the chapter. Based on rival op-eds by Taube and myself, I demonstrate that open-ended dialogue and cooperation have been severely undermined by the rise of a security state under Xi. Any future-oriented calls for renewed dialogue and cooperation with China are incomplete if they neglect to incorporate lessons learned from squandered leverage over more than forty years of German China engagement.

8.2 Unforeseen policy failure 3 | Cooptation of
German development agencies in China

OECD's Development Assistance Committee (DAC) defined ODA in 1969 as foreign aid provided by governments for the purpose of advancing economic development and welfare in developing countries. Before 2018, in order to qualify as ODA, foreign aid would need to be 'concessional in character and [convey] a grant element of at least 25 per cent (calculated at a rate of discount of 10 per cent)' (OECD, 2023). Since the early 1980s, Germany has provided substantial ODA to China. Between 1982 and 2018, annual ODA flows ranged from 100 to close to 600 million euros. The KfW state development bank has provided 'soft loans' to China as part of ODA flows to China that 'must be paid back in full at concessional terms and originate from market funds, which are formally approved, but not funded by the BMZ' (Zajac and Kaplan, 2021). Both Financial Cooperation (FC) and Technical Cooperation (TC) have traditionally aimed to reduce poverty and promote social development. State and non-state development agencies in Germany receive funding for TC from the Ministry for Economic Cooperation and Development (BMZ). But why have successive German governments continued to provide ODA to China, which experienced an economic boom after WTO membership in 2001 and hardly can be considered a developing country any more?

Public debate over German ODA flows to China intensified during the early 2000s. Following China's successful launch of its first manned space flight, *The Economist* published a widely noted cover story titled 'Congratulations, China (So no need for any more aid, then?)' (2003). German conservative politicians such as Steffen Kampeter and Eckard von Klaeden subsequently questioned the wisdom of continuing development aid to China (Blume, 2006). Along with these external pressures, ODA delivery modalities were criticized within the community of development practitioners. A call was made for more inclusive aid, or what is known today as political philanthropy. A complex system approach was needed to provide effective aid, critics argued, which required 'stepping back from the intricacies of individual projects and programmes and gaining an understanding of the relationships that link the various actors' (Hinton and Groves, 2004, 5). A key to achieving this was to reflect on the critical and dynamic choices of aid actors regarding (1) development approaches, (2) development methodologies, (3) core concepts or values, (4) perception of primary stakeholders, (5) accountability, (6) the relationship between aid providers and recipients, (7) procedures, (8) organizational pressures and (9) philosophy of change (2004, 7).

Participatory development vs. dialogue and network management

Back in the early 2000s, I was part of a community of social development professionals who were driven to reform the aid system. During 2003 to 2007, I worked simultaneously for German and Chinese aid agencies while writing my dissertation on Sino-German development cooperation. Between 2002 and 2004 I also served as an advisor to the BMZ-sponsored sector project

'Mainstreaming Participation' at the Policy and Strategy Division of Germany's bilateral development agency Gesellschaft für Technische Zusammenarbeit (GTZ) GmbH. I was the lead author for the country case study 'China. Authoritarian yet participatory?', which was commissioned by the BMZ and published by GTZ (2006). Study findings highlighted opportunities for political participation within existing Sino-German development initiatives. As part of its call for an active engagement with China, the study also explored strategies for supporting the development of China's nascent civil society. The study was aimed at helping the BMZ promote participatory development, which was 'defined as a process that actively and meaningfully involves people in all decisions that affect their lives' (BMZ, 1999).

The German Development Institute (DIE) published another study in 2006 commissioned by the BMZ that painted a strikingly different picture of Sino-German development cooperation. The study highlighted that when it comes to technical cooperation (TC) with China 'the role of TC experts in China is more that of dialogue and network managers and less – as in other developing countries – that of patient, long-term process support in the context of building local capacities and institutions' (Wolff, 2006). This insight is remarkable, as it suggests a highly circumscribed agency for German development practitioners. In the case of both financial cooperation (FC) and TC the DIE study also revealed that key Chinese partner organizations such as 'MOF and MOFCOM do not have a strategic view of German [development cooperation]. . . they do not see [it] as having the task of influencing internal processes and driving forward reforms, but only as an instrument to serve particular Chinese interests and the acquisition of know-how for individual institutions' (2006). The DIE study showed that in the case of Sino-German development cooperation, managerial approaches were seen as dominating the field. Rather than supporting comprehensive socio-economic and political change in China, Sino-German development cooperation was portrayed in a passive manner. Dialogue and cooperation with China was seen as an end in itself. Additionally, the DIE study suggested that Chinese cooperation partners had effectively coopted German development agencies. This is a very important finding, as the following discussion will show.

Policy to practice gap

Based on my practical experience in China between 2003 and 2007, I authored a PhD thesis on promoting participatory development in China (Fulda, 2009a). As a well-informed insider I could observe shifting organizational identities of German state and non-state development organizations. In my published monograph, I criticized the German government's policy to practice gap. While the BMZ had long claimed to be in favour of participatory development and the active involvement of citizens in processes that affect their lives (1999, 2), the institutional setting in autocratic China severely limited the effectiveness of individuals and organizations contributing to such outcomes. I was particularly critical of the German bilateral development agency GTZ, which had lost most of its organizational autonomy to MOFCOM, its main cooperating partner (Fulda, 2009b, 103–8). Additionally, I criticized German political foundations for their lacklustre attempts to engage with China's nascent civil society during the semi-liberal early years of the Hu administration (2009b, 111–14). As a final note, I advocated greater parliamentary oversight and assisted the Free Democratic Party (FDP) caucus of Germany in drafting a small inquiry (*Kleine Anfrage*) and a parliamentary motion in 2008, which was subsequently discussed in the German Bundestag (2009b, 115–18; Murphy and Fulda, 2011).

Reform efforts of this kind failed. In 2008 BMZ Minister Wieczorek-Zeul declared an end to financial cooperation with China, which should be replaced by 'a strategic partnership of the entire German government with China in order to advance reform processes there in the areas of justice, society and climate protection' (Asienhaus, 2008). In addition, following the General Election in 2009, the new BMZ Minister Dirk Niebel declared the end to technical assistance to China in 2012 (Fuchs and Thomas, 2009). Ironically, the China portfolio of the Center for International Migration and Development (CIM) was a casualty of this policy decision. Besides being a division of GTZ, CIM also forms a working group with the work placement agency Zentralstelle für Arbeit (ZfA). During the early 2000s Horst Fabian, the CIM's programme director for China, had placed numerous German and European experts in Chinese government-organized non-governmental organizations (GONGOs) as well as grassroots NGOs (Fulda, 2009b, 108–9). Between 2004 and 2007, I was an integrated CIM expert for the GONGO China Association for NGO Cooperation. CIM had created a cooperation channel for supporting the growth and maturation of China's nascent civil society where there was none before. It is not without irony that the *German side* terminated the highly innovative CIM programme in 2012.

Old wine in new bottles?

Paradoxically, Germany's *international cooperation* with China intensified even as *development cooperation* was formally phased out by the BMZ in 2008 and 2009. In subsequent years, German ODA to China increased substantially (Zajac and Kaplan, 2021). Besides the BMZ, which had traditionally been responsible for funding development aid, the Federal Ministry for Environment, Nature Conservation, Nuclear Safety and Consumer Protection (BMUV), the Federal Ministry of Education and Research (BMBF) and the Federal Ministry of Economics and Climate Protection (BMWK) became funders in their own right. After a merger of GTZ, DED and InWent on 1 January 2011 the Deutsche Gesellschaft für Internationale Zusammenarbeit (GIZ) GmbH was established (Nabiyeva, 2011). According to Thorsten Giehler, Country Director in China, GIZ operates bilingually and interculturally based on a 'broad network' in the state (2019). In his essay Giehler complained that 'the scale of exchange between Germany and China and between Europe and China remains relatively modest. Compared with transatlantic relations, mutual understanding and dialogue are still very limited' (2019).

Giehler had been more direct on his Twitter account. A now deleted tweet stated that '(the) biggest challenge is to redefine EU's foreign policy outside the Western alliance, being equidistant from the US and China. There is no "side by side with the US" in a #ColdWar' (@thorstenbenner, 2022). In 2020 Giehler also shared a tweet by the Qiao-Collective, which denied human rights abuses against the Uyghurs with the words 'interesting compilation of resources and studies' (Heide, 2020). As a result of public criticism, he first deleted his tweet and then his entire Twitter account (2020). While he had used the account in his private capacity, his profile picture had made it clear that he was representing GIZ (Heide, 2022). The journalist Heide has further outlined that '(not) only with this, but also with numerous other political posts on Twitter, he opposed his main client, the German government, and argued in favour of the Chinese state leadership' (2022).

Why did policy learning take sixteen years?

A leaked cable of the German Embassy in Beijing has revealed that as of 2022 patience with GIZ China is now wearing thin. In a confidential report a fundamental rethink of GIZ projects was called for. Signed by Frank Rückert, the acting Chargé d'Affaires of the German Embassy, the cable recommended that 'more than before . . . the cooperation measurably takes into account our goals and delivers sustainable results' (Heide, 2022). As part of a critical review of current cooperation more attention should be paid to risks such as 'one-sided knowledge and technology transfer, white- and greenwashing and the (involuntary) promotion of strategic Chinese interests' (2022). Furthermore, the cable's author argued that 'cooperative approaches in the climate and energy sector (. . .) face the challenge of not subordinating [Germany's] interest in combating global climate change to [China's] industrial policy interests in green technology and corresponding market leadership' (2022). The leaked cable from 2022 is remarkable insofar as many of the underlying problems were already known to the German Federal Government as early as 2006, when the aforementioned DIE study was published.

The DIE study had clearly shown that the Chinese party-state was instrumentalizing German development agencies like GTZ. The Twitter posts of GIZ Country Director Giehler revealed that twelve years later the GTZ successor organization GIZ had moved even closer into the orbit of 'official China'. From a longitudinal perspective, the German government could have known early on about the problem of party-state cooptation. Another learning opportunity was the parliamentary inquiry and the parliamentary motion of the German Free Democratic Party (FDP) caucus in 2008. In 2009, my PhD thesis criticizing Sino-German development cooperation was published as a German-language book. Due to the many learning opportunities for key stakeholders, it is remarkable that it took the German government until 2022 to reign into GIZ China operations.

This can be explained as follows: successive German governments had signalled that dialogue and cooperation with China is an end in itself. In my PhD thesis I had observed that '(more) important than the achievement of a specific political goal is the maintenance of cooperative relations, even if these can no longer be described as cooperative' (Fulda, 2009a, 114). Once international cooperation is seen as an end in itself, an overly pragmatic and procedural approach also means that partnership models are no longer sufficiently scrutinized: the key question of whether the organizational autonomy of GTZ/GIZ is still sufficiently protected was no longer asked.

8.3 Policy punctuation analysis 3 | Limits to dialogue and cooperation with autocratic China

In the first conceptual part of the book I discussed the role of paradigms in Germany's foreign policy behaviour towards autocracies. In Chapter 5, I asked the question whether the paradigms of 'Change through rapprochment', 'Rapprochement through interweaving' and 'Change through trade' had also shaped public debates in specific policy subfields. This second analytical step was recommended because policymakers and practitioners might defend their respective policy monopolies with policy images that differ from the three paradigms mentioned above.

The third policy punctuation analysis (PPA 3) is concerned with what principles and practices underlie international cooperation with China. Specifically, it addresses the issue of *dialogue* and *cooperation* under conditions of *censorship* and *coercion*. A remarkable op-ed by German economist and sinologist Taube was published in *WirtschaftsWoche*, a widely read business magazine, in June 2022. A striking policy image was at the centre of his argument. It consisted of a litany of complaints about the direction of travel under Xi Jinping in terms of empirical information. Among other things, Taube criticized the harsh Zero-Covid policy, the resulting lockdowns, human rights abuses in Xinjiang and the propagation of Russian war narratives. The author also criticized 'change through trade' because it implied that only liberal democracies could achieve economic success. 'Western transfers' created the economic basis of a regime incompatible with our values, according to Taube.

The emotive appeal that followed was surprisingly upbeat and contained a rhetorical question: 'And now? Should the West now withdraw from China, downgrade cooperation across the board and try to block China's further development? Certainly not. It is too late for containment' (Taube, 2022). The following two reasons make such an emotive appeal highly problematic. The first error Taube made was employing a straw man fallacy (Walton, 2013), attacking a position of *full decoupling* and *containment* that no one in the German discourse endorsed. As a second point, by claiming that 'it is too late for containment' Taube echoed what former deputy national security advisor Pottinger called 'United Front propaganda and psychology' (Policy Exchange, 2020) and the CCP's overseas propaganda theme 'we own the future, so make your adjustments now' (2020). I consequently offered *WirtschaftsWoche* to publish an op-ed in reply.

Is international cooperation with China an end in itself?

Two weeks later, my own op-ed in response to Taube's essay was published in *WirtschaftsWoche* (Fulda, 2022). While I affirmed the desirability of an open-ended dialogue with China I argued that Taube's advocacy for a 'values-based policy and corporate governance' was logically inconsistent with his call for 'unemotional' and 'free from ideology' engagement with China (2022). In my competing policy image, I criticized Kissinger's doctrine whereby in the pursuit of common interests with autocracies value differences should be downplayed. I also highlighted the aforementioned DIE study from 2006, which showed that Chinese authorities do not let their German partners have any meaningful input on internal reforms. In order to make the emotive case, I argued that dialogue and cooperation will degenerate into an end in themselves if the arbitrary restrictions imposed by China are not critically reviewed. There was an urgent need to evaluate current partner models and collaboration projects. German enlightened interests would be served by ending agreements if they were no longer cooperative and reciprocal (2022).

My contribution was later summarized as follows on the website of the Institute of East Asian Studies at the University Duisburg-Essen: 'Andreas Fulda pleads for renouncing dialogue with China if it is not possible to enforce "Western values" in the cooperations' (IN-EAST, 2022). My critique was caricatured instead of engaging it head on: a simplified version that made it appear I was arguing from the vantage point of cultural superiority.

Such a misrepresentation of my original argument is not only harmful to our culture of conflict (*Streitkultur*) but also does not contribute to our understanding about Germany's *bargaining leverage* vis-à-vis autocratic China.

Since Taube himself had argued in favour of a 'values-based policy and corporate governance' (2022) he should have also identified the available *levers* for the German state, private sector and civil society to put such values into practice. Instead, Taube's remedy was 'as much dialogue and contact as possible' (2022). This resembles what the international relations expert Tempel called the Steinmeier doctrine: 'infinite patience for talks under the most difficult conditions and an almost inexhaustible belief in the power of dialogue' (IPG, 2016). Here the problem remains that placating authoritarian partners in an unconditional China engagement requires the tacit acceptance of censorship and other red lines, for example, in terms of politically circumscribed dialogue topics, cooperation partners and collaboration methods. As the next sections will show such a strategic approach is ultimately self-defeating.

It takes two to tango

It is possible that sceptical readers will still not be convinced by my critique of Taube's op-ed. Didn't he also make valid points about finding common grounds for dialogue and cooperation, and slowly building a new mutual understanding and trust? (Taube, 2022) And wasn't it true when he pointed out that 'Europe and China have common interests' and that '(at) the top of the list are the green transformation and the realisation of global goals for sustainable development' (2022)? As far as I'm concerned, Taube's *ambitions* aren't the problem in this debate. In an ideal world, dialogue and cooperation should indeed prevail over conflict. But as the saying goes, it takes two to tango. While the German side can unilaterally signal their willingness for dialogue and cooperation, it is ultimately up to the Chinese Communist Party whether or not to accept such overtures. In other words, there can be no reckoning without the host.

The rise of wolf warrior diplomacy under Xi Jinping was already discussed in Chapter 3. A case in point would be a delegation of the Free Democratic Party (FDP) visiting Hong Kong before travelling on to mainland China in 2019. As part of the German delegation's visit to Hong Kong, it met with both members of the HK SAR government and opposition leaders. It is unfortunate that the German delegation was given the short shrift in Beijing, even though photos from the meetings in Hong Kong were posted on social media only after the visit to China. Retribution was meted out by cancelling meetings last minute. During one of the meetings which took place, a Chinese official reportedly shouted at the delegation for 30 minutes (Heide, 2019). Besides the lack of decor, such grandstanding indicates that dialogue with Beijing is not unconditional. In political and practical terms, this means that dialogue opportunities are withheld if and when representatives of the Chinese Communist Party believe their Western counterparts have crossed a red line (like meeting with democratic leaders in Hong Kong). Another prominent example is the reaction to Nancy Pelosi's visit to Taiwan in 2022. As well as sanctioning the Speaker of the House of Representatives, Beijing temporarily halted the US-China 'dialogue on climate change, military issues, and other cooperation in the fight against crime, drugs, and repatriation of illegal immigrants' (WirtschaftsWoche, 2022). Therefore, a compartmentalized approach to dialogue and cooperation with China does not solve the overall problem of dealing with political risks in the relationship. Even when Western officials tip-toe around party-state sensitivities, CCP officials can at any point tie perceived sleights in one policy arena to justify withholding dialogue and cooperation in another.

Growth of China's civil society and civil society links between Europe and China

In this context, it is crucial to highlight how much space has been closed for constructive engagement with Western China under the Xi regime. In Chapter 3 I argued that China was infinitely more open during the period of reform and opening up (1978–2012) in comparison to the Xi era (2012–). There were frequent people-to-people exchanges on political, economic and social levels. For Chinese reformers and their foreign supporters, there were at least some grey areas that could be creatively exploited. One example of this was the Fourth World Conference on Women in 1995, which helped kickstart China's NGO sector. And while in the following years China scholars held highly theoretical debates on whether or not the concept of civil society could be applied to China (Johnson, 2003, 551), Chinese citizens started establishing civic organizations which had at least some autonomy from the party-state. An organization of this type was the Institute for Civil Society (ICS) in Guangzhou. In 2011, Kamp described how ICS created itself enough space to run with the help of a collaborative relationship with the local government (2011).

One of its partners in Europe was the Stiftung Asienhaus, a non-profit organization based in Cologne. A workshop on 'Sustainable Community Building and Grassroots NGOs' was organized by both organizations in Guangzhou in 2010 (Stiftung Asienhaus, 2010). In addition, ICS became a partner of the EU-China Civil Society Dialogue Programme (2011–2014), a four-year dialogue and delivery initiative implemented by the University of Nottingham together with six consortium partners (Fulda, 2015). Support for this initiative came from the European Commission (EC) and the British Foreign and Commonwealth Office (FCO). It demonstrated that collaboration between the Chinese government and civil society could still be advanced with European support at the dawn of the Hu era and the beginning of the Xi era.

Such constructive cooperation between European and Chinese civil societies only lasted for a short period of time. In 2017, the party-state began implementing its draconian Overseas NGO Law (hence ONGO law). The impact of the law was well described by Sausmikat, a German sinologist and civil society practitioner with many years of collaboration experience: 'Ties that have grown over the years between China's civil society and the democratically formed societies of the West are obviously no longer wanted,' she was quoted. 'These bridges to Europe are in danger of being torn down. That is catastrophic' (Giesen and Strittmatter, 2017).

The Overseas NGO Law casting a long shadow

I would argue that anyone who still advocates continued Western China engagement in China's Xi era also needs to educate the German public about the detrimental effects of the ONGO law. It was announced by Yang Huanning in late 2014 that the party-state would no longer tolerate foreign NGOs by simply registering. As a result of a new law, they would be required to obtain express permission by the Ministry of Public Security (MPS) to operate in China (WirtschaftsWoche, 2014). A chilling effect was already felt before the new law took effect. I was unable to publish the fully transcribed and translated interview I conducted with a leading foundation representative in Beijing in Summer 2014 due to concerns within the organization that such an – in my opinion relatively harmless – interview might compromise its China operations. In an op-ed for the German newspaper *FAZ* two years later, German China scholar Lang offered the following policy image to describe the situation: the political climate was marked by suspicion about foreign infiltration, a disturbing trend towards instrumentalizing nationalist sentiments under Xi, and a growing discrimination against foreign organizations. With regard to its emotive appeal, Lang provided a bleak outlook 'for Chinese as well as foreign NGOs with political ambitions, life and work under the suspicious eye of the police ministry is therefore likely to become even more unpleasant in the future' (2016). Strittmatter quoted another Shi-Kupfer, another German China scholar, describing the situation as a 'selective closing' of China (2016b).

The highly illiberal ONGO law had the effect of further entrenching self-censorship among Western non-profit organizations. Kolonko cited a German NGO practitioner who observed that many foundations were refraining from addressing politically sensitive issues that they had previously addressed. Many foreign organizations had already scaled back or terminated their projects in

China prior to the enactment of the law (Kolonko, 2016). Moreover, three years after the enactment of the ONGO law, Böge stated 'you can tell how much pressure international organisations are under in China not by what they say, but by what they don't say' (2020). As Shi-Kupfer and Lang warned early on in a coauthored op-ed, 'putting pressure on the Chinese government can probably only help in individual cases; it won't bring about fundamental change. The new NGO law is here to stay and it's going to change the way liberal democracies in Europe and other parts of the world engage with China' (Shi-Kupfer and Lang, 2017). The following discussion will demonstrate that their bleak assessment turned out to be prophetic.

Effects of the ONGO law on European and Chinese NGOs

From 2017 until 2019 I was the principal investigator for a Ford Foundation-funded research project which monitored and evaluated the state of implementation of China's ONGO law. Together with a team of consultants we documented the intended and unintended consequences of the law for European non-profit organizations and their Chinese partners. Around twenty-four in-depth interviews with leaders and co-workers of European NGOs in Germany, Netherlands, France, United Kingdom and Italy were conducted. They informed seventeen anonymized case studies. The latter revealed that open-ended dialogue and cooperation had become a thing of the past. Civil society trust networks had been replaced by centralized and strictly controlled party-state power hierarchies (UoN, 2019a). A European organization saw its role changed from innovative driving force and know-how carrier reduced to that of a junior service partner and executing agency (UoN, 2019b). In the case of another organization the Chinese partners had started to dictate the rules of cooperation and – though the European organization was the funder – the price, too (UoN, 2019c). Yet another INGO could no longer continue its China-related activities and had to close its small grants programme (UoN, 2019d). What's more, a European NGO which worked on human rights and the promotion of the Sustainable Development Goals (SDGs) had to close its China programme and the European staff in China had to leave the country (UoN, 2019e).

More service-oriented European NGOs, on the other hand, fared better. One organization envisaged a permanent engagement with China and thus did not consider the restrictions a reason to disengage (UoN, 2019f). Another European social development NGO believed that an atmosphere of cooperation still existed, and that its local partners wanted it to succeed and continue their work (UoN, 2019g). An international campaigning organization reported that under the ONGO law informal meetings could still take place, but only with well-established Chinese contacts (Uon, 2019h). Another European organization noted that local partners now proposed much less adventurous project designs and that their appetite for overseas funding had considerably cooled (UoN, 2019i). This sentiment was not universally shared. While noting a greater cautiousness when working with international NGOs (INGOs), a European NGO specialising in children's rights did not notice that its partners feared political trouble or that they had withdrawn from projects (UoN, 2019j). In the case of an European NGO supporting agricultural cooperatives and farmer organizations the survival strategy has to be completely in line with the objectives of the party-state (UoN, 2019k).

Taking part is not everything

During the Hu era, Yunnan, a southern province bordering Vietnam, Laos and Myanmar, had a very active NGO scene. According to Böge, there were approximately 160 foreign organizations operating in the region by 2009, many of them motivated by Christian beliefs. As soon as they were required to register with a state organization, this number decreased to forty-eight. After the ONGO law came into effect in 2017, only twenty-five remained (Böge, 2018). As China expert Sidel correctly points out, instead of 'restricting civic space across the board . . . China is molding the kind of third sector it wants – one that is focused on service provision, charity and capacity building' (2019, 673). The new law also allowed the party to shape the political foundations of Germany in accordance with its own objectives. In Germany every major political party has an affiliated foundation. The German state funds these organizations and they are responsible for promoting democracy abroad (Pogorelskaja, 2002). In my published PhD thesis, I criticized that only two German political foundations – HBS and KAS – were willing to support China's growing civil society sector (Fulda, 2009b, 177). As a consequence of the ONGO law, the political foundations' work in China came to a grinding halt (WirtschaftsWoche, 2017).

Due to the foundations' legal limbo, then German Ambassador Clauß wrote a stern letter to China's powerful Central Political and Legal Affairs Commission (中央政法委) (Giesen and Strittmatter, 2017). According to Strittmatter, German support for a new –'people-to-people dialogue' proposed by the Chinese side was contingent on the party-state registering German political foundations (Strittmatter, 2017). Although such pressure paid off, the resulting dialogue forum was characterized as a 'people-to-government' meeting. Strittmatter cites an unnamed participant complaining that '(in) China, repression against civil society is on the rise and the influence influence of the West is being actively pushed back by the party . . and we are here as staffage for an event in which China wants to demonstrate to foreign countries how supposedly open they are' (2017). The political foundations KAS, HBS and RLS were subsequently coerced to partner with the Chinese People's Association for Friendship with Foreign Countries (CPAFFC) (CDB, 2017). Diamond and Schell note that CPAFFC is part of China's united front bureaucratic structure, which aims to enhance the rule of the CCP to increase the country's influence abroad (2018, 30). While the Merkel administration succeeded in registering three of five German political foundations, this 'success' in fact came at a very high price: the almost complete neutralization of German political foundations as critical actors in the aid system.

Have German political foundations become sitting ducks?

During China's so-called 'reform and opening up' period (1978–2012) increasing numbers of German political foundations set up their representative offices in China. There were many tangible benefits of having a permanent representative on the ground: they could gain a better understanding of the local situation and could develop relatively lasting and trusting relationships with their key partners (Erdmann, 1999, 144). In theory at least, this provided country representatives of German political foundations with the 'opportunity for direct value-oriented influence and debate' (1999, 146). It is important to point out that German political foundations should be regarded as mission-based organizations, not as self-styled 'neutral' service providers like GTZ/GIZ. Following the enactment of the ONGO law the previously existing limited space for active engagement however almost completely disappeared. The ONGO law and other anti-liberal laws such as China's National Security Law (2015), the National Intelligence Law (2017) or the recently revised Counter-Espionage Law (2014/2023) have considerably increased political risks for both foundation representatives and their staff.

In China's Xi era representatives offices of political foundations in China should no longer be considered an asset but a liability. The Friedrich Naumann Stiftung (FNS) had to close its Beijing office following a Tibet conference in Bonn in 1996 (Böge, 2020). In order to avoid the FNS' fate German political foundations with a representative office have always had a strong incentive not to engage in public activities in Germany which could be perceived as overly critical of the party-state. This means that while German political foundations could in theory warn the German public of pitfalls in Western China engagement, they are reluctant to do so, as this could jeopardize their China operations. The fate of the FNS office in Hong Kong is instructive here. It was opened in 2018 and closed only two years later due to the Hong Kong National Security Law (2020) (Paqué, 2020). The FNS subsequently relocated to Taipei (FNF, 2023). In 2020 the Konrad Adenauer Stiftung was also accused by the pro-Beijing newspaper –*Ta Kung Pao* to be 'the US Central Intelligency Agency's right hand in Europe' (Wenhui wangxun, 2020). During one of the many roundtable meetings which took place in Berlin to discuss the effects of the ONGO law I recall a stunning account of a German co-worker of a political foundation. The individual described how Chinese police officers had treated German staff like a criminal. The incident had taken place during a routine investigation of the foundation's filed paperwork. I was struck that this account did not prompt a wider discussion about the risks and demerits of keeping representative offices in China.

Who were the disruptors and what were their achievements?

The public debate about principles and practices of international cooperation with China was dominated by journalists and academics. The policy images employed in the debate were uniformly critical of Xi's hard authoritarian turn. As far as emotive appeals were concerned, there was a sense of resignation. Also noteworthy is the lack of voices from field practitioners. With the exception of Sausmikat, many prominent European civil society practitioners remained quiet. A good explanation for this is that many European non-profit organizations found themselves in an uncertain position because of the ONGO law. As part of our Ford Foundation project, we had to invest considerable time and energy into building trust with our European interviewees. To address concerns that participating in our study could jeopardize their organizations in China, we anonymized the seventeen case studies as much as possible. It is indicative of Beijing's power and reach that European non-profit organizations and their Chinese partners have been so cautious. The discussion also showed that three years before its enactment in 2017, the ONGO law was already casting a long shadow. Following its enactment, this law greatly increased self-censorship among European civil society practitioners. In the language of Anderson, the ONGO law can be considered as an example of the CCP's *destructive leverage* (2014, 7) over German and European non-governmental organizations.

Taube's call for dialogue and cooperation with China under conditions of censorship and coercion was unconvincing. It is not enough to praise dialogue and cooperation without taking stock of previous failures to establish a more collaborative relationship, I argued in my response. Developing a good relationship with China cannot be reduced to intercultural competence, either. China expert Heilmann predicted in 2016 that 'hard conflict' would become a defining feature of Germany's relationship with China which would require 'hard resistance' in response to Beijing's increasing interference in inter-societal exchanges (Strittmatter, 2016a). I also argued in my reply to Taube's op-ed that 'freedom of expression is the necessary prerequisite for intercultural dialogue' and that '(the) possibilities for dialogue and cooperation therefore depend on whether autocratic China will accept to tolerate differences of opinion' (Fulda, 2022). A better relationship between Germany and China arguably requires a more liberal political regime in Beijing, which doesn't seem likely to happen anytime soon. And as the CCP is already imposing conditionality for dialogue, Western China engagement cannot be unconditional either.

8.4 What can we learn from past failures and current headwinds?

The third unforeseen policy failure (UPF 3) is a textbook example of destructive learning. Repeated learning opportunities were squandered. In my PhD I had criticized the German government, more specifically, the Ministry for Economic Cooperation and Development (BMZ), for its failure to reign into the operation of GTZ. As the Giehler controversy has shown, the 'phasing out' of ODA did very little to help strengthen BMZ's ability to steer the GTZ successor organization GIZ in China. In this context one needs to be mindful that GIZ employees on secondment are very well paid: a parliamentary inquiry from 2019 revealed that whereas a GIZ project manager can earn from 57 650,71 euro to 109 787,08 euro (Band 4) per year, a senior professional with leadership responsibility for staff and employees of the Band 4 can earn between 67 779,40 euro and 120 868,67 euro annually

(Band 5) (Deutscher Bundestag, 2019). I consider such generous remuneration a key obstacle to reform from within the organization, since those who work for Sino-German development cooperation thus have very little incentives to question the modalities of existing partnership models.

I also find it particularly concerning that until the present-day German policymakers are trying to justify the current technical and financial cooperation in opposition to 'classical bilateral development cooperation' (*klassische bilaterale Entwicklungszusammenarbeit*) (Greive, Heide, and Stiens, 2023). Politicians and policymakers have repeatedly used this false dichotomy to justify the German government's passive China engagement. While it invokes a contrast between managerial and conventional charitable approaches, in my view the real dichotomy has always been between a *passive managerial* and *active political* approaches in development cooperation and international cooperation. In this context I also find it remarkable that any attempt to use existing German leverage in constructive ways was prematurely squandered. While it could be argued that the CIM programme supporting China's civil society would have run into headwinds due to Xi's hard authoritarian turn sooner or later, this highly innovative placement programme was prematurely terminated by the German side in 2012, without any obvious need to do so.

The third policy punctuation analysis reveals another case of (self-)destructive learning. What it shows is that it is not enough to reference the principle of dialogue and cooperation alone to justify a continuation of the status quo in international cooperation with China. The debate showed that the coercion of political foundations and German and European NGOs must be addressed, too. Advocates of dialogue and cooperation with autocratic China must also be able to explain how we can deal with the problem of cooptation (Weber, 2022). From the point of view of the Chinese Communist Party the Overseas NGO Law was a striking success. It not only prompted mission-based European NGOs to reduce or even terminate their China programme in its entirety. It also allowed the party-state to mould Germany's political foundations in its own image. While the Merkel administration managed to get all political foundations registered under the ONGO law, they have become proverbial sitting ducks. At any point the Chinese party-state can now threaten to pull the plug on one of its representatives offices, thus further enhancing its *destructive* leverage.

References for Chapter 8

@thorstenbenner (2022), 'German Government-owned GIZ Agency Is Literally the Last to Get the Memo. Its China CHIEF representative Thorsten Giehler (with Legendary Now Defunct @eurasiabridge Twitter Handle) Is Chief Advocate of Equidistance of Germany & EU Between China & US', *Twitter*, 9 March. Available online: https://archive.is/wDLtw (accessed 18 July 2023).

Anderson, D., ed. (2014), *Leveraging: A Political, Economic and Social Framework*, New York: Springer.

Asienhaus (2008), 'Berlin beendet Entwicklungshilfe für China', Available online: https://archive.is/Xxw6u (accessed 18 July 2023).

Blume, G. (2006), 'Keine Subventionen für Astronauten', *TAZ*, 19 May. Available online: https://taz.de/!430352/ (accessed 18 July 2023).

BMZ (1999), 'Übersektorales Konzept. Partizipative Entwicklungszusammenarbeit, Nr. 102, September 1999', Available online: https://conservation-development.net/Projekte/Nachhaltigkeit/CD2/Brasilien/Links/PDF/BMZ_1999_Partizipation_Konzept_102.pdf (accessed 18 July 2023).

Böge, F. (2018), 'Armes reiches Land', *Frankfurter Allgemeine Zeitung*, 20 November. Nr. 270: 3.

Böge, F. (2020), 'Auf Distanz zu China', *Frankfurter Allgemeine Zeitung*, 18 September. Nr. 218: 8.

CDB (2017), 'CPAFFC Appointed Government Supervisory Unit for German Foundations', *China Development Brief*, 27 May. Available online: https://archive.is/AtZW2 (accessed 18 July 2023).

Deutscher Bundestag (2019), 'Drucksache 19/8074', Available online: https://dserver.bundestag.de/btd/19/080/1908074.pdf (accessed 18 July 2023).

Diamond, L. and O. Schell, eds. (2018), *China's Influence & American Interests: Promoting Constructive Vigilance*, Stanford: Hoover Institution Press.

Erdmann, G. (1999), *Demokratie- und Menschenrechtsförderung in der Dritten Welt*, Wissenschaftliche Arbeitsgruppe für weltkirchliche Aufgaben der Deutschen Bischofskonferenz: Projekte 7.

FNF (2023), 'Taipei', *Friedrich Naumann Stiftung*, no date. Available online: https://archive.is/z74Om (accessed 18 July 2023).

Fuchs, R. and A. Thomas (2009), 'Germany Puts an End to Aid to China & India', *Deutsche Welle*, 30 October. Available online: https://archive.is/GxfH5 (accessed 18 July 2023).

Fulda, A. (2009a), *Förderung partizipativer Entwicklung in der VR China. Möglichkeiten und Grenzen politischer Einflussnahme durch Akteure der deutsch-chinesischen Entwicklungszusammenarbeit*, Wiesbaden: VS Verlag für Sozialwissenschaften.

Fulda, A. (2009b), 'Promoting Participatory Development in the People's Republic of China: A Case Study of Sino-German Development Cooperation (2003–2006)', *Internationales Asienforum*, 40 (1–2): 97–118.

Fulda, A. (2015), 'Civil Society Contributions to Policy Innovation in the PRC', in A. Fulda (ed), *Civil Society Contributions to Policy Innovation in the PR China*, Houndmills, Basingstoke, Hampshire and New York: Palgrave Macmillan, 3–30.

Fulda, A. (2022), 'Kooperation mit China ist kein Selbstzweck', *WirtschaftsWoche*, 1 July. Nr. 27: 42–43.

Giehler, T. (2019), 'Intercultural Bridge-Builders', *akzente*, January. Available online: https://archive.is/HJMHP (accessed 18 July 2023).

Giesen, C. and K. Strittmatter (2017), 'Jetzt hat die Polizei das Sagen', *Süddeutsche Zeitung*, 13 March. Nr. 60: 2.

Greive, M., D. Heide, and T. Stiens (2023), 'Bundesregierung stellt KfW-Kredite für China infrage', *Handelsblatt*, 19 January. Handelsblatt Archive.

GTZ (2006), *Autoritär und partizipativ zugleich? Regierungspraxis im Wandel*, Sektorvorhaben Mainstreaming Participation, Eschborn: Deutsche Gesellschaft für Technische Zusammenarbeit.

Heide, D. (2019), 'Eklat bei Chinareise: KP-Funktionär schreit FDP-Chef Lindner 30 Minuten lang an', *Handelsblatt*, 23 July. Handelsblatt Archive.

Heide, D. (2020), 'Thorsten Giehler in der Kritik – Der Fauxpas des China-Chefs der GIZ', *Handelsblatt*, 13 October. Handelsblatt Archive.

Heide, D. (2022), 'Handelspartner und Systemrivale: Deutschlands neuer Chinakurs wird konkret', *Handelsblatt*, 8 March. Handelsblatt Archive.

Hinton, R. and L. Groves (2004), 'The Complexity of Inclusive Aid', in L. Groves and R. Hinton (eds), *Inclusive Aid: Changing Power and Relationships in International Development*, London and Sterling: Earthscan, 3–20.

IN-EAST (2022), 'IN-EAST News', 1 November. Available online: https://web.archive.org/web/20220703051851/https://www.uni-due.de/in-east/news.php?id=1189 (accessed 18 July 2023).

IPG (2016), 'Steinbeißermeier', 28 November. Available online: https://archive.is/rsHEx (accessed 10 July 2023).

Johnson, I. (2003, September), 'The Death and Life of China's Civil Society', *Perspectives on Politics*, 1 (3): 551–4.

Kamp, M. (2011), 'Peking ist weit weg', *WirtschaftsWoche*, 25 June. WirtschaftsWoche Archive.

Kolonko, P. (2016), 'Agieren in der Grauzone', *Frankfurter Allgemeine Zeitung*, 29 December. Nr. 304: 2.

Lang, B. (2016), 'Kulturelle Soft Power aus *China?*', *Frankfurter Allgemeine Zeitung*, 7 May. Nr. 106: 8.

Murphy, A. and A. Fulda (2011), 'Bridging the Gap: Pracademics in Foreign Policy', *PS: Political Science & Politics*, 44 (2): 279–83.

Nabiyeva, K. (2011), 'In Sweeping Aid Reform, Merged German Agency Becomes Operational', *devex*, 3 January. Available online: https://archive.is/8obtz#selection-727.0-727.64 (accessed 18 July 2023).

OECD (2023), 'Official Development Assistance – Definition and Coverage', Available online: https://archive.is/u9CxB#selection-4617.0-4617.129 (accessed 18 July 2023).

Paqué, K.-H. (2020), 'Possibilities and Limits of Our Work', *Friedrich Naumann Foundation*, 26 November. Available online: https://archive.is/uoB1t (accessed 18 July 2023).

Pogorelskaja, S. (2002), 'Die parteinahen Stiftungen als Akteure und Instrumente derdeutschen Außenpolitik', *Aus Politik und Zeitgeschichte*, 22 May. Available online: https://www.bpb.de/shop/zeitschriften/apuz/27121/die-parteinahen-stiftungen-als-akteure-und-instrumente-der-deutschen-aussenpolitik/ (accessed 18 July 2023).

Policy Exchange (2020), 'The Importance of Being Candid: On China's Relationship with the Rest of the World', 23 October. Available online: https://archive.is/k2hjm (accessed 18 July 2023).

Shi-Kupfer, K. and B. Lang (2017), 'Overseas NGOs in China: Left in Legal Limbo', *The Diplomat*, 4 March. Available online: https://archive.is/muPNn (accessed 18 July 2023).

Sidel, M. (2019), 'Managing the Foreign: The Drive to Securitize Foreign Nonprofit and Foundation Management in China', *Voluntas*, 30: 664–77.

Stiftung Asienhaus (2010), 'Sustainable Community Building and Grassroots NGOs Workshop Report, Guangzhou, 9–11 July 2010', Available online: https://www.asienhaus.de/uploads/tx_news/12_Sustainable_Community_Building_and_Grassroots_NGOs_01.pdf (accessed 18 July 2023).

Strittmatter, K. (2016a), 'Beschränkter Dialog', *Süddeutsche Zeitung*, 13 June. Nr. 134: 6.

Strittmatter, K (2016b), 'Angst vor fremden Mächten', *Süddeutsche Zeitung*, 29 April. Nr. 99: 8.

Strittmatter, K (2017), 'Gabriel kann auch Diplomatie', *Süddeutsche Zeitung*, 25 May. Available online: https://archive.is/2nRjS (accessed 18 July 2023).

Taube, M. (2022), 'Für ein Containment Chinas ist es zu spät', *WirtschaftsWoche*, 17 June. Nr. 25: 44–45.

The Economist (2003), 'Congratulations, China', 16 October, Available online: https://archive.is/k02pj#selection-1039.0-1039.22 (accessed 18 July 2023).

UoN (2019a), 'Case Study 1', *University of Nottingham*. Available online: https://web.archive.org/web/20221027144639/https://www.nottingham.ac.uk/asiaresearch/documents/ffp-case-studies/case-study-1.pdf (accessed 26 October 2023).

UoN (2019b), 'Case Study 2', *University of Nottingham*. Available online: https://web.archive.org/web/20221027144650/https://www.nottingham.ac.uk/asiaresearch/documents/ffp-case-studies/case-study-2.pdf (accessed 26 October 2023).

UoN (2019c), 'Case Study 5', *University of Nottingham*. Available online: https://web.archive.org/web/20221027144648/https://www.nottingham.ac.uk/asiaresearch/documents/ffp-case-studies/case-study-5.pdf (accessed 26 October 2023).

UoN (2019d), 'Case Study 8', *University of Nottingham*. Available online: https://web.archive.org/web/20221027144657/https://www.nottingham.ac.uk/asiaresearch/documents/ffp-case-studies/case-study-8.pdf (accessed 26 October 2023).

UoN (2019e), 'Case Study 12', *University of Nottingham*. Available online: https://web.archive.org/web/20221027144619/https://www.nottingham.ac.uk/asiaresearch/documents/ffp-case-studies/case-study-12.pdf (accessed 26 October 2023).

UoN (2019f), 'Case Study 7', *University of Nottingham*. Available online: https://web.archive.org/web/20221027144636/https://www.nottingham.ac.uk/asiaresearch/documents/ffp-case-studies/case-study-7.pdf (accessed 26 October 2023).

UoN (2019g), 'Case Study 14', *University of Nottingham*. Available online: https://web.archive.org/web/20221027144642/https://www.nottingham.ac.uk/asiaresearch/documents/ffp-case-studies/case-study-13.pdf (accessed 26 October 2023).

UoN (2019h), 'Case Study 9', *University of Nottingham*. Available online: https://web.archive.org/web/20221027144621/https://www.nottingham.ac.uk/asiaresearch/documents/ffp-case-studies/case-study-9.pdf (accessed 26 October 2023).

UoN (2019i), 'Case Study 11', *University of Nottingham*. Available online: https://web.archive.org/web/20221027144633/https://www.nottingham.ac.uk/asiaresearch/documents/ffp-case-studies/case-study-11.pdf (accessed 26 October 2023).

UoN (2019j), 'Case Study 15', *University of Nottingham*. Available online: https://web.archive.org/web/20221027152321/https://www.nottingham.ac.uk/asiaresearch/documents/ffp-case-studies/case-study-14.pdf (accessed 26 October 2023).

UoN (2019k), 'Case Study 18', *University of Nottingham*. Available online: https://web.archive.org/web/20221027144622/https://www.nottingham.ac.uk/asiaresearch/documents/ffp-case-studies/case-study-17.pdf (accessed 26 October 2023).

Walton, D. (2013), 'The Straw Man Fallacy', in *Methods of Argumentation*, 249–86, Cambridge: Cambridge University Press.

Weber, R. (2022), 'At What Point Does Cooperation Lead to Complicity?', *China.Table*, 20 September. Available online: https://table.media/china/en/opinion/at-what-point-does-cooperation-lead-to-complicity/ (accessed 18 July 2023).

Wenhui wangxun (2020), 'Diaocha baodao: Me "bang shui" bu "wang" tudu zhongxiaoxue', 17 April. Available online: https://archive.is/zZA0J (accessed 18 July 2023).

WirtschaftsWoche (2014), 'China will ausländischeNGOs „regulieren"', 22 December. WirtschaftsWoche Archive.

WirtschaftsWoche (2017), 'Ausländische Stiftungen in China lahmgelegt', 12 March. WirtschaftsWoche Archive.

WirtschaftsWoche (2022), 'China stoppt Dialog mit USA zu Klimaschutz und andere Kooperationen', *WirtschaftsWoche*, 5 August. WirtschaftsWoche Archive.

Wolff, P. (2006), 'Entwicklungszusammenarbeit im Gesamtkontext der Deutsch-Chineseischen Kooperation: Eine Portfolioanalyse', *Deutsches Institut für Entwicklungspolitik*, Discussion Paper, November 2006. Available online: https://www.idos-research.de/uploads/media/Internetfassung_DiscPaper_11.2006.pdf (accessed 18 July 2023).

Zajac, K. and L. Kaplan (2021), 'Why Germany Should Continue Its Development Cooperation with China', Kiel Policy Brief, Nr 159, November 2021. Available online: https://www.ifw-kiel.de/fileadmin/Dateiverwaltung/IfW-Publications/-ifw/Kiel_Policy_Brief/2021/KPB_159.pdf (accessed 18 July 2023).

Chapter 9

EUROPE'S ARMS EMBARGO, DUAL-USE EXPORTS AND GERMANY'S INDIFFERENCE TOWARDS TAIWAN

9.1 *Towards a more robust diplomacy vis-à-vis China?*

In Chapter 2 I described the 'paradox' (Kundnani, 2015) or 'puzzle' (Maull, 2018) of German power. I outlined that in the aftermath of WWII and under US tutelage, Germany relinquished autonomous security policies (Maull, 1990/1991). This has constrained Germany's ability to project military power abroad. While such a self-limiting approach can be explained by the horrors of the Holocaust and the tragedy of WWII, with the benefit of hindsight we can recognize that Germany's political learning has also had a destructive dimension. As I will show throughout this chapter a strictly apolitical approach to security and defence policy reaches its limits when we are dealing with radical revisionist and expansionist powers like Russia and China. In Chapter 8 I showed why the Steinmeier doctrine with its 'infinite patience for talks under the most difficult conditions and an almost inexhaustible belief in the power of dialogue' (IPG, 2016) was insufficient in international cooperation with China. In this chapter I will show why a much more robust diplomacy – which includes the projection of hard military power – is required to safeguard secure and accessible seas in the Indo-Pacific.

Chapter at a glance

In the first part of the book chapter I explain how the harsh suppression of China's anti-corruption and pro-democracy movement in 1989 prompted the European Union to impose an arms embargo. The unforeseen policy failure 4 (UPF 4) centres around the difficulties of implementing the embargo. Much of the discussion revolves around the challenge of restricting the export of dual-use items which can either be used for civilian and military purposes. In the second part of the chapter and in the fourth policy punctuation analysis (PPA 4) I discuss Germany's dangerous indifference towards Taiwan. I offer a critical appraisal of the German government's strategic approach to the Indo-Pacific since 2020. I show how an overly deferential attitude towards China has hampered Germany's ability to engage with Taiwan more constructively. Drawing on recent examples of high-level diplomacy I discuss how much progress has been made in terms of Scholz's *Zeitenwende*.

9.2 Unforeseen policy failure 4 | 1989, Europe's patchy arms embargo, and the problem of dual-use exports

From Spring until Summer 1989 a nation-wide anti-corruption and pro-democracy movement took place (Fulda, 2020, 17–20). Over the course of a few months millions of Chinese citizens took to the streets in over 300 Chinese cities and demanded greater political freedoms (2020, 17–18). While demands for more democracy in China were couched in abstract terms, the China expert Unger has interpreted them to mean 'an independent judiciary, beyond the reach of a Party leader's sway' (1991, 4) and greater space for China's civil society to flourish (1991, 5). Among the more specific demands of movement leaders were freedom of speech, freedom of press and freedom of association (Fulda, 2020, 18).

The stand-off between movement leaders and senior CCP officials could not be resolved through dialogue. Student disorganization contributed to this outcome, which can be explained by a fear-laden atmosphere on Tiananmen Square. It made it very difficult for student leaders to reach consensus about their goals and tactics (Wright, 1999). But constructive dialogue between protest leaders and senior CCP officials was also undermined by a power struggle within the top echelons of the party. For weeks and months CCP leaders were in disagreement how to deal with the protester demands. Such ambivalence ended with a hard-line editorial in the *People's Daily* from 26 April 1989, which provided an early signal of an impending crackdown (Tiananmen Chronology, 2023). More moderate senior officials such as Zhao Ziyang and Hu Qili were subsequently sidelined and a decision was taken by Politburo Standing Committee members Deng Xiaoping, Li Peng and Yao Yilin to impose martial law, which came into effect on 19 May 1989 (Mufson, 2001).

In the night of 3–4 June 1989 a bloody crackdown started. Tanks started to roll through the streets of Beijing. PLA soldiers started shooting at civilians indiscriminately. Security forces were also deployed in other cities such as Chengdu (Kuo, 2019). Accounts of numbers of victims vary considerably. A report of 2,600 casualties by the Chinese Red Cross was soon retracted under pressure from the party-state (Frontline, 2019). According to a secret cable by Sir Alan Donald, then British Ambassador to Beijing, at least 10,000 people were killed by the Chinese army (Yu, 2019). When asked about his source Donald revealed that an unnamed member of China's State Council had passed along this information (Cheng, 2017). The real number of casualties will only be known if and when archives are opened.

Is Europe's arms embargo more symbolic than substantial?

Following the brutal crackdown on China's nation-wide anti-corruption and pro-democracy movement European governments took swift action. On 26 June 1989 the European Council of Ministers issued a joint statement. Annex II of the Presidency Conclusions included a political declaration on China. One of its most consequential measures was the 'interruption by the Member States of the Community of military cooperation and an embargo on trade in arms with

China' (Consilium, 1989). This political commitment by all EU member states could not mask the fact that the arms embargo was not legally binding. Initially it was also unclear which specific export items were actually covered under the arms embargo. The political declaration allowed each European member state to determine how the embargo should be interpreted 'in the context of their national laws, regulations and decision making processes' (SIPRI, 2012). While Kirchberger has convincingly argued that '(the) modernization of the PLA that started in the mid-1990s was long hampered by the Western arms embargo' (2021, 43), the overall effectiveness of the embargo should still to be questioned. EU member states had considerable discretion how to interpret it. A narrow interpretation – favoured by the UK and France – only covered 'lethal items and major weapon platforms' (SIPRI, 2012). The embargo initially also did not explicitly cover the export of dual-use technology.

In 1998 member states agreed on the European Union Code of Conduct on Arms Exports. It was 'designed to set common standards across the EU for the export of military equipment' (Bauer and Bromley, 2004). Export control experts Bauer and Bromley have argued that in 'a process of dialogue, negotiation and review based on practical experience . . . national governments have increasingly felt comfortable discussing arms export control in an EU context and have gained more confidence in the EU Code as a policy tool' (2004, 4). IR expert Casarini, on the other hand, has highlighted '(a) report by the European Parliament released in October 2004 [which] points out that, in the past, both the embargo and the EU Code of Conduct have been varyingly and erratically applied by EU member states' (2006, 33). He also stated that 'that in 2004 EU member states exported military equipment worth more than €340 million to China' (2006). Such findings suggest that while Europe's arms embargo was effective in preventing the sale of entire weapon systems, it could not prevent arms sales in their entirety. Throughout the late 1990s and early 2000s European governments continued to grant licences for items with potential military use to China.

Enhancing the party-state's security and surveillance capabilities

Annual EU reports have shown that between 2002 and 2012 'EU arms makers received licenses to export equipment worth three billion euros ($4.1 billion) to China' (Hancock, 2014). The Belgian newspaper *De Standaard* has furthermore reported that between 2013 and 2021 'EU countries issued an average of 188 licences a year for the export of military goods to China' (European Parliament, 2023). An independent report by the NGO Action on Armed Violence has underscored China as an important export market for UK-manufactured arms manufacturers. Between 2008 and 2017 'the UK approved £202m worth of military arms exports to China' government' (AOAV, 2018). In addition to single-use military exports dual-use items have included imaging cameras (1,355), cryptography equipment (647), corrosion-resistant chemical manufacturing equipment (570) and information security devices (320), just to name a few (2018). Such dual-use items have considerable value for the Chinese party-state to augment its security and surveillance capabilities. European studies expert Andreosso has criticized Europe's dual-use export controls as 'very lax and very loose' (Hancock, 2014).

Bräuner, Bromley and Duchâtel have shown that between 2008 and 2012 the French government authorized transfers or licenced production in the value of around €160–180 million per year (2015, 22). Between 2003 and 2012 'transfers to China were dominated by imaging and countermeasures equipment (42 per cent) and aircraft equipment (37 per cent), but also included electronic equipment (6 per cent) and "other"(13 per cent)' (2015). Airbus has been a long-term provider of aviation technology, which can be used both for civilian and military purposes. A report by Horizon Advisory has shown that Airbus 'China engagement entails ties to China's military and military-fusion apparatus, including in the form of supply dependencies, technology sharing, and research and development (R&D) cooperation' (2022, 1). Airbus' long-time cooperation partner AVIC is 'a Chinese State-owned aerospace conglomerate that the US Department of Defense has identified as a Chinese military company and the Department of Commerce has placed on the Entity list' (2022, 9). While the arms embargo put a stop to the sale of whole weapon systems from Europe to China, it was not designed to prevent such partnerships which have arguably strengthened China's military-industrial complex. So far I have drawn primarily on examples related to the United Kingdom and France. Germany is an important third example. The German Security and Defence Industry (SDI) is a major economic player, which in 2014 employed 135,700 people directly and generated more than 12 billion euros in gross value added (BDSV, 2014).

Is German technology powering the PLA navy?

Licensed production of military equipment in China has also led to public controversies in Germany. In 2021 *Welt am Sonntag* and public broadcaster ARD published findings from a joint investigation into the China operations of German mechanical engineering company MTU Friedrichshafen. The reports revealed that MTU, a wholly owned subsidiary of Rolls Royce Power Systems, up until 2020 had provided engines for guided-missile destroyers of the Chinese Luyang-III class (Tillack, 2021). It was also reported that MTU had supplied diesel engines for China's Song-class submarines in the past but had now stopped doing so (Deutsche Welle, 2021). In 2006 a Chinese Song class submarine had surfaced 'around 15km near the USS Kittyhawk, a US aircraft carrier that was on exercise in the East China Sea between Japan and Taiwan' (The Week, 2021). The particularly quiet diesel-electric engines had allowed the Chinese submarine to approach the US Navy ships escorting the aircraft carrier undetected (2021). MAN, a Volkswagen subsidiary, had also provided propulsion systems for Chinese warships (Tillack, 2021). Monitoring conducted by the Stockholm-based think tank SIPRI suggests that MTU engines are not only powering Luyang destroyers but have also found their way into Chinese corvettes of the Jiangdao type (Tillack, 2022). Both types of Chinese warships have been deployed to project the PLA Navy's hard military power in the South China Sea (2022).

Maritime security expert Kirchberger has noted that we are witnessing 'the largest peacetime naval buildup since at least the 1930s' (2021). She warns that 'China has been producing warships as if it were already at war, with shipyards reportedly working around the clock seven days per week, sometimes completing hulls ahead of schedule' (2021). This has alarmed policymakers in Washington DC. According to a report by the Congressional Research Service 'China is expected to field 420 ships by 2025 and 460 ships by 2030, the goal of the current U.S Navy shipbuilding plan is for a fleet of 355, with no set date for achieving it' (The Maritime Executive, 2022). US diplomats have lobbied successive German governments since at least 2007 to prevent German companies to assist with the PLA Navy's modernization (Tillack, 2022). Yet it took another ten years before such pressure bore fruit. Only in 2017 the German government finally introduced a requirement for authorization for the export of all submarine engines (2022). What explains the long timespan between the initial ask by US diplomats and the tardy response by the German government? As the following discussion will show it is difficult for state agencies to prevent the provision of dual-use technology by German companies.

Endangering US forward deployment in the South China Sea?

During the Cold War, Germany's export controls remained relatively lax. The Coordinating Committee on Multilateral Export Controls (CoCom) served as an informal agreement between the United States and NATO partners. While CoCom lists were supposed to restrict the export of high-tech items to Warsaw Treaty countries and China, in the mid-1980s Chancellor Kohl's administration signalled to the Chinese leadership that the German government would 'not be outdone by anyone in CoCom in terms of flexibility on CoCom-required exports to China' (Bösch, 2022). After unification Germany adopted a stricter export control regime. More specifically it consists of the 1990 War Weapons Control Act, the 2013 Foreign Trade and Payments Act as well as the 2013 Foreign Trade and Payments Ordinance (Bräuner, Bromley, and Duchâtel, 2015, 25). A Weapons of War List and Export List specify prohibited export items.

The latter Export List, together with Annex 1 of EU Dual-Use Regulation Recast (Sidley, 2021), also includes provisions for dual-use goods. The Federal Office for Economic Affairs and Export Control (BAFA), which comes under the Federal Ministry for Economic Affairs and Climate Action (BMWK), is tasked to either grant or deny licences for dual-use items which are not covered by the Weapons of War List (Bräuner, Bromley, and Duchâtel, 2015, 26). Since neither the MTU diesel engines for Chinese submarines nor the engines for guided-missile destroyers of the Chinese Luyang-III class were part of the Wassenaar control list, they were also not listed as prohibited items in BAFA's Export List and thus did not require an export licence. BAFA also has the authority to deny the export of unlisted dual-use items with the help of an individual intervention clause (*Einzeleingriff*) (Bräuner, Bromley, and Duchâtel, 2015). In practice, however, it has proven to be a rather blunt instrument. While it can lead to the attachment of further conditions to the export of sensitive dual-use goods, the export law expert Hohmann has shown that such BAFA interventions can also be successfully challenged by exporters (ExportManager, 2015). The BMWK also has the possibility to 'discourage' exporters with reference to potential reputational damage. Yet Bräuner, Bromley and Duchâtel have argued that '(this) approach can be especially difficult when other EU member states are already providing the same items to China' (2015, 28). And while it understandable that revising internationally agreed dual-use controls in a timely fashion can be very time-consuming, the slow pace of regulatory change has also meant that 'if the People's Liberation Army went to war tomorrow, it would field an arsenal bristling with hardware from some of America's closest allies: Germany, France and Britain' (Lague, 2013).

9.3 Policy punctuation analysis 4 | Germany's dangerous indifference towards Taiwan

For decades China has loomed large in the imagination of German politicians and industrialists. Only in recent years foreign and security policymakers in Berlin have started to recognize the downsides of limiting Germany's engagement in the region to Asia's economic powerhouse. In 2020, the German Federal Government published its long awaited 'Policy guidelines for the Indo-Pacific' (hence guidelines) (2020). According to this policy document '(the) Indo-Pacific is not clearly delineated in geographical terms and is defined variously by different actors. The Federal Government considers the Indo-Pacific to be the entire region characterised by the Indian Ocean and the Pacific' (Federal Foreign Office, 2020).

In the foreword of the guidelines then Foreign Minister Heiko Maas (2018–2021) acknowledged that for too long Germany had remained at the sidelines. In the context of EU, OSCE and NATO the Indo-Pacific region had only played a limited role for both Berlin and Brussels (Federal Foreign Office, 2020, 2). 'The prosperity of our society depends on open shipping routes, physical and digital connectivity and participation in functioning growth markets', the former Foreign Minister argued. Maas also acknowledged the need to take 'part in exercises and in collective security measures to protect the rules-based order when implementing UN resolutions' (2020). In a public comment on the guidelines Maas underscored Germany's desire to shape the future international order 'so that it is based on rules and international cooperation – and not on the right of the strongest' (Drüten, 2020). While his comments could have been interpreted as a rebuke of China's increasingly aggressive military posture, in fact he sent out a much more mixed message. In a swipe against China *and the* United States he expressed the desire to 'strengthen the idea of a multipolar world in which no country has to choose between poles of power' (2020).

Leithäuser has argued that the guidelines 'are not a counterpoint to German-Chinese relations, but they do place them in a new context: by strengthening and emphasising cooperation with Japan, India and Australia in the future – instead of the 'law of the strongest', rules and international cooperation should be the basis – China is moving from the role of the largest strategic partner to that of a political competitor and rival' (2020). In stark contrast China analyst Goldberg has pointed out that '(critics) of the plan . . . lament that it fails to grapple with the hard realities of Chinese power' (2020). As the fourth policy punctuation analysis will show Germany's approach to the Indo-Pacific region remains remarkably ambiguous.

Ignoring Taiwan in the guidelines: a textbook example of the 'black elephant' phenomenon

Following the publication of the guidelines former Foreign Minister Maas also penned an op-ed in *Handelsblatt* in which he described an 'Asia of geopolitics, with ever sharper nationalisms, territorial conflicts, arms races and the Sino-American rivalry' (2021). Such a stark policy image was cushioned by an emotive appeal to consider China was as a 'central economic partner' and as a partner in the global fight against climate change (2021). Whilst claiming to address geopolitical challenges in the region Maas was in fact pulling punches.

His caution was also reflected throughout the guidelines. Despite mentioning China sixty-two times in the policy document, its authors did not offer any advice on how to counter China's destructive regional influence. The following three examples illustrate this problem. Despite citing criticism of China's flagship Belt and Road Initiative, such as reckless Chinese lending practices that led to over-indebtedness, the guidelines did not offer any specific recommendations on how Germany can address existing power imbalances in the region. A vague preference for multilateral approaches was expressed instead. And as reasonable as it sounds to commit to strengthening regional multilateralism through close cooperation with ASEAN, such calls did little to address the specific challenges faced by emerging Chinese client states like Laos within ASEAN, or Pakistan outside of it. In the case of territorial disputes in the region, an inability to speak the language of power is also evident. Rather than reminding China to respect UNCLOS's ruling on China's claims vis-à-vis the Philippines (Hayton, 2018), the German government put its hopes in a Code of Conduct between ASEAN and China, which has not made much progress because of Beijing's intransigence (Strangio, 2022).

And as one of the region's biggest geopolitical hotspots, Taiwan was not even mentioned once in the guidelines. But without taking a stand against Xi Jinping's threat to annex Taiwan by military means, how can the German government claim to contribute to peace and security in the Indo-Pacific region? And how would Taiwan fare if it was to follow German policy advice of avoiding bipolarity? Without Taiwan's strong security partnership with the United States, would it even exist in its current form? I promised to outline the contours of the black elephant in Germany's relationship with China in the introduction. In Ho's words, a black elephant is a problem that everyone sees, but no one wants to deal with, so they pretend it doesn't exist. The way the guidelines ignore Taiwan should be considered a textbook example of the black elephant phenomenon.

What is the difference between Berlin's One China policy *and the Beijing's One China* principle?

Germany's relationship with Taiwan is anything but straightforward. Heide and Gillmann have provided a very concise summary of the rather ambivalent position towards Taiwan adopted by successive German governments: 'In fact, Germany has not committed itself to the "One China Principle", but is pursuing a "One China Policy". This is a big difference. While the "One China Principle" propagated by the Chinese leadership contains stipulations formulated by China, such as that Taiwan belongs to the territory of the People's Republic of China, the German government does not make any statement about this with its "One China Policy". It merely recognises that China is only represented diplomatically by Beijing' (2023). The two journalists also highlight Berlin's self-limitation on diplomatic exchanges, which currently rules out high-level visits of German and Taiwanese high representatives such the head of state, head of government, the vice president, the ministers of foreign affairs and defence, the president of parliament and the chief justice (2023).

Although Germany has a One China *policy* in place, it has been proven malleable over time. In 2020 two IR experts, a former German Ambassador to China and a prominent member of the European Parliament jointly drafted an open letter in which they called Europe to readjust its policy vis-à-vis Taiwan and the People's Republic of China (Bütikofer, Godement, Maull, and Stanzel, 2020). The open letter was co-signed by four active and one former member of the European Parliament. The nine signatories bemoaned the fact that the leadership in Beijing was undermining the status quo in the Taiwan Strait. They pointed out that Taiwan was facing ever growing diplomatic isolation as well as the threat of military coercion. By 'continuing its One China policy as before, Europe risks leaving Taiwan's citizens at the mercy of the Communist Party' the signatories argued. Doing so, would mean to 'abandon our commitment to work together for the liberal values of democratic societies and allow Beijing to fundamentally alter the international balance' (2020). In order to preserve the status quo the open letter writers called for (1) dialogue with holders of the highest offices in Taiwan, (2) Taiwan's membership in international organizations, (3) international cooperation with Taiwanese partners in the field of public health, (4) the establishment of dialogue on peace, security and stability with Taiwan, (5) a reorganization of critical supply chains to reduce dependency on China, (6) improved trade and economic relations with Taiwan and (7) support for the establishment of a Taiwanese satellite channel in Mandarin in Europe to move away from Beijing's monopoly on information in the Chinese language (2020).

Pelosi's visit to Taiwan and the end of self-imposed diplomatic restrictions

The open letter's first demand was for the European governments to 'conduct a dialogue with all key political actors in Taiwan including the holders of the highest offices in the country' (Bütikofer, Godement, Maull, and Stanzel, 2020). Yet it took

American leadership to overcome self-imposed restrictions for such diplomatic exchanges. In February 2018 the US Congress had unanimously passed the Taiwan Travel Act, which was signed into law by then President Trump in March 2018. In an editorial for the *Financial Times* White described the law as a 'break from precedent', which according to him could 'further destabilise [the US] relationship with China' (2018). Among others, the Taiwan Travel Act also made the high-profile visit to Taiwan by then US Speaker of the House Nancy Pelosi possible. Her stay in Taipei in August 2022 was the first since Newt Gingrich had visited Taiwan in 1997.

Pelosi's visit to Taiwan brought into relief the varying assessments of how to deal with Beijing's red lines. Critics employed policy images which painted her visit as symbolic politics. In terms of the emotive appeals commentators warned of an unnecessary provocation. A case in point is the op-ed by Rüesch, who considered it a 'a step towards the recognition of Taiwan's statehood' and a departure from the 'unsatisfactory but ultimately successful One-China policy of the past fifty years' (2022). Warning against 'preventative enmity', Fischer similarly argued that '(as) long as China refrains from bellicose actions and offers a hand in maintaining the status quo in Taiwan and to cooperation, the USA and the West should also respond with cooperation' (2022). Such viewpoints did not go unchallenged. According to Hulverscheidt 'the furious Beijing war cry that [Pelosi] triggered with her visit should have opened the eyes of even the last optimists in Berlin and Paris, Washington and London' (2022). Strittmatter has similarly argued that 'critics of Pelosi say she has put Xi under unnecessary pressure. In reality, however, it is the [Communist Party] itself that is putting itself under pressure and has created a logic of escalation in its Taiwan policy. It can and will look for as many occasions as it likes' (2022). Arguing along similar lines Shi-Kupfer's emotive appeal consisted of the warning that 'Beijing's provocations are not made more predictable and restrained by silent politics' (2022). In my own commentary for Sky News I criticized Beijing for manufacturing a crisis (Vimeo, 2022). In a subsequent in-depth interview about Taiwan with a leading Swiss online magazine I pointed out that the Chinese authorities had 'announced that they will do everything in their power to prevent the trip – and then they do not dare to do anything' (Blülle and Fuchs, 2022).

Following Czechia's lead?

On the European side Czechia has been a trail blazer in forging closer diplomatic ties with Taiwan. China expert Šebok has traced Czech delegations to Taiwan between 2016 and 2023. He notes that they are 'quite common' and that 'they have grown in profile in recent years' (2023). A noticeable example is the delegation led by Senate President Miloš Vystrčil, Czechia's second-highest-ranking official after the president. In response Chinese state media went into overdrive. A spokesperson for the International Department of the Communist Party of China Central Committee described the visit as a 'sinister political attempt' and 'erroneous practice' which was supposedly putting the China–Czech relationship at risk (People's Daily, 2020). An editorial of Beijing's nationalist mouth piece *Global Times* called his Taiwan visit 'vicious in nature' and labelled Vystrčil as a 'rule-breaker ' and 'political hooligan' (2020). Yet Šebok shows that 'despite harsh rhetoric, China did not take any tangible countermeasures, except for an odd case of a canceled piano purchase' (2023). More recently a large delegation of the Czech Chamber of Deputies visited Taiwan. Šebok has called it a 'milestone in the development of bilateral ties and Taiwan's global engagement, even as it loses official diplomatic allies' (2023).

Repeated visits by Czech politicians have shown European partners that the risks of diplomatic escalation by Beijing are manageable. In Spring 2023 Germany's Minister of Education and Research Bettina Stark-Watzinger visited Taiwan. This was the first time in twenty-six years that a German minister had visited the island. I consider it highly unlikely that Stark-Watzinger would have visited Taiwan if there hadn't been various European and American politicians who had successfully made such visits. Whereas Stark-Watzinger downplayed her visit as a 'normal work trip' (Hamacher, 2023), Chinese Foreign Ministry spokesman Wang Wenbin described her visit to Taiwan as 'vile conduct' (Reuters, 2023). He also called on the German government to 'immediately stop associating and interacting with Taiwan independence separatist forces, immediately stop sending wrong signals to Taiwan independence separatist forces, and immediately stop using the Taiwan issue to interfere in China's internal affairs' (2023). While highlighting that the visit to Taiwan was in line with Germany's One China policy, Stark-Watzinger did not hold back either. She is quoted as saying that 'China is increasingly becoming a competitor and systemic rival. That is why we should not only focus on Western countries such as Canada, but must also intensify the exchange with value partners in Asia who have the same standards in terms of the rule of law and academic freedom' (Gillmann, Heide, and Kölling, 2023).

What are Germany's primary interests in Taiwan?

At the heart of the German minister's visit were talks about battery research, green hydrogen and semiconductor research (Süddeutsche Zeitung, 2023). During Stark-Watzinger's visit a Germany-Taiwan Scientific and Technological Cooperation Arrangement was signed (National Science and Technology Council, 2023). While praising the agreement as a sign 'for enhanced cooperation based on the democratic values of transparency, openness, reciprocity and scientific freedom' (TAZ, 2023) the German minister also highlighted that Germany had more to learn from Taiwan than the other way around, for example, in terms of independent China competence through Chinese language learning as well as in the field of domestic microchip production (Pape, 2023).

Fischer has emphasized how dependent Germany has become on Taiwanese companies like TSMC and UMC, which are the world's largest and third largest contract microchip manufacturers, respectively (2022). In his emotive appeal he warns that '(without) chips that are at least partially produced in Taiwan, the automobile industry in Germany and the USA would hardly be able to produce on a regular basis' (2022). Fischer also highlights the willingness in Western capitals to 'initiate investments worth billions to become more independent in the promising field of semiconductor technology' (2022). *Handelsblatt* reporters Gillmann, Heide and Kölling have suggested that during the final hours of her stay Stark-Watzinger paid TSMC a visit. Neither the minister herself nor the company confirmed that this meeting took place. Such a possible meeting was seen as significant since there have been speculation that TSMC may build a factory in Dresden, Germany (2023b). Kölling has suggested that 'in the search for a location, Germany is considered the favourite' (Kölling, 2023b). He has also reported that German automotive supplier Bosch may become a joint venture partner for a European chip factory. According to Kölling the German car industry was in favour of TSMC. But due to higher production costs in Europe the amount of subsidies could prove decisive (2023). As Fischer argues, even if a decision to produce microchips in Europe was taken, attempts to develop greater independence from chip imports from Taiwan 'will take many years. Until then, Taiwan has strategic importance for all of them' (2022). This raises the question what Germany and its allies can do to promote peace in the Taiwan Strait and to deter the General Secretary from ordering a military annexation of Taiwan. As the following discussion will show, this scenario is increasingly taken seriously by German politicians.

An annexation of Taiwan by 2027?

The German politician Roderich Kiesewetter (CDU) has expressed concerns that 'the Chinese leadership could see a strategic advantage in an earlier attack, because the West is currently tying up a lot of capacity in the Russian conflict' (Süddeutsche Zeitung, 2022a). Chinese leader Xi Jinping has reportedly instructed his military to be ready to annex Taiwan by 2027, according to US intelligence (Hawkins, 2023). Görlach has argued that 'China's ruler is not bluffing: he is preparing the people for the coming war and has clearly called on the business community via party directives and texts in state media to prepare for war as well. In the People's Republic, this is not a friendly recommendation, but an order' (2023). Asian security expert Heginbotham on the other hand has expressed scepticism about the likelihood of an early war in the Taiwan Strait. Pointing out that in war games China has consistently lost, he has argued that '(if) China's capabilities are really growing compared to ours, then the longer they wait, the better off they would be' (Kölling, 2023a).

Jhy-Wey Shieh, Taiwan's Ambassador to Berlin, considers the 2027 timeframe realistic. He argues that if Xi 'were to delay the war any longer, he would probably be physically and mentally too weak to make it happen' (Álvarez, 2022). Heide, Gusbeth and Kölling have pointed out that it is anyone's guess how Xi assesses the chances of success and what price he would be willing to accept for it (2023). The German China expert and economist Zenglein has warned of underestimating Xi's willingness to pay a high economic price to realize his ambitions vis-à-vis Taiwan (Müller, 2022).

In light of the 2027 scenario the Federal Ministry for Economic Affairs and Climate Action (BMWK) reportedly produced a 100-page strong document which has analysed potential consequences of a war in the Taiwan Strait for Germany's economic relationship with China. The ministry's report pointed out that due to economic interdependencies Germany was highly vulnerable to blackmail. Whereas Germany exported 2.7 per cent of its total value added to China, China, on the other hand, imported only 0.8 per cent of its value added from Germany (Süddeutsche Zeitung, 2022b). Jhy-Wey Shieh has furthermore warned that '(the) West cannot afford for Taiwan to fall under the control of this communist country. This is not only about defending a democracy against a dictatorship, but 30 per cent of world trade passes through the Taiwan Strait. If China conquers Taiwan, they also control this lifeline of the world economy' (Álvarez, 2022).

Deployment of the frigate Bayern in the Indo-Pacific

The threat of war in the Taiwan Strait requires us to revisit the question of what steps the German government can take to contribute to peace and security in the Indo-Pacific region. One of the key principles which informed the aforementioned 'Policy guidelines for the Indo-Pacific' was a rules-based order: 'it is not the law of the strong that must prevail, but the strength of the law', the document stated (The Federal Government, 2020, 11). 'This also applies to the shipping routes through the Indian Ocean and the Pacific. The UN Convention on the Law of the Sea as a comprehensive maritime regulatory and cooperation framework and the freedoms of navigation enshrined therein are universal' (2020).

To underscore Germany's commitment to protect freedom of navigation in the Indo-Pacific region the German government deployed its frigate Bayern from 2 August 2021 to 18 February 2022 (Bundeswehr, 2022). Prantner has suggested that '(the) addressee of the message is above all China' (2021). Carstens has similarly suggested that '(the) warship with 243 crew members has the task of demonstrating to China that Germany stands for a rules-based world order. Also and especially on Beijing's doorstep' (2021). The German politician Mützenich (SPD) has been sharply critical of the deployment, comparing it to a Wilhelmine world view of a 'place in the sun' (Brössler and Szymanski, 2021). To pre-empt Beijing's overreaction Maksan reports that 'it was never planned to sail too close to territories that China claims for itself in the South China Sea, contrary to international law. Nor was a passage through the Taiwan Strait ever planned. And manoeuvres with allies in the South China Sea were not planned either' (2022). Further attempts to placate the CCP fell onto deaf ears. The Merkel administration had offered a port visit in Shanghai. This was declined with reference to a 'lack of trust' and a call on the German side to 'create favourable conditions for it" (Böge, 2021). Despite such frictions in the Sino–German relationship Frankenberger has considered the deployment of the frigate Bayern 'a symbol' (2021). He has argued that 'Germany will not become overly militarily involved in the region. Nor does it have to; it must fulfil its security tasks in and around Europe. But because the Indo-Pacific is increasingly becoming the epicentre of global politics, what happens there also concerns us' (2021). According to Frankenberger 'German security policy is learning slowly, but it is learning' (2021). In my view such an upbeat assessment of the slow pace of development of Germany's security and defence policy is hardly warranted, as it does little to help Taiwan deter the PLA from a possible military annexation in the future.

Who were the disruptors and what were their achievements?

In Chapter 5 I described the constant tug-of-war between *policy communities* and *issue networks*, and how policy images are used to either defend or challenge existing policy monopolies. The fourth policy punctuation analysis highlights this tension in striking ways. While the previous Merkel administration's 'Policy guidelines for the Indo-Pacific' suggest a pivot to the Indo-Pacific, a closer look revealed that these policy guidelines do not address existing shortcomings in Berlin's previous engagement with China. There were only hints at some of the challenges which Germany continues to face in its relationship with China. The omission of Taiwan in the document revealed a major black elephant in Germany's foreign and security policy towards the region.

The contentious debate about Pelosi's visit to Taiwan also revealed the shortcomings of an overly accommodating Western China approach. Whilst all commentators recognized the risk inherent for Pelosi travelling to Taiwan, their emotive appeals varied greatly. Some considered the visit as too risky and a threat to peace and stability in the region. Supporters of a more robust diplomatic approach, on the other hand, argued that it was in fact Beijing that was challenging the status quo in the Taiwan Strait. The discussion over upgrading diplomatic relations with Taiwan also revealed that Czechia has been pulling above its weight. Frequent delegations by Czech politicians to Taiwan normalized high-level exchanges between Europe and Taiwan. Both US and Czech leadership arguably paved the way for Stark-Watzinger's landmark visit to Taiwan in Spring 2023.

Controversies surrounding the deployment of the frigate Bayern are indicative of the glacial pace of change in German strategic culture. While some commentators have applauded the German government's recognition of the importance of freedom of navigation in the Indo-Pacific, the fact that the Bayern avoided any contested waters in the South China Sea and also did not sail through the Taiwan Strait show how reluctant Germany still is to project hard military power. And while Frankenberger is of course right in pointing out the need for Germany to do more to guarantee security in Europe, more could also be done by future German governments to enhance the US-led security architecture in the Indo-Pacific. A considerable reduction of Germany's economic footprint in China would go a long way to reduce the likelihood of blackmail in the event of a war in the Taiwan Strait. It is heartening that the BMWK is taking this scenario increasingly serious and is trying to reduce Germany's existing economic dependencies on China.

9.4 What can we learn from past failures and current headwinds?

The fourth unforseen policy failure (UPF 4) was rooted in the question of whether Europe's arms embargo is more symbolic than meaningful. The discussion showed that uneven enforcement of the embargo by the UK, France and Germany has already contributed to enhancing the party-state's security and surveillance capabilities. Even Germany's supposedly rigid export control regime could not prevent the provision of dual-use items such as engines for Chinese submarines and warships. While US government officials have warned successive German governments against contributing to military modernization in China since 2007, it took until 2017 for the Merkel administration to impose a licencing requirement for the export of all submarine engines. Whereas in UPF 3 I showed that it took the German government *sixteen years* to reign into the operations of its bilateral development agency GIZ UPF 4 showed that in the field of arms control the Merkel administration needed *ten years* to move from insight to action. This should be considered another case of destructive learning, as the German government's tardy response has aided the PLA Navy's modernization which is now endangering US forward deployment in the South China Sea.

The fourth policy punctuation analysis (PPA 4) is significant for revealing that neither Beijing's red lines nor Berlin's One China policy is set in stone. Despite highly militant language the CCP did not follow through with its many threats against Czechia. This is also evident from Stark-Watzinger's visit to Taiwan, which also prompted harsh political rhetoric but did not result in punitive actions against Germany. Gradual diplomatic upgrading with Taiwan thus is possible even under the conditions of Berlin's One China policy. Such political learning is significant, as it reveals that the widespread psychological dependence on China among many German elites'– more specifically, the fear of retribution for acts that are considered unfriendly towards the one party-state – can in fact be overcome. At the same time PPA 4 has also shown that it will not be enough to simply court Taiwanese investment in Germany. Much more needs to be done to help Taiwan protect itself militarily. The deployment of the frigate Bayern can only be considered a form of tokenism. And during a recent visit to Taiwan the Chairwoman of the Bundestag's Defence Committee made it clear that '(there's) no question to send weapons to Taiwan' (Deutsche Welle, 2023). She has also suggested that '(our) role is less military here" and that '(it's) an economic question' (2023). This suggests that when it comes to the Indo-Pacific in general and Taiwan in particular Germany has not yet made significant headway in terms of Scholz's *Zeitenwende*.

References for Chapter 9

Álvarez, S. (2022), '„Kann sein, dass der Krieg schon morgen beginnt"', *WirtschaftsWoche*, 13 December. WirtschaftsWoche Archive.

AOAV (2018), 'UK Arms Exports to China', November. Available online: https://aoav.org
.uk/2018/uk-arms-sales-to-china/ (accessed 19 July 2023).

Bauer, S. and M. Bromley (2004), 'The European Union Code of Conduct on Arms
Exports', *SIPRI*, Policy Paper No. 8, November. Available online: https://www.sipri.org/
sites/default/files/files/PP/SIPRIPP08.pdf (accessed 19 July 2023).

BDSV (2014), 'The German Security and Defence Industry', (no date). Available online:
https://archive.is/A4YAA (accessed 19 July 2023).

Blülle, E. and O. Fuchs (2022), 'Herr Fulda, wieso riskiert China so viel für diesen kleinen
Flecken Erde?', *Republik*, 18 August. Available online: https://archive.is/BrcYW
(accessed 19 July 2023).

Böge, F. (2021), 'Kein Vertrauen in die Fregatte', *Frankfurter Allgemeine Zeitung*, 18
September. Nr. 217: 5.

Bösch, F. (2022), 'Handel durch Wandel', *Frankfurter Allgemeine Zeitung*, 17 October.
F.A.Z. Archive.

Bräuner, O., M. Bromley, and M. Duchâtel (2015), 'Western Arms Exports to China',
SIPRI, Policy Paper 43, January. Available online: https://www.sipri.org/sites/default/
files/files/PP/SIPRIPP43.pdf (accessed 19 July 2023).

Brössler, D. and M. Szymanski (2021), 'Reise in die Untiefen der Weltpolitik', *Süddeutsche
Zeitung*, 4 March. Available online: https://archive.is/So8uE (accessed 19 July 2023).

Bundeswehr (2022), 'Indo-Pacific Deployment 2021', Available online: https://www
.bundeswehr.de/en/organization/navy/news/indo-pacific-deployment-2021 (accessed
19 July 2023).

Bütikofer, R., F. Godement, H. Maull, and V. Stanzel (2020), 'Europa muss seine China-
Politik ändern', *Handelsblatt*, 14 September, Handelsblatt Archive.

Carstens, P. (2021), 'Für eine regelbasierte Weltordnung', *Frankfurter Allgemeine Zeitung*,
30 July. Nr. 174: 8.

Casarini, N. (2006), 'The Evolution of the EU-China Relationship: From Constructive
Engagement to Strategic Partnership', *ISS*, Occasional Paper No. 64, October. Available
online: https://www.iss.europa.eu/sites/default/files/EUISSFiles/occ64.pdf (accessed 19
July 2023).

Cheng, K. (2017), 'Chinese Official Said 10,000 Died in 1989', *MCLC Resource Center*,
Available online: https://archive.is/fhA8M (accessed 19 July 2023).

Consilium (1989), 'Presidency Conclusions, European Council', June. Available online:
https://www.consilium.europa.eu/media/20589/1989_june_-_madrid__eng_.pdf
(accessed 19 July 2023).

Deutsche Welle (2021), 'German Technology Found in China's Warships: Report', 6
November. Available online: https://archive.is/uHXef#selection-1571.0-1571.59
(accessed 19 July 2023).

Deutsche Welle (2023), 'Germany Won't Arm Taiwan, Says Senior Lawmaker', 11 January.
Available online: https://archive.is/K0Ero (accessed 19 July 2023).

Drüten, C. (2020), 'Deutschlands neuer China-Plan', *Welt*, 2 September. Available online:
https://archive.is/qr91C (accessed 19 July 2023).

European Parliament (2023), 'Member States' Non-compliance with the EU Arms Embargo
against China', March. Available online: https://archive.is/QwYgx (accessed 19 July 2023).

ExportManager (2015), 'Aktuelles zum China-Waffenembargo', 14 October. Available
online: https://archive.is/hSQ5N#selection-907.3-924.0 (accessed 19 July 2023).

Federal Foreign Office (2020), '"Germany – Europe – Asia: Shaping the 21st Century
Together": The German Government Adopts Policy Guidelines on the Indo-Pacific
Region', September. Available online: https://archive.is/zsZfK (accessed 19 July 2023).

Fischer, P. (2022), 'Krieg um Taiwan? Hoffentlich siegt die Vernunft!', *Neue Zürcher Zeitung*, 5 August. NZZ Archive.

Frankenberger, K.-D. (2021), 'Nur ein Symbol? Immerhin!', *Frankfurter Allgemeine Zeitung*, 5 November. F.A.Z. Archive.

Frontline (2019), 'Timeline: What Led to the Tiananmen Square Massacre', 5 June. Available online: https://archive.is/U8Zen#selection-395.0-395.51 (accessed 23 July 2023).

Fulda, A. (2020), *The Struggle for Democracy in Mainland China, Taiwan and Hong Kong. Sharp Power and its Discontents*, Oxon and New York: Routledge.

Gillmann, B., D. Heide, and M. Kölling (2023), 'Stark-Watzinger warnt vor neuer Abhängigkeit von China', *Handelsblatt*, 22 March. Handelsblatt Archive.

Global Times (2020), 'Vystrcil's Taiwan Visit an Opportunistic Stunt: Global Times Editorial', 30 August. Available online: https://archive.is/2US9a (accessed 19 July 2023).

Goldberg, C. (2020), Germany's Indo-Pacific Vision: A New Reckoning with China or More Strategic Drift?', *The Diplomat*, 15 September. Available online: https://archive.is/b4SAE (accessed 19 July 2023).

Görlach, A. (2023), 'Bereitet Xi Jinping China auf den Krieg vor?', *WirtschaftsWoche*, 4 April. WirtschaftsWoche Archive.

Hamacher, F. (2023a), 'Taiwan Visit China Called "Vile" Is a "Normal Work Trip", German Minister Says, 22 March 2023', *Reuters*, 22 March. Available online: https://archive.is/DdU1Q#selection-471.0-471.78 (accessed 19 July 2023).

Hancock, T. (2014), 'European Companies Are Supplying China with Billions in Weapons and Military Technology', *Business Insider*, 30 April. Available online: https://archive.is/EJgpP#selection-2854.0-3019.87 (accessed 19 July 2023).

Hawkins, A. (2023), 'Taiwan Foreign Minister Warns of Conflict with China in 2027', *The Guardian*, 21 April. Available online: https://archive.is/9VB3d (accessed 19 July 2023).

Hayton, B. (2018), 'Two Years On, South China Sea Ruling Remains a Battleground for the Rules-Based Order', *Chatham House*, 11 July. Available online: https://archive.is/IO9L8 (accessed 19 July 2023).

Heide, D. and B. Gillmann (2023), 'Peking zeigt sich verärgert über Taiwanreise der deutschen Forschungsministerin', *Handelsblatt*, 17 March. Handelsblatt Archive.

Heide, D., S. Gusbeth, and M. Kölling (2023), 'Taiwan-Konflikt alarmiert die Wirtschaft', *Handelsblatt*, 17 February. Handelsblatt Archive.

Ho, P. (2017), 'The Black Elephant Challenge for Governments', *The Straits Times*, 7 April 2017. Available online: https://archive.is/tK2AD.

Horizon Advisory (2022), 'Risks of Airbus Ties to China', June. Available online: https://www.horizonadvisory.org/flight-risk (accessed 19 July 2023).

Hulverscheidt, C. (2022a), 'Die Welt sollte Pelosi dankbar sein', *Süddeutsche Zeitung*, 5 August. Available online: https://archive.is/3jhDm (accessed 19 July 2023).

IPG (2016), 'Steinbeißermeier', 28 November. Available online: https://archive.is/rsHEx (accessed 10 July 2023).

Kirchberger, S. (2021), 'Understanding Risk in the Great Competition with China', *Heritage*, 20 October. Available online: https://archive.is/V9keN (accessed 19 July 2023).

Kölling, M. (2023), 'TSMC zögert beim Bau der eigenen europäischen Chipfabrik', *Handelsblatt*, 17 April. Handelsblatt Archive.

Kölling, M. (2023a), 'China-Taiwan-Konflikt: Warum eine Invasion unwahrscheinlich ist', *Neue Zürcher Zeitung*, 21 February. NZZ Archive.

Kölling, M. (2023b), 'Auf Chinas Befindlichkeiten wird weniger Rücksicht genommen: Eine Zeitenwende in Deutschlands Asienpolitik?', *Neue Zürcher Zeitung*, 23 March. NZZ Archive.

Kundnani, H. (2015), *The Paradox of German Power*, New York: Oxford University Press.

Kuo, L. (2019), 'China's Other Tiananmens: 30 Years On', *The Guardian*, 2 June. Available online: https://archive.is/lmdGt (accessed 19 July 2023).

Lague, D. (2013), 'Special Report - Chinese Military's Secret to Success: European Engineering', *Reuters*, 19 December. Available online: https://archive.is/E9ykE (accessed 19 July 2023).

Leithäuser, J. (2020), 'In Konkurrenz zu China', *Frankfurter Allgemeine Zeitung*, 3 September. Nr. 205: 10.

Maas (2021), 'Wir brauchen eine europäische Strategie für den Indo-Pazifik', *Handelsblatt*, 11 April. Available online: https://archive.is/9XpAb (accessed 19 July 2023).

Maksan, O. (2022), 'Die Fregatte «Bayern» kehrt nach heikler Mission heim – Und die Ministerin hat keine Zeit', *Neue Zürcher Zeitung*, 18 February. NZZ Archive.

Maull, H. (1990–91), 'Germany and Japan: The New Civilian Powers', *Foreign Affairs*, Available online: https://archive.is/njjo5 (accessed 10 July 2023).

Maull, H. (2018), 'Reflective, Hegemonic, Geo-economic, Civilian … ? The Puzzle of German Power', *German Politics*, 27(4): 460–78.

Mufson, S. (2001), 'Documents Reveal Top Chinese Split Before Crackdown', *The Washington Post*, 6 January. Available online: https://archive.is/0rWeZ (accessed 19 July 2023).

Müller, F. (2022), 'China kann sich einen Krieg um Taiwan nicht leisten - Eigentlich', 10 August. Available online: https://archive.is/yThhX (accessed 19 July).

National Science and Technology Council (2023), 'A Historic Milestone in Taiwan-Germany Cooperation! First German Minister Visits Taiwan in 26 Years to Sign a Cooperation Ar-rangement with the NSTC', March. Available online: https://archive.is/ Fapza (accessed 19 July 2023).

Pape, L. (2023), '„Bildungsreise" in Taiwan', *TAZ*, 23 March. Available online: https:// archive.is/rT7aR (accessed 19 July 2023).

People's Daily (2020), 'Czech Senate Speaker Condemned for Interfering in China's Internal Affairs', September. Available online: https://archive.is/9qVA3 (accessed 19 July 2023).

Prantner, C. (2021), 'Fregatte «Bayern» läuft in den Indopazifik aus', *Neue Zürcher Zeitung*, 2 August. NZZ Archive.

Reuters (2023), 'China Protests "Vile" Taiwan Visit by German Minister', 21 March. Available online: https://archive.is/m1qE0 (accessed 19 July 2023).

Rüesch, A. (2022), 'Pelosis Reise ins Ungewisse: Amerika riskiert eine unnötige Krise mit China', *Neue Zürcher Zeitung*, 2 August. NZZ Archive.

Šebok, F. (2023), 'Czech Speaker of Chamber of Deputies Arrives in Taiwan on a "Mission"', CHOICE, March. Available online: https://archive.is/agtKI (accessed 19 July 2023).

Shi-Kupfer, K. (2022), 'Zu viel Zurückhaltung gegenüber China wäre ein Fehler', *Süddeutsche Zeitung*, 15 August. Available online: https://archive.is/cVSa4 (accessed 19 July 2023).

Sidley (2021), 'New European Union Dual-Use Regulation Enters Into Force', 9 September. Available online: https://archive.is/c3SqF (accessed 19 July 2023).

SIPRI (2012), 'EU arms embargo on China', November. Available online: https://archive.is /3q1LX (accessed 19 July 2023).

Strangio, S. (2022), Chinese FM Pledges Progress on South China Sea Code of Conduct, *The Diplomat*, 13 July. Available online: https://archive.is/0iX0V (accessed 19 July 2023).

Strittmatter, K. (2022), 'Auf Taiwan schauen - Und lernen', *Süddeutsche Zeitung*, 4 August. Available online: https://archive.is/3gMgT (accessed 19 July 2023).

Süddeutsche Zeitung (2022a), 'Deutsche Außenpolitiker warnen vor Eskalation im Taiwan-Konflikt', *Süddeutsche Zeitung*, 1 August. Available online: https://archive.is/NSerk (accessed 19 July 2023).

Süddeutsche Zeitung (2022b), 'Habeck-Beamte rechnen offenbar mit Annexion Taiwans bis 2027', 1 December. Available online: https://archive.is/vRdlZ (accessed 19 July 2023).

Süddeutsche Zeitung (2023), 'Deutschland und Taiwan vereinbaren Forschungskooperation', 21 March. Available online: https://archive.is/nLv9T (accessed 19 July 2023).

TAZ (2023), 'Forscher Besuch', 21 March 2023. Available online: https://archive.is/zOcoq (accessed 19 July 2023).

The Federal Government (2020), 'Policy Guidelines for the Indo-Pacific', 1 September. Available online: https://www.auswaertiges-amt.de/blob/2380514/f9784f7e3b3fa1b d7c5446d274a4169e/200901-indo-pazifik-leitlinien--1--data.pdf (accessed 19 July 2023).

The Maritime Executive (2022), 'Report: China Is On Course to Overtake America's Naval Capabilities', https://archive.is/EaB23 (accessed 19 July 2023).

The Week (2021), 'German Engines Powering China's Warships: EU Arms Ban Torpedoed by Dual-Use Tech', November. Available online: https://archive.is/9rX1d (accessed 19 July 2023).

Tiananmen Chronology (2023), 'It Is Necessary to Take a Clear-cut Stand against Disturbances', Available online: https://archive.is/6Sh6 (accessed 19 July 2023).

Tillack, H.-M. (2021), 'Deutsche Firmen lieferten Motoren für chinesische Kriegsschiffe', *Welt*, 6 November. Available online: https://archive.is/m5nky (accessed 19 July 2023).

Tillack, H.-M. (2022), 'Chinesische Aggression, deutsche Technik', *Welt*, 11 July. Available online: https://archive.is/tvdLD#selection-3649.0-3656.0 (accessed 19 July 2023).

Unger, J. (1991), 'Introduction', in J. Unger (ed), *The Pro-Democracy Protests in China: Reports from the Provinces*, 1–7, New York: M.E. Sharpe.

Vimeo (2022), 'Dr Andreas Fulda on Sky News 8 August 2022', August. Available online: https://vimeo.com/737797861 (accessed 19 July 2023).

White, E. (2018), 'US-Taiwan Relations Warm in Face of Beijing Protests', *Financial Times*, 16 March. Available online: https://archive.is/0fb1q (accessed 19 July 2023).

Wright, T. (1999), 'State Repression and Student Protest in Contemporary China', *The China Quarterly*, 157: 142–72.

Yu, V. (2019), 'Tiananmen Square Anniversary: What Sparked the Protests in China in 1989?', *The Guardian*, 30 May. Available online: https://archive.is/PI0RO (accessed 19 July 2023).

Chapter 10

CENSORSHIP, SELF-CENSORSHIP AND COMPROMISES
IN ACADEMIC COOPERATION WITH CHINA

10.1 How to deal with autocratic China in science collaboration?

In the previous empirical chapters I thus far discussed eight case studies of policy failure (UPF 1–4) and policy punctuation (PPA 1–4) in *industry policy, technology policy, development aid* and *security policy*. In this fifth and final empirical chapter I will dissect the topics of censorship, self-censorship and compromises in academic cooperation with China. The question how to engage with autocratic China has been subject to fierce public debates in Germany. Since I have been an active participant in these debates I would like to reiterate a point I already made in the fifth methodology chapter. I contend that while actively participating in a fast-paced and high-stakes public debate, one can also take on the role of a dispassionate researcher working on a fairly slow-paced book project. During the course of writing this book chapter, I had a chance to reflect on my own pre-scientific value orientations, tacit norms, approaches and theories, in addition to my perceptions of situations that led me to choose particular approaches. Also included in my reflections are the ways in which I have framed problems and my role within a larger institutional setting (Schoen, 1983, 62).

Chapter at a glance

Germany's half-hearted defence of academic freedom vis-à-vis CCP-led China is a central theme of the first part of this book chapter. Drawing on a discussion of fault lines in German China studies I ponder the question whether there is a lack of critical self-reflexivity in German Sinology. Following unprecedented sanctions by the CCP on European parliamentarians, lawyers and academics I describe the nature of a civil society-led pushback. In the fifth unforeseen policy failure (UPF 5) I also ask the admittedly provocative question whether academic freedom is still a shared value in Germany.

The second half of the book chapter centres around the German Sinology debate (2022–). Here I discuss what can be considered a fallacy of tactical compromises in academic cooperation with China. The fifth policy punctuation analysis (PPA 5) also discusses revelations by investigative journalists and independent scholars relating to the dangers of unregulated scientific collaboration with China.

10.2 *Unforeseen policy failure 5 | What explains Germany's half-hearted defence of academic freedom?*

The fifth and final unforeseen policy failure (UPF 5) revolves around Chinese Communist Party censorship and the resulting threat to academic freedom at home and abroad. The Hong Kong lawyer and writer Dapiran has aptly described the creation of an 'environment of fear' as the 'act of censorship' (2021). It is my contention that such an *environment of fear* has compelled not only Chinese academics but also many Germans to either practice self-censorship *actively* (conscious self-control) or *passively* (subconscious, internalized self-control). It is also my contention that German science policy towards China thus far has failed to address this major challenge.

In Germany, academic freedom is enshrined in the country's Basic Law under Article 5 ('Arts and sciences, research and teaching shall be free. The freedom of teaching shall not release any person from allegiance to the constitution') (Federal Ministry of Justice, 2023). German Sinologists Ahlers and Heberer have argued that '(in) principle, "academic freedom" in the European sense has not existed or does not exist in China' (2021). According to the two authors the instrumentalization of China's academia 'has not only been the case since the founding of the People's Republic in 1949, but is rooted in political culture and was not handled differently in the Republic of China in the 1930s and 1940s' (2021). This view is highly problematic, as it is not only ahistorical but also exaggerates the extent of 'coordination' (*Gleichschaltung*) of China's society, both past and present. The Sinologist Schell has highlighted that Chinese history is littered with examples of officials and scholars remonstrating against their rulers (1997). It should also be pointed out that during the Republican Era (1912–1949) the American philosopher John Dewey went to China and was able to give more than 200 lectures 'to large academic and general audiences on topics such as education, philosophy, and science' (Stroud, 2013, 97). Without some form of intellectual openness this certainly would not have been possible. And while the two authors are right in emphasizing anti-liberal traditions during the era of the People's Republic of China (1945–), they should have pointed out that the primary carriers of such an anti-liberal political culture have been CCP officials. Ahlers and Heberer also critique an emphasis on the control of the party-state over Chinese academia in the Western public discourse, as such criticism would supposedly run the danger of 'profiling' Chinese scholars and students (2021), who would be either seen as 'propagandists' or 'spies' (2021). Such framing is highly problematic, since it is of course possible to critique the party-state's anti-liberal approach to Chinese academia without pigeonholing Chinese academics and students.

Fault lines in German China studies

In my own contribution to the debate I highlighted how the rise of China's security state since 2012 undermines academic freedom in China and Germany

(Fulda, 2021a). Document No 9, a censorship directive from 2013, which according to Buckley claims bears 'the unmistakable imprimatur of Xi Jinping' (2013), had turned universal values, freedom of speech, civil society, the party's historical mistakes, among others, into taboo subjects. I argued that it marked a departure from the semi-liberal approach of Xi's predecessor Hu Jintao. Numerous anti-liberal party laws were subsequently passed under Xi's leadership, such as the Counter-Espionage Law (2014), National Security Law (2015), Cyber Security Law (2017), National Intelligence Law (2017) and Overseas NGO Law (2017). Charters of Chinese universities were amended to remove freedom of thought. A number of Chinese intellectuals who were critical of the regime were dismissed, had their pensions denied or were sentenced to long prison terms. In my op-ed I also explained that with its extraterritorial paragraph 38 of the Hong Kong National Security Law (2020) the CCP has criminalized independent Western China studies (2021a).

The dueling op-eds in *Forschung and Lehre* are an example of existing fault lines in German China studies. Charon and Vilmer have argued that 'a majority of researchers, shaped by interpersonal relationships they have built with their Chinese academic partners for decades, are closer to the discourse of the business class: China is not a threat, and the point is to try and deconstruct the prejudices and the ignorance vis-à-vis this original political system. They hope to work on a rapprochement and dialogue (notably through academic exchange programs)' (2021, 284–5). This finding suggests that foreign policy paradigms such as the Steinmeier doctrine 'Rapprochement through interweaving' and its historical antecedent – Bahr's Ostpolitik 'Change through rapprochement' – have been highly influential in the field of German China studies, too. According to Charon and Vilmer 'China-Versteher' were dominating the academic field whereas '(the) researchers considering China as a threat or those qualified as "China-Kritiker" are in the minority in Germany, and most do not have permanent positions in German universities' (2021, 285). To support this view they referenced an open letter in support of Canadian researcher Michael Kovrig, who was arbitrarily detained by the Xi regime. It 'was signed by MERICS experts, journalists, think tankers critical of China at the Deutsche Gesellschaft für Auswärtige Politik . . . but not by the crushing majority of university professors in Germany' (2021). In the view of Charon and Vilmer this 'revealed the invisible fracture between the "China-Versteher" and "China-Kritiker"' in Germany (2021).

Is there a lack of critical self-reflexivity in German Sinology?

While the term 'China-Versteher' (China understander) is frequently invoked in public debates, it is seen as pejorative by some. A case in point is a highly polemical essay by Monschein. In reference to an op-ed in *Deutschlandfunk* by the journalist Pamperrien titled 'The China-understanders and their democratic enemies' (2013) Monschein alternatively used the politically charged terms 'enemy scheme' (*Feindschema*), 'China-Bashing' and 'sinophobe propaganda' when responding to Pamperrien's criticism (2020). The fact that the Sinologist-turned-think tanker Shi-Kupfer (who by now has returned to academia) had developed a very similar critique of 'China-Versteher' didn't seem to matter much (2020). In her op-ed Shi-Kupfer had critiqued 'politicians, entrepreneurs, scientists, doctors, journalists and also China experts from liberal democracies' (2020) who, similar to Beijing's position, would accuse compatriots who are critical of the Chinese government of 'arrogance', 'racism' and 'double standards' (2020). Such a critique, according to Shi-Kupfer, would in fact promote racism and arrogance in China, as it was tantamount to shielding a Chinese government which was discriminating ethnic and social minorities. Those who were condemning critics of the Chinese regime as racists and agitators were 'guilty of disregarding the many courageous Chinese who oppose their government' (2020).

What can explain this schism in the field of German Sinology? I contend that the core of this debate is about researcher positionality under conditions of authoritarianism. A historical perspective can help shed light on yet another black elephant phenomenon (see also Chapters 2 and 9). The Sinologist Klotzbücher has pointed out that Maoism at German universities has remained a taboo topic. When German Maoists returned from China in the late 1970s and early 1980s many did not self-critically reflect on their *seduction experience*, thus burdening successive generations of Sinologists with 'emotionally strongly loaded taboos' (Klotzbücher, 2019, 448). Since the second generation remained dependent on the patronage of senior Sinologists, German Sinology as a whole did not develop the necessary self-critical reflexivity to further develop as an academic field, Klotzbücher argues (2019, 449). Only in Autumn 2023 and following the publication of a controversial op-ed by two former heavyweights in German Sinology (Strittmatter, 2023) did the Maoist past of the highly influential Sinologist Heberer gain more public attention (Grzanna, 2023). After the relativization of the human rights situation in the Xinjiang Uyghur Autonomous Region (XUAR) by Heberer and Schmidt-Glintzer in their op-ed in NZZ 'questions are being raised that shake the credibility of the discipline [of Sinology]' (2023).

It hasn't helped that the Chinese party-state has actively exploited existing tensions in the academic field. According to Charon and Vilmer, it has employed control tools ranging from (1) limiting field access for critics of China's political regime, (2) the creation of financial dependencies, (3) elite capture, (4) pressure by Chinese students on campus, (5) pressure on publishers, (6) pressure on PhD supervisors, (7) pressure on relatives, (8) arrest and intimidation of people with access to their field in China, (9) kidnappings, arbitrary arrests, disappearances, forced televised 'confessions', to (10) lawsuits (2021). Such measures have further contributed to self-censorship among Western academics. I have argued that '(while) individual self-censorship which aims to protect family and research partners in China can be justified, a sector-wide tacit acceptance of the CCP's political censorship regime would neutralise German academia as a realm of critical inquiry' (Fulda, 2021b). As the following discussion will show, this is not only a theoretical possibility but a tangible problem.

Civil society-led pushback against the CCP's targeting of independent scholars

As part of a coordinated international effort, the EU, the UK, Canada and the United States sanctioned four Chinese officials on 22 March 2021 over gross human rights violations in the Xinjiang Uygur Autonomous Region (XUAR) (Lau and Barigazzi, 2021). China's Ministry of Foreign Affairs (MoFA) announced countersanctions the same day against ten individuals, including eight European parliamentarians and two European scholars, Adrian Zenz, a Senior Fellow and Director in China Studies at the Victims of Communism Memorial Foundation, as well as Björn Jerdén, director of the Swedish National China Centre (2021). Moreover, the Chinese party-state retaliated against four European institutions, including the Berlin-based think tank Merics. A few days later, British China expert Jo Smith Finley (Newcastle University), who researches the suppression of Uyghurs, was also sanctioned (BBC, 2021). A ban on entry into China was imposed on targeted individuals and their families. Companies and institutions that were sanctioned were also prohibited from doing business in China. While German foreign minister Maas summoned the Chinese ambassador (Talmon, 2023), Chancellor Angela Merkel did not publicly respond (Fulda and Missal, 2021a). Stronger resistance came from European civil society. Thirty directors of European research institutes stated that they were 'deeply concerned that targeting independent researchers and civil society institutions undermines practical and constructive engagement by people who are striving to contribute positively to policy debates' (Statement by European Research Institute Directors, 2021). The German learned society Deutsche Vereinigung für Chinastudien criticized the sanctions against European China experts (DVCS, 2021). The Board of the European Association for Chinese Studies likewise critiqued the 'defamation of European researchers and research institutions as circulators of "lies and disinformation" by the P.R.C. government' (EACS, 2021).

Such pushback was not unanimous, however. In a public statement in 2020 the board of the learned society Deutsche Gesellschaft für Asienkunde (DGA) had lauded the virtues of taking a supposedly 'neutral' position when it comes to China (DGA, 2020). In its statement the DGA board argued that '(we), of course, accept if scholars engage in political discourses or reflect about their personal position to critical issues of our time' (2020). Free speech, however, was not unconditional. The DGA statement went on to argue that 'we oppose any attack against scholars for their scholarly attitude of questioning positions, for looking deeper and for sometimes opposing to the mainstream' (2020). The call for civility in public discourse was admirable; however, it also relegated academic freedom and free speech to what Frank Furedi refers to as a 'second-order value' (2016, 179). Despite the fact that 'opposing the mainstream' could be seen as granting academics licence to engage in contrarian thinking, the statement also argued that 'Cold war rhetoric and de-coupling fantasies are combined as if there were no alternatives. For many countries in Asia-Pacific and Europe this is no reasonable choice given the complex supply chain networks which have emerged over the past decades' (2020). As the global discourse about possible decoupling from China is relatively new, it became apparent that the DGA board was advocating a rather mainstream view held by German establishment academicians that there is no alternative to deepening Western economic entanglement with China. DGA board members therefore mirrored Merkel's mercantilist approach by advocating ever-greater economic integration between Europe and China. Germany's 'business first' approach in China policy thus was not supposed to be challenged. And by mentioning 'Cold War rhetoric and decoupling fantasies' the DGA statement's phrasing was not unlike that of the ultra-nationalist party-state mouthpiece *Global Times*. In another public statement from June 2021 the DGA board did not directly address the CCP's countersanctions (DGA, 2021). The China scholars Habich-Sobiegalla and Steinhardt have agreed with 'Fulda and co-authors' point that it is the task of academic organizations to take a stance against acts of repression against academics by the Chinese government' (2022). The two authors have also argued that 'that the DGA, of which we are both members, has not lived up to this task in its recent statements' (2022). As the following discussion will show, tensions in the field are not only limited to the positions taken by learned societies.

Is academic freedom still a shared value?

Another remarkable pushback against the CCP's countersanctions took the form of an open letter signed by 1,336 scholars worldwide. The open letter expressed 'solidarity with all our persecuted colleagues' (Solidarity statement, 2021), which included both non-Chinese and Chinese scholars. Signatories were 'calling on the Chinese government to revoke these unjustified sanctions and to accept that scholarship on China, like scholarship on any country, entails scrutiny of its policies, goals and actions. We also pledge to continue to be inclusive in our own work and engage with all academic views, including those the Chinese government is trying to marginalise' (2021). While attributing responsibility to the party-state the letter also demanded Western universities to enhance transparency and accountability in their engagement with autocratic states (2021).

Among the signatories were eighty China experts at German universities. But as Missal and I have pointed out in an op-ed '(not) everyone was on board, however. Many prominent German China scholars did not sign the solidarity statement' (Fulda and Missal, 2021a). Pointing out this fact would become a highly consequential speech act. In this context it should be noted that election law expert Muller has warned against over-interpreting missing signatures, suggesting that not signing an open letter should not be equated with tacit support for those who are criticized in it. And according to Muller open letters can have other defects, too: either they are 'watered down and sufficiently generalized to attain broader support' (2020) or they act as a form of virtue signalling to peers rather than serving the purpose of persuasion (2020). While Muller makes many good points, once applied to the case of the aforementioned open letter his criticism would hardly hold water. The open letter drafters made it very clear that '(the) measures against non-Chinese scholars, although singling out a few individuals and institutions, target and affect the entirety of the scholarly community working on, in and with counterparts in China, as well as those counterparts in Chinese academia' (Solidarity statement, 2021). In our commentary Missal and I also offered the following explanation for the reluctance among senior German China experts to co-sign. We argued that this was the case 'perhaps because they fear retribution or don't want to risk Beijing's support for their research projects, institutional partnerships, or consulting positions' (Fulda and Missal, 2021a). Little did we know at the time of publication of our op-ed that our criticism – as well as related critique of existing financial dependencies in German Sinology on party-state funding (Fulda and Missal, 2021a) – would trigger what has now become known as the German Sinology debate (2022–).

10.3 Policy punctuation analysis 5 | *The fallacy of tactical compromises in academic cooperation with China*

Both in past and present, the field of Sinology has been subject to fierce public debates. It is important to note that while Sinology has a strong linguistic and philological orientation, contemporary China studies as *area studies* have more in common with the social sciences. In Germany, the term 'Sinologist' is widely used to refer to academics with China expertise, regardless of whether they belong to the former or the latter academic field.

The state of the field of German Sinology has been critiqued both from *outside* and *within* academia. A case in point of the former is the journalist Strittmatter's critique of German Sinologists staying mum on the awarding of the Nobel Peace Prize to Liu Xiaobo (2010). In this article the freelance author Shi Ming described Beijing apologists as including old leftists, culturalists, relativists and those 'who would like to play door opener in China as advisors to German politicians' (2010). Strittmatter also cites the Sinologist Kühner as saying that there is 'a large group in German sinology [which] is about to become dependent' (2010). This was a critique of the proliferation of Confucius Institutes (CI) at German universities with the help of prominent German Sinologists.

Missal and I argued in our coauthored article that Confucius Directors sending an open letter to more than 200 parliamentarians in August 2020 justifying the existence of CI at German universities should be regarded as *lobbying* and a telltale sign of the formation of an *interest group* (Fulda and Missal, 2021b). We also discussed findings from our research article with a large group of German Sinologists during a webinar hosted by DGA's *Arbeitskreis Sozialwissenschaftliche Chinaforschung* (ASC) on 26 November 2021. Yet our critique from within the community of China scholars was not welcome and prompted strong emotional reactions. In retrospect, the frosty reception we received reminded me of observations by Dahrendorf about American Sociology in the 1950s. Dahrendorf detected an 'anxious profession' (1963, 173) that 'spends a disproportionate amount of time justifying and discussing their professional existence. The hedgehog position to the outside world, however, hinders, as always, the critical discussion within. The profession of sociology is like a nation at war. In this way, too, the development of the discipline itself is held back. One divides the supposed object into countless boxes or little gardens and allows everyone to fence in their little garden, but forbids them to even look critically over at their neighbour' (1963, 174). The resulting Sinology debate, which took the form of dueling op-eds in the *Frankfurter Allgemeine Zeitung* in Spring 2022, is a case in point.

The Sinology debate reloaded

On 9 March 2022 the two Sinology professors Alpermann (University of Wuerzburg) and Schubert (University of Tuebingen) published a German-language op-ed in *Frankfurter Allgemeine Zeitung* (2022a). They also translated their text into English (2022b; please note that all of the following direct quotes are not my translation but theirs). Academic discourse participants who were critical of self-censorship and appeasement towards the Chinese party-state in Germany's China studies would 'represent a new moral crusade' (2022b). Established China scholars were labelled as 'new crusaders' (2022b). Besides these ad hominem attacks, Alpermann and Schubert employed a policy image which dismissed existing arguments and research findings by stating that 'no proof' (2022b) existed demonstrating a growing Chinese influence on German China studies. The two authors also complained that Ohlberg, a China expert at the German Marshall Fund, was using 'a distinctly China-critical narrative in both the German and international media' (2022b) in order 'to exert considerable public pressure on otherwise-independent China researchers to embrace this narrative as their own' (2022b). Co-Founder and Director of the Global Public Policy Institute (GPPi), Thorsten Benner, tweeted that 'Alpermann and Schubert demonstrate a "most impressive capacity for cognitive dissonance when one claims"': 'Serious China research needs differentiation. Polarization makes it blind' and at the same time one calls dissenters 'moralizing crusaders' who have fallen prey to 'delusions of decoupling' (MCLC Resource Center, 2022).

In their op-ed Alpermann and Schubert argued that 'three things are needed to ensure appropriate and future-oriented China discussions: 1) Access to the country; 2) Rejecting the idea of any need for a "morality entrance exam" for China research; and 3) Maintaining a dialogue with Chinese universities' (2002b). Arguing that 'access to the country is absolutely essential' (2002b) Alpermann and Schubert spoke up in defence of 'tactical compromises in research design' (2002b). 'Tactical concessions', they argued, were required 'to keep the path to understanding China open' (2002b). They also complained about pressure on China scholars to 'publicly position themselves against grievances and political suppression in China' (2002b), be it in their media commentary or by signing an open letter in 'solidarity with colleagues hit with sanctions or with dissidents persecuted by the CCP' (2002b). Last but not least the two authors argued against a 'strict regulation or even the complete cessation of cooperation with Chinese universities' (2002b), claiming that at Chinese universities 'opportunities still exist for critical debates with western perspectives on China, and vice versa' (2002b).

Willing to compromise without limits?

On 16 March 2022 Fulda, Ohlberg, Missal, Fabian and Klotzbücher responded with a German-language op-ed of their own (2022). An English translation was provided via H-Asia (2022). Drawing on data obtained through more than 100 freedom of information requests (Missal, 2020), the five authors pointed out that there was ample evidence that 'that German universities receive several million euros from China every year without much effort, often several hundred thousand euros per university' (Fulda et al., 2022). In defence of Ohlberg, the five authors criticized Alpermann and Schubert from not '(shying) away from resorting to a popular motif of Chinese propaganda: Allegedly controlled by the United States, Western media paint as negative a picture of the People's Republic as possible. What they omit is how the Chinese government itself contributes to this image' (2022). And while Alpermann and Schubert's three demands were duly noted, the five authors countered by stating that 'they must not lead to a situation in which China research is blindfolded and only studies what is tolerated by the Chinese side', as '(this) kind of research would make itself obsolete' (2022).

A key criticism centred around the idea of 'creative research strategies' and 'tactical compromises in research design' to maintain field access in China. Drawing on Klotzbücher's research the five authors argued that 'field research by foreign China scholars in the People's Republic of China takes place in a highly monitored, politically restricted field. The act of self-censorship associated with the inevitable "embeddedness" that is consciously or unconsciously demanded, especially upon entry, must be disclosed and methodologically anchored' (2022). The five authors in particular took issue with Alpermann and Schubert's 'use of questionable crusader metaphors to devalue legitimate discourse about the self-understanding and norms of China studies' (2022). They also warned of academic cooperation with China 'with possibly bad compromises' (2022). Instead 'the goal must be to ensure academic standards: openness, authenticity, commitment to truth, the right of doubt and criticism' (2022). Such criteria would 'be difficult to enforce if the willingness to compromise demanded by the totalitarian party-state is signaled in advance as the price of academic cooperation' (2022). The dueling op-eds resembled the Lau vs. Sandschneider dispute in 2013, which I discussed in Chapter 5. Whereas the latter was a battle over German foreign policy's direction (Lau, 2013), the competing viewpoints expressed by Alpermann/Schubert and Fulda et al. in Spring 2022 could be seen as a microcosm of the larger debate on how to engage with China both critically and constructively.

Normative shackles?

In a subsequent letter to the editors Schubert and Alpermann doubled down on key assertions of their op-ed from 9 March 2022, arguing that even the documented evidence of Chinese financial influence was still insufficient (2022). Another assertion of their letter was met by derision by Klotzbücher. He tweeted: 'In a letter to the editors, two tenured professors, Björn Alpermann from @uni_wue and Gunter Schubert from @uni_tue claim that we put "normative shackles" on them.

With a discussion on methods? With insistence on truth and right of critics? Are you serious, dear professors?' (@sascha_kb, 2022) On 30 March 2022 the German Sinologist Roetz commented on the Sinology debate in his own letter to the editors (2022). He also provided an English translation via H-Asia (Roetz, 2022). He pointed out that Sinology was 'one of those unenviable disciplines that have to work in the shadow of a dictatorship' (2022). Roetz argued that 'China, it seems, is bringing to mind a problem that the humanities and social sciences, increasingly subject to economic constraints, have too much repressed in the name of value-freedom postulates and cultural relativism' (2022). He cast doubts about Alpermann and Schubert's suggestion that the acquisition of knowledge can be separated from the normative level. Roetz wrote: 'But how, the critics rightly object, is research supposed to produce the promised "empirically proven knowledge" that supposedly cannot be obtained in any other way, if it has to be conducted under the aegis of the Chinese Communist Party and its own normative agenda?' (2022) He also took issue with claims by 'the "researchers" [who] think they can outsmart the Chinese side through "tactical compromises" and "mimicry"' (2022). He also critiqued that '(it) is probably in the nature of things if it is not specified what such "compromises" look like. However, one has to ask oneself what understanding of science is actually involved if one thinks one can pursue it with the ethos of a secret service' (2022).

Germany's Sinology debate surfaced unanswered questions about researcher positionality and what kind of compromises are permissible in Western academic China engagement. It revealed that in German Sinology no consensus yet exists about what constitutes acceptable pragmatic research strategies and what should be considered compromised research in the service of the CCP. In an article I have argued that a step towards a more self-reflexive debate would be to acknowledge that China studies are a post-normal studies (Fulda, 2021b, 225), since it deals with issues which '[involves] risk' and is marked by an environment 'where facts are uncertain, values in dispute, stakes high and decisions urgent' (Funtowicz and Ravetz, 1993, 744).

China Science Investigation

As the following discussion will show autocratic China is not only a challenge for the arts and humanities and social sciences. In Chapter 3 I outlined how predatory technology transfers are key to Beijing's global ambitions. As part of the Military-Civil Fusion strategy (Weinstein, 2021) the Chinese party-state has taken particular interest in the STEM fields – including science, technology, engineering and mathematics – since breakthroughs in basic research can lead to highly innovative applied research for both civilian and military use. This has raised concerns about the security dimension of scientific collaboration between China and Europe.

But how concerned should we be about research security? The platform for investigative journalism Follow the Money 'went through 350,000 scientific papers to figure out where the Chinese government is looking for the knowledge to become the most powerful nation on earth' (2022) and 'made those available to a collective of eleven investigative desks from seven European countries' (CSI, 2022). The resulting 'China Science Investigation' identified that among the 353,546 scientific collaborations between China and Europe 2,994 were with the Chinese military (2022). Around 2,210 studies were conducted with China's National University of Defense Technology (NUDT) (Deutschlandfunk, 2022), which 'is the PLA's premier institution for scientific research and education' (ASPI, 2019). Since 2000 at least 230 academic publications were published in collaboration between German researchers and NUDT. German research institutions such as the Universität Hamburg and Max-Planck-Institut were at the top of the list (Deutschlandfunk, 2022). Hofmann, President of the TU München – one of the German technical universities whose researchers were also found to be collaborating with NUDT – has chafed at the thought of greater state regulation as a result of the China Science Investigation. He argued that prevention – not prohibitions or permits – was key to addressing such problems (Bovensiepen and Weinmann, 2022).

In this context it should be noted that German dual-use exports regulations already include 'immaterial research results' or 'technical support' should they be relevant for weapons of mass destruction. The problem here is that 'researchers themselves must check whether a research project or parts of it require approval' from the Federal Office for Economic Affairs and Export Control (BAFA) (Bovensiepen, Menner and Weinmann, 2022). Ohlberg has consequently called on German institutions to refrain from projects which could 'either feed the military apparatus or the security machinery in China' (Bovensiepen and Weinmann, 2022).

Should democracies draw redlines around research collaboration with China?

According to another study by CRSI, Germany's laissez-faire approach to research collaboration with China threatens national security, undermines the economy and compromises ethics (Stoff, 2023). Its author Stoff argued that unregulated scientific collaboration with China could enhance China's military modernization, undermine Germany's economic competitiveness and potentially contribute to human rights abuses (2023, 10). Stoff examined German-Chinese partnerships in the STEM fields. A review of over 43,000 articles published between 2016 and May 2022, which list coauthors from Germany and China, was conducted by the author. Similar to ASPI's *China Defence Universities Tracker*, Chinese entities were classified as critical, high and moderate risk. In the study, more than 100 Chinese entities were included (2023, 11). Stoff found that research collaborations with Chinese entities that pose high or critical security risks were widespread. A total of 835 articles revealed collaboration with 24 PLA organs and military institutes. Around 283 articles were authored by coauthors who were affiliated with China's nuclear and advanced weapons R&D complex. A total of 12 articles involved collaboration between Germany and the PLA's leading hypersonic testing facility. There were 94 articles involving 6 Chinese state-owned defence conglomerates and their subsidiaries, including the facility that manufactures missiles in China (2023, 12). Researchers published research with Chinese organs involved in mass surveillance and oppression, which has ethical risks associated with it. In 450 articles, computer vision was discussed, some of which raise ethical concerns about its potential use in mass surveillance (2023, 13). According to Stoff, there was a lack of understanding of the problem of exploitation and predation in the early stages of research and innovation. Moreover, there is a lack of fit-for-purpose risk assessment frameworks and a lack of capacity for due diligence on the part of individual research institutions (2023, 14).

Feldwisch-Drentrup cites Stoff as stating that 'scientific cooperation with the People's Republic of China increasingly runs the risk of supporting China's military modernisation – even through basic research' (2023). Stoff considered existing rules to prevent high-risk scientific collaboration with China 'completely inadequate or impracticable' (2023), and suggested that unethical behaviour was partly tolerated and would continue on a 'huge scale' (2023). His independent study, read in conjunction with the aforementioned China Science Investigation, suggests that the German state and civil society thus far have failed to develop policies and protocols which can help prevent playing into the hands of Beijing's Military-Civil Fusion strategy.

How to deal with the problem of espionage?

It should be noted that neither the China Science Investigation from 2022 nor the Stoff's study published in 2023 addressed the thorny problem of Chinese espionage in Germany. Stiens has rightly pointed out 'that not all 40,000 Chinese students in Germany are in fact malicious spies' (2023). But she also correctly notes that 'according to Chinese law, individuals as well as companies and research institutions are obliged to cooperate with the Chinese secret service' (2023). Álvarez and Stölzel warn that '(if) Chinese students spy out discoveries in which German researchers have invested time and money in, China will sooner or later overtake Germany' (2021). They have noted that '(there) are no official figures on how many suspected cases of espionage at German universities have been investigated, or how many cases have been confirmed. The Office for the Protection of the Constitution does not want to comment. No statistics are kept at the state level either, so there is no picture of the situation. Germany is flying blind' (2021). There are now signs that such secrecy is gradually coming to an end. In June 2023 Handelsblatt reported that German security circles had shared information about a typical case of Chinese espionage with journalists. The reported case involved a Chinese PhD researcher who had been involved in a project between a university and a medical technology company in northern Germany. The willingness by the Chinese side to cover all expenses and the researcher's strong interest in the company's technology had raised suspicion by the company manager. It later transpired that the Chinese researcher was in fact a spy, who registered the stolen technology as a patent in China under his name (Heide, Murphy, and Neuerer, 2023).

Due to a lack of publicly available statistics, it is difficult to determine the extent of such forms of espionage. Furthermore, it is important to point out that

PRC national students and scholars abroad are rarely spies. The real danger lies in the fact that Chinese state or non-state agents acting on behalf of the CCP may direct, task or incentivize them to engage in highly unethical and irresponsible behaviour, such as research misconduct with significant national and economic security implications and ethical issues. As a result, German universities and research institutes will need to critically evaluate their existing risk management procedures. A stricter vetting process should be considered for applicants with PLA backgrounds in particular. Information security policies and protocols could also be strengthened to mitigate existing risks. As the following discussion will show, there are however limits to what universities and research institutes can do on their own.

Risk management: how well prepared are universities and research institutes for due diligence?

As Hannas and Chang have shown, there are thirty-two methods of legal, illegal and extralegal transfer of technology (2021, 7). Irregular outflows of knowledge and technology harm the German economy. There is also a risk of unethical use of new technology in China. As the example of the Military-Civil Fusion strategy show, in China, politics, science and the military are not separated. Tatlow has pointed out that even in the case of seemingly non-political cooperation topics such as marine research, one does not see the potential military relevance at first glance. In an interview with *Süddeutsche Zeitung* she used research surrounding the island of Hainan in the South China Sea as an example to illustrate this point. The latter may be declared as serving tourism or the environment, but mapping the seabed with sonar can also have a military purpose, for example, allowing submarines to operate more effectively (Bovensiepen and Menner, 2022).

Tatlow has called for a much wider public debate about risks in Germany's scientific collaboration with China. She has also suggested that a specialized consultancy could provide advise for German universities and research institutes on due diligence and risk management (Bovensiepen and Menner, 2022). Gillmann and Heide have drawn attention to the fact that '(in) Germany, the DFG, universities, the Leopoldina Academy and research organisations have had internal guidelines on China for some time' (2022). The German Academic Exchange Service (DAAD) has also established Kompetenzzentrum Internationale Wissenschaftskooperationen (KIWi), which in 2021 alone received about 400 inquiries about Chinese universities (2022). In light of the China Science Investigation Gillmann and Heide have expressed skepticism about existing guidelines and advisory services, which 'have not been of enough use' (2022). In my view it hasn't helped that a key guideline document published by KIWi was given the title 'No red lines' (DAAD KIWi, 2020). For individual researchers it remains a challenging task to grasp what exactly the Chinese interest in collaboration could be. The problem can either lie in the topic of cooperation, the cooperation partner itself or further downstream the kind of public or private organizations the Chinese partner organization is working with. And the central problem for German universities is that not all of them will be able to develop the human resources and instruments to engage in political risk analysis. While due diligence could be the way forward, in reality many universities lack information and organizational China expertise to perform this task well.

Limits to top-down state regulation

In an interview Federal Minister of Education and Research (BMBF) Stark-Watzinger announced that the BMBF will 'continue to support universities and research institutions in developing their independent China expertise, i.e. advise on what is possible and what is not. Because even if there are good personal contacts to researchers in China, one must not be naive. In China today, everything serves the Communist Party' (Gillmann, 2022). In another interview she made it clear that in terms of Germany's academic cooperation with China 'academic freedom applies, but not without responsibility. Universities must therefore weigh things up carefully' (Kummert and Leister, 2023).

President of the German Rectors' Conference (HRK) Peter-André Alt expressed a similar sentiment in an interview with Feldwisch-Drentrup (Feldwisch-Drentrup, 2022). Reflecting on past experiences in the cooperation with universities in authoritarian countries such as Russia and China, Alt spoke of 'frustrating realities' and a 'learning process within academia' (2022). He made it clear that '(in) the future, we will certainly approach cooperations more cautiously and not continue some of them' (2022). It was now a matter of 'keeping an eye on the risks inherent in scientific cooperation' (2022). In the future, 'more attention will be paid to the risks and negative consequences of contracts' (2022). Alt spoke of a 'change . . . towards a critical realism' (2022).

While such political rhetoric by senior decision-makers should be welcomed, it needs to be said that in the case of Germany the central state and organizations such as the German Rectors' Conference have few instruments at their disposal to impose their will on German universities and research institutions. Dietmar Braun, an expert in comparative political science, reminds us that after World War II 'the Allies had also successfully sought to weaken the powers of the Federal government vis-à-vis the Länder' (1997, 214). Under federalism German universities and research institutions enjoy a lot of discretion how to self-regulate. And while I am generally sympathetic to the principle of subsidiarity, in the case of autocratic China it would be a mistake to rely on an exclusively bottom-up approach. As I have argued in a recent interview 'state intervention does not have to result in prohibitions of cooperation . . . But unfortunately we cannot rely on university self-administration' (Baumgärtner and Müller, 2023). In the future, the German state and society will need to seek common ground and reach a consensus on what is and isn't permissible in scientific cooperation with China.

Who were the disruptors and what were their achievements?

Germany's Sinology debate (2022–) has revealed both destructive and creative learning. At least parts of German Sinology appear not to be ready for a self-critical debate about existing problems in the academic field. The scholarship of Klotzbücher furthermore suggests that the undetermined issue of research positionality under conditions of authoritarianism could have something to do with the unresolved legacy of Maoism at German universities. According to Klotzbücher, the latter casts a long shadow and is affecting German Sinology to this day. And since the CCP continues to engage in transnational repression, I would argue that we could have a more productive and honest discussion about the challenges and opportunities involved in conducting research in this area, if we were more willing to acknowledge that China studies are post-normal studies. There is also a need to develop new methods and approaches to China studies that are more appropriate for the complex and uncertain socio-political environment we are operating in. It is heartening that during a recent conference in Olomouc, Czechia, close to fifty participants joined our panel on 'Dilemmas of academic freedom in China Studies and beyond: Censorship, self-censorship, voice and exit' (EACS, 2022). The debates addressed the issue of self-censorship head on and also dealt with researcher positionality vis-à-vis the party-state and Chinese cooperation partners. This gives me hope that greater critical self-reflexivity can be achieved over time.

The discussed CSI and CRSI studies paint a different picture. They come to show that there are serious shortcomings in existing policies and protocols relating to research security. I would argue that even a stricter export control regime will not be sufficient to deal with this problem. No amount of state regulation alone will be enough to prevent bad academic practices occurring again. Research security can arguably only be achieved with the active support from academics and researchers in Germany. Here, a tension exists between the demand put on modern-day academics to be entrepreneurial and to raise third-party funds, and the need to better protect research security in scientific collaboration with Chinese partners. In order to address this tension the German state and society will need to seek common ground on what is still permissible and what is not. It should be noted that this will also need to include prohibitions in particularly sensitive technology or military domains. Here it is the task of the German government to communicate very clearly in which areas scientific collaboration with China should no longer take place. While such prohibitions will not endear the German government to academics, such rail guards can also be justified with reference to national security.

10.4 What can we learn from past failures and current headwinds?

In addition to greater self-reflexivity among academics and researchers, I would argue that it is important for representatives of the German state and society to reach a consensus that scientific cooperation with China should neither legitimize the CCP nor strengthen the surveillance and military capabilities of the Chinese party-state. In order to achieve such a consensus, there needs to be a more honest debate within German academia about the current role of individual researchers. Tatlow has rightly pointed out that academic freedom cannot be absolute and that ethical, social and political considerations need to be given much more consideration (Bovensiepen and Menner, 2022). I would argue that cultural norms in Germany's scientific community will only be able to evolve if practitioners are willing to critically reflect on paradigmatic assumptions underpinning their professional self-understanding. Mulkay's research on models of scientific development teaches us that cognitive change is not inevitable. Drawing on Kuhn's scholarship Mulkay argues that 'most research consists of attempts to solve problems generated by the paradigm without bringing into question its basic assumptions' (1975, 514). This book chapter revealed an enduring influence of falsified foreign policy paradigms such as 'Rapprochement through interweaving' and its historical antecedent 'Change through rapprochement' on German academia.

Wietholtz, an expert in science management, early on categorized four types of reactions during discussions about research security and China: escapism, idealism, fatalism or relativism. To illustrate the reactions she described ideal types of colleagues in the field: a *basic researcher* who would deny any personal responsibility for applied research resulting from his or her scholarship (escapism); a *professor of technology* who would justify unregulated technology transfer in science collaboration with reference to German industry doing the same (fatalism); an *idealistic researcher* who believed that collaboration with autocracies would contribute to China's democratization (idealism); and a *value relativist* researcher who would rationalize the party-state's quest for technology leadership with reference to 'the Americans', who supposedly would do the same (2021). The BMBF and HRK, together with the help of learned societies, should enter a dialogue with academics and critically engage with such cognitive and behavioural predispositions. Without a robust debate about the underlying value orientations informing such attitudes, paradigmatic change will be impossible.

References for Chapter 10

@sascha_kb (2022), 'In a Letter to the Editors, Two Tenured Professors, Björn Alpermann from @uni_wue and Gunter Schubert from @uni_tue Claim That We Put "Normative Shackles" on them. With a Discussion on Methods? With Insistence on Truth and Right of Critics? Are You Serious, Dear Professors?', *Twitter*, 22 March. Available online: https://twitter.com/sascha_kb/status/1506167621342973956?s=20 (accessed 20 July 2023); see also Footnote 9 in Sascha Klotzbücher (forthcoming in October 2023), 'Die Zukunft der Chinastudien, aus der Geschichte einer Verführung betrachtet', in: Daniel Fuchs, Sascha Klotzbücher, Andrea Riemenschnitter, Lena Springer, Felix Wemheuer (eds), *Die Zukunft mit China denken*, Wien: Mandelbaum Verlag.

Ahlers, A. and T. Heberer (2021), 'Kooperation auf Augenhöhe?', *Forschung & Lehre*, 20 September. Available online: https://archive.is/CJkDD (accessed 20 July 2023).

Alpermann, B. and G. Schubert (2022a), 'Gegen das moralische Kreuzrittertum', *Frankfurter Allgemeine Zeitung*, 9 March. Nr. 57, N4.

Alpermann, B. and G. Schubert (2022b), 'An Argument Against Moral Crusading', *ResearchGate*, March. Available online: https://archive.is/7JM5r (accessed 20 July 2023).

Álvarez, S. and T. Stölzel (2021), '"An manche Kooperation mit China zu unvoreingenommen herangegangen"', *WirtschaftsWoche*, 8 December. WirtschaftsWoche Archive.

ASPI (2019), 'China Defence Universities Tracker. National University of Defense Technology', Available online: https://archive.is/G7zny (accessed 20 July 2023).

Baumgärtner, M. and A.-K. Müller (2023), '»Wollen wir warten, bis ein deutscher Wissenschaftler in China festgenommen wird?«', *Spiegel Politik*, 17 January 2023. Available online: https://archive.is/v38SK (accessed 20 July 2023).

BBC (2021), 'Chinese Sanctions on Newcastle Academic "Counter-Productive"', 26 March. Available online: https://archive.is/4yhHq (accessed 20 July 2023).

Bovensiepen, N. and L. Weinmann (2022), 'Blindes Vertrauen', *Süddeutsche Zeitung*, 20 May. Nr. 116: 8.

Bovensiepen, N. and S. Menner (2022), '"Warnsignale sind schon da"', *Süddeutsche Zeitung*, 20 May. Nr. 116: 9.

Bovensiepen, N., S. Menner, and L. Weinmann (2022), 'Profiteure der Freiheit', *Süddeutsche Zeitung*, 20 May. Nr. 116: 8.

Braun, D. (1997), *Die politische Steuerung der Wissenschaft: Ein Beitrag zum »kooperativen Staat«*, Frankfurt and New York: Campus Verlag.

Buckley, C. (2013), 'China Takes Aim at Western Ideas', *The New York Times*, 19 August. Available online: https://archive.is/rf9Oe#selection-309.0-354.0 (accessed 2023).

Charon, P. and J.-B. Jeangène Vilmer (2021), *Chinese Influence Operations: A Machiavellian Moment*, Institute for Strategic Research, Paris: Ministry for the Armed Forces.

CSI (2022), 'China Science Investigation', Available online: https://www.ftm.eu/chinasc ienceinvestigation (accessed 20 July 2023).

DAAD KIWi (2020), 'Keine roten Linien. Wissenschaftskooperation unter komplexen Rahmenbedingungen', Available online: https://static.daad.de/media/daad_de/pdfs _nicht_barrierefrei/infos-services-fuer-hochschulen/kompetenzzentrum/dokumente/ daad_kiwi_kompass_keinerotenlinien_2020.pdf (accessed 20 July 2023).

Dahrendorf, R. (1963), *Die angewandte Aufklärung. Gesellschaft und Soziologie in Amerika*, München: R. Piper & Co Verlag.

Dapiran, A. (2021), 'A 20th Procrastination: On Censorship', *Substack*, June 15. Accessed July 7. Available online: https://bit.ly/3yw78J2 (accessed 20 July 2023).

Deutschlandfunk (2022), 'Recherche analysiert über 350.000 wissenschaftliche Studien', 19 May. Available online: https://archive.is/5vqbQ (accessed 20 July 2023).

DGA (2020), 'Ein Plädoyer gegen Polarisierung', *Deutsche Gesellschaft für Asienkunde*, 12 June. Available online: https://archive.is/DMZv6 (accessed 20 July).

DGA (2021), 'Stellungnahme des DGA-Vorstands zur Lage der Asienforschung in Deutschland', *Deutsche Gesellschaft für Asienkunde*, 19 June. Available online: https:// archive.is/3RCSn (accessed 20 July 2023).

DVCS (2021), 'Stellungnahme zu Sanktionen des Außenministeriums der V.R. China gegen europäische Wissenschaftler:innen', *Deutsche Vereinigung für Chinastudien*, Available online: https://archive.is/Ra0cw#selection-73.0-75.50 (accessed 20 July 2023).

EACS (2021), 'Statement by the EACS Board Regarding the Sanctions Issued by the Chinese Ministry of Foreign Affairs Against European China Researchers', *European Association for Chinese Studies*, 12 April. Available online: https://archive.is/YhgZH (accessed 20 July 2023).

EACS 2022 (2022), 'Program for Friday, August 26th', *EACS 2022: The 24th Biennial Conference of the European Association for Chinese Studies (EACS)*, Available online: https://archive.is/pFamc (accessed 20 July 2023).

Federal Ministry of Justice (2023), 'Basic Law for the Federal Republic of Germany', Available online: https://archive.is/uSf96 (accessed 20 July 2023).

Feldwisch-Drentrup, H. (2022), 'Rektorenpräsident zu Russland: „Wir setzen unsere Prinzipien außer Kraft"', *RiffReporter*, 25 March. Available online: https://www .riffreporter.de/de/artikel/ukraine-russland-wissenschaft-kooperation-interview-hoc hschulrektorenkonferenz (accessed 20 July 2023).

Feldwisch-Drentrup, H. (2023), 'Deutsche Forscher kooperieren mit Chinas Militär', *Frankfurter Allgemeine Zeitung*, 13 January. Available online: https://archive.is/yMVMu #selection-3455.0-3455.48 (accessed 20 July 2023).

Follow the Money (2022), 'China Science Investigation', Available online: https://www .youtube.com/watch?v=5_TEA7WVNKA (accessed 20 July 2023).

Fulda, A. (2021a), 'Rote Linien längst überschritten', *Forschung & Lehre*, 13 September. Available online: https://archive.is/n74tV (accessed 20 July 2023).

Fulda, A. (2021b), 'The Chinese Communist Party's Hybrid Interference and Germany's Increasingly Contentious China Debate (2018–21)', *The Journal of the European Association for Chinese Studies*, 2: 205–34.

Fulda, A. and D. Missal (2021a), 'Mitigating Threats to Academic Freedom in Germany: The Role of the State, Universities, Learned Societies and China', *The International Journal of Human Rights*, 26 (10): 1803–21.

Fulda, A. and D. Missal (2021b), 'German Academic Freedom Is Now Decided in Beijing', *Foreign Policy*, 28 October. Available online: https://archive.is/YoC7H (accessed 20 July 2023).

Fulda, A., M. Ohlberg, D. Missal, H. Fabian, and S. Klotzbücher (2022), 'Grenzenlos kompromissbereit?', *Frankfurter Allgemeine Zeitung*, 16 March. Nr. 63, N4.

Funtowicz, S. and J. Ravetz (1993), 'Science for the Post-normal Age', *Futures: The Journal of Policy, Planning and Futures Studies*, 25 (7): 739–55.

Furedi, F. (2016), *What's Happened to the University: A Sociological Exploration of its Infantilisation*, London and New York: Routledge.

Gillmann, B. (2022), '„Man darf nicht naiv sein" –Forschungsministerin rät Hochschulen zu radikalem Schritt gegen China', *Handelsblatt*, 16 June. Handelsblatt Archive.

Gillmann, B. and D. Heide (2022), 'Nach der Industrie jetzt die Wissenschaft - Deutschland geht auf Distanz zu China', *Handelsblatt*, 24 June. Handelsblatt Archive.

Grzanna, M. (2023), 'Kommunismus und Klassenkampf holen die deutsche Sinologie ein', *China.Table*, 3 October 2023, Since this article is paywalled readers can access this X/ Twitter thread with excerpts and an English-language summary of Grzanna's article. Available online: https://archive.ph/g2TdI (accessed 28 October 2023).

Habich-Sobiegalla, S. and H. Steinhardt (2022), 'Debating Academic Autonomy in the German-Speaking Field of China Studies: An Assessment', *ASIEN*, 162/163. Available online: https://archive.is/vSdyO#selection-1217.26-1217.39 (accessed 20 July 2023).

Hannas, W. and H.-M. Chang (2021), 'Chinese Technnology Transfer: An Introduction', in W. Hannas and D. Tatlow (eds), *China's Quest for Foreign Technology. Beyond Espionage*, 3–20, Oxon: Routledge.

Heide, D., M. Murphy, and D. Neuerer (2023), 'Verstärkte China-Spionage alarmiert Bundesregierung', *Handelsblatt*, 7 June. Available online: https://archive.is/3SCcN (accessed 20 July 2023).

Klotzbücher, S. (2019), *Lange Schatten der Kulturrevolution. Eine transgenerationale Sicht auf Politik und Emotion in der Volksrepublik China*, Gießen: Psychosozial-Verlag.

Kummert, T. and A. Leister (2023), '"Wir müssen extrem aufpassen"', *t-online*, 5 May. Available online: https://archive.is/fApej (accessed 20 July 2023).

Lau, J. (2013), 'Die deutsche Liebe zu den Diktatoren', *Zeit Online*, 21 February. Available online: https://web.archive.org/web/20130224084420/http://blog.zeit.de/joerglau/2013 /02/21/schurken-die-wir-brauchen_5889 (accessed 20 July 2023).

Lau, S. and J. Barigazzi (2021), 'EU Imposes Sanctions on Four Chinese Officials', *Politico*, 22 March. Available online: https://archive.is/U2ErG (accessed 20 July 2023).

MCLC Resource Center (2022), 'Germany's Contentious China Debate', *Modern Chinese Literature and Culture*, 19 March. Available online: https://archive.is/WeoWR#selection -449.0-449.34 (accessed 20 July 2023).

Ministry of Foreign Affairs (2021), 'Foreign Ministry Spokesperson Announces Sanctions on Relevant EU Entities and Personnel', 22 March. Available online: https://archive.is/ Nd9GI (accessed 20 July 2023).

Missal, D. (2020), 'Chinas Geld an deutschen Unis', 7 September. Available online: https:// archive.is/ZspdL (accessed 20 July 2023).

Monschein, Y. (2020), '„Neuer" Kalter Krieg und alte Macht der Propaganda: „Ausweitung der Kampfzone" auf China?', *minima sinica*, 32 (2020): 99–145.

Mulkay, M. (1975), 'Three Models of Scientific Development', *The Sociological Review*, 23 (3): 509–26.

Muller, D. (2020), 'Why I Don't Sign Open Letters or Group Amicus Briefs', *Excess of Democracy*, 9 June. Available online: https://archive.is/goWGD (accessed 20 July 2023).

Pamperrien, S. (2013), 'Die China-Versteher und ihre demokratischen Feinde', *Deutschlandfunk*, 10 March. Available online: https://archive.is/ypSZc (accessed 20 July 2023).

Roetz, H. (2022), 'Germany's contentious China debate', *H-Asia*, 17 March. Available online: https://archive.is/rZ49o (accessed 20 July 2023).

Roetz, H. (2022), 'Kritik und Kompromiss', *Frankfurter Allgemeine Zeitung*, 30 March. Available online: https://archive.is/M3j65 (accessed 20 July 2023).

Schell, O. (1997), 'China's Tradition of Dissent', *Los Angeles Times*, 29 June. Available online: https://archive.is/bktED (accessed 20 July 2023).

Schoen, D. (1983), *The Reflective Practitioner: How Professionals Think in Action*, London: Ashgate.

Schubert, G. and B. Alpermann (2022), 'Keine normativen Fesseln anlegen', *Frankfurter Allgemeine Zeitung*, 19 March. Available online: https://archive.is/nEuKb (accessed 20 July 2023).

Shi-Kupfer, K. (2020), China-Versteher machen alles noch schlimmer, *Zeit Online*, 2 May. Available online: https://archive.is/ct09x (accessed 20 July 2023).

Solidarity Statement (2021), 'Solidarity Statement on Behalf of Scholars Sanctioned for Their Work on China / 学界联署声明：声援因从事中国研究而被制裁之学者', Available online: https://archive.is/nmJGb (accessed 20 July 2023).

Statement by European Research Institute Directors (2021), 'Statement by European Research Institute Directors', Available online: https://archive.is/Wp4I5 (accessed 20 July 2023).

Stiens, T. (2023), 'Bittere Realität: Technologieklau chinesischer Wissenschaftler', *Handelsblatt*, 6 June. Available online: https://archive.is/W4RqP (accessed 20 July 2023).

Stoff, J. (2023), *Should Democracies Draw Redlines Around Research Collaboration with China? A Case Study of Germany*, CRSI, Available online: https://researchsecurity.org/

wp-content/uploads/2023/01/Click-here-to-download-the-full-publication.-Stoff-Dra
wingRedlinesFINAL.pdf (accessed 20 July 2023).

Strittmatter, K. (2010), 'Das Schweigen der China-Kenner', *Süddeutsche Zeitung*, 10
December. Available online: https://archive.is/7KcwH (accessed 20 July 2023).

Strittmatter, K. (2023), 'Beschämend leichtgläubig', *Süddeutsche Zeitung*, 24 September.
Available online: https://archive.ph/OKk57#selection-519.0-519.24 (accessed 28
October 2023).

Stroud, S. (2013), 'Selling Democracy and the Rhetorical Habits of Synthetic Conflict:
John Dewey as Pragmatic Rhetor in China', *Rhetoric & Public Affairs*, 16 (1) (Spring):
97–132.

Talmon, S. (2023), 'Germany Defends Use of EU Global Human Rights Sanctions Regime
Against China', *German Practice in International Law*, 25 April. Available online:
https://archive.is/tkCh3 (accessed 20 July 2023).

Weinstein, E. (2021), 'Don't Underestimate China's Military-Civil Fusion Efforts', *Foreign
Policy*, 5 February. Available online: https://archive.is/W7wmJ#selection-829.0-834.0
(accessed 20 July 2023).

Wietholz, A. (2021), 'Dornröschen schlägt die Augen auf', *leibniz*, 8 June. Available online:
https://archive.is/P3QC8 (accessed 20 July 2023).

Chapter 11

TOWARDS GREATER AUTOCRACY COMPETENCE IN GERMANY?

11.1 Key takeaways

In the final chapter I will answer the research questions, revisit the initial research puzzle, provide eight recommendations and make the case for a German Foreign Agent Registration Act (FARA). I would like to begin by addressing the first research question: How does the Policy Equilibrium Theory (PET) explain punctuation during the final years of the Merkel era (2018–21) and the beginning of the Scholz administration (2021–23)?

In the conceptual *first part of the book* I argued that the period between 1993 – the year the Asia-Pacific Committee of German Business (APA) was founded – and 2018 Germany's China policy was marked by *stasis*. During this time Germany's foreign policy paradigms such as 'Rapprochement through interweaving' and 'Change through trade' were not sufficiently scrutinized. I described how contrarians' criticisms of Germany's mercantilist approach towards autocracies were ignored and critics were sidelined. Germany's business-friendly approach towards China consequently morphed from policy monopoly to *dogma*. First signs of *punctuation* only emerged in 2018, when various crisis converged: the US-China trade war was in full swing; evidence about re-education camps in the Xinjiang Uyghur Autonomous Region (XUAR) was mounting; and the National People's Congress rubber stamped the decision to abolish the two-term limit for General Secretary Xi.

In the empirical *second part of the book* I drew on a close reading of more than 300 media reports in the newspapers TAZ, SZ, FAZ, Handelsblatt, WirtschaftsWoche and NZZ. I analysed the *policy images* which either supported or critiqued established and emerging foreign policy paradigms during the final years of the Merkel administration. Reviewing the German-language media discourse allowed me to capture how Germany's changing relationship with China has been assessed by politicians, industrialists, journalists, academics and civil society practitioners. This qualitative research approach afforded me the chance to trace Germany's China discourse on the national level over a period of time; compare and contrast policy images with vastly different emotive appeals; and infer whether *creative* or *destructive* learning has taken place (more about this later).

How balanced is Germany's media coverage on China?

Reading the media coverage on China-related topics in five policy subfields revealed that the vast majority of reports were critical of developments in China under Xi. Yet journalists writing for the centre-left TAZ as well as centre-right NZZ at times also employed *policy images* with emotive appeals which were more friendly towards China. This reminded me of the fact that in foreign and security-related matters the political left-right divide does not necessarily play a decisive role. Furthermore, the German newspapers as well as online media such as China.Table or +49security also regularly publish op-eds by proverbial 'China understanders' (*Chinaversteher*) as well as regime critics (*Chinakritiker*), thus guaranteeing viewpoint diversity. This finding puts in perspective the critique of a study by Jia, Leutner and Xiao, in which they accused the German media coverage on China of reproducing 'a "Western" values agenda and a Eurocentric perspective' (2021, 10).

As I have argued in an op-ed, the study's editor pretended that China 'remains a closed book despite the intensive Western engagement with China and that the media are now pushing the country into the role of the enemy' (Fulda, 2021a). I argued that such a view was 'too short-sighted' since 'precisely because we are increasingly gaining experience in dealing with the People's Republic, the media essentially reflect what is learned from this interaction' (2021a). And while media framing clearly matters, the professionalism of German China correspondents needs to be acknowledged, too. Benner is right when stating that '(we) are fortunate to have some excellent and well-informed journalists working about and/or in China' (2023). Journalists such as Friederike Böge, Christoph Giesen, Marcel Grzanna and Kai Strittmatter know China very well. Often considerable China experience is coupled with subject matter expertise. For example Dana Heide has provided excellent in-depth reporting on topics where industry policy, technology and German–China relations intersect. The same could also be said about Nina Bovensiepen, Silke Wettach and many other German journalists.

Reading the more than 300 media reports for the empirical chapters also confirmed my assertion in Chapter 5 that we don't have a problem of *too little* available information but *too much*. Black elephant phenomena in foreign policy have precisely emerged not because of a lack of information, but as a result of key decision-makers turning a blind eye to openly available evidence. A striking example is Chancellor Scholz and his advisors who ignored important information regarding Putin's imperial ambitions until it was too late.

Information is not neutral, as it creates winners and losers

When conducting research for the five empirical chapters I learned that even a media discourse which is highly critical of autocratic China does not automatically translate into a new German China policy. With the exception of the tightening of Germany's Foreign Trade and Payments Ordinance (AWV), and some tinkering around the edges of the IT Security Act 2.0, Germany's pro-business China policy remains largely unchanged. Such minor policy changes can be considered a form of instrumental learning (May, 1992, 335). Resistance to policy change should not come as a surprise and is consistent with Baumgartner and Jones Policy Equilibrium Theory. In Chapter 5 I argued that a close-knit policy community of senior politicians and industry officials could utilize the paradigm of 'Change through trade', which supposedly settled for good how to handle autocratic nations. With the help of the 'Change through trade' mantra their *policy monopoly / dogma* was defended. Jones and Baumgartner are clear-eyed about the prospect of policy change when pointing out that 'changes may come, but they come grudgingly' (2005, 17). They highlight that those 'who fought long and hard to get a new policy implemented . . . do not suddenly admit mistakes; they resist, resist, and resist until either they are outmaneuvered or the evidence simply overwhelms them' (2005). According to the two authors '(in) politics, information is not neutral; it creates winners and losers. People prefer to be seen as winners and do not like to admit when they are wrong' (2005). This can explain the proliferation of highly problematic op-eds and public statements in favour of Germany's established foreign policy paradigms throughout the year 2023.

Strittmatter has thoroughly deconstructed arguments put forward by *status quo* defenders, according to which 'clear words towards China's leaders are either a cultural affront / counterproductive / dangerous'; '"burning bridges" . . . would be insanity, as would "an abrupt end to trade relations"'; 'it is wrong to explain system competition to China'; 'Europe needs strategic autonomy. We have other interests than the US'; 'an attack on Taiwan would "not be our crisis"'; 'human rights policy is naïve'; and 'Why do we always have to proselytize? "Why can't we leave them alone"'? (2023) In an op-ed I have furthermore argued that the *status quo* proponents' frequent use of logical fallacies and 'bogus arguments harm our democratic culture of debate' (Fulda, 2023). In a Spiegel interview I also pointed out that '(the) current China debate in Germany is too much dominated by people with agendas, and it is not always clear whether enlightened German interests or those of the party are being represented' (Baumgärtner and Müller, 2023).

The dangers of denial

Over the course of writing this book I also learned that failure itself does not necessarily translate into policy learning. As late as June 2023 – more than a year after Russia's full invasion of Ukraine – former Chancellor Schröder (1998–2005) has shown no sign of contrition for his close personal affiliation with Putin (Zeit Online, 2023). Similarly, former Chancellor Merkel (2005–2021) has refused to acknowledge any errors in the Russia and energy policy over the course of sixteen years in office. Boyse rightly points out that '(none) of those responsible for *Wandel durch Handel* have paid a political price for their mistakes, except perhaps for former Chancellor Schroeder, whose fall from grace was swift and steep' (2023). And while former Foreign Minister Steinmeier has acknowledged that adhering to Nord Stream 2 was a mistake, he has also deflected personal responsibility by suggesting that somehow *we* were collectively wrong (Deutsche Welle, 2022a).

What explains the inability of senior German politicians to admit responsibility for policy failure? May has pointed out that 'governmental leaders may be unwilling to acknowledge failure as required for political learning or to explore the reasons for failure of policy ideas as required for policy learning. Such reluctance is particularly strong in ideologically-dominated administrations for which acknowledging failure and learning from it would entail fundamental re-thinking of core, ideological values' (1992, 341). In his critique of the SPD's *Ostpolitik* of the 1980s Winkler has criticized the tendency among German Social Democrats 'to exaggerate their positions verbally, not to say ideologically' (2022). I would argue that acknowledging that 'Rapprochement through interweaving' and 'Change through trade' have been thoroughly falsified as foreign policy paradigms would be tantamount to admitting that many German elites – and to a certain extent also parts of the German electorate – have subscribed to what Groitl (2021), Büschemann (2021) and Thome (Dieckmann and Tartler, 2023) have called a life lie (*Lebenslüge*). Such an inability to admit failure has arguably also made it harder for policy entrepreneurs to chart a new course. Roberts and King remind us of the importance of political leadership when stating that '(change) is more than incentives. It is about persuading people to change the way they think' (1996, 216). Yet even the particularly outspoken ministers and China critics Baerbock and Habeck (Alliance 90/The Greens) and Stark-Watzinger (Free Democratic Party) have thus far been unable to convince Chancellor Scholz (SPD) to develop a more realistic and assertive German China policy. This raises the question what it will take for more *creative learning* to take place in the German Chancellery.

An echo chamber at the heart of the German government?

In November 2022 Der Spiegel reported that Germany's draft China policy was causing tensions between the Chancellery and Foreign Office. Was the new China strategy – expected to be finalized in 2023 – more likely to reflect Chancellor Scholz' business-friendly approach or Foreign Minister Baerbock's value-based vision? (Baumgärtner et al., 2022) In June 2023 another report by Der Spiegel described the growing rift between the Chancellery and the Ministry for Economic Affairs and Climate Action. Whereas Scholz and his SPD were 'fearing for jobs if relations with China deteriorate' (Kormbaki, Schult, and Traufetter, 2023), Habeck was keen to reduce Germany's growing dependencies on China, for example, by limiting investment and export credit guarantees for German companies in China (2023). Scholz also overruled Habeck when green-lighting Cosco's acquisition of a 24.99 per cent stake in Hamburg's Tollerort container terminal (von der Burchard, 2023). With this decision Scholz disregarded warnings by the US government, six German ministries and his two coalition partners (Deutsche Welle, 2022b; Pamuk, 2022). Scholz's position in the Cosco debate resembles the role which Schröder played in 2005. Against all odds Schröder had – albeit unsuccessfully – argued for a lifting of Europe's arms embargo towards China. Despite being almost completely isolated on the Cosco issue, in 2022 Scholz insisted on knowing better than Germany's allies and experts. *The Economist* has suggested that 'the problem lies . . . with the tightness of the ship he runs' (2023a). Scholz's proverbial praetorian guard would consist of Head of the Chancellery Wolfgang Schmidt; his official spokesperson Steffen Hebestreit;

advisor for finances and economics Jörg Kukies; as well as Scholz's foreign policy advisor Jens Plötner (2023a). The 'tightness of the chancellor's circle can both make it impermeable to useful information and create a siege mentality' (2023a).

Such an echo chamber at the heart of the German government not only limits 'the competition of beliefs and ideas' (May, 1992, 334) which are seen as central to policy-oriented learning (1992) but can also have potentially deleterious consequences in the future. In Chapter 2 I described in detail how Steinmeier's insistence on knowing better than seasoned security experts how to deal with Russia led to destructive learning. With reference to Janis's scholarship I also pointed out that a flawed group consensus could contribute to an 'illusion of invulnerability' (1971), which makes extraordinary risk-taking more likely. By limiting Chancellor Scholz's interactions with independent experts his special advisors now run the danger of creating blind spots, disrupting feedback loops and overlooking flaws in their paradigmatic foreign policy thinking.

How much legwork for the Zeitenwende *has been done?*

The second research question centred around the types of policy images which have challenged Germany's mercantilist China policy. The five policy punctuation analysis in the empirical part of this book have shown that in terms of policy images and related emotive appeals the pendulum has decisively swung from an emphasis on *opportunities* to a focus on *risks*. The resulting German China discourse is now very defensive in nature. Discourse participants seem to have given up on trying to influence the political trajectory of China. I would argue that this is actually a problem. While Germany neither has the levers to destabilize China nor the means to stabilize it, this does not mean that Germany does not enjoy at least some constructive leverage of its own.

Former China director at the US National Security Council Tobin has argued that US–China policy should affirm 'that the choice between democracy and dictatorship ultimately belongs to the Chinese people' (2023). This would require contesting the legitimacy of the CCP (2023). A purely defensive China policy may help to shield Germany from the worst aspects of the CCP's leverage, but would do little to address the root cause of the problem. It should have become increasingly apparent that the outside world is in fact paying a high price for China not democratising: under General Secretary Xi we are witnessing a continued militarization of state and society within China. We are also now facing the prospect of a potentially devastating war of aggression against Taiwan.

Which brings me to the third and fourth research questions: To what extent has Germany's China policy shifted as a result? And in terms of Scholz's *Zeitenwende*, what has already been accomplished? Findings from both the conceptual and empirical part of this book suggest that while in the public debate a paradigm shift is under way, the contours of the new paradigm(s) in German foreign policy remain sketchy. Only very little of the required legwork for the *Zeitenwende* has been done. In contrast, Görg, Kamin, Langhammer and Liu have argued that a new German China strategy should be embedded in a EU strategy (2023). Yet I would argue that their suggestions is the equivalent of German politicians hiding their inaction behind Brussels. Germany's inability to forge a national consensus on how to deal with autocratic China does not bode well for the search for a pan-European approach. As the German government is failing to find common ground among its coalition partners, how realistic is it that Berlin will be able to achieve a unified approach among 27 EU member states?

How liabilities of German businesses have become an intractable problem for the German state

In light of Chancellor Scholz's unwillingness to adjust Germany's China policy to changed geopolitical circumstances I would like to revisit the initial research puzzle. I asked why and how did Germany become entangled with an autocratic China. In the conceptual first part of the book I argued that during an unconditional engagement process German elites compromised democratic values while underestimating both conventional and non-conventional threats from a neo-totalitarian China. Flawed political and intellectual leadership by Schmidt, Kohl, Schröder, Merkel and Scholz led to a single-minded pursuit of foreign trade promotion and contributed to Germany's inadequate strategic culture vis-à-vis autocracies. As a result, Germany became entangled with autocratic China and became the victim of malign foreign interference.

In addition to misguided *political leadership* and an inadequate German *strategic culture* we also need to be mindful of *structural factors*. The empirical second part of the book revealed that a lack of receptivity to paradigm change and a refusal to unlearn can also be linked to Germany's corporatist political economy. In this context I would like to readdress Kundnani's clear-eyed comments on Germany as a geoeconomic power. With reference to Luttwak Kundnani described the relationship between the German state and business as marked by 'reciprocal manipulation' (Kundnani, 2011, 41). More specifically, Kundnani argued that 'German companies lobby the German government to make policy that promotes their interests; they in turn help politicians maximize growth and in particular employment levels the key measure of success in German politics' (2011).

When conducting research for this book I noted with interest that Felbermayer has described BASF and Volkswagen as 'too big to fail' (De Gruyter, 2022). I was also struck by the assessment by former Minister of the Environment Trittin, who has argued that the four German conglomerates VW, Daimler, BMW and BASF are of 'systemic importance from a German perspective' (China.Table, 2023a) and that they 'have an implicit state guarantee in Germany' (2023a). I consider both assessments to be correct. They are also crucial to explaining the immovability of German China policy. Corporate overexposure in China has created major liabilities, not just for the four conglomerates but for the German state as well. In view of major challenges such as VW's controversial factory in Urumqi, the difficulty of supply chain monitoring China, and the prospect of a Taiwan shock mounting material and psychological dependencies of Germany's big four corporations are a cause for concern.

The CCP as the third actor in 'reciprocal manipulation' between German politics and industry

I argued in Chapter 2 that when German foreign policy objectives align too closely with those of the private sector, there are conflicts of interest, a reduction in democratic accountability, the development of reciprocal dependencies and a compromise of transparency. But even if we were to put aside such shortcomings of 'reciprocal manipulation' between German politics and business, it should have now become clear that this Faustian bargain no longer delivers what was promised. A case in point is the announcement by BASF to 'downsize "permanently" in Europe' (Nilsson, 2022). This statement by the chemical group 'came after it opened the first part of its new €10bn plastics engineering facility in China a month ago' (2022).

This worrisome development has led me to reevaluate Kundnani's assessment from 2011. He wrote that 'German politicians are particularly dependent on exporters. However, because much of this growth has come from exports to economies such as China and Russia, where the state dominates business, exporters are also conversely dependent on the German government' (Kundnani, 2011, 41). I have come to realize that 'reciprocal manipulation' between German politicians and industrialists isn't sufficient to explain the issue, since the latter are also at the mercy of the Chinese party-state. This means that the CCP is in fact the third actor in this troublesome equation. In this context we should not forget that hybrid interference of autocratic regimes in liberal democracies is aimed at 'manipulation of other states' strategic interests' (Wigell, 2019, 262).

Throughout this book I have demonstrated that the CCP's *destructive leverage* has already contributed to *destructive learning* on the German side. This brings me to the second question of the research puzzle, which asked to what extent has the Chinese Communist Party been able to leverage Germany's entanglements with autocratic China? Here I would like to remind readers that 'the important point about failure as a stimulus for change and potential learning is that the objective reality of policy failure is less important than a perception of policy failure' (May, 1992, 341). I would not be surprised if following the publication of this book some critics may argue that none of the five unanticipated policy failures in the empirical part of the book actually constitute genuine policy failure, but should instead be seen as the price one has to pay for *Realpolitik*. But not only would such a relativization of failure be deeply cynical but it would also overlook the extent of destructive learning on the German side.

11.2 Destructive learning on the German side

It is important to point out that the question what kind of learning has occurred – whether creative or destructive – also depends on a readers' vantage point. Fischer reminds us that 'learning for one person may not be learning for another person with a different political ideology. No amount of data, regardless of how well tested and verified it might be, will convince a person that anything important or useful has been presented if, in his or her view, the findings lead to policy judgments that take him or her in the wrong direction, or at least down a road he or she is unwilling to travel' (Fischer, 2003, 111). This book suggests that the real-world damage inflicted by the CCP's destructive leverage over key German stakeholders is both considerable and highly consequential. I would like to highlight four specific examples, where the fear of retribution from Beijing coupled with political inertia in Berlin has already contributed to destructive learning on the German side.

(1) In order to protect Germany's automobile industry from Beijing's wrath, in 2012 the German government refrained from lobbying Brussels to impose sufficiently punitive tariffs on Chinese solar panel exporters. As a consequence the European solar industry went into a rapid decline (Chapter 6). In 2016, the attempt to build a German consortium to outbid Midea during the takeover of Kuka Roboter GmbH in part failed since automobile company Daimler reportedly did not want to upset the Chinese government by joining a rivaling German consortium. Germany lost a proverbial crown jewel of its industry as a result. And following Chinese Ambassador Wu Ken's threat to punish German automobile manufacturers at the Handelsblatt event in 2019, neither the outgoing Merkel administration nor the current Scholz administration has dared to exclude the Chinese IT company Huawei from 5G infrastructure building in Germany (Chapter 7).

(2) A DIE study informed the Ministry of Economic Cooperation and Development as early as 2006 that German development agencies were being instrumentalized by the Chinese party-state and that their function was reduced to serving particular Chinese interests. Similar findings from my PhD thesis about the loss of German government steering capabilities vis-à-vis the development agency GTZ informed a parliamentary inquiry and a parliamentary debate in 2008. Yet it took the German government until 2022 to reign into the operations of GIZ in China, the successor organization of GTZ. Remarkably, the German government has also been unable to protect the organizational autonomy of German political foundations operating in China. While they could register under the Overseas NGO Law in 2017, this highly illiberal law allowed the CCP to politically neutralize German political foundations as critical aid actors (Chapter 8).

(3) While the arms embargo of 1989 could prevent the sale of whole weapon systems from Europe to China, it was not designed to curb the export of dual-use technology, which can either be used for civilian or military purposes. A senior American diplomat advised the Foreign Office in Berlin as early as 2007 to prevent German companies from assisting with the modernization of China's army. Berlin's inaction on this issue allowed the German mechanical engineering company MTU Friedrichshafen to provide diesel engines for Chinese submarines and MTU engines for Chinese corvettes and destroyers. It took the Merkel administration ten years before it introduced a requirement for authorization for the export of all submarine engines in 2017. Yet by that time the PLA Navy's modernization had already made significant progress, thus greatly diminishing the effectiveness of subsequent export controls for such dual-use goods (Chapter 9).

(4) The German government also appeared flat-footed when the CCP imposed countersanctions on parliamentarians, lawyers and academics in response to the coordinated sanctions of the EU, UK, United States and Canada in Spring 2021. Chancellor Merkel did not publicly comment on the CCP's brazen attack on freedom of speech and academic freedom. The board of the learned society Deutsche Gesellschaft für Asienkunde (DGA) remained mum on the CCP's countersanctions on European academics. Perhaps because they feared retribution or did not want to risk Beijing's support for their research projects, institutional partnerships or consulting positions leading German Sinologists refrained from co-signing an open letter which called on the Chinese government to revoke the sanctions. Such half-hearted attempts to protect academic freedom were insufficient to persuade the Chinese party-state to lift the countersanctions (Chapter 10).

Such instances of destructive learning indicate a significant reduction in the 'reflective capacity that makes democratic societies more rational and resilient in the long run' (Emcke, 2022). In complex and dynamic systems destructive learning can be likened to a *downward spiral*, where disrupted feedback loops lead to unintended consequences. Left unchecked, destructive learning has the cumulative effect of undermining Germany's sovereignty. Reversing the dynamic from a downward into an *upward spiral*, or in the other words from destructive to creative learning, will require much greater critical self-reflexivity of key stakeholders.

Which external and internal factors have contributed to destructive learning?

If a repetition of harmful patterns of behaviour is to be avoided we need to understand the various factors which have contributed to destructive learning on the German side. In Chapter 3 I described how the CCP's threat of coercion hangs like a dark shadow over German–China relations. The five unanticipated policy failures in Chapters 6 to 10 furthermore provided ample evidence of the moulding of German stakeholders by 'official China' during a process of unconditional Western China engagement. While Germany has limited leverage over CCP-led China, the loss of Berlin's steering capabilities vis-à-vis the private sector and academia is alarming.

At the national level, the German government is increasingly acting as supplicant to the big four corporations VW, Daimler, BMW and BASF. And despite Deutsche Bahn being fully state owned and although the German state holds a blocking minority as shareholder at Deutsche Telekom neither the outgoing Merkel administration (2018–2021) nor the current Scholz administration (2021–) has been able to disentangle the two German corporations from the Chinese IT company Huawei. Even within the German state administration, a loss of steering control can be observed. The Federal Ministry for Economic Cooperation and Development (BMZ) has shown itself powerless to reign into the China operations of the federal agency GTZ and its successor organization GIZ. And the Federal Ministry of Education and Research (BMBF) has only limited levers which could be used to steer German universities and scientists when it comes to Sino-German academic cooperation.

This unfortunate state of affairs illustrates the downsides of a highly fragmented federal German system. Instead of joined up creative learning, we can see how in different policy subfields principal-agent dilemmas have contributed to destructive learning. In the principal-agent framework, it is apparent that principals – for example, German state officials, who are entrusted with regulatory or distributive tasks – are at a disadvantage compared to private or societal actors acting as agents on behalf of the state. The latter agents hold an information edge over the principals, which are a step removed from the frontline. Principal-agent relationships marked by information asymmetry (Lane, 2005, 40) can jeopardize German sovereignty when individuals or organizations start representing the interests of China's one-party state instead of working towards enlightened or material German interests. The unwillingness of senior German politicians to admit policy failure provides further cover for *moral hazard* in principal-agent relations.

How entanglement undermines freedom, prosperity and security

I would argue that Germany can no longer afford *not to learn* from past failure. This is especially so because Xi's growing security state is casting an ever longer shadow over Western liberal democracies. If Germany remains entangled with autocratic China our *freedom, prosperity* and *security* will be further undermined.

At the Munich Security Conference in 2023 Michael Kovrig, the former Canadian diplomat who was held hostage by the Chinese party-state for more than 1,000 days in retaliation for the persecution of Huawei CFO Meng Wanzhou by the US government, offered a blunt warning about the 'Leninist totalitarian DNA of the party-state' (@lukedepulford, 2023). He criticized that a 'fundamentally hostile outlook drives the political repression, selective disregard for international law, increasingly aggressive international behaviour. And these are not bugs in an otherwise reasonable governance system, they are features. It is a system that cannot trust anything it doesn't absolutely control. And if you want a preview of how that party-state will behave, how it will treat any geopolitical sphere that it is able to control, you really only have to look closely at how it treats dissenting or otherwise divergent from consensus citizens of its own state, from Xinjiang to Hong Kong' (2023).

(1) Undermining freedom. The threat which the Chinese Communist Party poses to open societies, both at home and abroad, should by now have become crystal clear. There is mounting evidence that state or non-state agents acting on behalf of the party-state are monitoring and intimidating members of the Chinese diaspora in Germany. The journalist Stremmel has documented how Chinese dissidents, Hong Kong democracy activists and Uyghurs, and even German academics, are subject to 'threats, intimidation, and stalking' (2023). The Berlin-based Chinese blogger Su Yutong received death threats after reporting about China's illegal overseas police stations (ZDF, 2023a). In an interview she complained that 'I was hoping for a safe environment here. But all this harassment worries me a lot' (2023a). And after investigating this topic for two months Stremmel himself received death threats (Y-Kollektiv, 2023). The Scholz administration has thus far been unable to better protect citizens from Beijing's long arm. While the German foreign office issued a verbal note to the Chinese Embassy in November 2022 demanding the closure of the overseas police stations operating on German soil, in Spring 2023 the Federal Ministry of the Interior had to acknowledge that two of the stations were still operational (Heide and Neuerer, 2023).

(2) Undermining prosperity. With its revised anti-espionage law the CCP has now greatly expanded the scope of what the Chinese party-state considers espionage activities or threats to national security. According to the US National Counterintelligence and Security Center (NCSC) the vague language means that 'US companies and individuals could "face penalties for traditional business activities" if Chinese authorities label them espionage or says they are assisting foreign sanctions on China' (The Guardian, 2023). The law now also puts German business people, academics and journalists in China at risk (Schmidt, 2023). Peter Humphrey, a British private investigator who was imprisoned in China after conducting a corporate investigation on behalf of the British pharmaceutical company GlaxoSmithKline (GSK) (Thorley and Fulda, 2020), has pointed out in an interview that '(any) form of information gathering on the part of companies can now be construed as espionage if arbitrarily defined by investigators as a threat to national security. Previously, such activities could only be prosecuted as "illegal acquisition of personal information". That then meant a few years in prison, as in my case. Now, in comparable cases, life imprisonment or even death sentences are threatened' (China.Table, 2023). German companies operating in China now face serious challenges in safeguarding their employees' well-being. And since due diligence on their supply chains now has become 'virtually impossible' (China. Table, 2023b), they also risk running afoul Germany's supply chain act, which went into effect on 1 January 2023.

Chancellor Scholz recently suggested that companies rather than countries must de-risk relations with China (Reuters, 2023). His comment revealed striking ignorance about the power relation between Western multinational corporations (MNCs) and the party-state. When discussing GSK's China engagement Thorley and I showed that '(when) pitted against a familial network that reaches into the heart of the [party-state], the MNC simply cannot win' (2020). Under Xi Jinping the party-state has developed an entire suite of laws and regulations which can be used to coerce Western businesses. A case in point is the 'unreliable entities' blacklist, which allows the CCP to penalize 'foreign company, organization or person which China says has "severely damaged the legitimate interests" of Chinese firms by not obeying market rules, violating contracts or blocking or cutting off supply for non-commercial reasons' (Bloomberg News, 2019). Another example is the Chinese Anti-Foreign Sanctions Law from 2021, which gives the party-state sweeping powers against anyone adopting '"discriminatory and restrictive" measures against Chinese citizen or China based organization or interferes in China's internal affairs' (Simmons + Simmons, 2021). And in June 2023 the CCP passed a Foreign Relations Law which 'deepens President Xi Jinping's control over the country's external relations' (White, 2023).

(3) Undermining security. Drinhausen and Legarda have rightly pointed out that 'the "securitization of everything" is here to stay and will likely accelerate' (2022). The two China experts have also made it clear that '(no) amount of engagement or cajoling will lead to Beijing shifting away from this security-focused, illiberal trajectory, short of major internal rethinking and reforms' (2022). This does not bode well since many of the aforementioned Chinese security laws are designed to insulate China against possible Western sanctions following an attack on Taiwan. It has been widely reported that Xi has tasked the PLA to develop the military capability to unify Taiwan with China by 2027. General Milley, chair of the Joint Chiefs of Staff, has rightly remarked that this does not mean that Xi has already decided to 'attack and invade' (Sharma, 2023). Other observers are less optimistic. Pomfret and Pottinger have argued that Xi's 'messaging about war preparation and his equating of national rejuvenation with unification mark a new phase in his political warfare campaign to intimidate Taiwan. He is clearly willing to use force to take the island' (2023). In the empirical part I cited different risk assessments of German politicians, industrialists, journalists and academics. While there are those who are downplaying the possibility of war in the Taiwan Strait, there are also growing concerns that Xi may indeed be willing to pay a very high economic price for his militaristic ambitions. This would mirror the recklessness of Putin's decision to order full-scale invasion of Ukraine in February 2022.

I contend that Germany is not prepared for such a 'Taiwan shock'. Whilst there are increasing concerns that Xi could order a military annexation of Taiwan by 2027, the German government has by and large pretended if such a geopolitical powder keg does not even exist. Taiwan was not mentioned once in Germany's 'Policy guidelines for the Indo-Pacific' (Federal Foreign Office, 2020). Germany's recently unveiled National Security Strategy reiterated the trifecta of China as a partner, competitor and systemic rival but also failed to mention Taiwan as a potential geopolitical flashpoint (The Federal Government, 2023). At the same time, Germany's economic dependencies on China has risen considerably. German direct investment in China reached 89 billion euros in 2020. It is likely that a war in Taiwan Strait would result in Western sanctions, which would put German companies' China assets at risk. The existing Sino-German Agreement on the Encouragement and Reciprocal Protection of Investments from 2003 would not provide any meaningful protection. The worst-case scenario would be a total loss of German investments from China following a hard decoupling. A disruption in procurement could destroy entire value chains. Germany would experience a deep recession.

Germany's new China strategy

On 14 June 2023 Germany's new China strategy was unveiled by Foreign Minister Baerbock at Berlin's think tank Merics. The strategy aimed to 'shows ways and instruments how the German government can cooperate with China without endangering Germany's free democratic way of life, sovereignty, prosperity and security' (Die Bundesregierung, 2023). Fahrion, Giesen, von Hammerstein and Schult have suggested that the government 'seems to have learned from decades of misguided Russia policy' (2023). Remarkably, such learning was primarily seen in the ability of the government to acknowledge the worsening human rights situation in China and the fact that Beijing had become an increasingly assertive geopolitical actor (2023). Benner has welcomed the China strategy as a 'a refreshingly realistic document with an ambitious amount of homework that now needs to be vigorously implemented' (Hasselbach, 2023). But he has also rightly pointed out that 'Beijing's system of one-party rule makes the desired open scientific and civil society exchange impossible' (Hasselbach, 2023). This shows the document marks a compromise between Chancellery and the Foreign Office.

The China strategy also remained vague in terms of policy solutions. The following three examples can illustrate this problem. Whereas 'risks to the freedom of research and teaching, illegitimate influence and one-sided knowledge or technology transfer must be minimised' the solution was seen in the strengthening of 'dialogue with universities and research institutions' (Auswärtiges Amt, 2023). Remarkably, the government felt compelled to state that 'we expect maximum transparency and publicity, especially when public funds are used for cooperation with China' (2023). A better approach would have been to suggest reforms to Freedom of Information laws on federal state level, which mandate that German universities have to answer FOI requests. Another example would be the situation of German political foundations in China. Here the government simply stated that it 'is committed to improving the working conditions of political foundations' (2023). No specific levers were identified how to accomplish this goal. A third and final example relates to the problem of transnational repression. Here the strategy document stated that the government was 'vigilant against all forms of illegitimate influence by official Chinese bodies' (2023) and suggested that it would 'dovetail our measures at the European level' (2023) and in exchange with both EU and NATO partners. What defensive measures could be taken beyond raising 'public awareness of the problem' (2023), for example, in the form of annual reports (*Verfassungsschutzbericht*) by the Office for the Protection of the Constitution, remain anyone's guess.

11.3 What can Germany do to disentangle itself without hard decoupling?

Both the ruling Social Democratic Party (SPD) and the oppositional Christian Democratic Union (CDU) have now published position papers in which decoupling from China is considered 'not the right answer' (SPD, 2023) and 'neither realistic nor desirable from a German and European perspective' (CDU/CSU-Fraktion, 2023). Both parties have advocated for embedding a German China strategy in a European and a transatlantic context. Strikingly, in both cases dependencies from China are almost exclusively seen through an economic lens. The position paper of the CDU/CSU parliamentary group only once mentioned that economic dependencies can also lead to 'political vulnerabilities' (2023, 6). The need for 'reducing vulnerabilities' (2023, 12), however, was once again limited to Germany's commercial relationship with China. In this book I have argued that in addition to Germany's three dependencies on *raw materials*; on *intermediate products* which are required for industry production; and on *revenues* generated in the Chinese market we also need to be aware of a fourth dependency: *psychological dependency*. The latter can be understood as *strategic blindness*, the illusion to be in control whereas in fact the CCP is already manipulating behaviour on the German side. Without an emancipation from the CCP's psychological control, how can individuals and organizations restore organizational and strategic autonomy? Those who frown at this admittedly provocative question need to be mindful of the following occurrence: at the end of the inter-governmental consultation between Germany and China in June 2023 the Scholz administration agreed to the CCP's demand that journalists should not be able to ask Li Qiang questions at a 'press conference' *in Berlin* (Metz, 2023). The studio director of Germany's TV channel ZDF Koll described this a 'clear Chinese blackmail: either like this or there will be no press conference' (ZDF, 2023b).

It doesn't have to be this way. In 2019, former US National Security Advisor Pottinger gave a widely noted keynote speech at the London-based think tank Policy Exchange. He spoke of the importance of *candor*, by which he meant 'the idea that democracies are safest when we speak honestly and publicly about and to our friends, our adversaries, and ourselves' (Policy Exchange, 2020). Pottinger criticized those who suggest that 'confrontational rhetoric turns countries into enemies' (2020). He suggested that '(clever) adversaries use such thinking against us. By portraying truth-telling as an act of belligerence, autocrats try to badger democracies into silence – and often succeed' (2020). In the following I will outline how greater candour – coupled with critical self-reflexivity on the German side – will be key to disentangling Germany from autocratic China.

Eight recommendations

Disentanglement does not mean cutting the proverbial Gordian knot in half. Hard decoupling would almost certainly incur very high costs. While a careful disentangling of German key stakeholders from autocratic China will also incur short-term costs, the upside of disentanglement would be the restoring of organizational and strategic autonomy, both preconditions for the protection of Germany's national sovereignty. The following recommendations are offered in the spirit of supporting Germany's disentanglement from autocratic China.

(1) Overcome *German Angst*. The historian Jan C. Behrends has remarked that German society lacks an 'empathic notion of freedom' (Volmer, 2022). In comparison to countries like Poland, France, America or the Ukraine Germany lacked the experience of 'successful liberation struggles' (2022). Behrends made this comments to explain German reluctance to provide military aid to Ukraine.

The Economist has similarly speculated that Scholz's caution to help Ukraine defeat Russia on the battlefield has much to do with the fear of Russia escalating the war (2023b). I would argue that deep-seated fear of military escalation or any other form of antagonistic political conflict – both at the elite and mass level – is key to understanding why Germany has thus far failed to adequately deal with both kinetic and non-kinetic threats. In an interview Science Minister Stark-Watzinger (FDP) has highlighted the scholarship of US psychologist Daniel Kahneman, according to which 'Germans feel losses emotionally twice as strongly, so they are more afraid' (portal liberal, 2022).

(2) Be more honest about the extent of Germany's entanglement with autocratic China. During a parliamentary debate in 2020 State Secretary Niels Annen (BMZ) has claimed that the '(the) Federal Government wants a China policy of partnership at eye level. In doing so, however, we are not naïve, but will safeguard and defend our interests and values' (@NielsAnnen, 2020). Here I would like to remind readers that the Federal Ministry for Economic Cooperation and Development (BMZ) remains one of the central funders of the German bilateral development agency GIZ. In light of the decade-long instrumentalization of GIZ and its predecessor GTZ by the Chinese party-state I consider it deeply cynical when a State Secretary speaks of a 'partnership at eye level'. It is also bewildering that the German state is still supporting the operations of German political foundations in China. As the space for genuine dialogue and cooperation with autocratic China has now firmly closed a more honest approach would be to ask German political foundations to leave China.

(3) Learn the language of power. In order to deal with the CCP's destructive leverage decisive political leadership is required. While Germany is unlikely to ever enter into a direct military confrontation with CCP-led China, we can still learn from the military doctrine of the German-American geostrategist Fritz Kraemer. He repeatedly warned of 'provocative weakness', whereby 'U.S. military weakness invites aggression by America's enemies' (Montgomery, 2023). The overly pragmatic and accommodating approach by German Chancellors Merkel and Scholz should be seen as a *civilian form* of 'provocative weakness', as it sent out a strong signal that they would not take a public stand against the Chinese party-state's clandestine diplomacy, economic coercion as well as mis- and disinformation campaigns. German Chancellors should be willing and able to engage in strategic communication about the hybrid threats Germany faces from autocratic China.

(4) Develop a more realistic view of the Chinese party-state. Scholz and his advisors still seem unaware that the CCP's foreign economic policy is strategically aimed at strengthening China's economic position and weakening that of democratic states. Here we need to be mindful that 'change through trade' could become a life lie since it allowed decision-makers to pretend that autocracies did not pose a fundamental threat to Germany's democratic system. At the same time the now falsified foreign policy paradigm legitimized a highly profitable commercial relationship. 'Anxiety about potential economic punishment by China and persistent optimism about the potential of the Chinese market' (Zenglein, 2023), according to Zenglein, 'are both important elements shaping German policymaking' (2023). Such groupthink will need to be challenged.

(5) Strengthen the role of the Foreign Office vis-à-vis the Chancellery. Throughout this book I have warned of the dangers of groupthink in German foreign policy. While the Berlin-based think tank GPPi should be commended for publishing numerous op-eds about Germany's new National Security Strategy (NSS) on its +49security website (2022), such inputs seem to have done little to shift the needle of the Chancellery's overly accommodating approach towards autocratic China. Fleck has bemoaned that in relation to China the published NSS 'says few things beyond the holy trinity of China as a partner, competitor, and systemic rival' (Atlantic Council, 2023). Kefferpütz and Rizzo have criticized the complete neglect for Taiwan in the NSS (2023). And commenting on the government's tug-of-war over the new approach to China, Demes has commented that 'the fact that someone at #Germany's Foreign Ministry felt compelled to leak its draft of the govt's new #ChinaStrategy speaks volumes for the lack of trust in the chancellor on matters of China policy' (@DemesDavid, 2022).

(6) Reduce corporate lobbying. In December 2021, the new Chairman of the Asia-Pacific Committee of German Business (APA), CEO of Siemens Roland Busch, issued a scathing attack on Foreign Minister Baerbock (Alliance 90/The Greens). He warned of a 'confrontational foreign policy' and called for a 'respectful interaction' with China (Business Insider, 2021). His Beijing-friendly argumentation mirrored the critique of former APA Chairman Hambrecht, who had criticized Chancellor Merkel's attempt to develop a more principled German China policy at the beginning of her Chancellorship. Throughout this book I have highlighted the outsized influence APA has had on German China policy over the past thirty years (1993–2023). If Berlin wants to reassert the primacy of politics over trade and investment, the German government needs to make it clear that the days of APA determining German China policy are over.

(7) Conduct outbound investment screening. There is a widespread misperception that decoupling would mean the complete cessation of trade with China. While trade imbalances have long existed between Germany and China, the real problem is that German companies now hold considerable fixed assets in China. In times of crisis – for example, a war in the Taiwan Strait – it could become impossible to repatriate them. In recent months Economic Minister Habeck has proposed US-style outbound investment screening (Sorge, 2023). But even if his proposal was implemented any time soon, it may come too late, given that German industrialists – encouraged by successive German administrations – have heavily invested in China over the past forty years. This is why I would suggest that in addition to outbound investment screening both Berlin and Brussels will need to make Germany and Europe, respectively, much more attractive for investors.

(8) Develop an industry policy for Germany and Europe. By repeating the mantra 'no decoupling' ad nauseam, German politicians and industrialists run the danger of creating a new dogma. I have argued in this book that at least *partial decoupling* from China will be required to counter CCP-led China as a power trader. In order to succeed the German government will need to develop both a new *China strategy* and an *industry policy* which would put economic resilience and national security first. Politicians and industrialists should have learned by now that CCP-led China will never be an ordinary market actor but a state-capitalist one. There are now growing calls for the EU to 'commit to the Single Market in actions and not only in words' (Eurochambers, 2019), to 'reduce complexity through better information online and digitalisation' (2019) as well as by providing 'a better legal framework adapted to the needs of SMEs' (2019).

11.4 Will the Zeitenwende *require a new German strategic culture, and if so, what must it entail?*

In 2023 the German government passed both the long anticipated National Security Strategy as well as the China strategy. Neither has offered specific guidance how Germany can disentangle itself from autocratic China beyond a very limited vision for de-risking in the economic sphere. Kundnani has offered a general critique on the proliferation of such policy documents. On Twitter he wrote that 'I always find it puzzling that so many foreign policy analysts, especially in Europe, pore over the details of strategy documents, and take them at face value, as if they represented the essence of a country's foreign policy. In reality, they are largely PR' (@hanskundnani, 2023). In Chapter 2 I had already expressed similar doubts when stating that a mere strategy document is unlikely to significantly influence the development of Germany's new strategic culture.

While I am optimistic that a more realistic and assertive German strategic culture vis-à-vis autocracies can indeed be developed, this process will take years if not decades. Paradigmatic change will also require the effort of both German state and society acting in concert. To speed up cognitive learning processes we should heed the advise of former President Gauck, who during a widely noted keynote at the Munich Security Conference in 2014 suggested that in order '(to) find its proper course in these difficult times, Germany needs resources, above all intellectual resources. It needs minds, institutions and forums' (Der Bundespräsident, 2014).

Giegerich and Terhalle have made the case for the development of strategic studies in Germany (2021, 35–9). Lough has argued that 'Germany needs to invest further in rebuilding Russia and Eastern European expertise' (2021, 253). When it comes to China studies, however, more money – on its own – is unlikely to solve existing problems in the academic field. Instead, I have argued that it is incumbent on 'China scholars to begin questioning rule-stabilizing, culturally relativistic and culturally essentialist as well as anti-praxeological traditions in Chinese studies' (Fulda, 2021b). There is also a need for learned societies to question existing norms in German Sinology and to encourage increased transparency in China research by disclosing premises, basic assumptions, positionality statements and compromises in academic publications. That being said I am confident that a German Sinology, which is no longer 'largely blind to China's expansive power politics' (Tatlow, 2018), could play a key role in enhancing autocracy competence in Germany.

What can be done in the meantime?

Marshalling intellectual resources to meet the challenges of autocracies should be considered a long-term task. This does not preclude the adoption of more immediate stop-gap measures. I have noted with concern that Germany's public discourse is all too often dominated by individuals with commercial interests in China. While news outlets by and large do a good job in highlighting institutional affiliations of interviewees or authors of op-eds, their commercial interests will not be obvious to a layperson.

One example is the participation of German academics in China's Thousand Talents Program, the CCP's flagship plan for talent recruitment. While the programme primarily targets Chinese scientists, I am aware of at least two German academics – an economist and a physicist – who have also participated in this overseas high-level talent plan. To be fair to both colleagues neither of them has made any attempt to hide their participation. Yet I still consider it to be highly problematic when beneficiaries of party-state resources praise the virtues of dialogue and cooperation with China, and talk of building bridges through academic exchanges. While such points of view are defensible, a potential conflict of interest arises when a German professor, whose salary is paid by the German taxpayer, also receives remuneration from organs under control of the Chinese party-state. In order to stop what I consider the *Schroederisation of academia* the German government should consider adopting a Foreign Agent Registration Act (FARA). In the United States the FARA was established in 1938 and 'requires certain agents of foreign principals who are engaged in political activities or other activities specified under the statute to make periodic public disclosure of their relationship with the foreign principal, as well as activities, receipts and disbursements in support of those activities' (U.S. Department of Justice, 2023).

German individuals registering under a FARA would still be able to accept CCP patronage. But a FARA-style declaration of political interests – when these are inimical to democratic values and goals – would also act as a deterrent and incur some form of reputational costs. Without a FARA, however, German politicians, business people and academics would be able to continue to take advantage of resources provided by the German taxpayer as well as the Chinese party-state. Such 'double dipping' is problematic since it creates conflicts of interest. Enhancing transparency and accountability of discourse participants would go a long way in ensuring a level playing field in the contentious debate about Germany's entanglement with autocratic China.

References for Chapter 11

@DemesDavid (2022), 'Call It a Power Move or a Hail Mary, the Fact That Someone at #Germany's Foreign Ministry Felt Compelled to Leak Its Draft of the Govt's New #ChinaStrategy Speaks Volumes for the Lack of Trust in the Chancellor on Matters of China Policy', *Twitter*, 17 November. Available online: https://twitter.com/DemesDavid /status/1593051245693980673?s=20 (accessed 21 July 2023).

@hanskundnani (2023), 'I Always Find It Puzzling That So Many Foreign Policy Analysts, Especially in Europe, Pore Over the Details of Strategy Documents, and Take Them at Face Value, as If They Represented the Essence of a Country's Foreign Policy. In Reality, They Are Largely PR'. *Twitter*, 17 January. Available online: https:// twitter.com/hanskundnani/status/1669973794755076096?s=20 (accessed 21 July 2023).

@lukedepulford (2023), 'Former Canadian Diplomat @MichaelKovrig, Who Was a Victim of China's Hostage Diplomacy and Incarcerated for Over 1000 Days, Speaks at @MunSecConf on the "Leninist Totalitarian DNA of the Party-State"', *Twitter*, 21 February. Available online: https://twitter.com/lukedepulford/status /1627993850227617793?s=20 (accessed 21 July 2023).

@NielsAnnen (2020), '„Die Bundesregierung will eine Chinapolitik der Partnerschaft auf Augenhöhe. Dabei sind wir jedoch nicht naiv, sondern wir werden unsere Interessen und Werte wahren und verteidigen"', Meine Rede zur China-Politik @ AuswaertigesAmt @GERonAsia @EU2020DE', *Twitter*, 10 September. Available online: https://twitter.com/NielsAnnen/status/1304090201313116165?s=20 (accessed 21 July 2023).

+49security (2022), 'About', Available online: https://archive.is/nXmoY (accessed 21 July 2023).

Atlantic Council (2023), 'The Hits and Misses in Germany's New National Security Strategy', 14 June. Available online: https://archive.is/Johis (accessed 21 July 2023).

Auswärtiges Amt (2023), 'China-Strategie der Bundesregierung', Available online: https:// www.auswaertiges-amt.de/blob/2608578/2b2effbc0886ef7ae0b22aaeacf199be/china -strategie-data.pdf (accessed 21 July 2023).

Baumgärtner, M. and A.-K. Müller (2023), '»Wollen wir warten, bis ein deutscher Wissenschaftler in China festgenommen wird?«', *Spiegel Politik*, 17 January. Available online: https://archive.is/v38SK (accessed 21 July 2023).

Baumgärtner, M., M. Gebauer, M. Knobbe, M. Kormbaki, A.-K. Müller, and G. Traufetter (2022), '»Lügen und Gerüchte«', *Spiegel Politik*, 25 November. Available online: https:// archive.is/MhgZh (accessed 21 July 2023).

Benner, T. (2023), 'The Lost Honor of the China "Bridge Builders"', *China.Table*, 26 June. Available online: https://archive.is/yOQN9 (accessed 21 July 2023).

Bloomberg News (2019), 'What We Know About China's "Unreliable Entities" Blacklist', 4 June. Available online: https://archive.is/h65Xk#selection-2435.0-2435.58 (accessed 21 July 2023).

Boyse, M. (2023), 'Germany Remains in Denial over Its Russia Policy', *Hudson Institute*, 1 February. Available online: https://archive.is/kORbH (accessed 21 July 2023).

Büschemann, K.-H. (2021), 'Kein Wandel durch Handel', *Süddeutsche Zeitung*, 14–15 August. Nr. 186, 22.

Business Insider (2021), 'Siemens-Chef kritisiert Außenministerin Baerbock für „konfrontative Außenpolitik" gegenüber China', 31 December. Available online: https://archive.is/wdhXv (accessed 21 July 2023).

CDU/CSU-Fraktion (2023), 'Souveränität aus eigener Stärke – Eckpfeiler einer neuen China-Politik', 18 April. Available online: https://www.cducsu.de/sites/default/files/2023-04/PP%20Eckpfeiler%20China-Politik%20neu.pdf (accessed 21 July 2023).

China.Table (2021a), 'Study on China Coverage Ignores Political Reality', 8 November 2021. Available online: https://archive.is/vZAQq.

China.Table (2023a), 'We Need to Rebuild a Solar Industry', 25 April. Available online: https://archive.is/eVqFQ (accessed 21 July 2023).

China.Table (2023b), 'This Law Makes Due Diligence Virtually Impossible', 25 June. Available online: https://table.media/china/en/feature/this-law-makes-due-diligence-virtually-impossible/#:~:text=This%20law%20makes%20due%20diligence%20virtually%20impossible.,illegal%20acquisition%20of%20personal%20information%E2%80%9D. (accessed 21 July 2023).

De Gruyter (2022), '„Wandel durch Handel funktioniert durchaus"', *De Gruyter*, 29 June. Available online: https://archive.is/DsESe (accessed 13 July 2023).

Der Bundespräsident (2014), 'Speech to Open 50th Munich Security Conference', 31 January. Available online: https://archive.is/BeThk (accessed 10 July 2023).

Deutsche Welle (2022a), 'German President Steinmeier admits mistakes over Russia', 4 May. Available online: https://archive.is/as2Re (accessed 21 July 2023).

Deutsche Welle (2022b), 'Scholz Criticized Over China's Cosco Bid in Hamburg Port', 20 October. Available online: https://archive.is/rYKOw (accessed 21 July 2023).

Die Bundesregierung (2023), 'Unsere Werte und Interessen besser verwirklichen', Available online: https://archive.is/0jlJl (accessed 21 July 2023).

Dieckmann, C. and J. Tartler (2023), 'Die Deutschen und Taiwan: „Es gibt Widersprüche zwischen unseren Wirtschaftsinteressen und unseren Werten"', *Tagesspiegel*, 19 March. Available online: https://archive.is/tBz8z (accessed 13 July 2023).

Drinhausen, K. and H. Legarda (2022), '"Comprehensive National Security" Unleashed: How Xi's Approach Shapes China's Policies at Home and Abroad', *Merics*, 15 September. Available online: https://www.merics.org/en/report/comprehensive-national-security-unleashed-how-xis-approach-shapes-chinas-policies-home-and (accessed 21 July 2023).

Emcke, C. (2022), '"Huch"', *Süddeutsche Zeitung*, 4–6 June. Nr. 128, 6.

Eurochambers (2019), 'Doing Business in the EU: Obstacles and Solutions', 14 October. Available online: https://www.eurochambres.eu/wp-content/uploads/2020/08/Doing-business-in-the-EU-obstacles-and-solutions.pdf (accessed 27 July 2023).

Fahrion, G., C. Giesen, K. von Hammerstein, and C. Schult (2023), 'Klare Kante', *Spiegel Politik*, 14 July. Available online: https://archive.is/oMw4y (accessed 21 July 2023).

Federal Foreign Office (2020), '"Germany – Europe – Asia: Shaping the 21st Century Together": The German Government Adopts Policy Guidelines on the Indo-Pacific Region', Available online: https://archive.is/zsZfK (accessed 21 July 2023).

Fischer, F. (2003), *Reframing Public Policy: Discursive Politics and Deliberative Practices*, Oxford and New York: Oxford University Press.

Fulda, A. (2021a), 'Study on China Coverage Ignores Political Reality', *China.Table*, 8 November. Available online: https://archive.is/vZAQq (accessed 21 July 2023).

Fulda, A. (2021b), 'The Chinese Communist Party's Hybrid Interference and Germany's Increasingly Contentious China Debate (2018–21)', *The Journal of the European Association for Chinese Studies*, 2: 205–34.

Fulda, A. (2023), 'We Need More Autocracy Competence', *China.Table*, 7 June. Available online: https://archive.is/N2jEY (accessed 21 July 2023).

Giegerich, B. and M. Terhalle (2021), *The Responsibility to Defend: Rethinking Germany's Strategic Culture*, Oxon: Routledge.

Görg, H., K. Kamin, R. Langhammer, and W.-H. Liu (2023), 'Auf falscher Spur mit der China-Strategie', *Frankfurter Allgemeine Zeitung*, 6 January. Available online: https://archive.is/2FULa (accessed 21 July 2023).

Groitl, G. (2021), 'Das Märchen vom Wandel durch Handel – Wenn seine Logik je funktioniert hat, dann umgekehrt: China führt mit seiner Wirtschaftsmacht die westlichen Demokratien vor', *Neue Züricher Zeitung*, 15 June. Available online: https://archive.is/36emA#selection-255.0-255.162 (accessed 12 July 2023).

Hasselbach, C. (2023), 'Germany's new China strategy: Critical but not decoupling', *Deutsche Welle*, 21 July. Available online: https://archive.is/FCMLO (accessed 21 July 2023).

Heide, D. and D. Neuerer (2023), 'Chinesische Polizeistationen in Deutschland sind weiter aktiv', *Handelsblatt*, 14 March. Available online: https://archive.is/ojQuA (accessed 21 July 2023).

Janis, I. (1971, November), 'Groupthink', *Psychology Today*, 43–6: 84–90. Available online: https://agcommtheory.pbworks.com/f/GroupThink.pdf (accessed 10 July 2023).

Jia, C., M. Leutner, and M. Xiao (2021), 'Die China-Berichterstattung in Deutschen Medien im Kontext der Corona-Krise', *Rosa Luxemburg Stiftung*, December. Available online: https://www.rosalux.de/fileadmin/rls_uploads/pdfs/sonst_publikationen/Studien_12-21_China-Berichterstattung_web.pdf (accessed 21 July 2023).

Jones, B. and F. Baumgartner (2005), *The Politics of Attention: How Governments Prioritizes Problems*, Chicago and London: University of Chicago Press.

Kormbaki, M., C. Schult, and G. Traufetter (2023), 'Die Zwei-China-Politik', *Spiegel Politik*, 22 June. Available online: https://archive.is/1d9pR (accessed 21 July 2023).

Kundnani, H. (2011), 'Germany as a Geo-Economic Power', *The Washington Quarterly*, 34 (3): 31–45.

Lane, J. (2005), *Public Administration and Public Management. The Principal-Agent Perspective*, London and New York: Routledge.

Lough, J. (2021), *Germany's Russia Problem: The Struggle for Balance in Europe*, Manchester: Manchester University Press.

May, P. (1992), 'Policy Learning and Failure', *Journal of Public Policy*, 12 (4): 331–54.

Metz, D. (2023), 'Wir sollten nicht Spielregeln aus Peking befolgen', *Frankfurter Allgemeine Zeitung*, 22 June. Available online: https://archive.is/sib3n#selection-3521.0-3521.49 (accessed 21 July 2023).

Montgomery, D. (2023), 'Kraemer, Fritz Gustav Anton', *The Scribner Encyclopedia of American Lives*, 29 June 2023. Available online: https://archive.is/huRj2 (accessed 21 July 2023).

Nilsson, P. (2022), 'BASF to Downsize "Permanently" in Europe', *Financial Times*, 26 October. Available online: https://archive.is/Je2cB#selection-1411.0-1411.40 (accessed 21 July 2023).

Pamuk, H. (2022), 'U.S. Cautioned Germany Against a Chinese Controlling Stake in Hamburg Port', *Reuters*, 2 November. Available online: https://archive.is/ZltiF (accessed 21 July 2023).

Policy Exchange (2020), 'The Importance of Being Candid: On China's Relationship with the Rest of the World, 23 October 2020', Available online: https://archive.is/k2hjm (accessed 21 July 2023).

Pomfret, J. and M. Pottinger (2023), 'Xi Jinping Says He Is Preparing China for War. The World Should Take Him Seriously', *Foreign Affairs*, 29 March. Available online: https://archive.is/yjxuF#selection-1095.0-1099.35 (accessed 21 July 2023).

portal liberal (2022), 'STARK-WATZINGER-Interview: Wir müssen selbst stärker werden', 17 June. Available online: https://archive.is/pXmhf (accessed 21 July 2023).

Reuters (2023), 'Companies Rather Than Countries Must De-risk Relations with China, Scholz Says', 30 June. Available online: https://archive.is/NwSK5 (accessed 21 July 2023).

Roberts, N. and P. King (1996), *Transforming Public Policy: Dynamics of Policy Entrepreneurship and Innovation*, San Franciso: Jossey-Bass Publishers.

Schmidt, E. (2023), 'Chinas neues Anti-Spionagegesetz: Firmen, Forscher und Journalisten im Visier', *ZDF*, 1 July. Available online: https://archive.is/mtyFV (accessed 21 July 2023).

Sharma, S. (2023), 'Xi Undecided on Whether to Order Military Unification with Taiwan by 2027, Top US Official Claims', *Independent*, 1 July. Available online: https://archive.is /QsDxz#selection-1479.0-1479.97 (accessed 21 July 2023).

Simmons + Simmons (2021), 'What You Need to Know About the Chinese Anti-Foreign Sanctions Law', 11 August. Available online: https://www.simmons-simmons.com/en/ publications/cks76w4g713a30a164jbve2zg/what-you-need-to-know-about-the-chinese -anti-foreign-sanctions-law (accessed 21 July 2023).

Sorge, P. (2003), 'Germany Considers Investment Screening to Reduce Reliance on China', *Bloomberg*, 10 May. Available online: https://archive.is/JDfmu (accessed 21 July 2023).

SPD (2023), 'Sozialdemokratische Antworten auf eine Welt im Umbruch', 20 January. Available online: https://www.spd.de/fileadmin/internationalepolitik/20232001_KIP .pdf (accessed 21 July 2023).

Stremmel, J. (2023), "Morgen bist du tot!", *Süddeutsche Zeitung*, 12 January. Available online: https://archive.is/cuqfS#selection-225.0-225.21 (accessed 21 July 2023).

Strittmatter, K. (2023), 'Es ist Zeit für eine neue China-Politik', *Süddeutsche Zeitung*, 11 May. Available online: https://archive.is/Fd9KU#selection-165.0-165.39 (accessed 21 July 2023).

Tatlow, D. (2018), 'Cultural Relativism and Power Blindness: Some Critical Observations on the State of Germany's China Debate', *LibMod*, 22 November. Available online: https://archive.is/uSdL7 (accessed 21 July 2023).

The Economist (2023a), 'Who Does Olaf Scholz Listen To?', 5 April. Available online: https://archive.is/2xss2#selection-1039.0-1039.31 (accessed 21 July 2023).

The Economist (2023b), 'A Meeting in Germany Approves More Arms for Ukraine, But No Leopard Tanks', 20 January. Available online: https://archive.is/l2cfn (accessed 21 July 2023).

The Federal Government (2023), 'Integrated Security for Germany: National Security Strategy', Available online: https://www.nationalesicherheitsstrategie.de/National -Security-Strategy-EN.pdf (accessed 21 July 2023).

The Guardian (2023), 'Fears for People and Firms as China's New Anti-Espionage Law Comes into Effect', 30 June. Available online: https://archive.is/0Y8cd (accessed 21 July 2023).

Thorley, M. and A. Fulda (2020), 'The Importance of Leverage in GlaxoSmithKline's China Engagement: A Revelatory Case Study', *Journal of Current Chinese Affairs*, 49 (2): 233–54.

Tobin, L. (2023), 'America's Goal Should Be a Democratic China', *Foreign Policy*, 5 June. Available online: https://archive.is/5PjDI (accessed 21 July 2023).

U.S. Department of Justice (2023), 'Foreign Agents Registration Act', Available online: https://archive.is/05cM2#selection-1317.0-1317.31 (accessed 21 July 2023).

Volmer, H. (2022), "'Einem großen Teil der SPD fällt es schwer, die Zeitenwende mitzugehen'", *n-tv*, 18 June. Available online: https://archive.is/r8QWr (accessed 21 July 2023).

von der Burchard, H. (2023), 'Germany's Scholz Overruled Habeck to Approve China Port Deal', *Politico*, 11 May. Available online: https://archive.is/D4R00#selection-2055.9 -2055.25 (accessed 21 July 2023).

White, E. (2023), 'China Passes Foreign Relations Law to Strengthen Xi Jinping's Response to Sanctions', *Financial Times*, 29 June. Available online: https://archive.is/gD99O (accessed 21 July 2023).

Wigell, M. (2019), 'Hybrid Interference as a Wedge Strategy: A Theory of External Interference in Liberal Democracy', *International Affairs*, 95 (2): 255–75.

Winkler, H. (2022), 'Als die SPD konservativ wurde', *Spiegel Politik*, 12 June. Available online: https://archive.is/sCU5D (accessed 26 July 2023).

Y-Kollektiv (2023), 'Chinas illegale Übersee-Polizei mitten in Deutschland? | Y-Kollektiv', Available online: https://www.youtube.com/watch?v=Pqpd8r8FirA (accessed 21 July 2023).

ZDF (2023a), 'Peking verfolgt Oppositionelle: China betreibt Übersee-Polizeistationen', 2 June. Available online: https://www.zdf.de/nachrichten/video/panorama-china -uebersee-polizeistation-deutschland-video-100.html (accessed 21 July 2023).

ZDF (2023b), 'Li bei Scholz im Kanzleramt: "Klare chinesische Erpressung"', 20 June. Available online: https://archive.is/sfHWc (accessed 21 July 2023).

Zeit Online (2023), 'Schröder hält seine Russland-Politik weiter für richtig', 28 June. Available online: https://archive.is/Y7URL (accessed 21 July 2023).

Zenglein, M. (2023), 'Germany Can Ignore Anxious CEOs While Setting China Policy', *Nikkei Asia*, 1 June. Available online: https://archive.is/bqenC#selection-2783.0-2783 .58 (accessed 21 July 2023).

REFERENCES

Albers, M. (2016), *Britain, France, West Germany and the People's Republic of China, 1969–1982*, London: Palgrave Macmillan.

Alpermann, B. and G. Schubert (2022a), 'Gegen das moralische Kreuzrittertum', *Frankfurter Allgemeine Zeitung*, 9 March. Nr. 57, N4.

Alpermann, B. and G. Schubert (2022b), 'An Argument Against Moral Crusading', *ResearchGate*, March. Available online: https://archive.is/7JM5r (accessed 20 July 2023).

Anderson, D., ed. (2014), *Leveraging: A Political, Economic and Social Framework*, New York: Springer.

Auer, S. (2021), 'Merkel's Germany and the European Union: Between Emergency and the Rule of Rules', *Government & Opposition*, 56: 1–19.

Auer, S. (2022), *European Disunion*, London: Hurst.

Barkin, N. (2020), 'Germany's Strategic Gray Zone with China', *Carnegie Endowment for International Peace*, 25 March 2020. Available online: https://archive.is/XsU1c (accessed 13 July 2023).

Baumgartner, F. and B. Jones (1993/2009), *Agendas and Instability in American Politics*, 2nd edn, Chicago and London: The University of Chicago Press.

Biel, H., B. Giegerich, and A. Jonas (2013), 'Introduction', in H. Biel, B. Giegerich, and A. Jonas (eds), *Strategic Cultures in Europe: Security and Defence Policies Across the Continent*, 7–17, Wiesbaden: Springer Fachmedien Wiesbaden GmbH.

BMZ (1999), 'Übersektorales Konzept. Partizipative Entwicklungszusammenarbeit, Nr. 102, September 1999', Available online: https://conservation-development.net/Projekte/Nachhaltigkeit/CD2/Brasilien/Links/PDF/BMZ_1999_Partizipation_Konzept_102.pdf (accessed 18 July 2023).

Bogumil, J. and J. Schmid (2001), *Politik in Organisationen. Organisationstheoretische Ansätze und praxisbezogene Anwendungsbeispiele*, Opladen: Leske + Budrich.

Bösch, F. (2019), *Zeitenwende 1979. Als die Welt von heute begann, 6. Auflage*, München: C.H. Beck.

Brady, A.-M. (2017), 'Magic Weapons: China's political influence activities under Xi Jinping', Wilson Center. Available online: https://www.wilsoncenter.org/sites/default/files/media/documents/article/magic_weapons.pdf (accessed 11 July 2023).

Braw, E. (2022), *The Defender's Dilemma: Identifying and Deterring Gray-Zone Aggression*, Washington, DC: American Enterprise Institute.

Buckley, C. (2013), 'China Takes Aim at Western Ideas', *The New York Times*, 19 August. Available online: https://archive.is/rf9Oe#selection-309.0-354.0 (accessed 2023).

Bulmer, S. and W. E. Paterson (2013), 'Germany as the EU's Reluctant Hegemon? Of Economic Strength and Political Constraints', *Journal of European Public Policy*, 20 (10): 1387–405.

Buzan, B. (1998), 'The Asia-Pacific: What Sort of Region in What Sort of World?', in A. McGrew and C. Brook (Hrsg), *Asia-Pacific in the New World Order*, 68–87, London: Routledge.

Cai, X. (2021), 'China-US Relations in the Eyes of the Chinese Communist Party. An Insider's Perspective', June. Available online: https://www.hoover.org/sites/default/files/research/docs/xia_chinausrelations_web-ready_v2.pdf (accessed 11 July 2023).

Cairney, P. (2011/2020), *Understanding Public Policy: Theories and Issues*, 2nd edn, London: Macmillan Education Limited.

Carrico, K. (2017), 'Putinism with Chinese Characteristics: The Foreign Origins of Xi Jinping's Cult of Personality', *The Jamestown Foundation*, China Brief, 22 December. Available online: https://archive.is/NQBbL (accessed 11 July 2023).

Charon, P. and J.-B. Jeangène Vilmer (2021), *Chinese Influence Operations: A Machiavellian Moment*, Institute for Strategic Research, Paris: Ministry for the Armed Forces.

Dahrendorf, R. (1963), *Die angewandte Aufklärung. Gesellschaft und Soziologie in Amerika*, München: R. Piper & Co Verlag.

Damm, J. (2023), 'China and Germany After the 2021 Election: Between Continuity and Increasing Confrontation', in S. Grano and D. Huang (eds), *China-US Competition Impact on Small and Middle Powers' Strategic Choices*, 159–90, Cham: Palgrave Macmillan.

Dapiran, A. (2021), 'A 20th Procrastination: On Censorship', *Substack*, 15 June. Available online: https://bit.ly/3yw78J2 (accessed 20 July 2023).

Daub, A. (2021), 'The Weird, Extremely German Origins of the Wirecard Scandal', *The New Republic*, 21 April. Available online: https://archive.is/RAuzv (accessed 12 July 2023).

Deutsch, K. (1973), *Politische Kybernetik. Modelle und Perspektiven*, Freiburg im Breisgau: Verlag Rombach.

Diamond, L. and O. Schell, eds (2018), *China's Influence & American Interests: Promoting Constructive Vigilance*, Stanford: Hoover Institution Press.

Erdmann, G. (1999), *Demokratie- und Menschenrechtsförderung in der Dritten Welt*, Wissenschaftliche Arbeitsgruppe für weltkirchliche Aufgaben der Deutschen Bischofskonferenz: Projekte 7.

Erling, J. (2014), 'Helmut Schmidt erklärt den Chinesen ihre Diktatur', *Welt*, 5 December. Available online: https://archive.is/kMP4c (accessed 12 July 2023).

Fedasiuk, R. (2020), 'Putting Money in the Party's Mouth: How China Mobilizes Funding for United Front Work', *China Brief*, 20 (16). Available online: https://archive.is/TOD08 (accessed 11 July 2023).

Fewsmith, J. (1999), 'Elite Politics', in M. Goldman and R. Mac-Farquhar (eds), *The Paradox of China's Post-Mao Reforms*, 47–75, Cambridge: Harvard University Press.

Fewsmith, J. (2007), 'The Political Implications of China's Growing Middle Class', *China Leadership Monitor*, No 21, July. Available online: https://www.hoover.org/sites/default/files/uploads/documents/CLM21JF.pdf (accessed 11 July 2023).

Fewsmith, J. (2021), *Rethinking Chinese Politics*, Cambridge: Cambridge University Press.

Fischer, F. (2003), *Reframing Public Policy: Discursive Politics and Deliberative Practices*, Oxford and New York: Oxford University Press.

Foot, R. (2000), *Rights Beyond Borders: The Global Community and the Struggle over Human Rights in China*, Oxford: Oxford University Press.

Ford, C. (2016), 'Realpolitik with Chinese Characteristics: Chinese Strategic Culture and the Modern Communist Party-State', in A. Tellis, A. Szalwinski, and M. Wills (eds), *Understanding Strategic Cultures in the Asia-Pacific*, 29–60, Seattle and Washington, DC: The National Bureau of Asian Research.

Ford, C. and T. D. Grant (2022), 'Exporting Censorship: The Chinese Communist Party Tries to Control Global Speech about China', *The National Security Institute*, March. Available online: https://nationalsecurity.gmu.edu/wp-content/uploads/2022/04/ Exporting-Censorship-FINAL-WEB-2.pdf (accessed 11 July 2023).

Franceschini, I. and N. Loubere (2022), *Global China as a Method*, Cambridge: Cambridge University Press.

Fulda, A. (2009), *Förderung partizipativer Entwicklung in der VR China. Möglichkeiten und Grenzen politischer Einflussnahme durch Akteure der deutsch-chinesischen Entwicklungszusammenarbeit*, Wiesbaden: VS Verlag für Sozialwissenschaften.

Fulda, A. (2015), 'Civil Society Contributions to Policy Innovation in the PRC', in A. Fulda (ed), *Civil Society Contributions to Policy Innovation in the PR China*, 3–30, Houndmills, Basingstoke, Hampshire and New York: Palgrave Macmillan.

Fulda, A. (2020), *The Struggle for Democracy in Mainland China, Taiwan and Hong Kong. Sharp Power and its Discontents*, London and New York: Routledge.

Fulda, A. (2023), 'We Need More Autocracy Competence', *China.Table*, 7 June. Available online: https://archive.is/N2jEY (accessed 21 July 2023).

Fulda, A. and D. Missal (2021a), 'Mitigating Threats to Academic Freedom in Germany: The Role of the State, Universities, Learned Societies and China', *The International Journal of Human Rights*, 26 (10): 1803–21.

Fulda, A. and D. Missal (2021b), 'German Academic Freedom Is Now Decided in Beijing', *Foreign Policy*, 28 October. Available online: https://archive.is/YoC7H (accessed 20 July 2023).

Fulda, A. and S. Klotzbücher (2022), 'Kooperation mit Autokratien: Still und heimlich schließen sich die Türen', *Tagesspiegel*, 7 October. Available online: https://archive.is/ sdsrt#selection-1493.0-1505.43 (accessed 13 July 2023).

Fulda, A., M. Ohlberg, D. Missal, H. Fabian, and S. Klotzbücher (2022), 'Grenzenlos kompromissbereit?', *Frankfurter Allgemeine Zeitung*, 16 März. Available online: https:// archive.is/xVZhQ (accessed 13 July 2023).

Funtowicz, S. and J. Ravetz (1993), 'Science for the Post-normal Age', *Futures: The Journal of Policy, Planning and Futures Studies*, 25 (7): 739–55.

Furedi, F. (2016), *What's Happened to the University: A Sociological Exploration of its Infantilisation*, London and New York: Routledge.

Garnaut, J. (2019), 'John Garnaut Takes a Deep Look at What Drives China and "What Australia Needs to Know About Ideology in Xi Jinping's China"', interest.co.nz, 20 January. Available online: https://archive.is/IIV5r (accessed 11 July 2023).

Giegerich, B. and M. Terhalle (2021), *The Responsibility to Defend: Rethinking Germany's Strategic Culture*, Oxon: Routledge.

Gold, T. (1997), 'Taiwan: Still Defying the Odds', in L. Diamond, M. Plattner, Y.-H. Chu, and H.-M. Tien (eds), *Consolidating the Third Wave Democracies: Regional Challenges*, 162–91, Baltimore: John Hopkins University Press.

Goodman, D. (2018), 'Social Mobility in China: Class and Stratification in the Reform Era', *Current History*, 117 (800): 203–8.

Grzanna, M. (2023), 'Kommunismus und Klassenkampf holen die deutsche Sinologie ein', *China.Table*, 3 October 2023, Since this article is paywalled readers can access this X/ Twitter thread with excerpts and an English-language summary of Grzanna's article. Available online: https://archive.ph/g2TdI (accessed 28 October 2023).

Habich-Sobiegalla, S. and H. Steinhardt (2022), 'Debating Academic Autonomy in the German-Speaking Field of China Studies: An Assessment', *ASIEN*, 162/163. Available online: https://archive.is/vSdyO#selection-1217.26-1217.39 (accessed 20 July 2023).

Hamilton, C. and M. Ohlberg (2020), *Hidden Hand: Exposing How the Chinese Communist Party Is Reshaping the World*, London: Oneworld Publications.

Hannas, W. and H.-M. Chang (2021), 'Chinese Technnology Transfer: An introduction', in W. Hannas and D. Tatlow (eds), *China's Quest for Foreign Technology: Beyond Espionage*, 3–20, Oxon: Routledge.

Heilmann, S. (2008), 'From Local Experiments to National Policy: The Origins of China's Distinctive Policy Process', *The China Journal*, 59 (January): 1–30.

Hirschman, A. (1945), *National Power and the Structure of Foreign Trade*, Berkely, Los Angeles and London: University of California Press.

Ho, P. (2017), 'The Black Elephant Challenge for Governments', *The Straits Times*, 7 April 2017. Available online: https://archive.is/tK2AD.

Hoffman, S. (2017), 'Programming China: The Communist Party's Autonomic Approach to Managing State Security', *MERICS*, Merics China Monitor, 12 December. Available online: https://merics.org/en/report/programming-china (accessed 22 October 2018).

Hofmann, G. (2011), *Polen und Deutsche. Der Weg zur europäischen Revolution 1989/90*, Berlin: Suhrkamp.

Hu, C., O. Triebel, and T. Zimmer, eds (2023), *Im Spannungsverhältnis zwischen Selbst- und Fremdverstehen. Globale Herausforderungen und deutsch-chinesische Kulturbeziehungen*, Wiesbaden: Springer VS.

IPG (2016), 'Steinbeißermeier', 28 November. Available online: https://archive.is/rsHEx (accessed 10 July 2023).

Janis, I. (1971, November), 'Groupthink', *Psychology Today*, 43–6: 84–90. Available online: https://agcommtheory.pbworks.com/f/GroupThink.pdf (accessed 10 July 2023).

Jia, C., M. Leutner, and M. Xiao (2021), 'Die China-Berichterstattung in Deutschen Medien im Kontext der Corona-Krise', *Rosa Luxemburg Stiftung*, December. Available online: https://www.rosalux.de/fileadmin/rls_uploads/pdfs/sonst_publikationen/Studien_12-21_China-Berichterstattung_web.pdf (accessed 21 July 2023).

Jones, B. and F. Baumgartner (2005), *The Politics of Attention: How Governments Prioritizes Problems*, Chicago and London: University of Chicago Press.

Kahneman, D. (2011), *Thinking, Fast and Slow*, London: Allen Lane.

Kampfner, J. (2020), *Why the Germans Do it Better*, London: Atlantic Books.

Karnitschnig, M. (2020), 'How Germany Opened the Door to China — And Threw Away the Key', *Politico*, 9 October. Available online: https://archive.is/AmKN7 (accessed 12 July 2023).

Kaufman, A. and P. Mackenzie (2009), *The Culture of the Chinese People's Liberation Army*, Quantico, Virginia: Marine Corps Intelligence Activity. Available online: https://info.publicintelligence.net/MCIA-ChinaPLA.pdf (accessed 11 July 2023).

Klotzbücher, S. (2019), *Lange Schatten der Kulturrevolution. Eine transgenerationale Sicht auf Politik und Emotion in der Volksrepublik China*, Gießen: Psychosozial-Verlag.

Klotzbücher, S. (2023), 'Die Zukunft der Chinastudien, aus der Geschichte einer Verführung betrachtet', in D. Fuchs, S. Klotzbücher, A. Riemenschnitter, L. Springer, and F. Wemheuer (eds), *Die Zukunft mit China denken*, 331–353, Vienna and Berlin: mandelbaum verlag.

Koselleck, R. (2004), *Futures Past: On the Semantics of Historical Time*, trans. Keith Tribe, New York: Columbia University Press.

Kundnani, H. (2011), 'Germany as a Geo-Economic Power', *The Washington Quarterly*, 34 (3): 31–45.

Kundnani, H. (2015), *The Paradox of German Power*, New York: Oxford University Press.

Lau, J. (2013), 'Die deutsche Liebe zu den Diktatoren', *Zeit Online*, 21 February. Available online: https://web.archive.org/web/20130224084420/http://blog.zeit.de/joerglau/2013/02/21/schurken-die-wir-brauchen_5889 (accessed 13 July 2023).

Lau, J. (2021), '„Wandel durch Handel"', *Internationale Politik*, 1 September. Available online: https://archive.is/VE5t7 (accessed 13 July 2023).

Lee, F. (2023), '„Wenpo, kannst du noch deine Muttersprache?": Wie Volkswagen in die Abhängigkeit mit China rutschte', *Tagesspiegel*, 16 March, Available online: https://archive.is/0XSAg (accessed 14 July 2023).

Leutner, M. (1995), *Bundesrepublik Deutschland und China 1949 bis 1995. Politik – Wirtschaft – Wissenschaft – Kultur. Eine Quellensammlung*, Berlin: Akademie Verlag.

Levitsky, S. and L. Way (2022), *Revolution and Dictatorship: The Violent Origins of Durable Authoritarianism*, Princeton: Princeton University Press.

Lough, J. (2021), *Germany's Russia Problem: The Struggle for Balance in Europe*, Manchester: Manchester University Press.

Lütjen, T. (2009), *Frank-Walter Steinmeier - Die Biografie*, Freiburg im Breisgau: Herder.

Maas (2021), 'Wir brauchen eine europäische Strategie für den Indo-Pazifik', *Handelsblatt*, 11 April. Available online: https://archive.is/9XpAb (accessed 19 July 2023).

Mattis, P. (2018), 'China's 'Three Warfares' in Perspective', *Texas National Security Review*, War on the Rocks, 30 January. Available online: https://archive.is/7BqGH (accessed 11 July 2023).

Maull, H. (1990–91), 'Germany and Japan: The New Civilian Powers', *Foreign Affairs*. Available online: https://archive.is/njjo5 (accessed 10 July 2023).

Maull, H. (2018), 'Reflective, Hegemonic, Geo-economic, Civilian … ? The Puzzle of German Power', *German Politics*, 27 (4): 460–78.

Maurer, H. and N. Wright (2021), 'Still Governing in the Shadows? Member States and the Political and Security Committee in the Post-Lisbon EU Foreign Policy Architecture', *Journal of Common Market Studies*, 59 (4): 856–72.

May, P. (1992), 'Policy Learning and Failure', *Journal of Public Policy*, 12 (4): 331–54.

Meijer, H. (2022), *Awakening to China's Rise: European Foreign and Security Policies toward the People's Republic of China*, Oxford: Oxford University Press.

Mo, Z. (2022), 'Is East Asia Becoming Plutocratic?', *Wold Inequality Lab*, Issue Brief 2022–11, November. Available online: https://wid.world/document/is-east-asia-becoming-plutocratic-world-inequality-lab-issue-brief-2022-05/ (accessed 11 July 2023).

Monschein, Y. (2020), '„Neuer" Kalter Krieg und alte Macht der Propaganda: „Ausweitung der Kampfzone" auf China?', *minima sinica*, 32 (2020): 99–145.

Moody, O. (2022), 'Why Is Germany Now Brutally Re-evaluating Angela Merkel's Legacy?', *The Times*, 16 July. Available online: https://archive.is/ym6QE#selection-805.0-805.65 (accessed 12 July 2023).

Mulkay, M. (1975), 'Three Models of Scientific Development', *The Sociological Review*, 23 (3): 509–26.

Murphy, A. and A. Fulda (2011), 'Bridging the Gap: Pracademics in Foreign Policy', *PS: Political Science & Politics*, 44 (2): 279–83. Available online: https://core.ac.uk/download/33563322.pdf (accessed 10 July 2023).

Nathan, A. (2003), 'China's Changing of the Guard: Authoritarian Resilience', *Journal of Democracy*, 1: 6–17.

NED (2017), 'Sharp Power: Rising Authoritarian Influence', *National Endowment for Democracy*, December. Available online: https://www.ned.org/wp-content/uploads/2017/12/Sharp-Power-Rising-Authoritarian-Influence-Full-Report.pdf (accessed 11 July 2023).

Nye, J. (2005), 'The Rise of China's Soft Power', *Belfer Center for Science and International Affairs*, 29 December. Available online: https://www.belfercenter.org/publication/rise -chinas-soft-power (accessed 11 July 2023).

Nye, J. (2018), 'China's Soft and Sharp Power', Available online: https://archive.is/ K6ahF.

Odell, R. (2023), '"Struggle" as Coercion with Chinese Characteristics: The PRC's Approach to Nonconventional Deterrence', in R. Kamphausen (ed), *Modernizing Deterrence: How China Coerces, Compels, and Deters*, 45–64, Seattle and Washington, DC: The National Bureau of Asian Research.

Oertel, J. (2023), *Ende der China-Illusion. Wie wir mit Pekings Machtanspruch umgehen müssen*, München: Piper Verlag.

Pei, M. (2016), *China's Crony Capitalism*, Cambridge: Harvard University Press.

Pogorelskaja, S. (2002), 'Die parteinahen Stiftungen als Akteure und Instrumente derdeutschen Außenpolitik', *Aus Politik und Zeitgeschichte*, 22 May. Available online: https://www.bpb.de/shop/zeitschriften/apuz/27121/die-parteinahen- stiftungen-als-akteure-und-instrumente-der-deutschen-aussenpolitik/ (accessed 18 July 2023).

Policy Exchange (2020), 'The Importance of Being Candid: On China's Relationship with the Rest of the World', 23 October. Available online: https://archive.is/k2hjm (accessed 18 July 2023).

Quarmby, S. (2018), 'What are the Implications of Complex Systems Thinking for Policymaking?', *LSE Blog*, 12 October. Available online: https://archive.is/4DR73 (accessed 13 July 2023).

Roberts, N. and P. King (1996), *Transforming Public Policy: Dynamics of Policy Entrepreneurship and Innovation*, San Franciso: Jossey-Bass Publishers.

Roetz, H. (1997), 'China und die Menschenrechte: Die Bedeutung der Tradition und die Stellung des Konfuzianismus', in G. Paul and C. Robertson-Wensauer (eds), *Traditionelle chinesische Kultur und Menschenrechtsfrage*, 36–55, Baden-Baden: Nomos Verlagsgesellschaft.

Roetz, H. (2007), 'China und die Standards einer künftigen Weltordnung: Eine kulturelle Herausforderung?', in D. Döring and E. Kroker (eds), *An der Schwelle zu einem „Asiatischen Jahrhundert"?*, 37–56, Frankfurt am Main: Societäts-Verlag.

Roetz, H. (2016), 'Der antike Legismus - Eine Quelle des modernen chinesischen Totalitarismus?', in H. von Senger and M. Senn (eds), *Maoismus oder Sinomarxismus?*, 75–99, Stuttgart: Franz Steiner Verlag.

Roetz, H. (2019), 'On Political Dissent in Warring States China', in K. Kellermann, A. Plassmann, and C. Schwermann (eds), *Criticising the Ruler in Pre-Modern Societies - Possibilities, Chances, and Methods*, 211–36, Göttingen: V&R unipress / Bonn University Press.

Roetz, H. (2022a), 'Germany's Contentious China Debate', *H-Asia*, 17 March. Available online: https://archive.is/rZ49o (accessed 20 July 2023).

Roetz, H. (2022b), 'Kritik und Kompromiss', *Frankfurter Allgemeine Zeitung*, 30 March. Available online: https://archive.is/M3j65 (accessed 20 July 2023).

Roetz, H. (2022c), 'Unterdrückung als kulturelle Besonderheit: Autoritarismus und Identitätsmanagement in China', *polylog*, 48 (Winter): 41–54.

Röttgen, N. (2022), *Nie wieder hilflos! Ein Manifest in Zeiten des Krieges*, Munich: dtv.

Safeguard Defenders (2022a), 'Patrol and Persuade - A Follow Up On 110 Overseas Investigation', 5 December. Available online: https://archive.is/TkjZh (accessed 11 July 2023).

Safeguard Defenders (2022b), 'Chinese Overseas Police Service Stations Tied to Illegal Policing in Madrid and Belgrade', 15 September. Available online: https://archive.is/ e3EhG (accessed 11 July 2023).

Sandschneider, E. (2012), 'Deutsche Außenpolitik: Eine Gestaltungsmacht in der Kontinuitätsfalle - Essay', *Aus Politik und Zeitgeschichte*, 1 March. Available online: https://archive.is/bHdQk (accessed 13 July 2023).

Sandschneider, E. (2013), 'Raus aus der Moralecke!', *Zeit Online*, 27 February. Available online: https://archive.is/gaTfZ (accessed 13 July 2023).

Sapio, F. (2015), 'Carl Schmitt in China', *The China Story*, 7 October. Available online: https://web.archive.org/web/20151020142101/http://www.thechinastory.org/2015/10/ carl-schmitt-in-china/ (accessed 11 July 2023).

Scharpf, F. (1988), 'The Joint-Decision Trap: Lessons from German Federalism and European Integration', *Public Administration*, 66 (3): 239–78.

Schmidt-Glintzer, H. (2022), 'Zur China-Wahrnehmung', in G. Thelen, H. Obendiek, and Y. Bai (eds), *Handbuch China-Kompetenzen. Best-Practice-Beispiele aus deutschen Hochschulen*, 21–35, Bielefeld: transcript Verlag.

Schmidt, H. and F. Sieren (2006), *Nachbar China*, Berlin: Econ.

Schneckener, U. (2022), 'Gestörter Empfang: Putins Kriegsnarrative und die deutsche Russlandpolitik', Zeitschrift für Friedens- und Konfliktforschung, 29 December, 279–93. Available online: https://doi.org/10.1007/s42597-022-00086-4 (accessed 10 July 2023).

Schneier, B. (2012), *Liars & Outliers: Enabling the Trust That Society Needs to Thrive*, Indianapolis: John Wiley & Sons, Inc.

Schoen, D. (1983), *The Reflective Practitioner: How Professionals Think in Action*, London: Ashgate.

Scholz, O. (2022a), 'Darum geht es bei meiner Reise nach China', *Der Bundeskanzler*, 3 November. Available online: https://archive.is/kEbMK (accessed 12 July 2023).

Scholz, O. (2022b), 'The Global Zeitenwende', *Foreign Affairs*, January/February. Available online: https://archive.is/y6WLU (accessed 12 July 2023).

Shambaugh, D. (2008), *China's Communist Party: Atrophy and Adaptation*, Washington, DC: Woodrow Wilson Center Press.

Shi-Kupfer, K. (2020), China-Versteher machen alles noch schlimmer, *Zeit Online*, 2 May. Available online: https://archive.is/ct09x (accessed 20 July 2023).

Shi-Kupfer, K. (2022), 'Zu viel Zurückhaltung gegenüber China wäre ein Fehler', *Süddeutsche Zeitung*, 15 August. Available online: https://archive.is/cVSa4 (accessed 19 July 2023).

Shi-Kupfer, K. and B. Lang (2017), 'Overseas NGOs in China: Left in Legal Limbo', *The Diplomat*, 4 March. Available online: https://archive.is/muPNn (accessed 18 July 2023).

Sidel, M. (2019), 'Managing the Foreign: The Drive to Securitize Foreign Nonprofit and Foundation Management in China', *Voluntas*, 30: 664–77.

Snyder, J. (1977), 'The Soviet Strategic Culture: Implications for Limited Nuclear Operations', *The Rand Corporation*, Santa Monica: RAND.

Steinmeier, F.-W. (2001), 'Abschied von den Machern', *Zeit Online*, 7 September. Available online: https://archive.is/WmfpA (accessed 10 July 2023).

Steinmeier, F.-W. (2006), '„Energie-Außenpolitik ist Friedenspolitik"', *Handelsblatt*, 22 March. Available online: https://archive.is/LAAVU (accessed 10 July 2023).

Steinmeier, F.-W. (2007), 'Verflechtung und Integration', *Internationale Politik*, 1 March. Available online: https://archive.is/DA9V5 (accessed 10 July 2023).

Stoff, J. (2023), *Should Democracies Draw Redlines Around Research Collaboration with China? A Case Study of Germany, CRSI*, Available online: https://researchsecurity.org/wp-content/uploads/2023/01/Click-here-to-download-the-full-publication.-Stoff-Dra wingRedlinesFINAL.pdf (accessed 20 July 2023).

Streeck, W. (2019), 'Reflections on Political Scale', *Jurisprudence*, 10 (1): 1–14.

Streeck, W. and M. Höpner (2003), *Alle Macht dem Markt? Fallstudien zur Abwicklung der Deutschland AG*, Frankfurt and New York: Campus Verlag.

Strittmatter, K. (2010), 'Das Schweigen der China-Kenner', *Süddeutsche Zeitung*, 10 December. Available online: https://archive.is/7KcwH (accessed 20 July 2023).

Strittmatter, K. (2023), 'Beschämend leichtgläubig', *Süddeutsche Zeitung*, 24 September. Available online: https://archive.ph/OKk57#selection-519.0-519.24 (accessed 28 October 2023).

Strittmatter, K. (2023), 'Es ist Zeit für eine neue China-Politik', *Süddeutsche Zeitung*, 11 May. Available online: https://archive.is/Fd9KU#selection-165.0-165.39 (accessed 21 July 2023).

Stumbaum, M.-B. (2009), *The European Union and China: Decision-Making in EU Foreign and Security Policy Towards the People's Republic of China*, Baden-Baden: Nomos.

Tatlow, D. (2018), 'China's Cosmological Communism: A Challenge to Liberal Democracies', MERICS, Report, 18 July. Available online: https://archive.is/WSgxD (accessed 11 July 2023).

Tatlow, D. (2019), 'Mapping China-in-Germany', *Sinopsis*, 2 October. Available online: https://archive.is/6tJ6z (accessed 11 July 2023).

Tatlow, D. (2022), 'Xi Jinping Ramps Up China's Surveillance, Harassment Deep in America', *Newsweek*, 12 March. Available online: https://archive.is/15kyQ (accessed 11 July 2023).

Tatlow, D. and A. Rácz (2021), 'Assessing China and Russia's Influence on the German Parliamentary Elections', *DGAP*, DGAP Kommentar. Available online: https://web.archive.org/web/20221208051421/https://dgap.org/de/node/35613 (accessed 11 July 2023).

Tatlow, D., H. Feldwisch-Drentrup, and R. Fedasiuk (2021), 'Technology transfer from Germany', in W. Hannas and D. Tatlow (eds), *China's Quest for Foreign Technology. Beyond Espionage*, 130–148, London and New York: Routledge.

Taylor, M. (2021), 'Assessing the Practical Implementation of the EU's Values in EU–China Dialogues', *Asia Europe Journal*, 19: 227–44.

Tellis, A., A. Szalwinski, and M. Wills (2016), *Understanding Strategic Cultures in the Asia-Pacific*, Seattle and Washington, DC: The National Bureau of Asian Research.

Terhalle, M. (2016), 'IB-Professionalität als Praxisferne? Ein Plädoyer für Wandel', *Zeitschrift für Außen- und Sicherheitspolitik*, 9: 121–38.

Terhalle, M. (2020), *Strategie als Beruf*, Baden-Baden: Tectum bei Nomos.

Thorley, M. (2019), 'Huawei, the CSSA and Beyond: "Latent Networks" and Party Influence within Chinese Institutions', *The Asia Dialogue*, 5 July. Available online: https://archive.is/gWV4D (accessed 11 July 2023).

Thorley, M. and A. Fulda (2020), 'The Importance of Leverage in GlaxoSmithKline's China Engagement: A Revelatory Case Study', *Journal of Current Chinese Affairs*, 49 (2): 233–54.

Tobin, L. (2023), 'China's Brute Force Economics: Waking Up from the Dream of a Level Playing Field', *Texas National Security Review*, 6 (1) (Winter 2022/2023): 82–98. Available online: https://tnsr.org/wp-content/uploads/2022/12/TNSR-Journal-Vol-6-Issue-1-Tobin.pdf (accessed 11 July 2023).

Tooze, A. (2022), 'Chartbook #168: Germany's Economic Entanglement with China', *Substack*, 6 November. Available online: https://archive.is/DeWnf (accessed 12 July 2023).

Tsang, S. (2009, November), 'Consultative Leninism: China's New Political Framework', *Journal of Contemporary China*, 18 (62): 865–80.

Umbach, F. (2006), 'Europas nächster Kalter Krieg', *Internationale Politik*, 1 February. Available online: https://archive.is/HFXWH (accessed 10 July 2023).

Umland, A. (2021), 'Germany's Russia Policy in Light of the Ukraine Conflict: Interdependence Theory and Ostpolitik', *Orbis*, 66 (1): 78–94.

Unger, J. (1991), 'Introduction', in J. Unger (ed), *The Pro-Democracy Protests in China: Reports from the Provinces*, 1–7, New York: M.E. Sharpe.

van Slyke, L. (1970), 'The United Front in China', *Journal of Contemporary History*, 5 (3): 119–35.

Weber, R. (2022), 'At What Point Does Cooperation Lead to Complicity?', *China. Table*, 20 September. Available online: https://archive.is/CJeK8 (accessed 11 July 2023).

Weinstein, E. (2021), 'Don't Underestimate China's Military-Civil Fusion Efforts', *Foreign Policy*, 5 February. Available online: https://archive.is/W7wmJ#selection-829.0-834.0 (accessed 20 July 2023).

Wietholz, A. (2021), 'Dornröschen schlägt die Augen auf', *leibniz*, 8 June. Available online: https://archive.is/P3QC8 (accessed 20 July 2023).

Wigell, M. (2019), 'Hybrid Interference as a Wedge Strategy: A Theory of External Interference in Liberal Democracy', *International Affairs*, 95 (2): 255–75.

Wittlinger, R. and M. Larose (2007), 'No Future for Germany's Past? Collective Memory and German Foreign Policy', *German Politics*, 16 (4): 481–95.

Wolff, P. (2006), 'Entwicklungszusammenarbeit im Gesamtkontext der Deutsch-Chineseischen Kooperation: Eine Portfolioanalyse', *Deutsches Institut für Entwicklungspolitik*, Discussion Paper, November 2006. Available online: https://www .idos-research.de/uploads/media/Internetfassung_DiscPaper_11.2006.pdf (accessed 18 July 2023).

Wright, T. (1999), 'State Repression and Student Protest in Contemporary China', *The China Quarterly*, 157: 142–72.

Xu, Z. (2020), 'Viral Alarm: When Fury Overcomes Fear', *ChinaFile*, 10 February. Available online: https://archive.is/HYUcH (accessed 11 July 2023).

Youngs, R. (2010), *The EU's Role in World Politics*, Milton Park: Routledge.

Zajac, K. and L. Kaplan (2021), 'Why Germany Should Continue Its Development Cooperation With China', Kiel Policy Brief, No 159, November 2021. Available online: https://www.ifw-kiel.de/fileadmin/Dateiverwaltung/IfW-Publications/-ifw/Kiel_Policy _Brief/2021/KPB_159.pdf (accessed 18 July 2023).

Zenz, A. (2018), '"Thoroughly Reforming Them Towards a Healthy Heart Attitude": China's Political Re-education Campaign in Xinjiang', *Central Asian Survey*, 38 (1): 102–28.

Zenz, A. (2022), 'Unemployment Monitoring and Early Warning: New Trends in Xinjiang's Coercive Labor Placement Systems, Jamestown Foundation, China Brief', Available online: https://archive.is/xVOeK.

Ziesemer, B. (2006), 'Die Konfuzius-Konfusion', Handelsblatt, 31 October. Available online: https://archive.is/jyvRx (accessed 12 July 2023).

Ziesemer, B. (2023), *Maos deutscher Topagent. Wie China die Bundesrepublik eroberte*, Frankfurt and New York: Campus Verlag.

INDEX